第三届中国（北京）国际服务贸
THE 3rd CHINA BEIJING INTERNATIONAL FAIR FOR TRADE IN SERVICES

# REPORT ON MAJOR VIEWS AT THE 3rd CHINA BEIJING INTERNATIONAL FAIR FOR TRADE IN SERVICES

Department of Trade in Services and Commercial Services
Ministry of Commerce of the People's Republic of China

National Academy of Economic Strategy
Chinese Academy of Social Sciences

International Economic, Trade and Finance Research Center
Chinese Academy of Social Sciences

2014

经济管理出版社
ECONOMY & MANAGEMENT PUBLISHING HOUSE

**图书在版编目（CIP）数据**

第三届中国（北京）国际服务贸易交易会重要观点报告/中华人民共和国商务部服务贸易和商贸服务业司等. —北京：经济管理出版社，2016.4

ISBN 978-7-5096-4361-7

Ⅰ.①第… Ⅱ.①中… Ⅲ.①国际贸易—服务贸易—研究报告 Ⅳ.①F746.18

中国版本图书馆 CIP 数据核字（2016）第 094537 号

组稿编辑：申桂萍
责任编辑：高　娅
责任印制：司东翔
责任校对：超　凡

出版发行：经济管理出版社
　　　　　（北京市海淀区北蜂窝 8 号中雅大厦 A 座 11 层　100038）
网　　　址：www. E-mp. com. cn
电　　　话：(010) 51915602
印　　　刷：北京九州迅驰传媒文化有限公司
经　　　销：新华书店
开　　　本：787mm×1092mm/16
印　　　张：28.75
字　　　数：600 千字
版　　　次：2016 年 5 月第 1 版　2016 年 5 月第 1 次印刷
书　　　号：ISBN 978-7-5096-4361-7
总 定 价：198.00 元（全书 2 册）

# CONTENTS

# Contents

## Part Ⅱ   Summary of Speeches at the Signing Ceremory

## Part Ⅲ   Summary of Speeches at the Summit High–level Forum

Contents

Contents

## Part Ⅳ   Summary of the Speeches on Theme Days and Special Activities

## Part V　Research on Hot Issues in the Fields of Trade in Services

Contents

Contents

# Part I

Summary of Summit and
Sub-forum Speeches

# Speech by WangYang, Vice–premier of China's State Council

## (Read by Zhong Shan, China International Trade Representative of MOFCOM)

On behalf of the PRC State Council Vice-premier Wang Yang, I will now read out his address to the 3rd CIFTIS Summit.

Distinguished guests, ladies and gentlemen,

On the occasion of the 3rd CIFTIS Summit, first of all, please allow me to extend my warm congratulations and sincere welcome to all the guests present on behalf of the Chinese government. With the theme of "The Role of Trade in Services in the Global Value Chain", this session will thoroughly discuss important issues such as the impact of the service industry on the development and transformation of the world economy, and the selection of policies regarding cooperation on international trade in services , which are of great significance.

The present era is the era of the service economy. With further developments in economic globalization and extensive application of information technology, international divisions of labor in the service industry have been deepening, and the level of service and technology has been improved gradually, step by step. Besides, service trade has undergone a rapid development in scale, sustained optimization in structure and continuous enhancement in investment cooperation, making it become an important engine for promoting recovery and transitional development of the world economy. Accelerating the development of the service industry is the inevitable choice in order for China to achieve steady growth, structure adjustment, employment expansion and benefits for its livelihood. In recent years, a series of policies and measures have been introduced to facilitate the development of the service industry and trade, enabling the service industry and trade to embark on the road towards fast development. The value added in the Beijing service industry has contributed to 77% of the GDP. Service export is basically equal to goods export. The fast development of the Chinese service industry has not only given a new impetus to economic growth and structure adjustment, but it has also become an important pillar for maintaining economic growth and an increase in employment.

It is also clear that the service industry is still a weakness in Chinese economic and social

---

development, for its ratio in the national economy is small, its development mode is extensive, its structure is not proper, its technical content and value added are not high, and the international competitiveness of enterprises is not strong. So the task that we face is to give full play to our strength in the scale of the large market and rich human resources and move towards marketization, industrialization, socialization and internationalization to energetically promote the increase in the speed, ratio and level of development of our service industry.

"To promote reform and development through the opening-up" is an important idea in order for China to develop its service industry. Since joining the WTO, we have honored our commitment to an open market in 100 service sectors, and we have improved laws and regulations concerning service industry management. In terms of China's utilization of foreign capital, the service industry has accounted for 52.3%. At present, the international community is looking forward to the opening-up of the Chinese service industry. Here, I would like to deliver the following messages to you:

Firstly, China will firmly adhere to the opening-up of its service industry. The Third Plenary Session of the 18th Central Committee of the CPC has explicitly proposed softening the access to investments, promoting an orderly opening-up in finance, education, culture, medical care, and relaxing the restrictions on the access of foreign investment in old-age care, architectural design, accounting, auditing, business logistics, e-commerce, etc. Since the direction of the opening-up of the service industry has been clearly set, China is actively and steadily moving towards it.

Secondly, the opening-up of the Chinese service industry advances step by step. We will, based on our development needs, grasp the opportunity, step, rhythm and mode of opening-up the service industry in order to integrate the service industry's speed of development and its level of opening-up with the degree of involvement. Last year, we eased market access in six service fields in the Shanghai Pilot Free Trade Zone. This year, we will expand the opening-up in more fields. Besides, we will draw experience from the pilot zone in due time and duplicate and promote it throughout the country.

Thirdly, the opening-up of the Chinese service industry has an institutional guarantee. Apart from expanding access to the market, we pay more attention to the innovation of the management system. By drawing on international experience, we have implemented the foreign investment management mode of "national treatment + negative list" in the Shanghai Pilot Free Trade Zone in an attempt to build a business environment in which domestic and foreign enterprises equally engage in fair competition, and in an attempt to relieve the problem of focusing on the approval procedure, ignoring supervision. Now we are studying and amending three Acts concerning foreign investment in order to define the final management mode in the legal system.

Lastly, the opening-up of the Chinese service industry is mutually beneficial. China is willing to actively participate in negotiations for an agreement regarding trade in services so that all involved will be able to work together to promote the liberalization and facilitation of trade in services, and we are also willing to discuss, with all countries and regions, a high-level service trade arrangement through adherence to the principle of equality and mutual benefit. We sincerely call on the international community to pay more attention to the appeal from developing countries and to help the less developed countries improve the level and capability of their services, thus promoting the balanced development of global trade in services.

CIFTIS is not only an important window for the Chinese service industry to open up to the outside, but it is also a crucial stage for China to deepen its cooperation in international trade in services. The Chinese government supports Beijing in taking the lead, through "CIFTIS", in leading the development and transformation of the service industry, and welcomes enterprises from all countries to attend CIFTIS in order to build up consensus and find business opportunities, jointly writing a new chapter for the prosperity of trade in services.

That's all, thank you!

# Summit Speech by Zhang Baowen, Vice-chairman of the NPC Standing Committee

Distinguished Ms Solvita Āboltiṇa, guests, ladies and gentlemen,

Today, we gather together to attend the 3rd China Beijing International Fair for Trade in Services (CIFTIS). First of all, please allow me, on behalf of the Chinese government, to express my sincere welcome to all of the guests present and warm congratulations on the holding of the 3rd CIFTIS. CIFTIS is the world's first international comprehensive fair specially designed for trade in services. It is a new platform for Chinese and foreign enterprises to carry out international exchanges and cooperation. The holding of the CIFTIS is a strategic move for China to expand its opening-up. It bears the historical mission of promoting the development of the service industry and trade.

The theme of the 3rd CIFTIS is "The Role of Trade in Services in the Global Value Chain". In sub-forums, discussions will be carried out on hot issues such as "The Role of Trade in Services in the Global Value Chain and its Importance", "The Development Channel of Information and Communication Technology as Service and Service Trade", "Opportunities and Challenges Faced by Developing Countries", which all conform to the general developmental trend of economic globalization and global economy servicizing, and they reflect the attention paid by national governments and international organizations to trade in services, as well as their desire to rebuild the global value chain and realize common development. The 3rd CIFTIS will facilitate the balanced development of global trade in services, even the global economy.

Firstly, the global value chain is increasingly prominent in the global economy, and trade in services has become an essential link. Under the background of economic globalization, factors of production such as international capital are re-reconfigured to form the global value chain. As a force of organization and governance, the global value chain can disperse various connections of one product to different countries. Economic globalization is constantly moving towards function integration and cooperation on international distribution.

With the increasing occurrence and organization of international trade, there has been a great change in the form, structure and growth rate through the global value chain in carrying out international trade. As the service economy era arrives, trade in services is booming all over the world, and has become a critical part of the global value chain. The OECD data reveal that 66% of global trade in goods originates in intermediate goods, while the ratio reaches 70% in trade in services, which shows that international trade has entered the age of the global value chain.

Secondly, China is becoming an important part of the global value chain that cannot be ignored, for it enjoys fast development in international trade. The process of China's reform and opening-up is also China's process of actively keeping up with trend towards economic globalization and constantly making efforts to be involved in the global value chain. Under the background of a slowdown in the growth of the global economy, a decline in global trade investment and the emergence of various risks in recent years, China has always stuck to its opening-up policy based on mutual benefit to continuously expand the breadth and depth of the global value chain and stimulate an open economy, so that new developmental progress will be achieved.

In 2013, China became the largest trading country in goods. The total export-import volume of goods trade amounted to 4.16 trillion USD, accounting for 12% of the global trade in goods. The total export-import volume of trade in services was 539.64 billion USD. According to an estimation, China will continue to be ranked 3rd in trade in services, demonstrating that China is an important part that cannot be ignored in the global value chain.

Currently, China is making efforts to develop its service industry, speed up the development of key and weak links in producer services and further optimize its industrial structure, thus promoting the transformation and upgrading from "Made in China" to "Created in China". As the opening-up of the service industry continuously goes on, more and more Chinese enterprises will be involved in the global value chain and play a greater role in driving the development of the world economy.

Last but not least, China will make a greater effort at promoting the development of trade in services, and actively participate in the optimization and upgrading of the global value chain.

China will adhere to the implementation of an active opening-up strategy to continuously improve its ability and level in the global value chain. Besides, China will take the service industry as the focus for its new opening-up strategy in order to further accelerate and accomplish the free flow of production factors, energetically develop two-way service outsourcing, and deeply integrate itself into the service-oriented global value chain, thus providing international support for the upgrading of service businesses and the overall industry.

Furthermore, China will further promote the transformation of foreign trade, vigorously develop trade in services, promote the export of services stamped with Chinese characteristics (such as traditional Chinese medicine, culture and art, cartoon games, radio films and television, press and publication, education and sport), emphatically foster modern trade in services in communication, finance, accounting, asset appraisal, computer and information services, media, consulting and exhibition, improve the laws and regulations regarding trade in services, standard systems and statistical systems, thus boosting the facilitation of trade in services. Service import is to be steadily expanded in order to allow importation to fully play its active role in promoting the development of trade in services.

The present world is an open world. Only by opening up to each other can various countries find more opportunities for cooperation. I hope various government and international organizations can strengthen cooperation, accelerate the extension of the global value chain to the service field and make concerted efforts to achieve trade liberalization, so as to create a good environment for the development of the global value chain, improve the global value chain and build a global integrated market.

Ladies, gentlemen and friends, I hope that all of you will take full advantage of the 3rd CIFTIS to carry out talks and communication to jointly push forward the development of global trade in services and the sustained development of a global economy. Finally, I wish complete success to the 3rd CIFTIS.

# Summit Speech by Cheng Hong, Beijing Deputy Mayor

Your Respected Excellency, Vice-chairman of the NPC Standing Committee, Zhang Baowen, Parliament Speaker, Solvita Āboltiņa, all guests, ladies and gentlemen,

On the occasion of the 3rd CIFTIS, I, on behalf of the organizing committee and the People's Government of Beijing Municipality, extend a cordial welcome to all delegations, enterprises and guests from 117 countries and regions, my sincere gratitude to all of the countries, regions, international organizations, international chambers of commerce, domestic ministries and commissions and provinces that provide energetic support to CIFTIS, and my honorable respect to all friends that dedicate their hard work and wisdom to the preparations for CIFTIS.

With the deepening of economic globalization, trade in services has become a fresh impetus to boosting the transformation and growth of the global economy, but it is also a new hot spot in international cooperation. CIFTIS emerges at the right moment. It bears the historical mission to expedite the development of the service industry and trade, and is meeting tremendous development opportunities. Thanks to concerted efforts and active participation of all the parties involved, CIFTIS has been held twice with success. As a demonstration of its thriving vitality and formidable vigor, it has become a significant platform for the transmission of ideas, for supplier-demander contacts, for the sharing of business opportunities and for the promotion of common development.

Distinguished guests and friends, relying on the synthetic advantages as the national capital, Beijing has been one of the most developed cities in the domestic service industry and service trade, and was the first to form an industrial structure dominated by the service economy. In 2013, value added in the Beijing service industry reached 150 million RMB, accounting for 77% of the regional GDP, of which producer services accounted for over 50%. The value of trade in services exceeded 110 billion USD, accounting for over 20% of local foreign trade and of national foreign trade, and accounting for 1.2% of global trade in services.

Characterized by intensive knowledge, industry agglomeration, high innovation vigor and increasing internationalization, the Beijing service industry plays an increasingly important role in supporting structure optimization and the sustained development of the capital economy. In the future, we will give full play to our strength in resources and in the service industry development comparison, deepen the reform in a comprehensive way, expand the opening-up of the service industry, intensify innovation, focus on building an integral service platform in an attempt to promote a sustained and sound development of a capital economy, and make unremitting efforts to push the development of regional economies, as well as of the domestic and even the global service industry and trade.

Distinguished guests and friends, all the activities in this session will start soon. As the hosting city, Beijing will earnestly accomplish all services and supports with greater inspiration and a stronger sense of practice. We hope all the guests and merchants present can take full advantage of the CIFTIS platform to enhance communication, exchanges and cooperation, and in this way, jointly promote the flourishing and development of the service industry and trade on the basis of mutual benefit and a win-win result. Finally, I sincerely wish all of you will be able to find business opportunities and accomplish cooperation and development, and I hope that the 3rd CIFTIS and summit is a complete success.

# Summit Speech by Mukhisa Kituyi, Secretary–General of UNCTAD

Respected Vice-chairman of the NPC Standing Committee, Zhang Baowen, Deputy Mayor, Cheng Hong, ministers, Heads of delegations, ladies and gentlemen,

I am very glad to attend the 3rd CIFTIS on behalf of UNCTAD. UNCTAD is very proud to be involved in the motion of the Chinese government and of the Beijing Municipal Government, and has carried out discussions regarding trade in services. I really appreciate the invitation from the Chinese government to attend this summit concerning the service industry and trade.

The 3rd CIFTIS creates a platform for us to have exchanges and discussions by regarding service businesses as a sector and an industry, and help other countries, especially developing countries, improve their capabilities in trade in services. Over the past few decades, the service industry has become an industry of high investment return, as well as a rapidly developing industry. There are two issues that may never be mentioned, but are important:

The first is the worldwide rapid development of trade in services, excluding North Africa. There are three symptoms: 1) the service industry has tremendous potential in job creation; 2) the service industry has the highest return compared with agriculture and the manufacturing industry; 3) the service industry has unique sustainability which is different from industry and agriculture, for it is a green industry and can better help women get a job.

The second is about the challenge encountered in the development of the service industry. On a global scale, the service industry makes a great contribution to promoting an increase in the GDP. For developing countries, 37% of the GDP originates in the service industry. However, there are still some weaknesses in trade in services for developing countries; for instance, it gives a low contribution to employment despite its high contribution to the GDP. The highest return of the service industry in developing economies mainly derives from the creation of jobs, especially low-level jobs in the value chain. It is a policy challenge to find a way to facilitate the development of the most easily tradeable service industry. It is a challenge to choose to push the development of the high-level or low-level service industry.

Upon discussion with the Chinese government and relevant departments, the solution is to find a way to integrate the relevant service industry and trade in the global value chain. 80% of global trade is the trade of intermediate products and services. Over the past decade, trade in services has turned into a task trade, which offers lots of opportunities to us and the return of service industry development. In the global context, trade in services accounts for 20% of global trade, and the export value added of the service industry reaches 50%. It relates to the relationship between services and development. Many emerging countries, including China, tend to make more efforts in industry, the manufacturing industry, the outsourcing industry, etc. However, the most advanced economy dominates upstream and downstream fields in the value chain, such as design, logistics, finance, distribution, after-sales services and legal consulting. The value of such fields is significantly greater than that created by trade in services of intermediate goods. China has taken a lot of measures over the past decades to enhance investment in research and development, to further expand the service industry to upstream and downstream fields, and to gradually extend businesses to other emerging economies. Besides, it can be seen that such policy reform makes contributions to the realization of the opening-up of the service industry. For instance, the deregulation policy plays a remarkable role in promoting the development of relevant fields.

As the service industry is of great significance to the development of global trade and economies of various countries, we need to pay more attention to multilateral trade negotiations. While enhancing cooperation and increasing investment, developing countries need to make a greater effort at becoming involved in the mainstream economy trade through applicable trade tools.

Finally, I would like to thank the Ministry of Commerce and the Beijing Municipal Government again for holding the event. I look forward to subsequent meaningful discussions.

# Summit Speech by William Danvers, Deputy Sectretary–General of the OECD

Good morning, everyone. I am very pleased to attend the 2014 China Beijing International Fair for Trade in Services (CIFTIS). I would like to express my deep gratitude to the Chinese Ministry of Commerce and the Beijing Municipal Government for holding the 3rd CIFTIS and inviting the OECD as the sponsor and supporter for three consecutive times.

Service trade is a very important issue which could help us together find the way of boosting economic growth through trade. In the past two decades, the global trade chain has become an essential element in worldwide trade, and the service industry has played an increasingly important role in the development of countries around the world. In cooperation with the World Trade Organization, we have conducted a great deal of work in terms of trade in value added and the global trade chain, which further demonstrates the importance of the service industry in the global trade chain. For OECD member countries, 50% of exports of value-added originate in the services sector, while this ratio in China now just reaches 30%. We need to further strengthen the smooth flowing of goods and services in the value chain, also first-rate R&D, design, marketing and other relative industries are required, and this means a lot to the development of the high-end manufacturing industry. Nowadays, the services sector contributes to 80% of the job creation and 75% of the GDP, which of course are the figures of developed countries, for China the ratio of the service sector in the GDP is 45%. In the "12th Five-Year Plan", China has especially pointed out that the ratio of the service industry needs to be raised, which would help China upgrade its status in the global value chain.

Two weeks ago, the OECD released a new tool used for service trade policy analysis, that is, the service trade restrictions index and database. The database includes data from 40 countries including China, as well as 18 service sectors. With the tool, we can compare the policies of various countries to help policy makers better evaluate and analyze measures to be taken in the reform of the service field and industry, and the impact such measures may bring. As a very useful tool, it plays a critical role in trade negotiations. Also, it can help enterprises better conform to local regulations before entering the foreign market.

None of the 40 countries in the database is on the list of the top three or the last three in all 18 service sectors, which shows that every country has its strengths and weaknesses in different service sectors, thus creating a good opportunity for various countries to make mutual exchanges and learn from each other.

We may, based on the specific condition of different service sectors, take some measures of reform. Even basic measures of reform can help increase the exports of the whole service industry by 3%–7%, which fully demonstrates the positive impact that the opening-up of the service industry brings. In addition, the opening-up also helps to improve the competitiveness of the domestic service industry and providers. As the global economy has been increasingly linked together, restrictions on trade in services, in fact, also exerts a negative impact on some downstream industries and enterprises. Therefore, the elimination of service trade restrictions will surely bring an active effect on many industries, including the manufacturing industry of electrical products, textiles and automobiles.

In the next three days, we will carry out very useful discussions by taking advantage of the CIFTIS platform. I believe such discussions are of great importance in the development of both the Chinese economy and the world economy. New tools introduced by the OECD such as the global value chain, trade in value added and the service trade restriction index, will help all countries find a way to further expand trade and make a positive effect on the development of our future economy.

Finally, I would like to thank the Chinese organizers again for inviting the OECD to attend the 3rd CIFTIS. I am very glad to attend the 3rd CIFTIS. I wish all of you benefits from the 3rd CIFTIS. Thank you!

# Summit Speech by Yi Xiaozhun, Deputy Director–General of the WTO

Ladies and gentlemen, good morning!

I'm very pleased and honored to be here today to attend the opening ceremony of the China Beijing International Fair for Trade in Services (CIFTIS).

I, on behalf of the WTO Director-General Azevêdo, express our sincere congratulations on, and best wishes to, the 3rd CIFTIS. He wanted to attend the 3rd CIFTIS, but unfortunately, his tight schedule prevented him from doing so. Mr. Azevêd has delivered a letter of congratulations to the CIFTIS organizing committee in the name of himself. He delegated my colleague, Hamid (Head of the WTO Trade in Services Division) and me to attend the high-level fair on behalf of the WTO.

I still remember the pomp of the 1st CIFTIS in 2012, as well as the effective delivery of Chinese policies. In the same year, China formulated and promulgated the "12th Five-Year Plan" where the development of the service industry was its principal element. Nowadays, the direction of the development of the Chinese economy is getting clearer, that is, China is in urgent need of energetically developing its service industry in order to make it the main pillar of its economic development. As a matter of fact, this year witnesses the ratio of the Chinese service industry value added in the GDP exceeding the ratio of the manufacturing industry for the first time. It is really worth celebrating. The blueprint of the current policy will intensify the development of the Chinese service industry, provide the necessary impetus for the transformation of the manufacturing industry to a higher level in the value chain, and guarantee the sustained development of the Chinese economy.

Though the speed of the transformation of the global economy is amazing, it faces unprecedented complexity. The most important part in the transformation is the rapid development of the complex and efficient service industry. This rapid development relies on the promotion of technology, global finance and an innovative business mode. In case of a lack of reliable and cost-effective services such as logistics transportation, finance service, communication, IT and other business services, the global production network and supply chain will be unable to play a role in the global economy. China's involvement in the global value chain and production chain is highly dependent on the service industry and trade. However, not many people have been concerned about or have understood Chinese trade in services when China became the world's largest exporting country of trade in goods. From 2002 to 2013, the Chinese commercial trade in services maintained a stable and sustained development at an annual growth rate of 11%. When joining the WTO in 2001, the exports of China's commercial trade in services was ranked 12th in the world. 12 years later, that is, in 2013, China had moved up to the 5th place. This rapid growth is largely attributed to China's determination to fulfill its commitments after joining the WTO, as well as its policy reform promotion and coordination.

When joining the WTO in 2001, China made wide and significant commitments in terms of the opening-up of its service industry, with the commitment level in excess of most developing member countries. It is generally believed that the commitments and reforms in the opening-up of the service industry have played a vital role in the rapid growth of the Chinese economy. Although it is crucial to consolidate domestic reform achievements, another issue is equally important for China, that is, China needs to negotiate with other member countries regarding broader trade freedom and predictive multilateral trade principles, thus creating a stable and predictable environment where China can maintain the increasing trend in its service trade exports. It should also be noted that China's foreign direct investment amounted to 88 billion USD in 2012, of which nearly 80% came from the service industry, such as transportation, logistics, distribution, finance, architecture and commercial services. A few months ago, WTO member countries reached the *Bali Package* in Indonesia, showing that we are working on the formulation of a comprehensive work plan to help us complete the Doha Round negotiations. Trade in services is of great importance in accomplishing the goal.

Multilateral trade negotiations need the active participation and strong support of China. We are very glad to see, at the Third Plenary Session of the 18th Central Committee of the CPC, the Chinese decision to further relax the restrictions on important service sectors, such as old-age care, logistics, accounting and audit services. Besides, the Chinese government has established a free trade zone in Shanghai, which will lead to more measures of reform, especially in the service industry. WTO member countries are greatly encouraged by such a bold initiative, and deem it a great contribution made by China to global trade liberalization. We hope to draw on the successful experience from the Shanghai Pilot Free Trade Zone and apply it to other regions. Again, I wish the 3rd China Beijing International Fair for Trade in Services complete success. Thank you!

# Summit Speech by Vince Cable, UK Secretary of State for Business, Innovation and Skills

Your respected Excellency of the NPC Standing Committee Vice-chairman, Deputy Mayor, guests, ladies and gentlemen,

I am very proud to deliver a speech at such an important fair and I am very glad to come to China again. My first trip to China was more than 20 years ago. Over the past 20 years, China has attained great achievements in economic and social development. Here, I would like to share my opinions on the opening-up of the economy and the service industry from the perspective of both China and the UK.

Of course, there is a great difference between China and the UK. However, both of them are undergoing very important or similar transformations. The UK is an important member of the Group of Seven who have just endured painful financial and economic crises. We are facing a series of structural challenges in many aspects, especially in the exportation of goods. In the meanwhile, China is also undergoing an important transformation. Xi Jinping, the Chinese President, has declared that China is currently in an important period of strategic opportunities, that is, a period turning from fast economic growth to a balance of sustained development. The period of strategic opportunities is of crucial importance.

We can see that since the beginning of reforms and the opening-up in 1979, which was put forward by Comrade Deng Xiaoping, China has been integrating into the international society and opening-up to the world by setting up special economic zones and by other methods as well. Such an opening-up theme has lasted until now. Reform measures issued at the Third Plenary Session of the 18th Central Committee of the CPC in 2013, for example, bringing more market vitality to state-owned enterprises, encouraging cross-border capital flow, and a batch of measures to reform supervision and better use international management experiences, all of these fully show the world the attitude and determination of China's opening-up, and the service industry and trade is going to play a very important role during this process.

The UK is also in an important transformation stage. China and the UK are highly complementary in terms of the economy. We are not only the core of the manufacturing industry, such as for example by exporting a great number of manufacturing products, but we also have the world world's first-class service industry, such as financial services. At present, as one of the world's most important financial centers, London has is rapidly developing RMB transactions. The financial industry consists of banking, insurance, accounting, audit auditing, and legal services, etc. The UK also houses many world-class universities. Educational output is also an essential element of service exports. At present, there are over 130,000 full-time overseas students from China in UK universities, which accounts for a very large ratio in among the UK UK's international students. Moreover, we have a significant amount of creative industries. For example, the UK TV series, like *Sherlock and Downton Abbey*, are very popular in China. We in the UK welcome the investment investments from all countries, including the direct investment investments from China. Of all the member countries of the EU, the UK has the largest scale of foreign investment, of which the ratio of Chinese investments is rising continuously. We welcome China's investments in building up our civilian nuclear energy, airport, water conservation and infrastructure. In the automobile industry, Chinese investments can also be found, such as SAIC MOTOR. I believe that in order to realize the free flow of capital effective international rules are needed, which should be formulated by the governments of all countries together. Regarding this, the WTO G20 and the UN should play a crucial role. We are particularly pleased to see China's intention to engage in the multilateral negotiation system of the agreement on trade in services. Activities such as CIFTIS will facilitate exchanges between China and other countries, and broaden the common ground.

It is really a pleasure to be back in China. I am pleased to see everyone has firm confidence in reform and opening-up. Thank you!

# Summit Speech by Solvita Āboltiņa, Speaker of the Parliament of Latvia

Respected Vice-chairman of the NPC Standing Committee, Zhang Baowen, Deputy Mayor, Cheng Hong, all guests, ladies and gentlemen,

I feel greatly honored to be here to attend the opening ceremony of the 3rd China Beijing International Fair for Trade in Services (CIFTIS).

The service industry is an important part of the economy of all countries, and it plays a vital role in global economic development. This is also true for Latvia. The service industry is crucial to the development of the Latvian economy. I am delighted to see Latvia has gotten out of the 2008 and 2009 financial crisis. Now, Latvia is one of the European countries that enjoys the fastest growth rate in the economy. I am pleased to be here to share our development experience with you.

Ms Christine Lagarde, the Managing Director of the IMF, said that "Latvia has found the right path towards development, for Latvia has achieved social stability, and the Latvian people have the common wish to drive Latvia to becoming a more prosperous and a stronger country". Early this year, a multitude of economic data further demonstrated that we have recovered from the crisis and have maintained a good developmental trend. Yesterday, I met and discussed with Premier Li Keqiang and the NPC Standing Committee Chairman, Zhang Dejiang. We reached a consensus that China and Latvia hold great potential for cooperation, especially in the field of traffic and transportation.

Latvia enjoys a superior geographical location and excellent conditions of its infrastructure, making it become a good portal for China's access to Europe. In the next couple of days, we will hold some meetings to discuss the transportation between China and the EU. I believe the discussion will further enhance the connection between China and Latvia.

Ladies and gentlemen, Latvia welcomes the Chinese investment in various fields, especially the field that China considers has advanced experience and technology. We Latvians have set up 15 industrial parks in various cities. Each one of them is equipped with a good business incubator, financial services and infrastructures. I believe they meet the requirements of Chinese investors. Latvia will serve as the presidency of the EU in 2015. We will be dedicated to strengthening the tie between China and Europe. Thank you again!

# Summit Speech by Juergen Fitschen, CEO of Deutsche Bank

Distinguished Vice-chairman of the NPC Standing Committee, Zhang Baowen, Deputy Mayor, Cheng Hong, guests, ladies and gentlemen,

I'm very pleased and honored to be here today to attend the opening ceremony of the 3rd China Beijing International Fair for Trade in Services (CIFTIS) and deliver a speech. The theme of the session is the service industry. During discussions in previous sessions themed "How to build smart cities and cope with economic challenges", one thing deeply impressed me, and that is, the ratio of Beijing's service industry in the GDP has reached 75%, the level of developed countries. Congratulations!

Beijing has achieved tremendous success in economic development. Today, I would like to discuss the trend in the development of the world economy. Just like many developing countries, China is undergoing transformation and facing population adjustment and change. With continuous population growth and aging, more and more services in medical care and social benefit are needed, and more challenges appear in the course of transformation. We need to provide more public and social services, construct more infrastructures such as water supply, waste disposal and transportation. All of these require more service input, meaning enormous potential for the development of the service industry. The trend towards urbanization will bring huge potential to the development of this industry. It is the basis for the realization of the development of economies of scale, and helps to further reduce developmental costs during the process of development, thus benefiting more people.

As CEO of Germany's largest bank, Deutsche Bank, I have to acknowledge that with the emerging and development of new technologies, such as big data and cloud computing, they really bring many uncertainties, but also lots of opportunities to the banking industry. To better cope with these challenges, it is necessary to re-evaluate and deliberate the operating mode of the banking industry to better meet customer's needs. For the establishment of a new economic mode, preliminary capital investment is of crucial importance. The banking industry will play a significant role in the preliminary phase. Without capital support from the banking industry, enterprises, especially emerging and innovative enterprises, will not be able to get sufficient funds, so that it would be impossible to achieve sustainable development of the economy. I believe in the next couple of days, CIFTIS will provide a good service platform for financing services.

I would like to point out in particular that every trip to China gives me lots of inspiration, and many of my past ideas and thoughts have been proved in China and in the world. I believe that if such ideas were put into practice further, the Chinese people, even the whole world, would get more benefits. Services link various countries together, improve people's lives and bring about infinite potentials and opportunities. Thank you again!

# Speech by Hamid Mamdouh, Director of Trade in Services Division of the WTO, at the Summit Sub-forum

I am glad to be here to share my opinions with you, and I would like to thank the organizer for giving me a chance to give a speech here. As we all know, the WTO has been engaging in negotiations regarding trade in services, which is an important issue in 2014. After successful negotiations in Pairs, we only hope to complete this round of negotiations as soon as possible. However, in such a scenario, we find a unique phenomenon; first of all, we haven't carried out official negotiations on services industry, such as negotiations on the opening-up of the service market. The WTO hopes to set up a legislation framework. The negotiation conference about market access may start in 5 years. Besides, there has been some progress in negotiations on agriculture. We also hope to establish a system or a legal legislation framework, which may also start in 5 years.

In the previous two decades, no serious discussion was carried out after the founding of the WTO. However, a new phenomenon keeps cropping up, for example, trade in services is booming, which is mainly due to the promotion of its liberalization, especially multilateral trade in services. Trade in services plays a vital role, which not only helps increase enterprise competitiveness but it also upgrades the status of a country in the global value chain. Nowadays, trade in services is becoming more and more important; particularly, it leads to the remarkable increase in social benefits. Look at our life, you will find you have enjoyed many social services such as medical insurance and your children's education.

The global value chain is a phenomenon of great interest. Before, we have mentioned the global supply chain. For the production or cross-border production of a product, the supply chain means a supply network that is supposed to be established for the circulation of products and service. It is not only designed for a single product. More importantly, it has a critical role in both the service supply chain and the business mode. Although the global value chain has made great contributions to the growth and development of global trade, it still suffers from problems in the following issues:

The first issue is the relevance to the enterprise. There is no need to push the development of the enterprise. There is enterprise, there is business. Therefore, our work is to promote innovation. However, we don't need to thrust innovation features onto technology, finance and enterprise, and just provide proper conditions for them.

The second is that we need to understand and handle things that are happening. Country is very important. Many national policies exert great effect on every supply chain and operation. We have realized the importance of high-level cooperation in such areas. But, unfortunately, most of the countries carry out management and policy formulation independently. As a whole, policy formulation can't meet the needs of cooperation among countries and regions in the global value chain.

The third is unity of international practices. For instance, in terms of law enforcement, the power of enforcement is required through laws and regulations. The same is true for the development of the enterprise. We can see that many practices require national cooperation. Only by national cooperation can, the desired results, be achieved.

# Speech by Qu Nianling, President of the China Information Technology Service Industry Alliance, at the Summit Sub-forum

I have been engaged in IT work for 33 years, which makes me feel that the focus of IT is always changing. Thirty-three years ago, our focus was hardware; 20 years ago, our focus moved to software from hardware; and 10 years ago, our focus moved to service from software. Nowadays, a great deal of IT work focuses on service. In 12 sectors of trade in services, a number of projects are inseparable from our work, such as the communication service and insurance finance. In fact, the global finance service depends on the support of the global Internet, so that trans-national finance service can be provided. In addition, there are many other fields that are based on IT service support, such as patent applications, franchise transfer and consulting services, not to mention computer and information services.

With the focus moving to the service industry, IT plays a critical role; for IT helps the whole service industry realize trans-national delivery, making trade in services have a huge development space. At the moment, we are specifically studying the process of Chinese trade. China is the world's largest country in goods trade, but its trade in services is still weak. In 2013, China achieved a trade surplus in goods, but a trade deficit in services, and the trade deficit came to 118.4 billion USD. Though the USA suffered a trade deficit in goods with China, it achieved a trade surplus in global service, with the amount exceeding 100 billion USD, thus forming both a trade surplus and a deficit between the USA and China, in the amount of 100 billion USD, so that the USA could achieve a trade surplus in services in China. The growth of the Chinese industry starts from its manufacturing industry. We spent 30 years making China become the largest country on the manufacturing scale. China has just occupied the first place in goods trade. The manufacturing industry requires the development of the service industry, which helps China blaze its road of trade in services.

Before, we communicated with the leaders of the Ministry of Commerce. Over the previous three decades, the Chinese manufacturing industry accumulated plenty of experience, laws and procedures, which are all designed for the manufacturing industry and trade in goods. Today, global trade in services has formed a large scale. However, from the WTO, the support system for trade in services is obviously not as mature as that for trade in goods. Therefore, a great deal of work still needs to be done.

China is also suffering from many problems; for example, how to support the development of trade in services and the transformation of the entire country. The development level of the service industry reflects the strength of a country. Therefore, the task that we face is to develop the support capacity for the service industry. In terms of talent education, laws and policies, China is also improving its abilities.

As a senior member of the IT industry, I am particularly hoping that IT service will play a significant role in supporting China's high-end trade in services with the extension of the Chinese trade in services, and that the Chinese government will help form an excellent system, legislation and policy framework in the service industry and trade.

Thank you!

# Speech by Margit Monat, the Chinese Business Executive of the Economy Division of OECD, at the Summit Sub–forum

As I am responsible for economic business in China, I will discuss trade in services, its ratio in the world economy and its overall productivity from the perspective of economic business in China. What is the major factor that promotes the economic development of China? Over the past decades, China has undergone dramatic changes in ratio of the service industry.

In comparison to trade in services, we compare the ratio of Chinese value-added service with that of OECD member countries, and discover that the ratio in China is lower than that of OECD member countries, and Russia and Brazil; it is only higher than that of Indonesia. According to the calculation based on the purchasing power parity, when purchasing, the power parity reaches 30,000 USD, the ratio of the service industry in economy normally increases to 70%, and at this time, the service industry maintains overall stability. Therefore, there is a tremendous space for the ratio of the Chinese service industry to rise.

Thanks to the rapid development of service productivity. The service industry, as well as service production efficiency, develops at a very high growth rate. Despite the fast increase in labor productivity, it still needs to be improved further, compared with other countries. China is smack in the middle level, and certainly has room for development. In terms of value added created by each employee, China tops the list among BRICS. In terms of the manufacturing industry, China has achieved a remarkable development, especially from 2000 to 2008. Compared with labor productivity, the total factor productivity of China is much higher than that of other countries. China enjoys a high growth rate in both the service industry and the manufacturing industry.

The ratio of commercial service in investments in the entire industry is very low, resulting in the slow development of industry. The slow growth of the manufacturing industry may be the result of the very low level of investment in the manufacturing industry. As the forum is about the ratio of Chinese trade in services, as we all know, the ratio of Chinese trade in services is very small, so the most important measure that we must take in order to increase the ratio of trade in services and further drive economic growth is to enhance the competitiveness of China's trade in services, which means we need to achieve a balance between overmuch and insufficient regulation. We can see that we exert heavy regulations and supervision in many industries, but few regulations and little supervision in other fields, which causes a fiercer competition in such fields. Therefore, we need better supervision and better protection for consumers if we want to create a more solid foundation for the service industry. Thank you!

# Speech by Yu Lixin, Director of the Research Center for International Finance of the Chinese Academy of Social Sciences, Deputy Secretary–General of Expert Committee for China Association of Trade in Services at the Summit Sub–forum

Good afternoon! This forum focuses on a discussion regarding the role of trade in services in the global value chain. China's reform and opening-up has experienced a history of 35 years; today, it stands at a crossroads. Therefore, the task we face now is to find a way to carry out transformation and upgrading. In the process, trade in services plays a significant role. Here, I will report two issues to you. The first issue is the weakness of the Chinese economy, that is, the producer service sector. The second issue concerns the role of our national producer service sector in upgrading China's status in the global value chain in the future.

In 2013, China's total foreign trade volume exceeded that of the USA, and was ranked first in the world. However, it is undeniable that we suffer from the three-industry structure problem, especially the tertiary industry, that is, a sluggish development of the service industry, which further results in the sluggish development of trade in both services and goods. Consequently, the transformation and upgrading of the manufacturing industry cannot meet the domestic need, and the only solution lies in importation. Hence, importation is the result of the huge trade deficit in services of China throughout the whole "12th Five-Year Plan" period.

It is known to all that the producer service industry, especially producer service trade, is beyond the national border from the perspective of the global value chain. It is an activity for meeting intermediate needs in the global value chain and providing various services in the production process of social items. For this reason, China needs to pay attention to the development of its trade in services, especially its producer service trade.

According to China's current statistical system, mainly China's *International Balance of Payment*, the ratio of the producer services (including communication services, finance services, computer and information services, patent application fees and other commercial services) in the whole, the service trade volume is 25%, showing that the scale of the producer service is not large. Moreover, trade in services doesn't correspond very much to trade in goods. In 2013, the ratio between the import-export volume of Chinese trade in goods and trade in services was 7.7:1, and the ratio in the world, in the USA and the UK was 4.2:1, 3.5:1 and 2.6:1 respectively. It can be seen that China's current trade in services, especially the producer service trade, suffers a sluggish development.

Traditional service items, especially tourism services, occupy a greater proportion of Chinese trade in services, while the real producer service trade only accounts for 25%. The imbalance of trade in services directly restricts the leap of the Chinese manufacturing industry into the exportation of high value-added producer service products. Besides, our China is weaker in capital-intensive and knowledge-intensive producer service, further resulting in low competitiveness. In the future period of time, the reduction of the trade deficit in services will depend on the conformance of reform to needs. The trade deficit will last if the domestic service fails to meet the needs.

How to vigorously develop the producer service trade to upgrade China's status in the global value chain? China's producer service trade is currently located at the low end of the global value chain. After relying on the labor and low-cost expansion mode for a long term, China is in the critical period of transformation and upgrading, during which it must give priority to the high value-added production link in order to improve its status in the global value chain.

The National Academy of Economic Strategy of the Chinese Academy of Social Sciences has conducted a 2-year survey on the east coastal area, Yangtze River Delta, Pearl River Delta and Circum-Bohai Sea Region. The *China Service Trade Research Report No. 2* is the report prepared by us according to the research on East China. At present, the major trouble faced by China in developing the producer service industry and the entire trade in services sector lies in the institution mechanism.

First of all, to upgrade China's status in the global value chain, we need to focus on the producer service industry and promote the value added space in the global value chain. Why is the producer service industry the focus? Although China is a manufacturing power in the world, it is far from the level of the developed countries in additional value of commodities. The producer service industry is still incorporated into the manufacturing industry, so that it fails to fully achieve a social division of labor. What is worse, the foundation of our producer service industry is not solid and strong.

In the producer service industry, the core that we should emphasize is the R&D capacity. It is crucial for China to develop its R&D capacity to strive to push the development of the producer service industry forward. The next thing we have to emphasize is that China attaches great importance to technological research and development and creates a good environment for them.

Second, proper actions are taken to make the producer service industry burgeon. Last month, the Chinese Academy of Social Sciences founded the Internet Integrity Alliance which pays close attention to emerging producer service industries in the era of big data, including Internet financing and international express and distribution logistics. Such emerging fields are critical for China if it wants to climb to the high end of the global value chain in the future. Big data and cloud computing are prevalent in such fields. The revolution of information technology creates an emerging service mode, which not only offers more convenient services to consumers and clients, but it also completely breaks the traditional service mode, thus shortening the composition of the value chain and improving the additional value of it in various linkages.

It is the new trend in development. China is standing at the crossroads now. It is the first time for China to be on the threshold of establishing international trade rules. We pay attention to the development of the emerging service modes, such as Internet financing and cross-border services. Since China has a huge market and a market population, it can formulate standards and rules in the domestic market. It is the mission that era gives to China. China needs to create rules and power of discourse in the market.

The emerging service fields in the future will help not only attain the strategic goal of China's service status in the world, but it will also help correct the current trade deficit in services. In the meanwhile, for the first time, China faces new opportunities in promoting a steady development of the global trade, especially the formulation of international rules. That's why the Chinese Academy of Social Sciences established the Internet Finance Integrity Alliance which is aimed at formulating new operational rules, including supervision and industry standards. How to accomplish this goal? Our suggestion is that a sound and practical macro-control system must be established at the governmental level, as well as an integrated ministry-level coordination operation mechanism. Without such reforms, the development of Chinese trade in services will be seriously hampered. Thank you!

# Speech of Li Gang, Director of the International Trade in Services Research Institute of the MOC Research Academy, at the Summit Sub–forum

The topic of my speech is to review and gradually reduce the policy barrier in trade in services. Nowadays, IT and Internet technology have penetrated into every walk of life, including the area of services. In such a scenario, we will discuss the new challenges facing trade in services policies in terms of its development, the formulation of policies in the various countries, and supervision.

How to deal with the policy barrier in trade in services? In a positive light, a country's policies regarding trade in services may intervene in the following three aspects. The opening-up of various areas of the service industry and trade decides the access of foreign enterprises or companies. More detailed requirements may be defined in market access, such as the permission of sole proprietorships, the proportion of joint ventures, qualification requirements and specific conditions in professional services, domestic rules and systems, specific systems and standards involving industry and department administration.

In a negative light, the aforesaid content is exactly the policy barrier. On a global scale, as far as I am concerned, different degrees of trade policy barriers exist in both developed countries and developing countries, and even in some emerging economies.

Regarding the policy barrier in Chinese trade in services, so far, we have honored the commitment to the opening-up 9 fields and 100 sub-sectors. Our commitment to the WTO is based on China's development level and the opening-up support of the industrial structure at that time. Today, of course, we have more fields that can stand an external impact, so we can expand the opening-up.

There are some restrictions on some fields. However, it is necessary to impose some access restrictions. Some improvements still need to be made. All countries may need to carefully review and consider the restrictions on the investment proportion and qualification requirements on professional services, which the governmental departments cannot avoid.

It is true that China suffers from some problems in the real opening-up, such as an incomplete opening-up. Besides, there are also some problems in the marketization of its system mechanism, as well as the "glass door" and "spring door" phenomenon. Therefore, a new challenge has also presented itself for the system requirements.

A country's policies regarding trade in services are really inseparable from the level of the national economic development. It is important to discuss trade in services policies because they are a very important part of the overall national trade policy. A country's policies regarding trade in services are also an integral part of the macroeconomic policy. Now, China is experiencing the transformation from an industrial economy to a service economy. Therefore, great concern and attention should be given. In the formulation of its trade policy, a country is making a balanced decision between free trade and protective trade, that is, the balance between rights and obligations. It needs to be considered seriously, especially in the performance of the WTO agreement. For those sectors already opened to the outside, free trade is implemented, but does it mean there is no limit to it or any restriction and supervision involved? For this point, I agree with the opinions of experts from the OECD, that it is necessary to seriously consider the implementation of proper supervision and the challenge proposed by the governmental departments in the course of the integration of the global value chain, the supply chain and the industrial chain in the era of IT. Therefore, we come to the conclusion that the policies regarding trade in services cannot be universally considered as a trade barrier. Full recognition should be given to proper policies. Improper policies against the access of foreign manufacturers are trade barriers, however, and should be gradually diminished.

China has done a great deal of work at attempting to eliminate and reduce the policy barrier in trade in services. The Chinese government has shown the world that it will expand the opening-up of the service industry. It will firstly perform an independent opening-up in various industries, such as finance, culture, education and medical care, as well as sub-sectors that were originally committed to opening up. Making commitments in trade cooperation in such fields is not required.

In terms of further relaxing access and qualification conditions, measures should be implemented step by step. In terms of deepening reforms, the administrative approval procedures need to be reduced and simplified. In the process, reform still means a lot. More efforts need to be made concerning the role of the market in resource configuration as determined during the Third Plenary Session of the 18th Central Committee of the CPC, and a clear definition by the government in tangible aspects. In addition, we also discussed new management modes such as the national treatment of access rights in the field of foreign capital. For those that are formulated by domestic departments and industries but do not conform to specifications and standards, a review should be carried out institutionally.

For the core field involving the national security and interest, we should be cautious about its further opening-up, and may promote the opening-up in the precondition of controllable risk. For the international coordination and management, China has shown it will actively participate in WTO negotiations. All of these reflect China's ambition and confidence in the opening-up of the service industry and trade. We really hope China can achieve a substantial participation rather than being excluded from WTO negotiations. We notice that the Chinese government has made positive declarations with respect to peripheral fields such as ITA and GPA. We hope China can promote negotiations regarding such fields because they are greatly associated with the further promotion of trade in services. Now, China is actively pushing forward its FTA strategy and facing a global high-level FTA network. We look forward to more involvement of trade in services in the FTA and RTA negotiations. We especially hope that new rules are manifested in the future FTA and RTA.

As we all know, new BIT negotiations are being carried out between China and the USA or between China and Europe, which surely involve new issues relating to the opening-up of the service industry. Finally, I am firmly convinced that China will make more progress in independent opening-up in the future, and balance between policy supervision and liberalization will be achieved in the field of trade in services. Thank you!

# Part Ⅱ

Summary of Speeches at the
Signing Ceremory

# Speech by Fang Aiqing, Vice Minister of Commerce, at the Signing Ceremony of the 3rd CIFTIS

Distinguished guests, ladies, gentlemen and friends,

Good afternoon! The five-day event of the 3rd China Beijing International Fair for Trade in Services (CIFTIS) will close today. This session witnesses splendid exhibitions, outstanding discussion themes, practical and efficient transaction negotiations, fully showing the important role as the Chinese opening-up window and the stage for deepening international trade in services cooperation. Here, I would like to, on behalf of the CIFTIS organizing committee, express sincere gratitude to leaders at all levels, domestic and foreign guests and media friends, for your consistent concern and support for the development of CIFTIS.

With the idea of "pragmatism, cooperation, integrity and simplicity", exhibitions, forum activities and trade negotiations have been arranged uniformly. There were 133 activities held altogether, which have attracted 153,000 representatives and operators from 117 countries and regions, showing a further improvement in internationalization, professionalization and marketization, and an increase in international influence. The success of CIFTIS lies not only in the concentrated displaying of the achievements of the development of Chinese trade in services , but also the full manifestation of trade in services as a new international cooperation hotspot. Here below is my reporting on three aspects, i.e., CIFTIS background, CIFTIS characteristics, and CIFTIS achievements.

Ⅰ. CIFTIS background.

This session of CIFTIS is different from previous sessions. Nowadays, the global economy is slowly recovering, and the service industry and trade have become new engines and impetus for driving its recovery. With the deepening of economic globalization, various countries have been increasingly integrated into the economy, and the international division of labor is extending from a traditional manufacturing linkage to a high-end linkage such as the producer service industry, which has triggered the adjustment and upgrading of the global economic structure and driven the fast development of trade in services. Under the background of the decline in total goods of the trade in services volume in 2013, the global trade in services increased by 6.1%, becoming the new growth point in global trade. Besides, trade in services and investment have become the new hotspot of international economic cooperation.

Transnational companies will speed up the transfer of producer services such as research & development, consulting and information to the developing countries. Meanwhile, the traditional trade in services has been transformed into a technology-intensive modern trade in services, and 60% of global transnational investments originate in the service industry. The acceleration of the transnational investment in service industry provides hard-won opportunities for the development of trade in services.

The current period is the period of important strategic opportunities for China to vigorously develop its service industry and trade. Foreign investments in the Chinese service industry have exceeded those in the manufacturing industry in the three consecutive years from 2011. The ratio of foreign investments in the service industry was 52.3% in 2013; in 2012, the service industry became the largest industry in creating jobs, exceeding agriculture for the first time, in 2013; the value added in the Chinese service industry accounted for 46.1% of the GDP, which was, for the first time, superior to that for industry, so that the service industry became the leading industry in the national economy. A sustained and sound development of the service industry lays a solid foundation for the development of trade in services. In the past ten years, Chinese trade in services developed at an annual growth rate of nearly 18%. In the first three years of the "12th Five-Year Plan", the ratio of trade in services in Chinese foreign trade continuously increased and reached 10.3%, 10.8% and 11.5% respectively. In the first quarter of the current year, the ratio climbed to 12.8%. In 2013, the total volume of Chinese trade in services amounted to 539.6 billion USD, which was ranked third in the world. The Chinese government has explicitly proposed to establish a strategic status of its trade in services and considers it as a strategic focus of its economic development. Trade in services will be energetically developed to accelerate the transformation of the economic development mode, in order to improve the international competitiveness of the industrial chain, and actively participate in cooperation concerning the global value chain.

As a unique integrated global trade in services exhibition, CIFTIS bears the historical mission to promote the development of the Chinese service industry and trade. The establishment of CIFTIS is really an important measure for China to boost a fast development of its service industry and trade. In the context of foreign and domestic economic development, at present, the 3rd CIFTIS closely keeps up with the developmental trend and the hot spots of trade in services, and outlines the role of trade in services within the global value chain, with the theme of "expanding the opening-up of the service industry". Focusing on trans-boundary integration of various industries, CIFTIS has been an important platform for China and other countries to reach a consensus and negotiate cooperation over three years of development, which makes a great contribution to promoting the development of global trade in services.

II. Characteristics of the 3rd CIFTIS.

The 3rd CIFTIS continues to acquire concern and support from the CPC and State leaders. Wang Yang, Member of the Political Bureau of the CPC Central Committee and Vice-premier of the State Council, visited CIFTIS pavilions in person and delivered a speech at the Summit. Besides, Zhang Baowen, Vice-chairman of the NPC Standing Committee, attended the Summit and delivered a speech as well. The 3rd CIFTIS focuses on the theme of "expanding the opening-up of the service industry" and has the following four outstanding features:

(i) The theme of "expanding the opening-up of the service industry" has been highlighted.

The CIFTIS organizing committee always earnestly implements the important spirits proposed in the Third Plenary Session of the 18th Central Committee of the CPC and in the 2014 Report on the Work of the Government in the whole process of the preparation for and the holding of CIFTIS; it also focuses on the theme of "expanding the opening-up of the service industry" to carry out the preparatory work. It has cooperated with the OECD to jointly hold the summit of "The Role of Trade in Services in Global Value Chain"; it will continue to cooperate with the WTO and UNCTAD to give China a voice in promoting the common development of global trade in services. Nine professional forums closely follow the theme of "expanding the opening-up of the service industry" and witness discussions and  exchanges concerning various fields such as the exhibition industry, the express industry, E-commerce, culture trade and international economic cooperation, showing the world the confidence and determination of various fields of the service industry in expanding the opening-up. China's Ministry of Commerce has put forward a proposal for establishing CIFTIS as an important platform of exchanges within and cooperation on trade in services in the Memorandum of Cooperation of Trade in Services signed together with several countries. Beijing actively fosters CIFTIS as an important carrier for expanding the opening-up of the service industry.

(ii) The idea of "improving the quality of the services" has been highlighted.

Centered on meeting the needs of exhibitors and purchasers, the CIFTIS organizing committee actively explores the trade in services exhibition rules, makes an overall arrangement of displaying, a forum of discussions and transaction  negotiations according to features of the industry in order to facilitate the conclusion of business and improve the level of the services. In terms of exhibition consulting, a call center and a "24-hour bilingual service" are provided to respond to foreign and domestic consulting; in terms of newspaper office services, an online newspaper office system is experiencing its first trial run; the networking and automation of the commercial newspaper office are promoted; in terms of the layout of the exhibition environment, the idea of "frugality" is observed, so that booths  are constructed by using loadable modules and reusable articles such as  flags and guiding marks continue to be used; in terms of on-the-spot services, various professional services and public services are clearly and explicitly presented to exhibitors through a variety of carriers such as a website, brochures, on-the-spot touch screens and sign systems have been installed in the exhibition hall; in terms of standardization of transaction negotiation, negotiation activities are under a uniform arrangement, and are classified based on type, and standardized based on the negotiation organization mode and process arrangement.

(iii) The method of "establishing a cooperation mechanism" has been highlighted.

On the basis of the summarization of the experience of the first two sessions, good working methods have been established to form a long-term effective mechanism. The cooperation with three major international organizations has been strengthened, leading to a preliminary cooperation mechanism for taking turns to jointly hold the summit. The cooperation with 17 national ministries and governmental agencies such as the Ministry of Foreign Affairs, the Ministry of Education, the Ministry of Industry and Information, the Ministry of Finance, the Ministry of Transport and the Ministry of Culture is enhanced to make them continue to serve as the support units for the 3rd CIFTIS. The cooperation with provinces and cities has been enhanced. A number of groups from 31 provinces, Xinjiang Production and Construction Corps and 5 municipalities have come to attend CIFTIS. The activity of the theme day has been conducted in nine provinces and cities such as Beijing, Shanghai and Hubei. The ministry-city consultation mechanism has been enhanced, and the work mechanism also continues to be intensified, such as a joint consultation by ministries and cities with respect to the significant issue, and cooperation and a labor division of executing agencies, so as to give play to the strength in the ministries and cities, thus providing first-rate meeting experience for exhibitors and operators.

(iv) The role of information technology in the holding of the fair has been highlighted.

Information technology is widely used to further improve the CIFTIS information level and quality of its services, as well as to increase the operators' satisfaction. The 3rd CIFTIS makes full use of an on-the-spot automatic control system, and outlines the intelligent management of exhibition control, electronic monitoring, security and firefighting. By drawing on experience from the on-line and off-line E-commerce mode, a trade matching information platform has been constructed for CIFTIS, and in addition, a 3,500-m$^2$ trade matching hall is built in the venue. In accordance with the process of "merchant registration, matching application, matching confirmation, off-line negotiation", trade matching between supplier and demander has been strengthened through an "on-line search of the negotiation object, and an off-line one-to-one contact".

III. The 3rd CIFTIS has attained great achievements in the following aspects.

(i) Show the world China's determination to expand the opening-up of the service industry.

Wang Yang, the State Council Vice-premier, has clearly showed the international community China's confidence and determination in expanding the opening-up of its service industry in the speech delivered at the CIFTIS Summit. Zhang Baowen, Vice Chairman of the National People's Congress, outlined China's involvement in the service-oriented global value chain through the expansion of the opening-up of its service industry. Mukhisa Kituyi, the UNCTAD Secretary-General, stated that the speech of Vice-premier Wang Yang impressed him when he said that the "Chinese government has determined to further expand the opening-up of the service industry market, and has made commitments, showing that the Chinese government has grasped the key point of the future development of the economy". William Danvers, the OECD Deputy Secretary General, stated that "the speech of Vice-premier Wang Yang impressed him regarding the determination of the Chinese government to reform the service industry and in pursuing the global leadership of the service industry"; he was also impressed with the fact that "the Chinese government has put the service industry as the core of its overall reforms". The Summit and a series of professional forums  have showed China's unswerving attitude towards the expansion of the opening-up of the service industry, which increases the confidence of the outside world in China's expanding the opening-up of its service industry and promoting a sustainable development of the economy.

(ii) Expand the space and field of international cooperation within trade in services.

The 3rd CIFTIS has further deepened the exchanges and cooperation among various countries, international organizations and industrial associations and has seen the attendance of 91 important foreign and domestic important, governmental ministers, ambassadors, the heads of various international organizations and industrial associations, as well as presidents of transnational companies. Apart from the summit held in cooperation with the OECD, it has also held "small conferences for ministers" in cooperation with UNCTAD, and will continue to hold the "WTO and China: Beijing International Forum" and the UN service procurement seminar. Leaders from the World Trade Point Federation, the International Trade Center and the International Center for Trade and Sustainable Development attended the 3rd CIFTIS activities. Groups from 21 international industrial associations and foreign commerce associations, such as the International Designers Federation, the Global Association of the Exhibition Industry and the European E-commerce Association, participated in the exhibition and fair. Groups from 17 foreign countries and regions such as the UK, Germany, Singapore, Korea and India, took part in the exhibition; among the world's top 10 enterprises in trade in services, 6 enterprises formed a group to attend the exhibition; there were 12 overseas countries and regions that held national theme day activities and special activities to have

exchanges and cooperate in terms of culture creativity, information technology and tourism services.

(iii) Promote the trans-boundary integration of industries and the transitional development of the service industry.

CIFTIS has focused on the innovative achievements in the field of trade in services, and has explored the developmental trend of the international service industry, which not only creates opportunities for integration and development of various service industries, but also builds a bridge for the integration between the service industry and other industries. At the Forum of "E-commerce Innovative Development" held on May 30, leaders from e-commerce enterprises and industrial organizations focused on the new social marketing mode (such as the E-commerce platform, the on-line and off-line E-commerce mode, the new mobile e-commerce trend, electronic invoices, cross-border e-commerce), new fields (such as e-commerce of community agricultural products), big data, e-commerce challenges and opportunities for discussion in the Internet finance age, so as to promote exchanges and cooperation in the related fields. With the theme of trans-boundary integration, the Seminar on the International Sports Service Trade Development was held and foreign and domestic experts, scholars and enterprise leaders were invited to attend it in order to find out a way to break through the industrial boundaries and achieve effective connections and deep integration among industries. StoryDrive meetings not only provided valuable trade information for exhibitors and professional buyers, but they also led to successful trans-boundary publications, so that a 360-degree conversion of stories was realized. Stories were presented in many media forms such as books, movies, games and electronic publications.

(iv) Promote trade matching among enterprises.

In the CIFTIS trade matching system, there are altogether 1,042 enterprises that apply for the trade matching service, of which 531 enterprises are willing to engage in international trade. Besides, there are 2,011 trade matching confirmation records, and 1,596 face-to-face business talks. The Chamber of Digital Commerce and Business Conferences received more than 2,000 professional visitors on May 29, 2014, with the number of one-to-one business talks reaching 350 and the amount of intentions for cooperation reaching 2.06 billion RMB. In terms of express services, nearly 400 enterprises attended the Forum of On-line and Off-line E-commerce Mode, with an amount of contracts of intention nearly 50 billion RMB. The Seminar on the International Sports Service Trade Development facilitate 33 signed projects in the area of sports services, including the 2014 Champion's Trophy, the 2014 Red Bull Air Race World Championship, and NBA Broadcast rights purchased by Letv.

Dear guests and friends, the 3rd CIFTIS is coming to a successful conclusion, and the 4th CIFTIS preparation is going to start. We will center on professionalization, internationalization

and marketization to show the world a more splendid fair. We will continue to consolidate the basic framework of the exhibition, forum and business talks, explore proper exhibition modes corresponding to the characteristics of trade in services, create a CIFTIS brand forum and improve the effectiveness of the business talks. We will deeply expand the space for and the mode of international cooperation, fix a long-term effective mechanism for holding a high-level forum together with three permanent supporters to strive to make more international organizations become CIFTIS international cooperative agencies and deepen the cooperation with overseas governmental chambers of commerce and transnational entreprises, thus further improving the international level of CIFTIS. Besides, we will explore an operational mode suitable for the marketization of CIFTIS in order to boost the sustainable development of CIFTIS.

The success of the 3rd CIFTIS shows the tremendous achievements in the development of the Chinese service industry, and numerous potential business opportunities in global trade in services. The concern and support of friends from all walks of life is absolutely essential for the success of CIFTIS. We will continue to solidify the cooperation with friends from all walks of life to drive the transformation and upgrading of the service industry and boost a fast development of trade in services, thus making more contributions to Chinese economic upgrades and promoting a healthy and fast development of the global service industry and trade.

Thank you!

# Speech by Cheng Hong, Deputy Mayor of Beijing at the Signing Ceremony of the 3rd CIFTIS

Just now, Vice Minister Fang Aiqing made a comprehensive summary about the 3rd CIFTIS, and made a brief introduction to the future plans.

As an organizer, we are very pleased and gratified to see the pomp of CIFTIS. Founded three years ago, CIFTIS has developed greatly under a meticulous fostering. Today is Children's Day, a special day that means growth, vitality and hope. With the development of the past three years, although CIFTIS is a new brand, it is thriving. We are glad to take the opportunity to share the history of the development of CIFTIS in the previous three years with you. It is precisely the common efforts that have achieved today's accomplishments. Here, I want to add that CIFTIS has shown the following characteristics regarding four aspects over the past three years.

The first aspect is the increasing growth. The number of exhibitors continues to grow year by year. In the current year, there are 153,000 people from 117 countries and regions participating in CIFTIS activities, of which the number of professional operators is 145,000, 20.8% more than the previous year. Yesterday, which was the first day of the 3rd CIFTIS, saw over 7,200 visitors. In addition, there is also a notable surge of enterprises. In the 3rd CIFTIS, the number of enterprises reached 2,524, with an increase of 33% over the last session and more than 800 over the first session. Besides, the number of professional buyers exceeds 210, with a rise of 17 over the last session. The 3rd CIFTIS for the first time has attracted operators from 20 countries and regions ranked in the world's top 20 in global trade in services. Particularly, I am pleased to tell you that there has been a marked rise in signed projects throughout the country and the world. In the 3rd CIFTIS, the number of signed projects has reached 236 and the amount of contracts of intention has reached 81.83 billion USD, of which the amount of international project contracts of intention is up to 35.5 billion USD, 3.3 times as much as that of the 2nd session, and accounting for 43% of the total amount of contracts of intention, with a growth of nearly 30%, revealing that the role of CIFTIS in enhancing cooperation in global trade for services enterprises has further increased. Moreover, the amount of contracts regarding domestic (excluding Beijing) projects reaches 34.36 billion USD, 2.1 times as many as those of last session, accounting for 42% of the total amount of contracts, with a growth of 21 percentage points over the last session, reflecting the role of

CIFTIS in services and in boosting domestic trade in services, which has also increasingly intensified.

Hence, the 3rd CIFTIS sees both old and new friends, old cooperation projects and new upgrading. For example, both of the two famous international exhibitions introduced an upgrading in their CIFTIS activities. For instance, the "StoryDrive China" has been upgraded to "StoryDrive Asia" in the current year. Juergen Boos, Chairman of the Frankfurt Buchmesse, has always said that, "I hope Beijing creates a Pan-Asia platform, enabling Asian publishers to realize exchanges and transactions without the need to go to the Frankfurt Buchmesse." In addition, "SmartCity China" has been upgraded to "SmartCity Asia" in the current year; the international participation rate has reached 72% , with a year-on-year growth of eight percentage points; the German exhibition group has organized more than 30 NRW enterprises, most of them were the first to come to China. Therefore, you can meet many new faces and friends in the 3rd CIFTIS.

The second aspect is the increasing attraction. This is shown in the increasing initiative of international organizations, countries, regions and enterprises in attending the CIFTIS. We can see that the three major organizations that play a decisive role in global trade, i.e., UNCTAD, OECD and the WTO, are all permanent supporters of CIFTIS. They have carried out a great deal of practical work for CIFTIS.

In the current year, the International Trade Center has expressed its strong will to establish a close cooperative relationship with CIFTIS. Bruno, Chairman of the World Trade Point Federation, has attended CIFTIS three times, and set up the Federation's secretariat in Beijing during the current year. Besides, there are 21 international industrial organizations and overseas chambers of commerce that are attending the 3rd CIFTIS, which was mentioned by Vice Minister Fang. Such a figure is nearly two times as large as that of the previous session. There are also many operators from trade in services from powerful countries and regions. There are even 55 countries and regions that have been involved in CIFTIS activities for three consecutive years. Of the world's top 20 countries and regions involved in global trade in services, 18 of them have been involved in CIFTIS activities for three consecutive years. Eight countries and regions, such as the UK, Singapore, Japan and Korea, have taken part in the CIFTIS exhibition for three consecutive years. India is our neighbor; Only Indian enterprises came to attend the 1st session, while the 2nd session saw groups of Indian industrial associations participating in special activities; In the 3rd session, apart from exhibition participation and participation in group work, theme day activities are also carried out. A number of world-famous enterprises are closely cooperating with CIFTIS, and many of them have attended CIFTIS for three consecutive years, such as Siemens, Carrefour, China Post, JD. com and Tongrentang, and they have obtained great results.

The third aspect is the constant improvement in its effectiveness. Vice Minister Fang has mentioned that the characterizing feature of the 3rd CIFTIS lies in the enhancement of on-line and off-line interaction and on-the-spot business talks. The 3rd CIFTIS has seen notable yields in many aspects, and has a great number of highly active trade and business talks. Moreover, the volume of transactions has repeatedly set a new high. For example, in terms of express services, the amount of contracts was 5 billion RMB and 20 billion RMB in the 1st and 2nd session respectively, while the amount in the 3rd session climbed to 50 billion, an increase of nearly 10 times over the 1st session.

The fourth aspect is the constant increase in the attention given CIFTIS. The attention from media, networks and insiders is rising year by year. Up to this morning, 1,437 reporters from 262 media have been making news reports on CIFTIS, with a total of 908 original reports, 4,131 reprinted reports, 150,000 Weibo topics, and more than 750,000 pieces of CIFTIS information on the Internet. In terms of website attention, the number of total visits to the CIFTIS official website exceeds 2,815,000, of which the number of visits from foreign websites is up to 1,324,000, accounting for 47% of the total visits. Besides, the total visits from Spanish, Russian, French, Arabic, Korean and Japanese websites all exceed 140,000. In terms of attention by industries, several modules are in a good situation, including the well-known Electronic Commerce Professional Conference, which attracts a number of visitors each year. For instance, this year, we have prepared a venue that holds 1,000 participants; the number of the actual participants exceeds 1,500; in the International Express Industry Development Conference, 800 seats are arranged, but the number of the actual attendees reaches 900. For the China International Exhibition Development Conference, the number of the attending applicants is 400, but the number of the actual attendees exceeds 500. Besides, in an Internet Seminar for Exhibition Marketization, the admission ticket is not cheap, around 1,000 RMB, but they are in short supply. The number of attendees is set at around 100, but the actual number reaches 200. It is our joint participation, concern and support that make CIFTIS flourish and yield such fruitful results.

Dear guests and friends, thanks to concerted efforts of all workers and volunteers, the 3rd CIFTIS has offered first-class service in all aspects, such as exhibition services, guest reception, security guarantee and service assurance; there have been zero safetyaccidents, reception errors and intellectual property complaints, and we have received unanimous acclaim from both foreign and domestic guests.

Dasio, the Brazil Federation of Trade in Services and International Marketing Represen-tative said that "CIFTIS grows larger and attracts an increasing number of exhibitors, creating more and more opportunities". Besides, he added that the most immediate and obvious feeling at the 3rd CIFTIS is the increasing number of purchasers, and many professional purchasers from Europe, Asia and North America bring valuable trade in services orders to CIFTIS.

In an interview, Mr. Li Xinqiang, President of the Law Society of Hong Kong, said that "CIFTIS is expanding in its scale, revealing much attention from the state and central government regarding trade in services, and regarding the growing influence of CIFTIS".

All guests and friends, the 3rd CIFTIS is coming to an end. It has drawn enthusiastic responses, and obtained notable results. Its success is ascribed to the objective background of the accelerated development of global trade in services, and the orientation of the Chinese policy of energetically developing the service industry. Furthermore, its success is inseparable from the strong support of international organizations and chambers of commerce at home and abroad, from the support and assistance of national ministries and central government departments, from the elaborate sponsoring of foreign and domestic institutions, from the active participation of 31 provinces (autonomous region, municipality), Xinjiang Production and Construction Corps, five cities with separate planning, and Hong Kong, Macao and Taiwan, and most importantly, from the professional planning and hard work of the media present. Friends from the press dig out the highlights of this session from special perspectives, seize wonderful and memorable moments and build an efficient bridge between CIFTIS and global operators, and between CIFTIS and numerous visitors. So here, I would like to take this opportunity to express a sincere gratitude to all friends that have shown concern and support to CIFTIS, including the media present here.

The success of the 3rd CIFTIS lays a solid foundation for subsequentCIFTIS events. Under the leadership of the Ministry of Commerce, CIFTIS will continue to follow the idea of "serving operators first, and centering on business talks" to increase the level of internationalization, enhance the professional capacity and stick to market-based development. We will listen to opinions and suggestions from all parties to further improve the organization, optimize the activity arrangement and improve the conference level to attempt to make CIFTIS more attractive, thus making new contributions to the development of the Chinese trade in services, the upgrading of the structure of foreign trade and the development of global trade in services.

At last, I, on behalf of the the organizing committee, sincerely invite all of you to attend the next session of CIFTIS and gather together again in Beijing. All guests and friends, I look forward to seeing you at the 4th CIFTIS. Thank you!

# Part III

Summary of Speeches at the
Summit High-level Forum

# Speech by Zhou Liujun, Director General of the Department of Trade in Services and Commercial Services of the Ministry of Commerce, at CIFTIS· the 8th International Trade in Services Forum

Distinguished Chairman Liu, Chairman Qian and all experts,

I am very pleased to be invited again to attend the CIFTIS—International Trade in Services Forum. First of all, I want to say that today is the third day from opening day and this session of CIFTIS is the 3rd one. This session is showing new changes, improvements and highlights. It should be noted that Vice Premier Wang Yang in charge of the commercial work agreed to attend the opening ceremony and deliver a speech, but unfortunately, an important conference held by the CPC Central Committee prevented him from attending this event. In spite of this, Vice Premier Wang Yang sent his written speech, which was read out by the international trade representative at the summit. The speech is wonderful; it specially discloses governmental information about the development of trade in services in four aspects. The first one is that China will firmly adhere to the opening-up of its service industry. The second one is that the opening-up of the Chinese service industry will advance step by step. His speech points out that China will integrate the developmental speed and the level of the opening-up of the service industry with the degree of involvement, and specially mentions the market access in six service fields which have been facilitated in the Shanghai Pilot Free Trade Zone. The third one is that the opening-up of the Chinese service industry has an institutional guarantee. The opening is neither restricted nor arbitrary. Apart from the market access, China pays greater attention to institutional design. The last one is that the opening-up of the Chinese service industry is mutually beneficial. The Chinese government welcomes investments from all countries and encourages domestic enterprises to go outside; in addition, it shows its willingness to actively participate in negotiations on trade in services agreements so as to be able to work together in order to promote the liberalization and facilitation of trade in services. Vice Premier Wang Yang's speech further demonstrates China's firm confidence and determination in expanding the opening-up of the service industry, and points out the direction of its opening-up and of the development of trade in services in the coming days, which is of great significance.

Next I want to stress that, compared with the previous two sessions, the influence of the

3rd session has further increased. On the first day, the 3rd session witnessed 36,000 visitors (a 46% increase) from 117 countries and regions, with an increase of 20 units. And there are 55 countries and regions that have been involved in CIFTIS activities for three consecutive years. At the CIFTIS, there are 133 activities such as exhibitions, forums and business talks. As we all know, it is hard to hold a trade in services fair, and the CIFTIS is the world's first comprehensive fair. Yesterday, Vice Premier Wang Yang came and we accompanied him to visit the exhibition hall; the visit lasted 50 minutes. He perceived the difference between the trade in services fair and the trade in goods fair. We made him notice that the trade in services fair houses exhibitions, forums and business talks, which is a harmonious interaction. The exhibition is the garden for showing the development of trade in services; the forum is the vane for determining and studying the developmental trend of trade in services; the business talk is the platform for enterprises to realize cooperation and win-win results, which is the cornucopia of trade in services. We introduced the specific meaning of garden, vane and cornucopia to Vice Premier Wang Yang. During the summit forum, leaders from three major international organizations, as well as senior managers of transnational companies, gave speeches and expressed their incisive opinions concerning the role of trade in services within the global value chain; they also made an optimistic predication about the future development of global trade in services.

During the 3rd CIFTIS, a great number of activities are being carried out. I have been attending the CIFTIS for three consecutive years, which is highly appreciated by Chairman Qian and Chairman Wang. In my opinion, the CIFTIS is going on a different path, which embodies people's wisdom, vision and attention, manifests people's persistence and expresses people's expectations and wishes. To sum up, Chinese trade in services will surely enjoy a steady, rapid and sound development, it will surely make great contributions to the improvement of the global value chain and it will surely play an increasing important role in the transformation and upgrading of our national economy, achieving the Great Chinese Dream and the improvement of people's welfare. Since its first session, the CIFTIS has closely followed the theme of time, the background and pulse of the development of trade in services, enabling the participants to make analyses and offer advice and suggestions from the point of view of globalization. I am very delighted to see the accomplishment of the thesis contest held by our Academy and I would like to extend my congratulations on participants' gains. The titles and accomplishments of these theses are of great pertinence, theoretical value and practical significance. I hope the Academy will be able to take full advantage of such accomplishments, just as before. I will ask my colleagues to carefully read every paper in which wise suggestions may be transformed into policies for the future. In the past, the transformation of accomplishments was carried out well. However, I believe we will do better in the future. We may invite some authors and experts to attend the forum to make some exchanges. I would like to make a proposal, that is, one or two thesis winners are invited to deliver a speech during the successive forum. The attendees of the forum not only include senior authoritative experts like me but also up-and-coming youngsters; we are all growing along with the service industry. I believe Chinese trade in services and its corresponding industry will be beneficial to many industries and fields, such as outsourcing services, cultural trade and academic achievements of domestic and foreign scholars who devote themselves to studying the service industry and trade in services.

What is new in this session is that I will give some answers to your requests. As I have just mentioned, in the process of the fast development of trade in services, we should pay close attention to the trade deficit that is increasing with each passing year. This happens because, according to a research report, the unfavorable balance of trade in services will exceed the favorable balance of trade in goods by 2017 based on the current speed of development. The research report, prepared by Li Gang, was submitted to the State Council, and the State Council has introduced relevant policies. It is a typical example of interaction between the government and academic institutions, which is conducive to promoting the completion of work. The key to facing and solving problems is what you think about the problems and what should be done. Today, I will focus on talking about how to enhance our capacity of service exportation and accelerate the formation of new advantages in foreign trade competition. I want to share my ideas about what to do and what we can do with regard to the increasing deficit.

It is known to all that Chinese manufacturing was renowned in the world during the three decades before the reform and the opening-up, enabling China to become the world's factory. In 2013, China reached 4.23 trillion USD in the total volume of import and export goods, and the first in the world. Since the rise of Chinese manufacturing, Chinese service has been on its way into the world, and trade in services has been developing rapidly. Especially since joining the WTO, China's service industry has been deepening at an opening-up level, expanding in scale and optimizing in structure. In 2013, China achieved 539.6 billion USD in the total volume of service imports and exports, with a year-on-year increase of 14.7%, accounting for 11.5% and 6% of the total Chinese foreign trade volume and worldwide total foreign trade volume respectively; and it was ranked 3rd in the world, only after the USA and Germany. Under the background of a 1% decline in the import and export of goods in the first quarter in 2014, trade in services is increasing, and the total trade in services volume reached 138.8 billion USD in the first quarter, an increase of 15.6%. All of this shows that trade in services has become the new highlight and an important growth point in Chinese foreign trade.

Besides, we should consider that China is a large trade in goods country rather than a trading power. It is because our added value in foreign trade is small, which is the result of the lagging development of trade in services and the small proportion of trade in services in foreign trade. Therefore, the only way for China to realize the transformation and upgrading of its foreign trade is go from Chinese-made to Chinese service, and from a large trading country to a trading power. Both national leaders and scholars believe that trade in services will play an increasingly important role in the process of moving towards becoming a trading power from its current position as a large trading country. We in China will continue the process of moving towards becoming a trading power more smoothly only when we can overcome the weakness in our trade in services, and improve out value added in goods service and service export capacity through the development of producer services and trade in services. So we must seize the opportunity offered by the adjustment of the structure of the global industry and by the accelerated transfer of the service industry to significantly enhance the service export capacity and create new advantages in foreign trade competition while energetically boosting trade in services.

Next, I will share my opinions about how to strengthen the service export capacity.

First of all, I believe that the enhancement of the service export capacity is the key to accelerating the formation of new advantages in competition regarding international economic cooperation. The Third Plenary Session of the 18th Central Committee of the CPC decided to accelerate the formation of new advantages in international competition and to promote reform through the opening-up; moreover, it has specifically proposed to promote an orderly opening-up in various fields, such as finance, education, culture and medical care, and ease access restrictions on foreign investments. Besides, the Central Economic Working Conference held last December also put forward the idea of maintaining traditional advantages and innovating new comparative advantages and competitive advantages. With the increase in the quality of talent and the dynamic adjustment of comparative advantages, service exports are expected to obtain a new competitive advantage, and trade in services will play a leading role in fostering new advantages in foreign trade. From the colorful activities that have been carried out in a few days, we realize that it is of far-reaching significance to set up bases and innovative carriers for talent cultivation, and we hope the bases and carriers named today will run practically and adopt new ideas and methods. As talent quality is the most important resource and internal motivation in the service industry and trade, we will further expand the opening- up of the service industry and attempt to carry out the management mode of national treatment+negative list concerning foreign investment. To grasp the new trend in the development of the service industry and trade, we must center on talent, strengthen international exchanges and cooperation, get involved in competition through the introduction of an advanced operation and management mode, foster domestic industry competitiveness and improve our service export capacity. Improving our service export capacity is a necessary requirement for driving the upgrading of our foreign trade structure and creating economic upgrading as well. In recent years, due to the decline in resource and population bonus and the rise in operation and salary costs, our low-cost international competitiveness in a labor- concentrated industry has been greatly impacted. At present, manufacturing industry servicizing has been a new direction and highlight in the development of world economy. The constant upgrading of our demand structure, the increasing expansion of a high-education population and the improvement of the industrial matching ability lay a solid foundation for expanding service exports. Enhancing the service export capacity and expanding service exports will efficiently further eliminate restrictions on resources and on the environment, take the development of the service industry a great leap forward, improve the quality benefit of economic growth, increase the overall operation efficiency of the national economy and promote the upgrading of the economy.

Do you know why Beijing makes such great efforts to hold the CIFTIS? As Secretary Guo put it, "Beijing considers the development of the service industry and trade as an important and unique choice". Last year, 77% of the GDP originated in the Beijing service industry. Beijing is promoting the CIFTIS and the Zhongguancun Innovation Center by regarding them as two strategic platforms. Let's take a simple example. China has an adverse surplus of the capacity for steel and cement production because of rigid constraints on demand. On the contrary, the culture trade is free from such restrictions. At a time of good development of the economy, people tend to need culture, they go to the opera and participate in the Music Carnival; at a time when the development of the economy is poor, people tend to be in a bad mood and need more comfort and consolation culturally than before. The food we can eat in one week is limited, but we can appreciate the opera repeatedly without a problem of "overnutrition". The service industry is subject to demand, but the supply is adequate and can create demand. Before the development of Dashilan, people did not tend to visit the Great Wall and Thirteen Ming Tombs, but after the development of Dashilan and the 798 Art District, more and more tourists prefer to go to there to experience China's long-standing and profound culture. It is the charm of trade in services and cultural trade which can create demand. Another example is Taobao: no matter what efforts a store makes to promote a product, it is impossible to achieve an incredible surge of shopping on November 11. It is the result of reforms in the service industry brought by new service means, distribution channels and e-commerce support.

Second, I believe that the enhancement of the service export capacity will provide energetic support for improving the overall competitiveness of the industry chain and getting involved in the international division of the value chain. In the scenario of economic globalization, a country's international competitiveness in industry depends on the overall competitiveness of its industrial chain, and product profits gradually derive from the two-end services of the value chain. The enhancement of the service export capacity in transport, finance and insurance will provide strong support for trade in goods to relieve the impact of the rise in the cost of manpower on international competitiveness in the manufacturing industry, thus improving the overall competitiveness of our industrial chain. Besides, the enhancement of services such as R&D service is conducive to involvement of Chinese enterprises in the two ends of the value chain, thus increasing the value added in the international industrial chain. The latest research report on the global value chain issued by the United Nations Conference on Trade and Development shows that since a great number of different services are applied in the production of an export product, trade in services makes an outstanding contribution to the added value in foreign trade. Nearly 50% of global export value added originates in service sectors, which was stressed by the Secretary-General of UNCTAD in his CIFTIS talk. Lately, I had a chance to attend an important meeting where leaders of the central authority were present. In the meeting, the leaders clearly pointed out that "we have enough even excess capacity of producing commodities and goods. But the products that have been produced still suffer from the problem of competition on the overseas market". And he said with good humor: "our suppliers and export merchants on the overseas market are strangers in a distant land, but they are afraid of meeting an old friend in a distant land; otherwise, it is inevitable to compete with each other through price reduction, resulting in no profits gained by any of them." For example, Zhang San and Li Si, et al. all select to produce cups and sell them overseas. It is inevitable for them to compete with each other. Consequently, both the environment of foreign trade and the forming of a Chinese manufacturing industry brand will be greatly affected. We should not settle for a large trade country, instead we should manage to improve the added value of our products. If a cup is painted with Beijing opera types of facial makeup, the cup will be a cultural cup, which may be purchased by a foreign consumer as a piece of artware and placed on the shelf. If a cup is painted with facial makeup of a male character, a female character, a painted face character, a middle-aged male character and a clown, the cup will be more than a cultural product; it will be a collectable. Moreover, if the product is produced in a limited edition in Jingdezhen, the cup will be a treasure among cultural trade products. It is the power of design, research and development. Therefore, added value embodies our originality and efforts.

Third, the enhancement of the service export capacity is an important way to improve cultural influence and national soft power. As we all know, nowadays, it is the Western culture relying on economy and commerce that is prevalent in the world, and American movies stand at the top of the international film-television industry. For instance, the box-office revenue of the movie Avatar exceeds the box-office revenue of all domestic films in a year. McDonald's and Kentucky Fried Chicken form the fast-food culture that is popular in the world. Thus, China needs to improve its cultural influence and national soft power. The exportation of cultural products and services is a direct way to build a powerful International cultural influence and improve cultural soft power. The enhancement of the service export capacity not only helps improve the international competitiveness of the service industry and foster Chinese service brands, but it is also conducive to the transformation of Chinese advantages in a huge trade volume and a profound cultural history into an international cultural influence and international rule discourse power, so as to promulgate Chinese ideas to the world and establish a positive Chinese image. Hence, the far-reaching significance of expanding service opening-up does not lie simply in trade volume or trade in services deficit correction, but in the embodiment of a national strategy, the improvement of new advantages in overall foreign investment competition, the abundance of connotations, and the extension of denotations.

Besides, I want to analyze and review the status and difficulties of our service exports.

First, in recent years, our service trade has made some progress. Our importation is ranked 3rd in the world, but exportation is ranked 5th. On the whole, the conditions of our trade in services have not been changed yet. The ratio (6%) of trade in services in global trade in services is only about 1/2 of the ratio (11%) of trade in goods, and in addition, the ratio (11%) of service exports is only about 1/2 of the world's average level (over 20%), showing that our trade in services is still at the initial stage, and international competitiveness of service exportation is weak. To be specific, the growth rate of service exportation is slow. From 2006 to 2013, the average annual growth rate of service exportation was 12.7%, 5.8 percentage points lower than that of service importation. Since the outbreak of financial risks, service exportation has dramatically declined. The year 2009 witnessed a year-on-year decline of 12.2%, the year 2010 a rebound of 32.4%, but the years 2011 and 2012 had a decline of 7% and 4.5% respectively. Trade in services has been in a deficit state for a long time, and the deficit is gradually increasing. In 2008, the deficit balance exceeded 10 billion USD for the first time, and five years later, it reached 118.5 billion USD.

Second, the exportation of services in high value added is growing rapidly, but its proportion is not high. For the past few years, the exportation of services in high value added, such as consulting, computers and information, finance, insurance and patent royalties, has been increasing rapidly. From 2006 to 2013, the average annual growth rate of such services was 26.5%, 26.6%, 53.6%, 32.8% and 23.3% respectively, and the average annual growth rate of transport exportation was only 8.7% and 6.2%. The ratio of services in high value added is relatively small. In 2013, the ratio of consulting, computers and information, insurance and patent royalties was 11.3%, 7.3%, 1.4% and 1.9%, while the ratio of traditional services in transport, tourism and architecture was 47.5%. Hence, the impetus of exportation remains to be improved.

Third, our overall competitiveness in service exportation is weak. From an analysis of the index for the comparative advantage in international trade, the index of comparative advantage of our service exports varied from 0.44 to 0.48 from 2006 to 2012. It is known to all that the index below 0.8 indicates that the industry is weak in international competitiveness. Over the years, the overall competitiveness of our service exports has been in a weak position, and the exportation of tourism, transport, insurance and patent royalties are all in a state of deficit except service outsourcing. Especially, China is a large marine country, but it does not have a pricing power and a discourse power on the international shipping market, and it has not achieved the transportation of Chinese-produced goods via Chinese transporters. Transp- orta- tion is a field that has a serious deficit, so there is a lot of work to be done.

Fourth, from the perspective of policy, our policy support for service exportation is not strong enough. In the promotion of service exportation, we do not make as much effort as trade powers, so it is necessary to make a greater effort to promote trade in services, especially in carriers, means and policy measures. Currently, domestic industrial policies and financial policies are still limited to the manufacturing industry and to trade in goods, and a special poli- cy system in support of the development of the service industry and trade has not been estab- lished yet; moreover, no institutional arrangement that will benefit many fields, such as export rebates, has been made in the field of trade in services. What's more, unreasonableness such as double taxation still exists in service exportation. At present, only research & development services and design services provided by international transportation service agencies and o- verseas agencies can enjoy export rebates, and the services on which value added tax is im- posed instead of business tax, so exportation of most services must still be taxed. In terms of fund support, although service outsourcing, cultural exportation and technology enjoy fund support, their proportion in service exportation is small. For instance, in 2013, the total funds for service outsourcing, which is a National public fund without local funds included, did not reach 600 million RMB; the funds from the Ministry of Commerce for cultural exportation were only over 200 million RMB, and the funds for technology trade was only 270 million RMB. However, trade in services involves 12 fields and more than 160 sub-sectors, so the fi- nancial support is not enough for all service fields. Moreover, in terms of export credit insur- ance and export credit, service exportation is far below goods exportation. Supervision innova- tion lags behind and the facilitation in personnel mobility, foreign exchange settlement and customs clearance is not adequate. According to feedback on many performance groups, it is very difficult to handle customs clearance and visas. The same is true for senior software engi- neers who provide professional services. It is the result of industrial competition, and the lack of support policies, trade facilitation and the expansion of the opening-up.

After analyzing the above-mentioned difficulties and problems and the importance of trade in services, we can come to an initial conclusion that we are at a stage of an important strategic opportunity to foster national export capacity. The stage for strategic opportunities is fleeting and will not be long. We believe that the "12th Five-Year Plan" is the important strategic opportunity stage for the development of trade in services. To energetically develop trade in services will be the key to promoting the development of foreign trade in a comprehensive way during the period of the "12th Five-Year Plan" and in the following days, and it will be the new requirement for further expanding the opening-up and realizing an economic upgrading. We must be based on new stage, seize new opportunities, conform to new trend, foster international competitiveness in trade in services and create new advantages in service exportation.

First, new stage. The service industry is facing a historical opportunity and is about to enjoy fast development, which is mainly manifested in the following aspects. First, the service industry surpassed the manufacturing industry in the absorption of foreign investment for the first time in 2011, and the proportion was up to 52.3% in 2013, and the ratio of the service industry in the GDP was 47% in 2013. Second, the urbanization rate exceeded 50% for the first time in 2011. As we all know, every increase of 1% in the urban population will exert a great impact on the service industry and on consumption. A constant increase in the urbanization rate is of vital importance to leading and promoting the service industry and trade. Thirdly, the service industry surpassed agriculture and became the largest industry for job creation for the first time in 2012. The current year may witness the "hardest employment season" again. If employment was hardest in the previous year, it is harder in the current year, not to mention the conditions in the following year. But fortunately, central leaders have told us not to be worried about employment because the service industry has been developing rapidly and it is the most efficient industry with regards to job creation. Nowadays, due to the subscription of enterprise-registered capital, undergraduates are willing to set up an enterprise with cultural originality, even an enterprise in their hometown. Many industries concerning cultural creativity are experiencing trans-boundary integration, which is in urgent need of high-quality and creative youngsters to set up studios and entrepreneurship teams through tax-exempt policies and petty loan policies. The service industry is the industrial foundation for trade in services. The four aspects mentioned above are all signs of an accelerated development of the service industry. The good development of the service industry will support and lay a foundation for trade in services.

Second, new opportunities. We must take full advantage of the WTO rules in order to fully support the development of trade in services. We have told many departments under the State Council that the Doha Round of talks is stagnant, and any subsidy for trade in goods has been "cancelled". We must be careful of our products. The subsidy for service happens to be in a window period without strict rules and regulations. We are now in a weak position. Without subsidies and support, opportunities are missed. When you are ready to give subsidies and support, it may be too late. At that time, the Doha Round may have reached a consensus, which might just possibly worsen the situation. Therefore, we must take full advantage of the window period to follow the formulation of foreign subsidy policies and foreign measures in finance, transportation, tourism, commerce, culture and entertainment to support the development of such industries through tax preference, direct subsidies and concessional loans. Besides, we should make unremitting efforts in research innovation under the framework of the WTO and centralize policy advantages to actively foster our service exportation capacity. I notice that there is a policy interpretation for cultural trade in the forum. I really think that the forum organizer is of keen perception, because the State Council has just issued a document requiring policy interpretation. All of you present have put forward many helpful ideas, which are conducive to the formation of policies by the State Council. In cooperation with the Reform Office of the Propaganda Department of the Central Committee of the CPC, we spend nearly one year in drafting and finishing the document. In the first quarter of the current year, No. 2014 (13) document was issued, which contains many important policies with high gold content. All of you should carefully read, take advantage of, and actively implement them. Next, we will gradually introduce sub-policies. Now, we and the Ministry of Finance are focusing on the formulation of property tax policies and then trade facilitation policies.

Third, new trend. It can be seen that trade in services is rapidly changing in structure and is developing toward technology-knowledge intensiveness, which is manifested in two aspects, i.e., manufacturing industry servicizing and trans-boundary integration of many new business types in the service industry. Speaking of service outsourcing, now there are many emerging industries that are making their debut in the 3rd CIFTIS. For instance, translation & interpreting is known as a language service industry now. I notice that the Microsoft machine translation platform has realized real time translation. With Microsoft equipment, a guest from Portugal and I can directly talk to each other and understand each other. Therefore, in the future, the elderly at the age of 60 and 70 may go on a tour round the world using this equipment with no concerns regarding language exchanges. However, I believe that a machine is a machine, and it is still necessary to cultivate foreign language talents because sometimes the sense of language can be understood but it cannot be described. For example, I say, "come here"; it can be expressed by 12 tones and 12 facial expressions. Innovation on the type of operation may lead to dramatic change. For example, when it comes to traditional Chinese medicine, veteran doctors of TCM, with a white beard and four ways of diagnosis (observation, listening, interrogation, and pulse-taking) will come to our mind automatically. But now, observation and pulse-taking are done by equipment. You just need to sit there for about 10 minutes, and then all of the pulse conditions will be detected, and then the condition of heat, heart rate, sphygmus and blood pressure will be delivered to the TCM doctor, who will make a prescription according to such data. In terms of trans-boundary integration, the outsourcing is now called crowdsourcing. For example, the Department of Trade in Services and Commercial Services wants to seek advice on service export rebates, and I publish the subject on the internet, and there may be tens of institutions, enterprises and research institutions that are interested in the subject and provide me with their research accomplishments and suggestions. The process is very fast. As a result, you need to conform to the trend in order to expand service exports and enhance service export capacity.

Next, I will report the overall thoughts and focus of the work regarding the expansion of service opening-up. We should seize strategic opportunities at home and abroad to lay down appropriate developmental strategies, sort out ideas and define the emphasis to vigorously foster the international competitiveness of Chinese services and promote the fast development of trade in services in the following aspects:

The first aspect is to determine the strategic status of trade in services so as to make it one of the strategic priorities in national economic development in the coming days. The development of trade in services is of great importance in foreign trade. With respect to actively expanding service exports, we set the goal of "Chinese Service, Global Sharing" to strive to realize "scale expansion, structure optimization, balance adjustment and facilitation promotion", form the developmental pattern of "Chinese services and Chinese manufacturing" for foreign trade, improve the international competitiveness and discourse power of Chinese services and attain the goal of becoming a trading power.

The second aspect is about the general idea of expanding service exports. It can be summarized in the following points. The first point is that the most important thing in expanding service exports is to motivate it by expanding its opening-up. The expansion of exports should not be arbitrary, and should be carried out after the expansion of service opening-up. Therefore, we should take the opportunity to accelerate the construction of free trade zones to implement the policy of service opening-up and independent opening-up in order to promote reforms through the opening-up and promote development through competition, to gather the impetus of opening-up and to enhance the premium benefits of the service industry, thus comprehensively improving the international competitiveness of the service industry. In my opinion, the first stage is exportation by transnational companies in cooperation with us to drive the development of our domestic service industry, because it is impossible to do better than enterprises that have been functioning for more than 100 years or 50 years, and transnational companies. It must be a process of opening-up, expanding, introduction and cooperation. The second point is that trade in services should be led by a macro planning commission. We should strengthen top-level design and macro planning of trade in services in order to be able to evaluate the "12th Five-Year Plan" of trade in services and study the "13th Five-Year Plan" of trade in services, so as to enhance the planning and guidance of critical service exports. Besides, for the industries in which exportation is planned to be expanded, we should make a careful analysis of advantages and disadvantages in the "13th Five-Year Plan", and put forward a developmental schedule, a mission book and indicate a responsible department. The third point is that we should center on fostering advantages and at the same time, consolidate scale advantages in traditional industries, and we should not pay attention only to emerging industries. Besides, we should enhance the export capacity of emerging businesses and high value added services, foster and dig out the advantages of distinctive features, determine a group of leading enterprises, actively help enterprises explore the international market and speed up the cultivation of key enterprises with international competitiveness in service exports. The forth point is that we should take advantage of a policy of optimization as a breakthrough point. We should seize the window period when the WTO has not set rules on subsidies for trade in services to establish and improve the policy support system for trade in services, introduce promotion policies in fiscal areas, taxation, finance and foreign exchanges, and significantly improve service trade facilitation. Even for an enterprise enjoying good development, the lack of an easing policy and facilitation will prevent it from going out to the world. The overall policies of trade in services ought to conform to and combine with our national foreign investment strategy and "going outside" strategy. For example, in terms of our technology, as reported by foreign media, General Secretary Xi is the salesman for Chinese nuclear power, and Premier Li the salesman for Chinese high-speed railways. In the field of nuclear power and high-speed railways, apart from the engineering construction, there are plenty of technologies, closely followed by our cultural trade. Can we play Chinese video programs, Peking Opera and travel video programs on television in high-speed trains? Can we paint the facial makeup of the Beijing Opera on a cup? Can we embroider a distinctive Chinese pattern on a slipper? All of these are worthy of studying. In fact, our people are very smart. For Example, there is a brand called FAPAI in Wenzhou. A few years ago, FAPAI invited Clinton to be the spokesman for its brand. At that time, the foreign media trumpeted the news and reported that "Clinton has agreed and will come to Wenzhou soon after and visit the company". All the media followed the progress of this event and made publicity. However, upon discussion and review of the relevant departments, the invitation proposal was rejected. The next day, the media reported that "Clinton will not come to Wenzhou to be the spokesman of FAPAI" and then analyzed the reasons. The event was hyped for nearly one week. At last, the Clinton team delivered an address and published a video during the brand's press conference. Without any cost, FAPAI had been widely propagandized by Clinton and had thus become known to everyone. This is the power of marketing. Therefore, we should utilize tactics to make our service go out to the world. Especially in cultural trade, insurance and finance, it is necessary to study national policies, marketing channels and strategies.

The third aspect is about the emphasis on exports. You must be concerned about the next direction of trade in services. First of all, we should continue to consolidate the scale advantages in our traditional service export industry, and expand the exportation of services such as transportation and business travel based on the export-oriented manufacturing industry in an attempt to realize the transportation of Chinese-made goods by Chinese transporters. Besides, we should make full use of the information regarding demand brought about by the re-industrialization of advanced economies so that we can energetically develop international engineering contracting services and drive construction service exports forward. Second, we should guide and support the exportation of emerging service fields. For this, we should be dedicated to carrying out the following work: develop Chinese services by relying on Chinese manufacturing, expand the exportation of services such as insurance, communications, research & development, and design, grasp the opportunity brought by the acceleration of the pace of Chinese enterprises to go outside, vigorously develop the services such as law, consulting and accounting, grasp the opportunity of new international industrial transfer, give full play to the strength of human resources, actively explore the overseas market, promote the exportation of services using computer and information technology, and increase the share of service outsourcing. Third, we should actively expand the exportation of distinctive services, strive to develop the exportation of services with Chinese characteristics and unique advantages, strengthen international cooperation, develop new products for the international market, and impel the exportation of services such as culture originality, art, radio, film, television, education, traditional Chinese medicine, technology, catering and housekeeping. For instance, in the activity of "Chinese Meals Approaching the United Nations", the Secretary-General of the United Nations, accompanied by senior officials, came to the booth to see the making of stretched noodles. With the cook's craftsmanship, a lump of dough was finally made into thin noodles narrower than a human hair, which really shocked the Secretary-General. The foreigners were unaware of the making of glue pudding; so we made a joke and told them the stuffing was injected into the glue pudding, and we told them that the pizza was the failure of our pie, because foreigners did not know how to put the stuffing into the pie, so they have to put the stuffing directly on top of the pie. Therefore, we should be confident about our culture, after all, what is national is international.

The fourth aspect is that we should speed up the formulation of new measures to form new advantages in service exportation. For this, first of all, we should set up a promotional system to support service exports, including the preparation of documents, the establishment of a trans-department work mechanism and the formulation of a coordination policy to jointly promote enterprise services. Second, we should further improve fiscal, tax, financial and trade facilitation policies, work out and release a guidance directory for key export fields, set up a zero tax rate policy concerning the exportation of industrial services that meet encouraging conditions, carry out innovation of our financial support policies, create new financial products based on features of trade in services, promote the construction of a mid-and small-scale enterprise credit guarantee system, refine our export credit guarantee mechanism, simplify the claims settlement procedure and quicken the speed of resolving claims. Besides, we should try to promote trade facilitation to make exit and entry easier, help international enterprises obtain the necessary qualifications to enter the international market, and make it convenient for professional talents and services to go out to the world. Third, we should enhance and expedite the construction of a platform and demonstration carrier. In the modern service industry pilot project, the pilot free trade zone and "the Belt and Road" cooperation, we should launch a series of projects and set up a group of bases to expand service exports. Fourth, we should expedite the opening-up of the service industry in an orderly way. According to the spirit of the Third Plenary Session of the 18th Central Committee of the CPC, we should strive to remove the glass door and the swing door in the utilization of foreign investments by our service industry. Although China opens its door to the world, many small doors in a number of fields are still closed, and phenomena such as the glass door and the swing door still exist. The going outside of the service industry is the vital engine for promoting the exportation of services. Enterprises are encouraged to set up research & development centers and design centers overseas. Fifth, we should further consolidate the foundation of trade in services. For this, we must quicken the pace of the formulation of service export and import management rules, gradually refine the management and promotional law framework for trade in services, further improve trade in services statistics, deepen the theoretical study of trade in services, and make a greater effort at studying the trend in and the rules regarding trade in services. Now, we have realized that the research institution is our think tank and talent pool, and we hope that all of you enthusiastically offer your intellectual support and advice to our governmental organ in theoretical study, policy study, industrial development study and planning study. Besides, I hope our academy and research institution can lay more stress on national research. When it comes to national research, people expect a detailed research on industries, involving over 160 sub-sectors. For example, regarding research on the going outside of traditional Chinese medicine, it probes into the industry, field and country, etc. Another example, concerning some research on the way of expanding exports, specific items in export expansion may be studied, as well as the rebound due to export expansion and the reason for export expansion through import expansion. After we introduced our advanced ideas and modes for the expansion of importations, we may be able to improve our domestic service industries that are weak in international competitiveness, and then export such services, while at the same time, focusing on the "The Belt and Road".

I would like to thank Chairman Liu and Chairman Qian for giving me the opportunity to report our work and share my opinions. It makes me deeply understand the importance of exchanges among the government, producers, universities and researchers, as well as the attention and support of scholars for trade in services. Such support gives an impetus to the advancement of the expansion of our service exports. We believe that Chinese trade in services will enjoy a more stable and better development under the guidance of national transformation, upgrading and policies, thus making more contributions to the realization of the Chinese dream and trading power. Welcome all peers and experts' criticism and correction, thank you!

# Speech by Li Gang, Director of the International Trade in Services Research Institute of the MOC Research Academy, at CIFTIS·the 8th International Trade in Services Forum

Fellow delegates, good afternoon! I am very glad to attend this trade forum, and give a speech during this sub-forum on urban economic development and service industry development. The topic of my speech is *Expanding the Opening-up of the Service Industry and Promoting the Development of Trade in Services.* In the field of the service industry, the opening-up of this industry is closely associated with trade in services. In the four transaction modes of trade in services, business is a basic mode of trade in services for going outside, and it is also an important part of trade in services. Hence, expanding the opening-up of the service industry and promoting its development share the same internal logic. My topic is actually a circular argument.

The first aspect is that the opening-up of the service industry dramatically promotes the development of the Chinese service industry and trade. I will make a brief review of the opening-up and development of the service industry and trade in accordance with the basic requirements for the WTO and GATS, and for the WTO accession protocol since joining the WTO. I will analyze the issue by looking at the following aspects. The first point is the status quo of the Chinese service industry. By fully implementing the WTO accession protocol, the Chinese service industry has entered a new stage of the opening-up. Though China has participated in the Uruguay Round of Negotiations, China did not join the WTO as an original member and a major contracting party before the official founding of the WTO in 1995. At that time, we were paying attention to the development of the service industry, and after the holding of the Sixteenth National Congress, we started to pay more attention to this industry. But the real development and opening-up of the service industry and the development of trade in services were implemented in accordance with the accession protocol.

In the 12 fields, there are 9 fields opened up. From our commitment, the opening-up level of China in those 9 fields and some sectors is higher than that of developing economies, and even higher than some developed economies in certain fields. Therefore, from my point of view, the opening-up level for which China made a commitment is ahead of the actual level of Chinese development level at the end of 2001, when China joined the WTO. Where conditions permit, we in China still made commitments with respect to what developed countries offer. Therefore, at that time, the reform was promoted by the opening-up, and the opening-up of some service fields was further promoted, thus leading to a remarkable development in all industries excluding finance and telecommunications.

The second point is that since joining the WTO, we have been actively exploring the implementation of the strategy of free trade zones, which was eventfully determined in 2007. However, in fact, before officially joining the WTO, China had attempted to make such arrangements and agreements in the free trade zone of China and the Association of Southeast Asian Nations. Therefore, the CEPA signed with Hong Kong and Macao or the RTA signed with countries and national groups was all a critical part of the whole opening-up strategy of China.

We have been adding some elements of the opening-up of the service industry and of service field investments during the course of the implementation of the strategy of free trade zones, which substantially boosts the opening-up and development of our service industry.

In addition, in terms of independent domestic opening-up, we have also made some other efforts. All of you must know about the pilot project in the Shanghai Pilot Free Trade Zone. It is a new way to explore the opening-up of the service industry, an essential goal conforming to the construction of a socialist marketing economy in a new round of opening-up, and a new independent pilot with an institutional guarantee.

In terms of laws and regulations in the service industry, we have abolished many laws and formulated many new laws at the beginning of our membership in the WTO. As far as I am concerned, there are many problems with the process. In the agriculture and manufacturing industries, abolishing laws and formulating laws may be carried out thoroughly, which might be impossible in the service industry. Therefore, law abolishment and formulation fail to be carried out thoroughly due to management problems within the service industry, most service fields and other industries, and in addition, reforms can also not be made in accordance with the requirements of marketization, which results in many problems. However, on the whole, the new round of reforms promotes constant improvement of domestic rules.

A few days ago, in the round-table conference organized by the Norway CP Organization, I talked about the fact that the opening-up of the service industry and trade has three levels, that is, market opening-up, market access and domestic rules. The restrictiveness index for trade in services issued by the OECD is also promoting and exploring the actual opening-up of a country based on these three levels. As a result, we may have made some progress, but it is far from enough.

The third point is that the development of the service industry has attained tremendous achievements in developmental speed and in the level of international service. Besides, it drives the development of trade in services.

Based on the adjustments to the statistical approach and to the caliber of the service industry by the National Bureau of Statistics, some services in primary industry and in secondary industry are separated from the primary industry and the secondary industry and put in the service industry; moreover, the service industry itself also enjoys some growth, so that the whole industry presented a growth trend in the first quarter of the current year, and the ratio of the service industry in the GDP added value increased to 49.1% from 46.1%. In my opinion, the ratio may exceed the critical point of 50% in the current year based on the current trend.

I agree with Director Zhou's opinion that only a thorough reform of the statistical system can really promote the development of the service industry. Investments in public goods depend on the ratio of various sectors in the GDP, and on the important ones. In fact, the policies are related to the central government, the local government and the department of industry. If you underestimate the importance of an industry in the national economic development, it is conducive to the development of the whole economy. Now, the reform of the statistical system and the development of the service industry have reached a point where it will be possible to exceed 50% of the value added after a short time.

Next, I will share my thoughts with you about the gap, the problems and its causes in the development of the service industry.

Regarding the gap, from my point of view, there are two large gaps; namely the ratio of value added in the service industry in the GDP is small, so is trade in services volume. In fact, from the ratio, a comparison may be made based on different ways. However, the real problems are not the same as the problems in the level or structure of the national economic development or in the specific developmental phase. Against such phenomena, I want to describe the issue from different perspectives.

First, the problems in the opening-up of the service industry include the inadequate level of the opening-up on the whole and an excessive opening-up in certain fields. In some ways, the inadequate level of opening-up on the whole may be measured by different methods. Now, the World Bank and the OECD have doubts about the level of the opening-up of the Chinese service industry, and place our market at about 80th in the list of 160 or 170 economies. Apart from the 30 member countries of OECD, BRICS and Indonesia are included in the trade in services index system for evaluation. In the past two days, OECD experts in charge of trade in services statistics and index construction have communicated and made exchanges with other department experts. Although the index indicates the existence of problems in the opening-up of the service industry, the information regarding institutional law that they have gathered is not comprehensive because China is not engaged in index construction. Consequently, it is inevitable that the evaluation of China is partial. We need to be clear about the inadequate level of the opening-up on the whole and the excessive opening-up in certain fields. Our commitment in the opening-up of certain fields even surpasses that of developed countries. For example, in the field of sea transportation, the opening-up of China's shipping surpasses that of America, according to our commitment. Our commitment is based on overall national benefits and takes national security into account.

Second, there is a gap between nominal opening-up and real opening-up. In the performance of our commitments in the WTO protocol, due to an error of understanding of industrial departments and incomplete adjustment to some laws, some problems arise, such as "the external door is open but the internal door is still closed", the "glass door" and the "swing door". Moreover, a monopoly on the market and excessive competition exist, which are not to be discussed in detail here because we have not made a commitment to open up the finance and telecommunication fields. However, in the course of the opening-up, the problems of a monopoly on the market and excessive competition are severe in some fields, and in addition, some service fields with fierce competition also suffer from the problem of excessive competition.

Third, the causes for restrictions on the opening-up of the service industry include ideology, institutional barriers and interest group interference. We have completely fulfilled our basic obligations to the WTO, and basically fulfilled our obligations under the WTO accession protocol. In terms of our reform later, upon evaluation of Chinese trade by the WTO, it is sharply pointed out that Chinese reform has been stagnant to a certain extent since 2007 because the level of the opening-up of the market in certain fields declined instead of showing an increase, as well as some problems in the process of the opening-up.

Next I will share with you some new understandings and judgments on major issues concerning the opening-up under the new situation. The service industry enjoys a new situation of opening-up. On the whole, we have still not gotten out of the post-crisis era. Although European, American and Japanese economies present a trend towards recovery, there are many obstacles in the development of the world's economies, including developed economies. At the same time, the globalization of the service industry in the post-crisis era also shows some new features. In the course of the globalization of the service industry, the service industry and trade have been a new engine for economic growth in various countries, or an important pillar in the development of the economy. In sum, the service industry and trade are playing an increasingly important role.

The negotiations on the multilateral trade agreement dominated by developed economies (which are also the WTO members) such as TISA, or GATS and GATS+, including the rules of the opening-up of trade in services, are all important worldwide issues, which may bring serious challenges to the development of the Chinese service industry and trade in the future. Moreover, we must pay great attention to the addition of the service industry in the TPP and the TTIP against the background of the implementation of a two-ocean strategy of the USA, as well as the direction of the opening-up of the service industry in the regions of those partnerships.

All of you must be familiar with our domestic situation. I have mentioned some important information before; for example, the valued added in the tertiary industry exceeded that of the secondary industry for the first time last year. The same is true for job creation, which can be proved by the latest statistical data released by the National Bureau of Statistics from January until April. The service industry has become not only a new breakthrough point in the new round of reforms and development, but also a new impetus for development. China is actively participating in the process of formulation of new international trade rules. We are eager to be involved in this, so we have decided to participate in TISA negotiations according to the official declaration last September 30. America has some doubts about us. However, we really want to make a difference in this aspect.

Next, let's share some understandings and opinions regarding major issues in the opening-up of the service industry within the new situation. As far as I am concerned, China realized industrialization in 2010 as the Chinese automobile industry achieved a sales volume of 18 million cars, which is far more than America's sales volume (nearly 17 million cars) in the peak period. Now, we have been capable of manufacturing an assembly based on thousands of parts in the automobile industry. Apart from our trade in services, our manufacturing industry, represented by the automobile industry, has surpassed that of the USA and is ranked 1st in the world. In addition, Chinese gross industrial production exceeded that of the USA for the first time in 2010 and 2011. At that time, the ratio of the Chinese gross industrial production was 19.1%, and the ratio of the American gross industrial production had declined to 16.9% from nearly 20% . Therefore, China was at the stage of transformation from a manufacturing economy and an industrial economy to a service economy, as well as a stage of fast development of the service industry.

We should reconsider our status in quasi-industrialized countries and quasi marketized countries. Our country has always been considered a large developing country in either international exchanges or international negotiations, which is not really accurate. In terms of our economic magnitude, the World Bank puts China in first place in the world. Therefore, we should have our own judgment on our status under the new situation. We always say China is a country at the primary stage of socialism, a developing country subject to the primary stage of socialism and an industrialized country subject to the status of a developing country. Therefore, we do need to make careful considerations in order to have a clear understanding of our status in the new environment, at the new level of development and at a new stage.

At last, I want to talk about the idea of further expanding the opening-up of the service industry. For this, the first key point, as mentioned by Director Zhou in the morning, is to determine the strategic status of our service industry and trade within the national economic development, which has been widely recognized at high levels and within the academic circle. However, there are still some practical problems. As a result, we must consider combining several aspects. No matter what the opening-up is expended for, such as the reform and opening-up, opening-up and protection, risk control, external and internal opening-up, or open protocol and independent opening-up, the most important premise is to open up to domestic enterprises, national enterprises and local enterprises before the Chinese market is open up to the outside.

The second point is that we should explore new ways to open up our service industry. Based on the Sino-American BIT negotiations by Xi Jinping and Obama, we explore new modes, including the pilot project in the Shanghai Pilot Free Trade Zone. Both the exploration of modes and the amendment to three foreign investment laws involve new ways of utilizing foreign investments. However, the mode is not unique. In my opinion, the mode needs to be further tested in future practice. Besides, as far as I am concerned, the ultimate Chinese opening-up mode may be a mixed type, which will not fully follow the ideas proposed by America.

We look forward to more multilateral, regional and bilateral negotiations and agreements in the future. In the era of technological innovation, we should hold a more optimistic and open attitude toward ITA and GPA agreements and participate in plurilateral agreement negotiations. In the meanwhile, we need to construct a global FTA network concerning the world's highest standards. In the process, we should apply the FTA agreement in our service industry. Besides, the independent opening-up fields, including finance, culture, education and medical care, should be opened step by step according to the basic requirements proposed by our leaders in the Third Plenary Session of the 18th Central Committee of the CPC, and the restrictions on five other fields should be eased, which will promote the advancement of the opening-up.

There are some other problems which need to be considered carefully in the promotion of regional financial development. Now, the layout of our domestic regional economy has reached a new stage, in which a significant adjustment is being carried out in some new concepts and regionalization.

The third point is that the measures for further opening-up our service industry should be promoted. For this, the key is to innovate the system and the mechanism because these kinds of innovation are rare. Since the reform in 2003, many problems still persist. Hence, in the

Part III  Summary of Speeches at the Summit High-level Forum

process of promoting the opening-up of the service industry, it is difficult to achieve coordination because of the restrictions on departments and industries, and the hidden rules gradually established by various departments. Without the elimination of these hidden rules, it will still be hard to solve the problems in spite of the availability of a trans-department coordination mechanism. Therefore, in the innovation of the system and the mechanism, it is necessary to comprehensively deepen reforms so as to promote the opening-up of our service industry. In the meanwhile, work on law abolishment and formulation should be carried out in the service industry. If fundamental problems are not solved, domestic adjustment as stipulated, as well as commitments on the opening-up of and access to the market, will not be fulfilled. Now, in terms of interference by governmental "tangible hands" and market "intangible hands", we expect the chambers of commerce and associations to give full play to their functions and roles during the process. With regard to functions undertaken by the government, I hope they are market-oriented to fully play their role.

Besides, for regional differences in the implementation of independent opening-up, we should consider making adjustments on the traditional mindset. Coast cities are not the unique choice for the opening-up of the service industry. There is another alternative, that is, a first pilot opening-up in the central and western regions. In the new stage, it is still crucial to enhance the fundamental work of the service industry and trade, apart from the statistics. According to the theory of market dominance, it is better to apply the ideas put forward in the evaluation of the "13th Five-Year Plan" and the "12th Five-Year Plan".

That is all that I want to share with you. I really expect to have exchanges and discussions with you about our recent research achievements. Thank you!

# Speech by Wan Lianpo, Vice Director of the Department of Trade in Services and Commercial Services of the Ministry of Commerce, at CIFTIS· the 8th International Trade in Services Forum

I am very delighted to be here to talk to all of you present. First of all, I would like to extend my gratitude to the academy for focusing on the study of trade in services and outsourcing annually by carrying out activities and research. I think it is an important support for the government to develop trade in services and outsourcing. Thanks a million. What's more, I would like to take this opportunity to report to you on the overall condition of the development of our national service outsourcing industry, as well as some current major problems and the approach to solving such problems in the future.

First of all, I will make a brief introduction to the developmental conditions of service outsourcing in recent years. The service industry is an important field and industry in trade in services at present. It is defined as an industry by the State Council. The Ministry of Commerce organizes relevant departments including the Ministry of Industry and Information Technology and the National Development and Reform Commission to jointly formulate policies that support the development of the service outsourcing industry so as to explore the international market. In terms of the positioning of service outsourcing, I believe it is different from that of other businesses. As we all know, the function of the Ministry of Commerce is a market-related function. However, regarding service outsourcing, apart from a function of market exploration, the Ministry of Commerce also undertakes another important mission from the State Council. To increase our share of the international market, it is necessary to have an industry that possesses international competitiveness to provide support. Therefore, the mission assigned to the Ministry of Commerce is to improve International industrial competitiveness, so that service outsourcing is different from other businesses where market expansion is mainly achieved through multilateral and bilateral policies, coordination and encouragement measures. Apart from multilateral and bilateral work, the improvement of industrial competitiveness is the focus of service outsourcing. The information industry is closely associated with service outsourcing as service outsourcing starts from the information industry in order to conform to the No. 18 and No. 4 documents issued by the State Council and to promote the development of the software industry. Over the years, we have achieved a good performance in the exportation of software products with independent intellectual properties. In terms of quantity, the scale of software and information service is larger than that of the products. So, the Ministry of Commerce suggests that we should encourage the exportation of not only software product services but also software and information services. As a result, software outsourcing has been developing vigorously, and up to now, our international service outsourcing industry has formed a scale.

Next, I want to share some data with you. The scale of our industry and market has been expanding continuously. We started to encourage the development of service outsourcing in 2006 and we started to collect data for statistics in 2008. What was our market share on the international market in 2008? The outsourcing volume was not greater than 5 billion USD in 2008, but it was over 60 billion USD in 2013. From this, it can be seen that the growth rate from 2008 to 2013 was very high. Besides, in 2013, China was the second largest country undertaking international service outsourcing in the world, only following India. Our market share on the international market was 27% in 2013, much higher than that in 2008, that is, 7%, showing that our market enjoys a fast increase in scale and development. Our market is mainly supported by industry. In 2013, there were altogether more than 24,800 service outsourcing enterprises and 5.36 million service outsourcing personnel, of which the number of personnel with a bachelor's degree was 3.559 million, accounting for 66.4%. Such data show that the service outsourcing industry is an industry of high competitiveness thanks to the support of policies, and the scale of enterprises, personnel; the whole industry develops very fast at an annual average growth rate of 40%-50%. Under the high pressure within both the world economy and the domestic economy, such a growth rate is hard-won compared with the growth rate of the entire national economy, trade in goods and trade in services. Currently, trade in services is in a state of deficit, and the deficit is expanding, but service outsourcing is developing at a growth rate of 40%-50%, which is really a gratifying achievement.

What about market expectation in the future? According to a prediction by the international data corporation, the international service outsourcing market will maintain a growth rate of 15.8%, near 16%, from 2014 to 2020. Based on the growth rate of 15.8%, the scale of the global service market will reach 1.8 trillion USD by 2020, of which offshore service outsourcing will be nearly 500 billion USD. According to such a prediction, our market share will be dramatically increased by 2020 if the growth rate is maintained. These are our achievements in industrial development, market exploration and in future predictions.

As our service outsourcing industry started later, there is a large gap between our country and India in spite of the fast growth rate and development. It is mainly manifested in the following aspects. The first is market share. In 2013, our share of the international market was 27%, but India's share was 51%. Secondly, in terms of industry, we have more than 20,000 service outsourcing enterprises, of which small and medium-sized enterprises occupy a large proportion, and the number of enterprises with thousands of personnel dedicated to service outsourcing is very small, while India has a great number of enterprises with thousands and even hundreds of thousands of personnel. The third gap is talent scale and structure. China and India have more than 5 million and 3 million service outsourcing personnel respectively. However, from the point of view of structure, most of those 5 million service outsourcing personnel are basal talents who graduate with a bachelor's degree and are capable of handling ordinary service outsourcing businesses, while 1/4 of the 3 million service outsourcing personnel are mid-to-high-end talents who take the lead in a group and are capable of handling orders and proposing solutions. In this respect, we need to learn from India. These are our weaknesses. Nevertheless, we also possess some strengths. Compared with India, we have a variety of industries, while Indian industry is not variegated. Especially in the manufacturing industry, India is very weak. As I mentioned before, the information industry promotes the integration of other industries. Why does the IDC predict that we will catch up with India by 2020? It is because we have had a strong recent development.

Next, let's turn to difficulties and problems faced by service outsourcing during its development. As a whole, such difficulties and problems refer to problems that arise during the course of development. From 2006, central and local governments have been promoting the development of the service outsourcing industry and attempting to create a proper environment suitable for the development of this industry, which means a lot to its development. With years of development, the scale of the industry, its enterprises and its market have been increased remarkably compared with the years 2008 and 2006. We could sense that the original polices do not apply under the current situation. Let me take a simple example, I began to get in touch with service outsourcing enterprises in 2000 and the number of thousands of personnel enterprises was still small until 2006, but now, the largest enterprise has nearly 30,000 personnel. There are great differences in management, innovation capacity and market exploration capacity between a thousand-personnel enterprise and a 10 thousands-personnel enterprise. So, the demand of such enterprises has changed. In the past, what the enterprise with thousands of personnel needs was innovation equipment and talent, while now what the enterprise with tens of thousands of personnel needs is improvement in international competitiveness. For example, if an enterprise with tens of thousands of personnel intends to merge with an American enterprise overseas, its focus lies in support, such as foreign exchange support or financing support; besides, when it comes to talent, the focus of such an enterprise lies in its talent structure instead of the quantity of its talent, and it is in urgent of high-end talents. Hence, we should carry out a study on new policies based on enterprise scale and demand. Upon close communication and investigation, we find that one of

Part III  Summary of Speeches at the Summit High–level Forum

the developmental bottlenecks of the service outsourcing industry is talent. Talent is the primary production factor in the development of the service outsourcing industry. It is different from the manufacturing industry, in which the main input is fixed asset, plant, equipment and means of production, and the human factor can be neglected. However, in the service outsourcing industry, 70% of the cost is human cost, and 15% is fixed asset production cost and the remaining 15% is integrated operation cost. So in the proportion of production factors, the service outsourcing industry is opposite to the traditional manufacturing industry. The most serious problem faced by the service outsourcing industry is talent scale and structure. The lack of talent will result in a slow scale of development of the industry; similarly, the irrational structure of talent will lead to weak industrial competitiveness. Recently, central leaders such as Premier Li Keqiang and Vice Premier Gao Li have been putting pressure on us to give them suggestions as soon as possible. Regarding how to further promote the development of the service outsourcing industry, we find, during our studies, that enterprises and relevant departments have reached a consensus, and that is, the problem of talent is the core problem of the development of the service outsourcing industry. Talent scale and structure determine the developmental scale and quality of the service outsourcing industry. In my opinion, the study on service outsourcing talent really grasps the core and lifeline of the service outsourcing industry. In the formulation of the next round of policies, we will take some measures concerning talent cultivation, talent structure adjustment and a suitable increase in talent scale.

Among the functions and tasks of the Ministry of Commerce assigned by the State Council, we will only focus on two issues. The first issue is market strategy to expand market share as far as possible, and the second issue is talent strategy which guarantees that the service outsourcing industry will have a certain foundation in international competitiveness. The international competitiveness of the service outsourcing industry mainly derives from talent competitiveness; to be specific, the international competitiveness lies in whether talent scale can meet the needs of industrial development and competitiveness. The day before yesterday, we proposed an idea to the leaders of the Ministry of Education, who quite agreed with it; and they expressed their willingness to support talent cultivation and introduction and enhance cooperation with us in the cultivation of mid-to-high-end talent, in the formulation of standards and talent cultivation or introduction. Apart from the cooperation with the Ministry of Commerce, cooperation with the Ministry of Education, enterprises and various parks may all be strengthened. In the course of the development of the entire service outsourcing industry, the State Council has determined 21 demonstration cities which are the focus of our work; international market businesses of such 21 demonstration cities account for 97% of the nationwide international market businesses. Besides, most enterprises engaging in offshore outsourcing services are concentrated in the 21 demonstration cities. In terms of talent cultivation and introduction, the 21 demonstration cities have their own policies apart from national policies. We may establish a cooperative relationship with the 21 demonstration cities.

Service outsourcing will play a vital role in the adjustment of our national economic structure and in the transformation of our growth mode, especially in the local and the entire foreign trade. Moreover, the transboundary and innovation trend of the service outsourcing industry is very clear. If the service outsourcing industry were to achieve a better performance in transboundary integration and innovation, the status of the Chinese economy would be improved constantly, and in addition, the value of the Chinese economy would be better manifested in the global value chain.

At last, please allow me to express my sincere gratitude to all of you present for your concern and support regarding the service outsourcing industry on behalf of the Department of Trade in Services and Commercial Services. Service outsourcing not only contributes to the Chinese economy in figures, but it also brings about dramatic changes in the mode of transboundary integration and the mode of production and people's lifestyle. As for the transboundary integration, the most specific and efficient way is service outsourcing. If our institutions, even our individuals, were to be used to purchase a professional service, a fundamental shift would occur in the division of social labor, production mode and people's lifestyle. As I mentioned before, the mobile terminal that contains many service outsourcing elements is changing our lives, and even our lifestyles. That is all for my speech. Thank you!

# Speech by Allan Conway, Dean of Odette School of Business, University of Windsor, at CIFTIS·the 8th International Trade in Services Forum

I am so glad to be here to give a simple lecture to you. In the past few years, I have been mainly engaged in the work of the insurance industry, which is a very important service sector. I have cooperated with Michael E. Porter, a prestigious service strategist, from Harvard University, conducting research related to the development of the regional economy and of the service industry. As of late, he has shifted his research interest into the development of banking services. I focus on the research of regional economic development so as to provide services to all types of economic developmental committees. Odette School of Business, University of Windsor, has set up the Center of Entrepreneurship to facilitate closer communication and connection between universities and entrepreneurs.

The topic for this speech is comparatively much easier as it is about the promotion of the development of the service industry. I would like to talk about some basic concepts and the relevant practice and experience in Canada.

The first major problem is how to create an environment to promote service industry development in any place, but the key lies in its competitiveness. We may set up several big companies in the local area. Most importantly, the economic development environment will be integrated with other environments as a whole and they will not be separated from each other.

In view of enterprises, particularly for service-based enterprises, they should have competitiveness and the key abilities. As for production enterprises, they often engage in affairs related to the service industry, thus developing their core competitiveness. In view of service enterprises, they are required to have competitiveness and must make the key choices on the local market, which must be uniquely distinctive in order to guarantee sustainable development with strong competitiveness. In making a choice, they must decide what products they are going to manufacture and who the specific customers are, and in what environment and area they can obtain favorable development.

When we talk about competitiveness, all barriers will be continuously reduced, so the whole world becomes more and more globalized, say, market globalization, capital globalization and knowledge globalization. If we can deliver these products to every part of the world, service can be more easily flown all around the world. In view of competitiveness, even a production enterprise has some key departments closely related to the service industry. Particularly, the Canadian *City on Wheels* manufactures heavy-duty products. "City on Wheels" does not mean that all automobile design and research departments are located in the local area. The R&D departments may be affiliated to the enterprises and the R&D service may be purchased from other enterprises.

Cost is a very important problem. Particularly the productive enterprises used to depend on cost but now cost is becoming much higher, and their competitiveness gradually fades away. How to solve those problems needs more study. All changes require enterprises to make continuous adjustments to guarantee their competitiveness.

I will further elaborate on the correlation of production and service. I used to provide the relevant consulting service to nearly 100 large enterprises to help them complete the analysis of the competition among enterprises in the auto industry. Even for this automobile production industry, there is a separate service sector to provide an analysis service for all functions. Production enterprises should be combined with the relevant services in many cases.

In 1998, Michael E. Porter's diamond model explored how to guarantee the competitiveness of the whole field or of the entire industry. In this model, the most fundamental part is to take these features into account at the income end of the enterprises, including all kinds of resources, human resources, capital resources, technical resources, infrastructures and the specialization degree in other aspects, etc. At the other end of the service enterprises, namely the demand end, it is necessary to ensure that they have the consumer groups with enough complicated demands so that enterprises can seek continuous development. The entire model can be applicable to several key enterprises according to the features of enterprises and consumers. This kind of continuous pressure can force enterprises to continue to improve themselves; however, some enterprises will make a natural choice, or will even be eliminated.

After we talk about the competitiveness model, we will consider development in any proper region and what key factors are involved. Although they can adapt to the majority of factors in various environments, in most cases, it is necessary to decide how to develop according to the specific features of a certain area. In view of the features or advantages of a certain area, we can consider creative ability, which is roughly a most essential part. Creation is the core ability, which is very important for service enterprises and likewise important for traditional and classic production enterprises. Development cannot do without the relevant fund support, borrowing for investments and supportive national policies.

Just as stated above, we cannot guarantee that there are any key competitive enterprises. At the same time, we must pay attention to some problems which may hinder the development of the service enterprises. So in view of the possible barriers, first of all, we shall pay attention to the problem of corporate management, which may affect the development of an enterprise without vitality. Second, we should have enough talents, particularly service-oriented talents, who are not easily trained or cultivated.

In the meanwhile, we find that there are not enough complicated demands. We listed several key factors. The most important one is the transformation of our concepts. When we say that a certain product has competitiveness, that is not enough; only when we truly have competitiveness can we have development. We may have a few advantages in some fields, but when we continue to improve and strengthen these advantages we can seek continuous development. So, we suggest that you can make good on a deficiency within the coming years so that you are able to promote the development of the service industry in seeking development in a certain region.

We suggest that different areas may take different policies by sharing the experience of cities in Canada; we can attract enterprises in all service sectors into all cities. The high value-added industries may select different areas. The problem is how we can attract these high value-added industries into the specific areas. For example, we are all familiar with the US Silicon Valley and Boston 1280, which is an IT clustering area. Although they have all types of enterprises with different features, they have something in common, as they basically have the best universities. In Silicon Valley, Stanford University is its very center. Boston 1280 is in Massachusetts Institute of Technology.

Take Boston for instance, when Boston becomes a magnet that will attract and integrate advantages in Hi-technology, economy and education, thus having the high value-added service industries, including universities, enterprises related to insurance, finance, strategy, consultation, particularly BCG, which is highly prestigious in the world, some of the reasons lie in that Boston has a lot of colleges and universities. In addition, the reason why there are so many universities and enterprises lies in the fact that Harvard University and Massachusetts Institute of Technology are in the area. Their graduates want to stay in the city and they want to be very close to each other for the better use of local resources. In view of the financial service industry in Boston, there are two important consulting enterprises, one of which is named "State Street Bank", to provide large trust services to all the enterprises.

Now let us talk about Ontario Province in Canada; its largest production enterprise is in the manufacturing industry or the automobile industry, both of which prospered in 2002. However, they have taken a downturn trend in the past 13 years. Many service industries are beginning to seek their development in areas other than Toronto, but Toronto remains the financial center. People are beginning to think about the decline of the manufacturing industry, there being a behavioral change from a pure manufacturing behavior to services. In some large and medium-size cities in Southern Ontario, which used to be the center of car manufacturing for all kinds of assembly and processing of parts and components, they now need transformation. We have selected this city as it has something to do with the service industry of the state-owned banks and international banks in Canada.

The first behavior is involved with a large bank in Toronto, where its Canadian headquarters is located.

First of all, Toronto is the largest city in Canada. Though it is not as large as Beijing, it has the same traffic jams as Beijing does. The local government wants to transfer many financial businesses from Toronto to a small city in Southern Ontario. The feasibility of this move is closely related to a provincial minister who wants to spread the service industry around the entire province so as to save money. Banks pay more attention to whether they can ensure stronger computer talents for normal business operations. They think that, although the service might not be offered in the same city, they can ensure that there will not be many problems in traffic service as they can provide prompt service as the occasion requires.

This small city is very close to the USA, which is a geographical advantage. If they can move the back-office business of large banks into this small city, they can easily enter the relevant banking sectors in the USA. Another move is that the mayors of these large and medium-size cities decide to move the Canadian head offices of the super-large US banks into this city, but their intention was not to move them to Toronto, but to here, and for what reason? As a result, there appears the demand of the super-large banks, and of the local schools of business, that must provide training services to the bank employees who have to serve the banks. We have just talked about a small city in Ontario. Now I would like to talk about a small city on the Eastern coast of Canada or on the edge of the Atlantic.

Five or six years ago, this city mainly had traditional industries. As we know, the unemployment rate in the sectors of coal mines and fishery is very high. With a view to changing the high unemployment rate, this city identifies its banking sector as a breakthrough sector. As a global director of a transnational corporation put it, we think that Halifax will become the core of business in Canada. When we move the financial industry into Halifax, it may save costs in the amount of roughly from 15% to 56%. This city is actually a far more remote place. Most importantly, the large banking institutions need to find the talents in this place. One of the reasons lies in the fact that Halifax has the most number of colleges and universities in Canada. Although this city does not have an ideal climate, it might attract talents there for a better life, who would then be willing to stay on. This area has become a financial business cluster and the very center that attracts the insurance industry in Canada. The largest global insurance company has its regional headquarters there, so their initial strategy was to attract the financial industry for development there and then to attract the headquarters of the financial sectors for development there so that the headquarters of the non-financial sectors would be attracted into Halifax for further development.

The successful experience of this city proves that the model just analyzed by us can further develop its feasibility. The major factor lies in the fact that Halifax has become the center with a sustainable impact. From now on, we can find out whether this model might still work after 5 or 6 years.

Before I finish the speech, I would like to talk about how to guarantee the sustainability of this developmental model, particularly from the perspective of the leaders regarding how to guarantee its success.

The first class of leaders are the entrepreneurial ones who are responsible for finding the target and seeking the resources for enterprises' further development; the second class of leaders are the administrative leaders who can guarantee that everything can be operated in an orderly manner without errors. The third class of leaders are the individual leaders who are responsible for working out and implementing the strategy. But what is more important lies in how we can establish corporate value and culture.

In view of the entrepreneurial leaders, the very key lies in that, in formulating their strategy, they must not say: I will do as you do. There are too many enterprises which try to learn from others when they see the success of other enterprises. We should learn, but we should pay attention to the changes and identify our own advantages. In view of the administrative leaders, the key to guaranteeing a balanced corporate operation is the combination from top-down to bottom-up. In view of either a region or an enterprise, the important thing is that the full use of talents can guarantee its development, which is the very key, or the critical success factor; most enterprises fail to do this: make the joint change from top-down to bottom-up.

In view of the personal charismatic leaders, the key lies in identifying the value and core values. This value mainly lies in that a technical or higher employee clearly knows where his or her values are in the enterprise. In establishing the values, the important thing is to take into account your employees rather than your work. So if you pay attention to work instead of money, you must have a higher life aspiration.

In the process of different communication and exchange processes in China, and even all over the world, the important thing is that there must be all kinds of colleges and universities in the area which can provide the corresponding talents. Service industries of whatever kind, even in our area, have this kind of service and processing, etc., across the Detroit River. The students of our school of business created the first technical enterprise incubator or accelerator as their entrepreneurial place. Our students have the opportunity to get their social practice in the service industries related to the automobile spare parts industries. The students are quite young, but they know how to conduct marketing in enterprises with a developmental history of 50 years, 60 years, 70 years or even 80 years, and they know how to promote the development of the service industry.

My idea is that we should encourage students to act in this way and that the colleges should also behave like this. Also at times, we should require them to behave in this way as it is the best method by which we can guarantee that we will have enough talents to bring success to your regional development.

Thank you!

# Speech by Fang Aiqing, Vice Minister of Commerce, at the China (International) Conference on the Development of the Convention and Exhibition Industry

To all guests, ladies and gentlemen,

Good morning! I am very pleased to attend the China (International) Conference on the Development of the Convention and Exhibition Industry and to discuss the new idea of encouraging the market-oriented development of China with you. The convention and exhibition industry is a key component of the modern service industry; it is a bridge and link connecting production and consumption, not only interfacing the supply and demand and expanding the circulation channels, but also boosting regional and industrial economic development. The convention and exhibition industry is a booster of economic growth. According to statistics, the direct economic benefits of the global convention and exhibition industry are more than 300 billion USD, and the total economic growth brought to the world's economy is more than 3 trillion USD, accounting for 4% of the total GDP in the world.

The convention and exhibition industry is a booster for urban development. Various conventions and exhibitions gather flows of people, materials, capitals, technologies, and information, and effectively drive the growth of catering, accommodation, traffic, retail and tourism. The convention and exhibition industry is an absorber of labor employment and provides a lot of employment opportunities. Analysis shows that, once every 1,000 square meters of exhibition area is added, almost 100 employment opportunities can be created.

With the rapid development of the Chinese economy, China's convention and exhibition industry has become a new power for boosting economic and social development. It plays an active role in transforming economic development, optimizing the industrial structure and upgrading the Chinese economy, with features as follows:

I. Continuous growth of conventions and exhibitions. According to preliminary statistics, in the year 2013, China held more than 7,000 conventions and exhibitions, increased by almost 6 times compared with the number in 1997. At present, there are more than 300 convention and exhibition halls in China, and the area for exhibitions is more than 12 million square meters. Based on relevant data, the net area, the area dedicated to professional halls and indoor exhibitions occupied by foreign economic and technological exhibitions in China, ranks No. 2 in the world.

II. Centralized regional distribution. The construction of exhibition halls, conventions and exhibitions in China are mainly located in the economically developed Bohai Rim, Yangtze River Delta and Pearl River Delta. According to statistics, the number of conventions and exhibitions and the area available for exhibitions in the Bohai Rim, Yangtze River Delta and Pearl River Delta accounts for 62% and 69% of the total number in China.

III. Diverse sponsors. Governments, industrial associations and various ownership enterprises play their roles in the market of conventions and exhibitions. With an area of more than 5,000 square meters, the exhibitions held by enterprises account for 57%, the ones held by industrial associations account for 20%; the ones held by the Party and the Government, and by people's organizations account for 23%.

IV. The rapid development of emerging conventions and exhibitions. With the rapid development of conventional conventions and exhibitions, transportation, financial insurance, cultural tourism and a series of emerging trade in services exhibitions have developed rapidly, and some conventions and exhibitions with vivid industrial features and remarkable industrial influences have begun to take shape, such as the China (Beijing) International Fair for Trade in Services(CIFTIS), the leader in trade in services, the China International Cultural Industry Fair (ICIF), which aims at boosting cultural transactions, and the China (Shanghai) International Technology Fair which promotes technological transactions.

Today, we are holding the China (International) Conference on the Development of the Convention and Exhibition Industry with the theme of the market-oriented developmental path of the convention and exhibition industry in China. My opinions are given as follows:

First, the market-oriented developmental path is inevitable for the rapid and sound development of the convention and exhibition industry.

The Third Plenary Session of the 18th Central Committee of the CPC proposed that the market should play a decisive role in resource allocation. The core of market operation for the convention and exhibition industry is to run according to the law of the market and give full play to the decisive role of the market in resource allocation within the convention and exhibition industry. To be specific, the convention and exhibition industry should be operated by the market, meeting the needs of the market and in accordance with the law of the market.

In recent years, the convention and exhibition market in China has been geared to the international market. The scale of conventions and exhibitions is increasing, the industrial chain has extended and developed further, the convention and exhibition industry with a wide design domain and covering all industries has been shaped, and the healthy and sustainable development of the convention and exhibition industry in China has benefited from the market-oriented path. At present, compared with the developed countries, the convention and exhibition industry falls behind and is in a transition period, changing from a large convention and exhibition country to a powerful convention and exhibition country. Its rapid and sound development can be achieved by taking the market-oriented developmental path.

Under the new situations, the Chinese government should accelerate functional transformation, innovate with a management mode, provide high-quality public services, lead rational layout and industrial self-discipline, accelerate the market-oriented process of the convention and exhibition industry, encourage industries to be on the road towards the orientation of a brand market, and provide a unified, open and orderly competitive market environment for the development of the conference and exhibition industry.

Second, the convention and exhibition industry should be clearly positioned to meet the market demands to the full.

The convention and exhibition activities are demand-oriented economic behaviors, and their supply and demand relations reflect the basic rules of the market. Therefore, the convention and exhibition organizer and provider should fully know about market requirements, the basic rules of convention and exhibition activities and their positioning; the organizer and provider should also become the bridge and link between exhibitors and buyers, and realize the functions of publicity media, information communication, exhibition and show, trade negotiation and market exploration.

Third, the convention and exhibition enterprises should innovate with modes, run operations and provide services with information technology.

With the prosperous development of the Internet, mobile Internet technology and multimedia video and audio technology, the convention and exhibition activities and network information platforms are quickly combined and mutually promoted. The convention and exhibition mode has been constantly changed, and traditional conventions and exhibitions have provided services and management with information technology, they have caused the traditional conventions and exhibitions to change their original mode, break the time and space barriers of conventions and exhibitions, shape an online and offline integrated service system, realize an organic combination of network information platforms and conventional exhibition platforms, thus becoming more vigorous.

Fourth, the market of conventions and exhibitions should be in order to reinforce the protection of intellectual property rights and the building of a credit system.

In recent years, while the conference and exhibition industry in China was developing, low-level repeated exhibitions, out-of-order competition and vicious cheating have still existed, which disturbs the market and the financial order, impairs the public image of conventions and exhibitions in society and affects the long-term and healthy development of the Chinese convention and exhibition industry. To standardize the market of the convention and exhibition industry, combined with industrial features and market demands, we will reinforce the protection of the intellectual property rights of the convention and exhibition industry, support and encourage the sponsors to protect intellectual property rights by patent applications, trademark registration and other means. We will also further prepare promotion and services, energy conservation, staff qualification, post specifications and information technology and other industrial standards. We will also carry out further research, establish the credit system for the industry, and explore the establishment of credit files and a disclosure system for the violation of organizational information. We will also actively promote and establish nationwide convention and exhibition industry associations and improve the self-discipline of the industry.

Fifth, the convention and exhibition industry should reinforce reforms and perfect the construction of a system of laws and regulations.

The establishment of a rational, scientific, orderly and efficient system of laws and regulations for the convention and exhibition industry is the key prerequisite and a key for a healthy development and a market-oriented developmental path of the convention and exhibition industry in China. To guarantee the development of the industry, we will actively involve the establishment and perfection of a system of laws and regulations of the convention and exhibition industry, increase the strength of reforms, release the approval authority, simplify administrative procedures, innovate the management mode, perfect the market operation mechanism, establish clear policies and rules that guarantee fair competition, break glass doors and spring doors affecting the healthy development of the convention and exhibition industry, promote orderly competition and push the market-oriented and professional developmental path of the convention and exhibition industry forward.

Ladies and gentlemen, as an international and comprehensive trade in services transaction platform, CIFTIS creates rare opportunities for exchanges and cooperation within the convention and exhibition industry. I sincerely hope that colleagues of the convention and exhibition industry can fully utilize this platform and seize the opportunities to communicate experiences, gather information and carry out widespread cooperation. The journey will not be made in vain, and I believe that more contributions will be made to the rapid and sound development of the convention and exhibition industry in China.

May the conference be a complete success. Thank you!

# Speech by Ren Xingzhou, Director of the Market Economy Research Institute, the Development Research Center of the State Council, at the China (International) Convention and Exhibition Industry Conference

Distinguished leaders and guests,

Good Morning! I am so pleased to attend the China (International) Conference on the Development of the Convention and Exhibition Industry again. Today, many new and familiar friends gather here to discuss the issues of the market-oriented development of the convention and exhibition industry in China. I think it is crucial. Then I have several key conditions on the market-oriented development of the convention and exhibition industry in China for all of you.

I suppose that market orientation is a trend. There might be several key issues to be solved, and what remains is not a problem. If a proper system and mechanism and market demands are required, market supply must be available. If some key issues are not solved, the market orientation would not be solved. Then, what are the key conditions and key issues for the market orientation of the convention and exhibition industry? I want to share them with you.

The decisive function of the market in resource allocation was mentioned in the *Decision* in the Third Plenary Session of the 18th Central Committee of the CPC. The former fundamental function was changed into the decisive function, and the difference between the meanings of the 2 words is great. It is an improvement of the connotation of the socialist market economy of China, it is the greatest highlight, the key theoretical innovation and a breakthrough for liberation. Meanwhile, the theory makes reform fall within the principle and the dimension of testing, and if the reform is in place? How can it be tested? The test is to check whether the market plays a decisive role in resource allocation. Let's take a look at the development of the convention and exhibition industry under the prerequisite of a theoretical breakthrough. There are several key conditions for market-oriented development:

Ⅰ. First, I suppose that the most crucial issue is to delineate the function and role of government in the field of conventions and exhibitions. This issue is unlikely to be a great issue in other countries. But for China, this is a core and key issue, because we are in a transition from a planning economy to a market economy. The field of conventions and exhibitions has mainly been led by the government, and it is a field that is approved by the government to a great extent. How does the government handle the relationship with the market? How does the government play a role in resource allocation? These are the issues to be addressed in China.

The government should take the lead in resource allocation, but not allocate resources directly. The government's "visible hand" is not allowed to override and should fill the vacancy in time. I think that there are several aspects for the transformation of the functions in the field of conventions and exhibitions: First, release the control, cancel or lay down the administrative approval, and reduce the items to be approved. Second, apply a scientific kind of management of categories. Do not apply the same identical management system for conventions and exhibitions, a scientific category is required. Different management modes are used for different types of conventions and exhibitions. Some important ones should also be managed by the state, such as some key conferences. You know that the CICA was just held in Shanghai. A particular kind of management was applied to very important international conferences like that one. Different management modes should be used for ordinary market-oriented conferences. Third, clarify the mechanism that allows access to the convention and exhibition as well as qualification conditions of the subjects, that is change from an approval system to a registration system. Over the past decade, the convention and exhibition industry has developed a lot, and the conditions for change from an approval system to a registration system are allowed.

Besides, conventions and exhibitions should be changed from government-oriented to market-oriented, which will cut down resource allocations in the aspect. We can understand that, at the beginning of the development of the convention and exhibition industry, as for China, without a lead from, support by and a link to the government, the development of the convention and exhibition industry may encounter many difficulties. The market has been developing for more than 10 years, and after about 20 years' development, the conditions for market orientation should be met and allowed. The government should be transformed from being in the forefront to being on the backstage, and the operation of the market should be forwarded to the subject of the market.

What should the government do? The government should prepare the industrial planning, reinforce the supervision, maintain the market order, oppose unfair competition, enhance the supervision, transformation and law enforcement and prevent market failure. As for the convention and exhibition industry, its market orientation cannot solve all of the issues, and some of them need the assistance of the government. The government's visible hand should play its own functions, such as building an appropriate environment, maintaining order, supplying and reinforcing public services, reinforcing the environment for the convention and exhibition, creating building and infrastructure services.

With the help of relevant policies, clearly delineate the relations between the government and the market, and this is crucial in China. Without this demarcation, the handling of relations between the government and the market cannot be achieved, and the market-orientation of the convention and exhibition industry would be tough.

II. In my opinion, the second key condition is to make the market mechanisms of the convention and exhibition field perfect.

In terms of market resource allocation, once the field is opened up by the state, it must be out-of-control. What is the reason? Only when standard market mechanisms are available can the resource allocation play a decisive role. So the market resource allocation is not blind and it is limited. The following mechanisms are required:

(1) Clarify the access mechanism, establish an open, transparent and public market rule, and follow the principle of introducing negative lists into the market access. Then, which resources related to the conventions and exhibitions should be managed by the government or allocated by the market; the access code should be clear.

(2) Make the market system perfect, and a unified, open and orderly convention and exhibition market system is required. With the complete upper and lower reaches, the entire ecological chain makes up an organic system.

(3) The first is the transparent supervision mechanism. Apply effective market supervision, clear and remove provisions and practices affecting fair market competition, and oppose local protection monopolies and unfair competition. In the field of conventions and exhibitions, finding out how to break the barrier between regions and industries is inevitable.

The second is a strict mechanism to punish dishonesty. Just now, Vice Minister Fang mentioned the establishment of an industrial credit system and the application of severe punishment for dishonesty. A credit is the pass for the honest, and dishonesty is the epitaph for the dishonest. A mechanism to punish dishonesty is necessary.

The third is the mechanism of price determined by the market. With a developed market orientation of the convention and exhibition industry, the pricing mechanism must be formulated according to the price determined by the market. If these mechanisms are continuously established and perfected, a market system and a market mechanism bearing resource allocations will be formed.

III. The third key condition is that the country must create an environmental system for equal development and fair competition for the different conventions and exhibitions. To do this, we must do the following things:

(1) Promote a joint development of the professional and market-oriented convention and

exhibition subjects of various ownerships. At the very beginning, there were many state-owned convention and exhibition companies. In recent years, many private-owned companies, even some overseas companies have entered China, and a joint development of diverse and various ownership entities have been formed, and in the future, the market for the convention and exhibition industry must be a market with the competition from a lot of entities.

(2) Protect the property rights. Production elements are used to participate in market competition and they involve lawful protection and legal supervision. All ownership subjects should be treated equally. For only that way can fair competition among all subjects be promoted. Regardless of ownership, if they are competitive and follow the rules of the market, they will have the opportunities for fair competition.

(3) Promote the development of private convention and exhibition enterprises. In recent years, private convention and exhibition enterprises have been developed rapidly with a higher ratio. The activity of private capital has yielded in investments on exhibition halls and the market orientation is very high. The government opened the field earlier. After opening the field to private capital, many private exhibition halls and exhibition companies were born.

Of course, the role of state-owned subjects in the convention and exhibition industry should be played out. They are subjects, and the state-owned economy should be developed. Of course, in the development of a state-owned economy, the administrative power will penetrate into convention and exhibition enterprises; this should be prevented. Some convention and exhibition enterprises should be separated from relevant government organizations and become the real market subjects; by not putting many government resources and intangible resources into the Company, the subjects compete on a fair platform.

Of course, we create environmental development for small and medium-sized enterprises, and many countries support these enterprises. We hope that the convention and exhibition industry will become larger and more powerful. The enterprises are of different sizes on the ecological chain, and we will provide sound conditions for convention and exhibition enterprises to provide these professional services.

IV. The fourth key condition is to reinforce the protection of intellectual property rights and encourage innovation.

We should encourage and support the innovation of convention and exhibition enterprises, in particular to original thoughts. At present, many conventions and exhibitions are borrowed, by importing overseas exhibitions or attracting already-developed domestic exhibitions. We do not have enough originality and innovation. What is imitation innovation? We should have a proper definition for it. It is important to encourage such innovation and to encourage imitation innovation.

Of course, against this background situation, the protection mechanism of the intellectual property rights regarding conventions and exhibitions must be established, behaviors infringing the intellectual property rights must be investigated so as to form a virtuous industrial code. At present, the innovated conventions and exhibitions are easily copied by many toughs, and a conference and an exhibition are copied with a non-identical order, so the market is disordered. Without the protection of intellectual property rights, who will innovate? Without innovation, how will China march forward? How can we develop originality in conformity with China's situation? We must protect the intellectual property rights.

Of course, how to explore the patent and professional service brand in the field of conventions and exhibitions is important. For which of these can we apply for patents, and what kind of special trademark and brand can be chosen as one's own? These should form a system, so as to protect the original and innovative enterprises for further development.

Ⅴ. The fifth key condition is to make tax collection and the financial support policy in the field of conventions and exhibitions perfect.

Based on a scientific and rational category, we should make the tax collection and the financial support policy in the field of conventions and exhibitions perfect. As for convention and exhibition programs in key fields and related to the national livelihood, the environmental protection and eco-friendly programs should be financially supported. For example, if the conventions and exhibitions are large, the government does not necessarily provide financial support but it provides financing support. The support must be given to conventions and exhibitions led by the country, such as support in tax collection and miscellaneous issues. A perfect system must be formed.

Ⅵ. The sixth is to establish a professional and qualified training system for talents.

To make conventions and exhibitions larger and China more powerful in this field, other systems and mechanisms are important, and talents are, too. Just now, I talked with the Deputy Mayor of Chengdu City. He said that the convention and exhibition industry of Chengdu has developed a lot, but insufficient professional staff was still a bottleneck. I suppose that Chengdu and other cities will encounter this problem. We lack in convention and exhibition talents, and talents are required for market operations by the convention and exhibition industry. How to form such a talent system? First, the cultivation by regular institutions of higher education is of importance. We should set up the corresponding disciplines and provide such training. Second, training by professional training organizations and targeted training is a key. Third, the cultivation through continuous education is important. In summary, we should have integrity complete system composed of regular colleges, professional training in society and continuous education for the cultivation of inter-disciplinary talents in the convention and exhibition field.

We can push the market orientation of conventions and exhibitions forward with talents and the just-mentioned market mechanism. All of these are crucial, and they make up the key condition for market operation of the convention and exhibition industry in China. With a good mechanism and system, supply would be available for the convention and exhibition industry, and I believe that supply must be rooted in demand. According to market rules, many people can create market demand without the government's worry. If the market subject is perfect and fair, system, mechanism and talents are key conditions, plus the protection of the intellectual rights.

Against such a background, the development of a market orientation of conventions and exhibitions would propose new requirements for the convention and exhibition industry.

First, in order to research the rules of the market orientation of conventions and exhibitions in China, the market resource allocation should be in conformity with the laws; what are the rules of the market orientation of the convention and exhibition industry with Chinese characteristics? There are many similarities to and differences from overseas countries. What are the rules of conventions and exhibitions for us? This needs our examination in practice.

Second, how to subdivide the market, and how to form the industrial chain, the service chain, the ecological chain of conventions and exhibitions to increase the value. For example, the ecological chain of the convention and exhibition industry is made up of convention-running subjects, local governments, convention and exhibition enterprises, exhibition halls, service subjects, marketing teams, publicity media which make up an entire industrial chain, the service chain and the ecological chain. How can we form such a chain? Besides, our market will be finer, and what is our market segment? We also need to examine this in practice.

Third, building and development of brand conventions and exhibitions and how to demonstrate the value of the brand.

Fourth, how to apply modern information technology and hi-tech means to the convention and exhibition industry, to which field should we apply frontier technology.

Fifth, combination of online and offline conventions and exhibitions. How to combine the development of the Internet t with the convention and exhibition industry; pushing this industry forward is a realistic issue. Some people say that, in theory, the Internet impacts the conventional industries, and the original industries will be adjusted, integrated, and re-shuffled. Then, how to form a new pattern under the development of the Internet and modern information technology? This issue also needs our examination and study.

Sixth, conventions and exhibitions. We talk about conventions and exhibitions, both of which have their rules. How to combine conventions and exhibitions and how to coordinate them will be discussed in market orientation.

Seventh, convention and exhibition planning, marketing and its own developmental rules. There are many good practices in overseas countries. How to form our own rules of conventions and exhibitions on the basis of reference?

Eighth, the necessary one is the development of coordination among conventions, exhibitions and cities. Just now, I talked with the Deputy Mayor; the conventions and the exhibitions should be the organic combination between the city and the conference, and between the brand city and the brand conference with one city, as a carrier and as a platform, and it must have Chinese characteristics. We have many good cases. Guangzhou comes to mind when the Canton Fair is mentioned, and Beijing, Chengdu, Shanghai, Yunnan, Kunming come to mind when conventions and exhibitions are mentioned.

Ninth, the opening of the convention and exhibition industry to the outside. The key conditions also include opening the doors to the outside and going global, and this is a key issue that we must face.

Tenth, about the role and function of Chinese associations, chambers of commerce and research institutes. Against the background of market orientation, the direct interference in and participation by the government will be weakened, and the convention and exhibition industry must have professional industrial management organizations, such as associations, chambers of commerce and research institutes. We should further research on how to seek the rules and how to form the development of the convention and exhibition industry with Chinese characteristics.

So these industrial management organizations and research organizations should play their roles in the road towards market orientation. It is a key one in the ecological ring of conferences and exhibitions. The above is a speech to be studied and discussed in the convention and exhibition industry, which concerns the market orientation of the said industry in China. Any mistakes are welcome for correction. Thank you!

# Speech by Chen Xianjin,  Executive Vice Chairman of the Global Association of the Exhibition Industry, at the China  (International) Convention and Exhibition Development Conference

Distinguished leaders and friends of the convention and exhibition circle,

Good morning! In the second half of last year, according to the principle in the notice issued by the General Office of the Central Committee of the CPC and the General Office of the State Council, the Ministry of Commerce stated that any festival, forum, convention or exhibition activities, sponsored by the Party, Government authorities and people's organizations, for the purpose of solving the issue of positioning, role and function of the government in the convention and exhibition industry, are aimed at accelerating the market orientation of the convention and exhibition industry. This matches the requirement that the core issue of the reform of the economic system is to handle the relations between the government and the market, and to make the market play a decisive role and yield to the government's function, which was proposed in the Third Plenary Session of the 18th Central Committee of the CPC.

Today, I wish to share some practices and experience in the convention and exhibition industry by other countries and exhibition enterprises. My speech is divided into 3 parts: The 1st part introduces the basic practice of the global exhibition industry in terms of investment and management of the exhibition halls, organization and operation of exhibition projects, and the function and position of the government; the 2nd part summarizes some features and trends of market orientation of the international exhibition industry; the 3rd part makes some suggestions about accelerating the market orientation of the exhibition industry in China.

Part Ⅰ: Current situations of the market orientation of the global exhibition industry.

1. Investments and management of the exhibition hall.

To make the more representative cases, in order to make comparisons, I selected the United States as the sample from North America, Germany, France, Italy, Spain and the U.K. as the samples from Europe, and Japan, Korea, Thailand, Singapore, Taiwan and Hong Kong areas as samples from Asia. Investments in and management of the exhibition halls in the countries are in accordance with the local situations. Almost all the exhibition halls and convention centers in the USA are run by the government. The government is not the central government but the local government. Investment and management modes of European halls are subject to the situation in the various countries. In countries with a well-developed exhibition industry, such as Germany, France, Italy and Spain, the exhibition halls are run by the government and managed as companies. The situation in the U.K. is different; the exhibition halls are run and managed by private enterprises. In Asia, the modes of investment and management of the exhibition halls are diverse. In Japan, Korea, Hong Kong, Taiwan and other countries and regions, the government or the government's delegate, such as semi-official trade promotion organizations, becomes the investor and manager of the halls. The two largest halls in Thailand are run by private enterprises. Singapore is a hybrid type. Of the three largest halls in Singapore, two halls are run by private enterprises and one is run by the government.

2. Organization and operation of exhibition projects.

We divide them into 3 categories in terms of organizer and operator of the exhibition projects. The 1st category is the exhibition hall. If the exhibition hall is run by the government, they are state-owned enterprises. The 2nd category is the industrial association. The 3rd category is the exhibition sponsors. They refer to private enterprises or listing companies. In countries with a relatively developed market economy, there are no exhibition sponsors of state-owned ownerships. The exhibition sponsors from the USA clearly know that 70% of trade exhibitions are sponsored by industrial associations and 30% of exhibitions are sponsored by private enterprises. The hall owners are not the sponsors in the USA. Of course, I will talk about the changes that have come about in the past 1 or 2 years. More than half of the exhibitions in Germany, Italy, France and Spain are organized and operated by the exhibition halls, so they are the owners and the guests of the hall, and the function of dual role makes them control and lead the market. Of course, these exhibitions are supported by and involve with the industrial associations; the function of private exhibition companies is limited in these countries. It is different in the U.K., because the exhibitions are led by private exhibition companies. The modes in Asia and the modes of investment in Asian halls are diverse. Associations and companies are dominant in Japan and Singapore, government or investment trade prevails in Korea, Taiwan and Hong Kong, and private enterprises are rare. Thailand is the combination of private halls and the operation of the government.

3. Positioning and function of the government.

The government is classified into several hierarchies; the 1st hierarchy is the central government, the 2nd hierarchy is the local government, the 3rd hierarchy is the city government, and so the companies are controlled by the government. Their functions are divided into investment in halls, organizations and exhibitions, industrial promotion and market standardization. We can see that the investment in halls by the central government is rare and almost non-existent, but it is common that local and city governments are investors in the halls. Of course, companies controlled by the government can be seen but they rare. The central government, the local government and the city government are not in charge of organizing the exhibition, I mean the economic and trade exhibitions. The companies controlled by the government are the organizers, and the central, local and city governments are responsible for the industrial promotion. The central government and the city government do not attach great importance to the standardization of the market; the enterprises do not concern themselves with it, and the local government contributes a lot to it.

The USA is a typical market economy, and the government never participates in organizing exhibitions, except for investments in halls. There is a kind of tax, called hotel tax, in the USA. After the local government collects the tax, the tax is used for operating and expanding the halls that have received the investments. Therefore, the exhibition companies and some industrial associations of the USA may receive discounts indirectly; the government does not run the exhibitions. The exhibition hall owners in Germany, France, Italy and Spain are owners and guests, and they are run by local governments and local chambers of industry and commerce. However, there are some private exhibition companies in these countries. So standardizing the market and ensuring fair competition is a key assignment of the government. Then the government or the government's delegate, such as some organizations of exhibitions, standardizes the market by laws or some rules and the systems prepared by these organizations.

The exhibition industry in Asia was developed recently, so the government is just at the beginning in its control of the market. Korea never passed a law on exhibitions, Singapore never made a program encouraging exhibitions. Thailand issued a rule on encouraging exhibitions. I checked these rules and found that they were used to attract exhibitions to be held in these countries, and they were not used to control the market. There are rare rules used for controlling the market and guaranteeing fair competition. This is the first part of my introduction of information on foreign countries.

Part II: Features and trends of the market orientation for the international exhibition industry. It mainly includes one mode, two kinds of weaknesses and three hot issues.

One mode. The unified mode without the global market orientation of the exhibition industry is the one mode. Due to different historical backgrounds, the stage of economic development, the market subjects, the system and mechanism of the market orientation of exhibitions are not the same in the various countries. The countries design and carry out their market orientation in accordance with local features, and diversity and diversification are features of the mode. We should not be proud or modest regarding the issue of the market-oriented mode. When talking with colleagues, I find that they appreciate Germany's mode and they think that it is very good. Why? Of the top commercial exhibitions in the world, approximately 60% of the projects take place in Germany. The way Germany's mode started is special: First, after World War Ⅱ, most German cities were destroyed, including the exhibition halls and ancillary facilities. Second, after World War Ⅱ, the German economy needed to be rebuilt. The German government needed to recover, and a lot of work was led by the government. Third, some German traditions had been inherited before World War Ⅱ.

The above three reasons are the foundations of the mode of the exhibition industry in Germany. In the circle of the international exhibition industry, people think that such a mode cannot be copied easily. This is the first feature of the market orientation for the international exhibition industry, that is the issue of mode.

The second feature is that the government's involvement needs to be weakened in two areas. The first area is the government's involvement in commercial exhibitions. In countries with a market economy, the government does not involve itself in economic and trade exhibitions. First, the government does not approve these exhibitions. Second, the government does not utilize administrative resources to assist the exhibitions in attracting businesses. Third, the government does not use its budget to subsidize these exhibitions. Finally, even in market-oriented countries with a developed economy, in terms of titling, sponsors of trade and economic exhibitions rarely include the names of the country, department or city.

The second area that should be weakened is the government's financial support via investment in, operation and management of the exhibition halls. As mentioned above, most exhibition halls and convention centers in the USA are run by the government, and the local governments establish the hotel tax to support the operation and expansion of these exhibition halls. For the past two years, the American Government has cut down the funds, and many exhibition halls have to earn more income on their own. They have increased the rent of the exhibition halls; they wish to involve the sponsorship of exhibitions and become the sponsor of the exhibitions. The above aspects, in particular the latter one, disturbs the existing industrial associations and private exhibition companies. The American industrial associations are discussing with local American governments and doubt the practice of the exhibition halls.

Three hot issues. The basic subjects and the main interest groups of the exhibition markets are classified into three categories. The first category is the exhibition hall, the second category is the exhibition sponsor and the third category is the exhibition supplier. The service subject and the investor are classified into: Government investments and private investments. Therefore, various relationships regarding interest and competition are complicated and each individual overlaps the others. At present, we are discussing three hot issues.

First, the relationship of supply and demand of the exhibition halls is out-of-balance. When there are several exhibition halls in a city, or the total supply of halls is more than the market demand, the competition among the exhibition halls or between the exhibition hall and the sponsor is severe. One the one hand, the exhibition sponsors have more options, and they can receive more discounts; on the other hand, the change of the exhibition order will bring new challenges. Here is an example. In Hong Kong, there was only one exhibition hall, the Hong Kong Convention and Exhibition Center. Two years ago, the AsiaWorld-Expo was established near the airport. There are two exhibition halls in Hong Kong. After the AsiaWorld-Expo, both exhibition halls hold exhibitions with the same themes and contents occasionally. For instance, an exhibition is held at the Hong Kong Convention and Exhibition Center, and, on the same day, another exhibition is held at the AsiaWorld-Expo with the same theme. The organizers holding the exhibition at the AsiaWorld-Expo dispatch many volunteers to the intersections of the Hong Kong Convention and Exhibition Center to persuade the professional visitors to go to the Center, register in on the spot and then pick up them at the AsiaWorld-Expo and using free shuttle buses, transfer many professional visitors. Of course, the sponsors holding the exhibition at the Hong Kong Convention and Exhibition Center feel uncomfortable about this. They tell the sponsors of the exhibition hall that this is unfair competition. They reply that it is difficult to handle. The volunteers stand out of the exhibition hall, on the road, a public place, and the sponsors of the hall have no power to control them. Hong Kong is a place full of free competition. After the AsiaWorld-Expo, two exhibitions, with the same theme and contents, are held in order to create competition. This is the first hot issue; they are discussing how to deal with it.

The second "hot issue" is that the exhibition hall operators become exhibition organizers. Most exhibition companies do not hope that the operators of the exhibition companies become exhibition sponsors. They hope that the owner and the guest play their respective roles and do not disturb each other. In fact, the views are not feasible. The exhibition hall owner, acting as the exhibition sponsor, is common practice in many countries, not just in Europe, but also in America. I hold the opinion that, requiring the owner and the sponsor to play their respective roles, is not a rational request, and this should be an issue to be discussed. If the exhibition hall owners become the sponsors, it is essential that they set up an open, fair and transparent hall-renting policy, and that they treat the customers' exhibitions and their own exhibitions equally. The government should make efforts here and supervise as required.

Third, theme protection. To protect the exhibition, some governments apply theme protection, namely, after a high-quality exhibition a second exhibition of the same type will not be approved within a certain period, such as one month, three months or longer. The current issue is that the market economy encourages competition, and progress can be made by competing, which benefits the consumers. Obviously, the dominant enterprises in the market do not welcome such competition, and the protective measure regarding the theme considers the expulsion of the enterprises involving the second competition. We never said that we opposed repeated exhibitions. Then we found that the slogan was problematic, and it was changed into opposing low-level repeated exhibitions. Should we consider canceling the measure of theme protection? If new competitors are qualified and have a more advanced philosophy and means concerning the operation of the exhibitions, the government should welcome them. Competition removes enterprises with low efficiency and poor benefits, and finally, there are benefits for exhibitors and visitors.

Part III: Three suggestions on improving the market orientation of the exhibition industry in China.

Seen from what has been introduced, including one mode, two areas that need to be weakened and three hot issues, we can clearly see that, in order to improve the market orientation of the exhibition industry, the key is to handle the relationship between the effective market and the active government. We are not new to a convention and exhibition market economy. The development of China's exhibition industry over the past 30 years, especially the development in the past 20-plus years, cannot be planned. From the state-owned exhibition companies of the past to the well-developed exhibition companies of various ownerships nowadays, and from zero ancillary facilities for exhibitions to the complete exhibition industrial chain are wonders created by the market economy. We can see that the trial period of the reform of the Chinese economic system is not a free and developed market economy, but a planned economy strongly disturbed by the government. The key to the market-orientation of the convention and exhibition industry is to remove the government involvement and solve the issues of unavailability of the government's function, and its overriding and not-in-place in the convention and exhibition industry. The following three suggestions are proposed:

1. Follow the basic rule of the market economy.

The mode of commercial exhibitions led by the government should be ended as soon as possible. Whether the economic and trade exhibitions should be held or not? Who should operate them? Where to operate? How to operate? All of them should follow the market demands and not depend on the government's subjective ideas. The Government should transform its functions and be separated from sponsoring the projects and being involved in the convention and exhibition operation, and not act as an athlete. We can see that, when the Political Bureau held the collective study on May 20, the General Secretary proposed that the government should reduce its direct control over microscopic economic activities, and that the market should play its full role. Hence, I think that the first suggestion is to follow the basic rule of the market economy.

2. Reform of the approval system.

Prior approval of sponsoring of international, economic, technological and trade exhibitions has been the responsibility of the government since the reform and the opening-up. In view of history, such an approval system plays an active role in promoting the internationalization of the Chinese exhibition industry, importing advanced technology and equipment and accelerating the reforms, the opening-up, etc. We know that the approval system solved the bottleneck issues in the mechanism and system arose from unitary exhibits used at the exhibitions due to foreign currency control and import control at the time being. After 30 years of reforms and opening-up, these issues do not exist. I think that prior governmental approval for international exhibitions in China is not fair to the market. It intensifies the power of the government, limits the efficiency of the market and produces rent-seeking space.

As introduced above, the approval system does not exist in countries with a developed market economy; we should reform these approval systems immediately. As the first step, we should change the approval system into a verification system. Namely, the government releases the conditions, and replies whether the applicant is qualified or not within a specified time and give the reason, if the application is denied. Or the system should be changed into a registration system, from prior approval into supervision afterwards. The applicant can operate after submitting the registration information, without the government's consent, and the government should investigate if any problems occur.

3. Establish a fair, open and transparent market rule.

What should the government do for the rapid development of the Chinese convention and exhibition industry? Hold government-led conventions and exhibitions? Of course not, because this is the governmental overriding, and whether or not the government should control the industry in terms of total volume, conforming procedures, optimal structure, proper layout and time efficiency? Of course not, this is governmental malposition to some extent. What should the government do at present? To do those when the government is omitted or not in place; That is, to reinforce supervision and establish a fair, open and transparent market rule. The main principle is that the subjects of various ownerships should be equal, have the same power, position, follow the same rules and bear the same responsibilities.

All of you know that the government is a visible hand. Since it is a visible hand, we want to know the function of that hand. I will provide two examples as an explanation or as reference.

The first example is that the largest exhibition hall in France is called Viparis. It was run by the Government of France at the beginning. During the year 2006, the French Government planned to transfer the management of such a large hall, from the government to a private company, which was the largest exhibition sponsor. At that moment, the government also worried that the largest exhibition sponsor would cause unfair competition in the hall. To avoid such situations caused by private companies, under the leadership of the Ministry of Finance of France, the investor in the hall, namely the Government of France and the Chamber of Industry and Commerce in Paris, signed an agreement with the management company. I never checked the agreement, and it might be helpful to us to do so. Some principles exist in the agreement. The principle of hall renting is explained below.

It mentioned three principles, and the general subject is called non-discrimination, and includes three parts. The first part concerns the principle of key exhibition, and each key exhibition is entitled to have priority in renting the hall. What is the definition of key exhibition? The key exhibition is defined on the basis of areas. The exhibition covering an area of 100,000 square meters or above is defined as a key exhibition and is entitled to priority in renting. The exhibition hall will release the theme of each key exhibition, and there may be 10 or 15 key exhibitions to be held each year. The organizers of key exhibitions are required to sign a contract 20 months before the exhibition. If not, the time for the exhibition can be sold to organizers of smaller-scale exhibitions, and this is the first principle. I have given this principle a name: "small-sized exhibition inferior to large-sized exhibition".

The second principle is the condition of master and slave. If you run airline companies, you are certainly very familiar with it. That is to say, whoever held the exhibition here has priority for a second event; for example, let's say you held an exhibition in 2014 or before, so you are entitled to priority in holding another one. Of course, the exhibition time has a variation of approximately 10%. I have also given this principle a name: "new exhibition inferior to old exhibition".

The third principle is interesting. As the hall managers also run exhibitions, they also run new exhibitions. If the new exhibitions are in conflict with the existing exhibitions on the market, how can this be dealt with? According to terms and conditions, you must give the existing exhibitions a chance; what is this? I have given this a name as well: "host exhibition inferior to guest exhibition".

The rules prepared by the French Ministry of Finance are fine and they were released to the public; the planning and scheduling of exhibitions are carried out based on the rule above. So the non-discrimination rule is very obvious. Of course, there is a pricing principle. The government manages too much, but it does not manage all of it. Since it is the largest exhibition hall in Paris, the fee cannot be fixed without any considerations. The index for the standards of architecture is used for pricing. The third principle is interesting, that is, who finishes the ancillary services in the hall. This principle divides the services into three ancillary ones: Compulsory, exclusive and competitive. The services that are compulsory and exclusive are specified.

I was very inspired, and the government's hand is visible and clear. Then the Government of France appoints a delegate to mediate any disputes in the hall. The Company's CEO told me that, after they took over in 2007, the delegate from the French Ministry of Finance did not receive any complaints. He was proud of it, and he managed well in the renting of the hall.

The second example is the news received from the website of the Wall Street Journal at the beginning of April, CCI Penalizes ITPO WRs6.75, what does it mean? CCI is the Competition Committee of India, and how about the example? The exhibition association of India submitted a complaint to the Committee and filed a case. In Deli, the largest hall manager is ITPO, equal to China Council for the Promotion of International Trade (CCPIT), in fact the trade promotion council of India. Then the exhibition association of India submitted a complaint to CCI, or the Anti-monopoly Committee, for it thought that ITPO applied unfair competition means in managing the hall. In the year 2007, ITPO specified the interval for holding two exhibitions of the same kind. In the year 2011, ITPO revised the rule and leased the hall according to the rule. The exhibition association of India thought that, after the rule was revised, the rule was beneficial for ITPO and constituted unfair competition to external exhibitors. Then they filed a case to the Anti-monopoly Committee of India. According to the judgment, ITPO lost and was fined for 67.50 million Rupees, equal to 1.25 million USD. It is strange that ITPO is a governmental body, equal to the trade promotion council of China. The Anti-monopoly Committee thinks that such a rule misuses your leading standing and causes unfair competition on the market. This is the second example.

The above two examples demonstrate that the government's managerial function is very important in market supervision and in protecting fair market competition so as to establish an open and transparent mechanism. Establishing a fair, tolerant, non-discriminative and barrier-free system is necessary, and an industrial mechanism without an industrial monopoly and local protection. The resource allocation can play a role, but not a decisive role. It should be restricted by laws, so the government should not be weakened in its function but it should play a more powerful role in maintaining social justice and fairness.

Success does not always come easy. All levels of government should concentrate on managing and release the power in place. Once the invisible and visible hands are united and promote each other, the market-orientation of the exhibition industry will be improved, and the ideal of becoming a powerful exhibition country is sure to be realized. Thank you!

# Speech by Bu Zhengfa, President of the China National Light Industry Council at the Global Design Trend Conference and the 2014 China International Design Industry Union Conference

Distinguished Chairman Zhang, all leaders, guests, ladies, gentlemen,

Good day! The Global Design Trend Conference and the 2014 China International Design Industry Union Conference are being magnificently held in Beijing today. First of all, please allow me, on behalf of the China International Design Industry Union, extend warm congratulations on the holding of the conference, and a sincere welcome and gratitude to all guests present.

China is currently in the critical period of economic structure adjustment and industry transformation and upgrading. In recent years, China has formulated and promulgated a group of policies and measures aimed at boosting the development of its design industry, showing China's high attention to design. On January 20, 2014, the Executive Meeting of the State Council made arrangements for promoting the integration of culture creativity and design service into relevant industries, and put forward supportive policies and measures in terms of five aspects, such as good environment creation, talent construction, market condition and finance services. Besides, on May 14, the Standing Committee of the State Council specially proposed to encourage the development of industrial design companies to boost the market for research & development and design, centering on the acceleration of the development of the producer industry. All of these made great contributions to the development of industries.

Light industry is closely connected to the life of every person. Industry design has played a crucial role in the course of the development of light industry, with tremendous achievements in promoting independent enterprise innovation, improving the product value added and creating an international brand. In recent years, designed innovation has been combined with technological innovation, service innovation and brand construction. The huge value created by the design industry has a profound influence on the structural adjustment of light industry and the transitional upgrading of the industry, so that it has become an organic component of inducing structural adjustment and increasing the industry's competitiveness and brand influence. The enterprise is the theme of innovative practice, the creative system for the construction of the design industry, and the key to promoting the integration of the design

Part III  Summary of Speeches at the Summit High-level Forum

service into light industry. Enterprises should make unremitting efforts to enhance the momentum in design innovation in order to form a market-oriented industry, a design innovation system, focusing on the enterprise and integrating the "industry-university-research institution", so as to accelerate the industrialization of design and the cooperation of various forms, promote innovation of the service mode and boost the concentrated development of industrial design, thus further improving the level of the internal opening-up. The industrial organizations play an irreplaceable role in the upgrading, integration and development of industries. Now, the China National Light Industry Council is actively constructing a basic assessment system of design innovation so as to guide the design innovation of light industry enterprises, improve the design innovation capacity, foster the establishment of more famous brands in light industry, thus enhancing the quality and efficiency of the development of light industry enterprises.

Since its founding in 2012, the China International Design Industry Union has actively carried out work on coordination by relying on its multi-level platforms by holding various activities, such as CIFTIS, the Global Design Trend Conference, the China International Design Industry Union Conference and the High-Level Forum, which increases the international influence of the Chinese design industry. The Union Secretariat offers membership service, which enhances communication and exchanges among its members, promotes design cooperation between design institutions at home and abroad and enterprises, while also creating new systematical platforms and mechanisms for its members.

Distinguished representatives, today, we still face a tough and arduous task regarding industry design innovation. We need to take the opportunity that this conference offers to consolidate the results of previous work, further give play to the strength in resources and talents, actively explore an efficient approach to the integration of the design service into industry, and intensify the service capacity and its effect, thus making great contributions to the upgrading of the light industrial economy.

At last, may the conference be a complete success.

Thank you!

# Speech by Zhang Longzhi, Vice–chairman of the China Association for the Promotion of Industrial Development at the Global Design Trend Conference and the 2014 China International Design Industry Union Conference

Distinguished Chairman, Bu Zhengfa, all guests,

Good morning, first of all, I would like to extend, on behalf of the China Association for the Promotion of Industrial Development, my warmest congratulations on the holding of this conference.

In recent years, design service, as an emerging industry, has been highly regarded and fostered by China. In 2011, the "12th Five-Year Plan" program outline pointed out the direction of the development of industrial design. In 2012, the *Industrial Transformation and Upgrading Planning (2011–2015)* issued by the State Council made explicit dispositions regarding the promotion of the development of industrial design. Due to this great attention, the Political Bureau of the Central Committee has promoted the development of the design service industry at a national level, as well as the transformation and upgrading of the industry's structure, so that the Chinese design service industry will surely achieve great accomplishments. Until now, the Chinese design service industry has developed considerably, with a gradual expansion in the scale of its services and a marked increase in service employees. A survey shows that 70% of the colleges throughout China have launched design-related majors, with the number of undergraduates specializing in design-reaching a total of more than 1 million, and in addition, the number of design institutions is increasing with each passing year, with the number of large design companies more than 1,200. Furthermore, there are 16 provinces that house industrial design promotion institutes, which lead to the prominence of innovative products, further boosting the flourishing of the design service industry.

Besides, to support the design innovation of Chinese enterprises, since its founding, the China International Design Industry Union has, by relying on the platform of international design resources, played a positive role in uniting a wide group of design colleagues in order to vitalize design. Hence, it has acquired wide recognition and praise from all parties concerned. As one of China International Design Industry Union's guiding units, the China Association for the Promotion of Industrial Development will, as always, strongly support the design industry union, and conduct work in conformity with applicable national policies and the articles of association of the union. I hope the union will absorb more excellent entrepreneurs in design to further expand its coverage, enhance its influence, unite the members to closely follow and analyze foreign and domestic design industry development dynamics, unite the industry organizations and enterprises at home and abroad in order to try to create a harmonious and vigorous international design resource platform, and provide a high-quality and high-efficiency service to resource design; in this way, it will be able to build itself an industrial union organization with an enormous influence, absorption and cohesion. In the meanwhile, I hope the union will strengthen its self-construction, create its own brand, stimulate and maintain the industry and market order according to relevant provisions, promote cooperation among its member units, thus realizing mutual benefits and win-win results.

May the conference be a complete success, thank you!

# Speech by Hu Jinglin, Assistant Minister of Finance, at the Professional Service Industry Development and Professional Talent Growth Conference

All distinguished guests, friends and comrades,

Good morning! During the 3rd CIFTIS, the Chinese Institute of Certified Public Accountants is holding a forum and a series of activities taking "Professional Service Industry Development and Professional Talent Growth" as the theme. I, on behalf of the Ministry of Finance, want to extend a heartfelt thanks and my sincere respect to all guests, the Ministry of Commerce, the People's Government of Beijing Municipality and the related departments which show great support for the activity, as well as to people from all walks of life who care for and have supported the financial work and the industrial development of certified public accountants for a long time!

At present, the global economic pattern is deeply changed, international competition is increasingly fierce, the transfer of industrial upgrading and production factors caused by the new technological revolution is accelerating, and the service industry is becoming a new direction to promote world economic recovery and lead the development of the economic transformation, and also a new impetus for China's economic development, quality improvement, industrial optimization and upgrading. The State Council of the Party Central Committee pays great attention to the development of the service industry. The 18th National Congress of the Communist Party of China proposes to accelerate the changing of the economic developmental modes, promote strategic adjustments to the economic structure, advance the sound development of the strategic emerging industry, and drive the service industry, especially the modern service industry, to development and expansion. The Third Plenary Session of the 18th Central Committee of the CPC further promotes an orderly opening of the service industry field and a relaxing of investment access as the important content for constructing a new open economic system, providing favorable strategic guidance, policy support and market environment in order to develop a modern service industry. The Ministry of Finance carefully implements the spirit of the instructions, focuses on playing the role of the service industry in the transformation and adjustment of the economic structure, introduces a series of fiscal taxation policies, and actively guides and promotes the development of the modern service industry.

As an important force within the professional service industry, the certified public accountant industry plays an important role in constructing quality accounting after 30 years of development, becoming one of the industries with the most degrees of standardization, professionalism and internationalization in China's professional service industry. As the competent department of the certified public accountant industry, the Ministry of Finance has always paid special attention to the development of the industry, fully supporting the management and services of the Chinese Institute of Certified Public Accountants. For the past few years, firmly centering on the spirit of General-Secretary Xi Jinping's instructions that the "certified public accountants should grasp the theme of serving the national construction and the mainline of credit construction", the Ministry of Finance actively implements, guides and supports five strategies of the industrial development to increase the industrial level. Up to now, China has 98,207 certified public accountants, 98,162 non-professional members, more than 300,000 practitioners, 8,283 accounting firms, 40 qualified securities firms, and 11 qualified H-share firms, providing professional services of auditing and authentication for more than 2,500 listed companies. In 2013, the industry achieved a business income of 56.3 billion RMB, maintaining a double-digit rapid growth for the successive years, much higher than that of the same industry worldwide.

The Third Plenary Session of the 18th Central Committee of the CPC determined the strategic objective of comprehensively deepening reforms, and takes the development of the strategic emerging industry of the modern service industry as an important hold on economic transformation and industrial upgrading. The professional service industry is coming to an encouraging historic period of opportunity. I would like to take this opportunity to put forward some suggestions regarding the development and construction of the professional service industry:

1. Fully play out the important role of the professional service industry in comprehensively deepening reforms.

The professional service industry has a huge developmental potential and a space in the general national construction layout. Its development is not only an internal requirement for adjusting the industrial structure, but it also provides important intellectual support for the transformation and upgrading of other industries and other service industries, playing a promotional role. The modern professional service industry is also essential for the improvement of social management, the national self-management system and the self-management ability. To comprehensively deepen the reforms, concept innovation and institutional innovation are needed. We should fully realize the value and the role of the professional service industry, and strengthen the research policy and support of this industry;

other things need to be done as well: further transform the governmental functions, and strengthen the government's purchase of professional services; actively support and guide the professional service industry to expand its field of business according to market functions and the professionalism of the service industry; respect the internal laws and value characteristics of the professional service industry, standardize the market order and the bidding/tendering of professional services, and try to create a fair and orderly market environment; further strengthen the publicity of the economic functions, professional services and service value of the professional service industry, deepen the understanding of the professional service value of all departments and of the entire society, and continuously stimulate and release internal demands for professional services on the market.

2. Strongly strengthen the talent teambuilding of the professional service industry. Development of the professional service industry is actually the development of talent. Talent is the core of the professional service industry, and professional ethics and professional skills of professional talent determine the width and depth of this industry. Centering on the new situation and the new requirements of China's economic construction, we should cultivate and develop professional talent as an important category, and make efforts to create a batch of talent that meet the requirements of professional service development and that can serve international and domestic markets; establish a standard industrial access evaluation mechanism, strengthen the continued education of industrial talent, and particularly maintain and improve the professional infiltration capacity and expand the market supply of professional services in line with new fields and new requirements of the national construction; strengthen restrictions on professional ethics and supervision on public social media, and establish a perfect professional ethics system for the professional service industry. Shape people with professions, cultivate people with professional self-disciplining, restrict people with professional self-disciplining, improve professional quality and credit and take talent as a foundation to create a century-old shop of the professional service industry.

3. Widely carry out international cooperation within the professional service industry. The international professional service industry has accumulated rich experience. We should cultivate professional talent, formulate professional standards and develop international professional cooperation; enhance the institutional innovation ability of the professional service industry, accelerate internationalized development, make a breakthrough and progress in international network construction of institutions and national project development, and improve brand reputation and the influence of China's professional service industry on the global market; strengthen the connection between international and domestic markets and a link with professional service institutions and market demand subjects, and expand professional trade in services; actively participate in the international governance of the

professional service field to promote the global development of the professional service industry.

4. Make efforts to develop organized construction of the professional service industry. Both international experience and China's practice show that a strong industry cannot do without powerful industrial organizations. Industrial organizations have unique advantages in the law recognition of industrial development, in professional market development and innovation as well as in industrial supervision and management; moreover, they are important forces to guide and promote the development of the professional service industry. We should create a good relationship between the government and the market, and hand the main industrial responsibilities over to social organizations so as to achieve a good mechanism of complementing each other and the mutual promotion of governmental supervision and management of industrial organizations; strengthen the self-disciplining system, build up the self-disciplining ability of industrial organizations, stick to the unification of industrial management and management services and the unification of serving members and society; improve the democratic decision-making and management mechanism, expand management service fields, improve management service functions, and really undertake industrial responsibilities of the innovation of the social governance mechanism.

Friends and comrades, the development of an economic society brings about a rare development opportunity for the professional service industry. Comprehensively deepening reforms creates higher requirements for the service connotation, service ability and service quality of the professional service industry. This is an opportunity and also a challenge. Let's further deepen our understandings, update our concepts, make full efforts to improve the level of development of the professional service industry and promote the professional service industry to a new stage, so as to make more contributions to China's economic transformation and upgrading as well as to foreign economic exchanges and cooperation. Thank you!

# Speech by Li Yuan, Deputy Inspector of the Department of Trade in Services and Commercial Services of the Ministry of Commerce, at the Professional Service Industry Development and Professional Talent Growth Conference

Distinguished Assistant Minister Hu Jinglin, all guests, ladies and gentlemen, friends,

Good morning! I'm glad to have been invited to attend the Professional Service Industry Development and Professional Talent Growth Conference, an accounting service trade platform of the 3rd CIFTIS. I, on behalf of the Department of Trade in Services and Commercial Services of the Ministry of Commerce, want to extend my warm congratulations to this activity, a heartfelt thanks to the Ministry of Finance and the Chinese Institute of Certified Public Accountants for their great support of the CIFTIS, and a warm welcome to all guests!

Since entering the new century, the global service industry and trade in services have vigorously developed, becoming an important means for the promotion of industrial transformation, an impetus to promoting a new round of economic growth and a hot spot of focus and competition for all countries. The Chinese government pays great attention to the development of trade in services, and actively promotes changing the method of foreign trade development. The 18th National Congress of the Communist Party of China explicitly proposed developing trade in services, and a balanced development of trade. In 2013, China's service trade volume reached 535.6 billion RMB, with a year-on-year growth of 14.7%, ranking third in global imports and exports, wherein service exports ranked fifth and service imports ranked second.

Greatly developing the professional service industry plays an important role in adjusting China's economic structure and promoting transformation. Particularly, against the background of economic globalization, cross-border activities of commodities and capitals rely on the improvement of the level of professional services. During China's enterprises "going out", certified public accountants actively provide such services for enterprises as strategic planning, merger and restructuring, accounting and risk control, and they support enterprises in catching up with international standards in terms of financial management and participating in international innovation in higher fields.

Acceleration of the professional service industry is the basis of expanding trade in services. For a long time, the Ministry of Commerce has been paying attention to the development of the professional service industry, including certified public accountants, deeply promoting various supporting policies to develop professional trade in services, actively building and utilizing international platforms and trade exchange channels including the CIFTIS, supporting the improvement of the level of the professional service industry and effectively expanding the exportation of professional services. Particularly, the Ministry of Commerce implements the *Several Opinions on Supporting Accounting Firms to Expand Service Exports* jointly issued by nine ministers and commissions of the government, takes professional services of certified public accountants as a service trade field with emphasized cultivation for a long term and incorporates it into the service trade category, and promotes the international development of the certified public accountant industry, to make contributions to the structured upgrading of China's trade in services.

At last, I wish the activity a complete success and I also hope the certified public accountant industry and accounting trade in services will achieve greater development. Thank you!

# Speech by Gao Xiaoping, Executive Vice President of the Chinese Public Administration Society, at the Professional Service Industry Development and Professional Talent Growth Conference

Honorable leaders and friends,

Good morning! First of all, I want to extend my thanks to the Chinese Institute of Certified Public Accountants for giving me such a chance to deliver a speech. I will make a brief speech centering on three issues, i.e. the position and function of the professional service field in the national economy, bottlenecks affecting the development of the professional service industry, and promoting the development of the professional service industry by talent teambuilding.

Now, the professional service industry is not a complete concept, social public cognition is not clear, and professional orientation is not definite. Since the 1960s, the industrial structure of developed countries has started to transform from industry-oriented economies to service-oriented economies, and the role of the service industry role in social development has been more and more obvious. In the meantime, the social division of labor has gradually refined, and the development of the service industry makes it gradually show a subdivision. The professional service industry is separated from the traditional service industry, characterized as highly knowledge-intensive, highly capital-intensive and professional.

The WTO classifies professional services into the category of vocational services, including services provided by accounting, auditing, law, taxation, construction, engineering, urban planning, medical services, midwifery, nursing, physical therapy, attendants, etc. With the development of the national economy and the improvement of the social governance structure, the professional service industry is playing a more and more important role in the national economy and in social development.

First, the professional service industry becomes a sign for measuring the degree of social and economic development. The proportion of the service industry in the GDP is an important index for determining a country's degree of economic development. As a provider and disseminator of professional knowledge, the modern professional service industry contributes knowledge and wisdom to the development of other industries in terms of management, law, auditing, design, consulting and other aspects, playing a role of knowledge base and consultant, and promoting the rapid development of a knowledge economy by producing and disseminating knowledge. Therefore, the level of development of the professional service industry directly determines the level of development of the entire service industry. To expand the service industry, the professional service industry must first be expanded and become strong.

Second, the modern professional service industry is an important channel through which to absorb social employment. The service industry is a natural channel through which to absorb employment. Compared with other industrial departments, the professional service industry has a low elasticity of employment with its labor-intensive, employment-intensive and knowledge-intensive characteristics, and has unique advantages in absorbing employment, which absorbs not only different laborer employments, but also drives other employees with high-knowledge employees. Economic fluctuation has the smallest influence on employment in the modern professional service industry. Compared with the employment elasticity of industry and agriculture, that of the service industry is at a low level. The professional service industry has the lowest employment elasticity level, thus it has much room for employment. According to the general law of economic evolution, after per capita GDP exceeds 5,000 USD, the employment structure enters an important intersection, the proportion of agriculture employment diminishes, industrial employment gradually declines after reaching its peak, and the proportion of employment in the service industry substantially increases. At present, China is entering a period of professional development in the modern service industry, which will provide much room for employment.

Third, the modern professional service industry is an important impetus for the optimization and upgrading of the industrial structure. International experience shows that, when the economy develops to a certain extent, further development of the secondary industry needs effective service industry support. If the service industry keeps lagging behind, it will certainly hinder economic development. To accelerate the development of the service industry, we must first accelerate the development of the high-end service industry, because the professional service industry is playing a leading role in the whole service industry, and it will become an important impetus in changing the methods of economic development. To achieve a change in the methods of economic development economic development needs to be based on structural optimization, efficiency improvement, consumption reduction and environmental protection. As a smokeless industry with high knowledge and high innovation, employment within the modern professional service industry has nothing to do with tangible assets. It has advantages in converting existing knowledge to ability, effectively reducing resource consumption and pollutant emission, and improving other industries' efficiency in energy conservation and environmental protection by developing the professional service industry.

The second issue is the bottleneck that is affecting and restricting the development of the modern professional service industry, mainly talent.

China's professional service industry started late and at a low level, and it is not developing rapidly. In order to develop the professional service industry well, the shortage of talent is the first problem that needs to be dealt with. The modern service industry is a typical, and even a specific, knowledge talent-intensive industry. The development of such professional service industries as law, finance and accounting, consulting, intellectual property, public relations and property transaction, high-end service talent must be taken as a basic support. With talent, anything can be done. So, whether high-level talent meeting international market competition requirements can be cultivated becomes the key to a rapid and sound development of the professional service industry. Provision of sufficient talent for the upgrading of the  internal industrial structure within the professional service industry becomes a way to develop the industry itself.

Now, the talent resources of China's modern professional service industry have some problems, such as undersupply and a large gap in the market, existing accumulation is obviously low, and in particular, there is a more serious gap in high-technology talent, core talent and international talent, which makes it difficult to meet the active demands generated within the development of the modern service industry. In such fields as engineering, finance, accounting, doctors and life science, China's job seekers have a qualified rate of less than 10%. Skilled talent is very short in Beijing Municipality. During the "12th Five-Year Plan", Beijing's skilled talent had a gap of 600,000, and 130,000 for high-skilled talents. Among the 15,000 hi-tech enterprises in Zhongguancun, IT enterprises account for more than half, and software professionals account for one third, but the gap in talent in Zhongguancun is 60,000–70,000 each year.

The low level of talent is also an important problem. After developing over years, China has accumulated a group of excellent talents in the modern service industry; these people have a certain ability, but professional business still lacks high-quality talent. Particularly, leading influential talents inside the industry are few. To accelerate the development of the professional service industry, a group of talented people who are professional, who have mastered foreign languages, who have planning and marketing skills and who are good at management is absolutely necessary. There is a shortage of talent and the level of that talent is insufficient. Modern senior logistics management talent, financial consultants, investment consultants, intermediary service talent, digital communications engineers and foreign-related law talents are the most important soft factors for the development of the modern service industry, and the people talented in these areas are extremely few in number now. With economic development and especially the high-end and international development of the service economy, there is an urgent need to expand talent teams and improve their level.

The third issue is to promote the development of the professional service industry by talent team building.

First, the key to accelerating talent teambuilding within the modern service industry is to efficiently deal with the relationship among the government, the market and society. There must be an insistence on government orientation, and on the application of policies and laws in order to guide the flow of talent into the professional service field. We should learn from the experience of the Chinese Institute of Certified Public Accountants and use it for reference; moreover, we should further emancipate our minds, promote the updating of the concept of talent development, deepen the reform of the talent work mechanism, change our ideas, explore and innovate, convert from supply orientation to demand orientation, learn from international talent training experiences and use them for reference, and promote the building up of a talent system through the joint cooperation of the government, scientific research institutions, and enterprises by virtue of upper and lower linkage.

1. Arrange and coordinate industrial development planning and talent development planning, refine the core talent development planning of the high-end service industry, formulate a series of supporting policies and deeply develop human resources through innovation-driven strategies.

2. Construct diversified talent input systems, establish and improve a mechanism to increase input with governmental orientation and an organic combination of various inputs, and accelerate the construction of innovative entrepreneurship service platforms.

3. Accelerate the improvement of building a system of related laws and regulations regarding the development of high-end service industry talent so as to effectively guide talent development. Current laws and regulations are apparently lagging behind the developmental needs of the professional service industry field: one defect is that laws and regulations are not perfect, and the other is that industrial standards are not unified, causing a bad environment of competition. Competition does not guide people to focus on the quality of professional services, but rather to consider professional services equal to general commodities and to ignore the quality of services, and thus competition in prices is directly created. In this way, the quality of professional services cannot be guaranteed. So, we should strictly formulate laws and regulations, study and standardize them by combining the particularities of professional services. Meanwhile, we should also grasp international and domestic talent markets, integrate regional talent resources, promote the integration of a system for talent cultivation for the high-end service industry, accelerate the integration of central and local talent, and achieve the

exchange and sharing of talent resources and win-win investments through counterpart study, training, two-way temporary practice, joint tackling of topics, and project coinciding; moreover, we should consider establishing regional talent cooperation, accelerate the improvement of regional human resource integration, and particularly strengthen talent exchanges with eastern coastal areas.

Second, accelerate professional talent teambuilding, with the market as an impetus. To develop the professional service industry, we must play out the decisive role of the market in configuring human resources. Through deepening reforms, improving social division of labor based on specialization and promoting externalization of internal professional service activities of the manufacturing industry and the marketization of professional trade in services, we lay a solid human resource market foundation for the development of the professional service industry.

1. Promote institutional innovation and adjust the framework of the system of market supervision regarding the professional service industry. Accelerate the cancellation of the discriminatory treatment of social organizations and enterprises within the non-public economy. The service industry belonging to private products should firmly promote its marketization and industrialization to further play the role of social organizations within the non-public economy as an investor and a development subject.

2. Promote service innovation and form good abilities for the development of the professional service industry. Increase new service categories and businesses, improve the internal structure of the professional service industry, raise the level of the technical equipment of the professional service industry, increase knowledge intensity and the content of the professional service industry, enhance its stability, cultivate new growth points of the professional service industry, and strengthen cross-regional and cross-professional radiating capacities of the professional service industry.

3. Gather an ecological base for the professional service industry by virtue of regional advantages. The professional service industry is characterized by high intensity of commercial areas and knowledge, and industrial agglomeration leads to knowledge sharing. Central commercial areas in metropolitan zones have a series of industrial clusters, e.g. they achieve core clusters of finance, accounting, commerce and services by taking central commercial areas as a carrier and a platform; take hi-tech technical parks as a platform to form an environment characterized by product R&D, and expand the professional service space in a diverse way, to make a value chain of professional services that will extend overseas.

Third, accelerate the talent teambuilding of the modern service industry, and form a diversified mechanism for the social cultivation of talent, by relying on society. ①Improve the cultivation system and accelerate high-skilled talent growth space. Through school cultivation, post-training and base cultivation, cultivate professional talent in various forms to gradually build high-quality talent teams. ② Establish systems, and adopt scientific, standard, effective and convenient evaluation methods to evaluate the technical level of skilled talent. ③ Strengthen service systems and optimize the environment for talent growth. By continuously strengthening service awareness, provide excellent service to improve professional talent skills, establish stages for skilled talents to show themselves, improve the flow service system, and strengthen publicity to create a social environment conducive to high-skilled talent growth. ④ Establish an incentive system for professional technicians. Establishing an incentive mechanism for professional service talents and implementing various treatments for professional technical talents are strong guarantees that professional technical talents will be encouraged to start a career and be successful.

Besides, we should get social organizations and all circles to play an important role in forming many talent cultivation modes such as combination of schools and enterprises and combination of industries, schools and scientific research institutions. Take related industrial knowledge as training focus and achieve conversion from order to customized talent cultivation form, especially advanced customization and private customization. Enterprises provide talent internship and experimental areas for schools. According to talent employment and knowledge skills, establish a mechanism to guide education where practitioners participate in guiding the work of universities and colleges, and cultivate more professional talent that will meet professional needs through two-way guidance of schools and industries.

In general, the development of China's professional service industry has a great amount of space for improvement. If we continuously adjust policies, innovate management and strengthen services, I believe we will blaze a new path towards the development of the service industry with Chinese characteristics and a new path towards adjusting our industrial structure with Chinese characteristics; moreover, we will be able to develop a socialist market economy with Chinese characteristics. Thank you!

# Speech by Lv Jijian, Depaty Director General of the Department of Trade in Services and Commercial Services of the Ministry of Commerce, at the China Science and Technology Service International Cooperation Conference

Distinguished guests, ladies and gentlemen,

Good afternoon! I am very glad to have been invited to attend the 3rd CIFTIS China Science and Technology Service International Cooperation Conference. First of all, please allow me to extend my warmest congratulations for the holding of the conference and a sincere welcome to all its guests on behalf of the Department of Trade in Services and Commercial Services of the Ministry of Commerce.

Since the beginning of the new century, the world economy and the industrial economy have gradually turned into a service economy. At present, 60% of the GPD originates in value added in the global service industry, and the ratio reaches over 70% in developed countries. Besides, investments in the service industry account for over 60% of global foreign direct investments, and trade in services around 20% of the global trade. All of these show that the service industry and trade have been the hot spots and new impetus in international economic cooperation. The Chinese government is actively promoting the transformation of the economic development mode and paying high attention to the development of the service industry and trade. In the scenario of a complex worldwide economic situation and economic downturn in 2013, the Chinese service industry realized a value added of 2,622.04 million RMB, with a growth of 8.3%. The ratio of value added in trade in services in the GDP for the first time exceeded the secondary industry, and reached 46.1%. As a result, the service industry becomes more and more important in the development of the Chinese economy.

The level of development of the modern service industry is a significant mark for measuring the level of comprehensive competitiveness and modernization of a country or a region. As an important component of the modern service industry, the science and technology service industry develops and grows with the introduction of sci-tech economy and information technology. It offers a knowledge-based and a high value-added science and technology service to society and plays an important role in supporting and guiding the development of the modern service industry, so that it is the main driving force for the rapid growth and development of the service economy.

Since the reform and the opening-up, China's science and technology service industry has accumulated a fairly solid foundation with the rapid development of its economy and society, and has made great progress in the areas of patent application, science and technology input, technology market, trading volume, etc. Nowadays, global science and technology are experiencing a rapid development and an increasingly fierce competition. A number of emerging industries represented by high technology is gaining dominance in economic development. In the context of structural adjustment and mode transformation, China is actively promoting enterprise self-independent innovation and managing to improve core competitiveness, which creates good opportunities for the development of the Chinese science and technology service industry. Science and technology service is a critical module in CIFTIS. It is aimed at fully encouraging the development of the Chinese science and technology service to have a positive impact on the development of the global science and technology service industry.

I am pleased to see a great number of international organizations and leading enterprises dedicated to scientific and technological innovation and engaged in science and technology service industry attending this conference, which fully demonstrates good prospects for the international community and transnational companies within the Chinese market. I hope technology and business élites from all countries will be greatly inspired through in-depth exchanges, and that the Chinese enterprises can take this opportunity to have a better understanding of the developmental trend and frontier dynamics of the global science and technology service industry, and that the foreign enterprises can enjoy better prospects for development as well as more cooperation opportunities in China.

Finally, I wish the conference a complete success, and I hope that the science and technology service industry will enjoy a flourishing development. Thank you.

# Speech by Ralph Haupter, Corporate Vice President of Microsoft, at the China Science and Technology Service International Cooperation Conference

Ladies and gentlemen,

I am very delighted to be here to deliver a speech. Today, I would like to discuss the issue of growth. In fact, we are making constant efforts to promote the growth of products and services. Therefore, I want to share with you some ideas about how Microsoft operates as a Chinese company and a Chinese cooperative partner.

Of course, Microsoft is a transnational company, but we pay great attention to China. We have set up 4 research and development centers in China, and we invest 10 billion USD in research and development on a global scale. Besides, we have 21 technological and innovation centers and 29 offices in the USA, with 13,000 employees. It can be seen that many employees of each of our partners work with us. Therefore, we help the Chinese IT industry to develop as a medium-sized enterprise.

In fact, we at Microsoft are also growing. You may think Microsoft is a seller of software. I would like to take this opportunity to impress on you that Microsoft is transforming from a software seller to an "equipment + service" seller. The service normally refers to transformation business, and cloud service is exactly our transformation purpose. Cloud service is a crucial business in China, which shows the great transition of our company. We are managing to transform ourselves into a service enterprise and a growth enterprise.

To attain this goal, our approach is to fully transform our business model. Our products are developing based on the cloud, as well as our technology and services. It is unique. Such transformation has been a great over the past 40 years. Now, what we need to do is to make users and enterprises get access to their proper technology. We are standing at the frontier of transformation. In the course of transformation, we focus on the following four aspects. We hope that our clients and partners can achieve transformation along with us.

The first aspect is digital work, which affects the daily working manner and the way of raising individual productivity.

The second is digital life, which refers to our behavior of acquiring digital information and using IT technology to improve ourselves.

The third is cloud service, which is provided on the basis of local operators and our technologies.

The last is our mode of consumption. In terms of consumption, we may consider equipment. If we consider the manufacturing industry, we can see it involves sensors and different technologies and products. In other words, it means how we consume the service. Technology is revolutionary, because it brings great changes to everyone's way of working and to the way of acquiring information, as well as the structure of our costs and infrastructure. In fact, it also has a great impact on Chinese society; for example, it helps enterprises reduce expenditures in hardware purchasing, and provides enterprises with excellent technology to make them rapidly offer service to global clients in an advanced way.

Cloud solution is also very strong. One of our typical client cases may show you how we offer service in a brand new way in China. Yunhe is one of our partners, which also uses a cloud service. It has established ERP infrastructures used for medical treatment, health care and education, which are services. Actually, we transform our product to service, which is exactly what we are doing with our local investment partners.

To take another example, GMW is a media industry, which in fact also provides a good cloud service platform for media so that they can better serve their clients, without any hardware investment.

We have developed a good cooperation relationship with Wenzhou. We provide small enterprises with office software as a service, such as office, TV video conferencing and a network presentation mode. As a matter of fact, such small enterprises do not need technology input and only need to pay monthly expenses like water or electricity charges. At present, our service in this aspect is also enjoying a notable development.

In addition, I would like to talk about our growth in China. The growth has mainly been achieved in equipment, such as mobile equipment, tablets, computers and PCs. Here, I want to talk about a different kind of equipment, similar to a sensor. China is a very critical market, so is our operation mode on the Chinese market. Recently, we announced that we are willing to provide free Windows packages for small devices. Besides, according to the level of technology, last Tuesday, we recommended that domestic clients should purchase an 8-inch tablet PC at the price of less than 800 RMB. This tablet PC is equipped with a good, safe operating system, which manifests our outstanding capacity in product and design. Seventy percent of the products produced by our partner are for exportation, contributing to its marked growth.

Next, I'd like to talk about innovation in cloud service and equipment. Both our industry and the enterprises taking the leading role in our industry share an important responsibility for privacy and security, which is exactly what I want to highlight. As our service is supported by

China and developed locally, it completely complies with international laws and Chinese laws. Our operating partner in China is 21vianet.com. It operates service in a compliant manner, which completely complies with Chinese laws and regulations. As a member of CCOPSA, we can have a better understanding of Chinese security laws and regulations. Besides, we have cooperated with the Chinese government to offer it security assurance and share a source code with it. In terms of consumer and corporate users, we are trying our best to protect their security and privacy, which fully complies with Chinese laws and regulations. It is of great importance to us, because we are trying to open a new field in the service industry, and we need to consider security and privacy in a new way. As a leading company, we should make unremitting efforts in this respect so as to develop and promote industrial standards.

In summing up, I hope my speech will help you learn more about how Microsoft promotes the growth of the entire industry and the development of enterprises in the Chinese service industry. Finally, may the conference be a complete success. Thank you.

important role in promoting social employment, industrial transformation and upgrading, and driving the growth of global trade.

According to statistics, China's E-commerce volume of trade in 2013 broke through 10 trillion RMB, quadrupling in 5 years. The number of people for online shopping has reached 302 million, and online retail has exceeded 1.85 trillion RMB. The proportion of the total retail of consumer goods increased from 1.2% in 2008 to 7.8% in 2013. E-commerce has become the largest online retail market in the world, and it plays an obvious role in promoting employment. Researches show that China's online retailing enterprises have created more than 9 million jobs, and are expected to reach 30 million in 2015. E-commerce also promotes an efficient establishment of domestic and foreign market integration, and cross-border E-commerce has become a new method for China to accelerate the transformation of the development of foreign trade. According to statistics, more than 80% of the foreign trade enterprises in China have started to apply E-commerce to explore overseas markets. Viewed from the developmental trend, E-commerce will show the following characteristics next:

1. The innovation of information technology will greatly promote the development of E-commerce. The application of the Internet of Things will be expand rapidly. Cloud computing and big data will promote changes in operation methods and service modes of E-commerce enterprises, driving a fine development of E-commerce. E-commerce enterprises can make marketing plans with more market competitiveness, and their level of service and operational efficiency will increase continuously. In the meantime, with the popularization and application of 4G technology, mobile terminals will become an important field for the future development of E-commerce.

2. E-commerce will accelerate its extension and expansion. More E-commerce enterprises will carry out cross-border operations, and their business will develop towards logistics, the supply chain, finance and advertising. Cross-border operations will become a strategic combination of large-scale E-commerce.

3. New modes of E-commerce, such as online and offline integration, will lead the transformation and upgrading of traditional enterprises. Different enterprises will use the development mode of online and offline integration to actively adjust their original operational methods and utilization systems, and properly solve the interest impact of the traditional industry caused by E-commerce, promoting the transformation and upgrading of entity enterprises to E-commerce.

4. The ability to provide services will become the core of the competitiveness of E-commerce enterprises. As consumers are more and more rational and the market becomes gradually more mature, the operational ability, the ability to provide services and the innovation ability of E-commerce enterprises will become key factors for winning markets and consumers.

5. Internet Finance will be developing and improving gradually. Internet Finance is a product of the innovative development of information technology, E-commerce and finance, and it is an important supplement and improvement of the financial ecosystem. On the basis of effective regulation and the improvement of the mechanism for risk control, Internet Finance will develop gradually and will gradually become mature and perfect.

6. E-commerce will constitute a breakthrough in the changing methods of economic development under policy support. The government will study and make policies for the problems and difficulties encountered in the development of E-commerce to further promote it.

China's E-commerce has also had some contradictions and problems during its rapid development, e.g. its rules and integrity are not perfect, the regional development is not balanced, the system is not developed and we are short of E-commerce talents. The Ministry of Commerce has always assisted the promotion of a sound development of E-commerce as an important grasp of its work in the new era. Stick to the principles of market orientation, enterprises as the main body, standardization in development and development in standardization. By virtue of government guidance and standardization, drive the market power to jointly promote the development of E-commerce. In order to solve the problems of development we should do the following:

First, strengthen the environmental construction. As for current problems in E-commerce, we should improve the regulations, actively promote the formulation of E-commerce law, advance the revision of related laws of E-commerce, such as the consumer protection law, food safety law, contract law, and advertising law; moreover, we should formulate, along with the National Development and Reform Commission, the Ministry of Finance, the People's Bank of China and other departments, a series of policy documents to promote the development of E-commerce, such as the *Notice of Further Promoting the Sound and Rapid Development of E-commerce*; in addition, we should issue a series of departmental regulations and standards, including E-commerce mode codes and online shopping mode codes, and actively construct uniform monitoring and credit systems regarding E-commerce.

Second, we should actively promote application. Support the online retail platforms in the retail field. Further expand coverage, and innovate the service modes. Support the traditional circulation enterprises, rely on offline resources to carry out E-commerce, and achieve online and offline resources complementarity as well as coordinated application. In the area of foreign trade, we need to actively implement the *Opinions on Related Policies of Promoting E-commerce Retail Export*, forwarded by the General Office of the State Council, and make efforts to break the bottleneck of foreign trade regulations that are not adapted to the development of cross-border E-commerce. It is also necessary to accelerate the construction of E-commerce foreign trade platforms and the publishing of E-commerce facilitation measures. Another thing that needs to be done is to further improve the network infrastructure, payment, regulation and other credit systems. In the field of agricultural products, we should establish and improve E-commerce standards of agricultural products, standardize the logistics and distribution system, encourage the connection of E-commerce enterprises with traditional agricultural product enterprises, and promote agricultural enterprises and agricultural E-commerce enterprises to carry out branding and standardized operations of agricultural products. Moreover, we need to construct and put online a national business information service platform for agricultural products, cultivate the E-commerce market in rural areas and promote the circulation of agricultural products. In the field of social services, we should promote the construction of a community facilitation E-commerce platform, and encourage E-commerce application serving the residents' daily life. In addition, we need to actively carry out E-commerce demonstration pilot programs and establish a demonstration system of E-commerce innovation and application as well as fully play the leading role of E-commerce demonstration cities, demonstration bases, demonstration enterprises and promote the innovative development of E-commerce.

Third, improve the E-commerce service system. We should: carry out the construction of E-commerce logistics system, promote a logistics and distribution system adapted to the development of E-commerce, encourage electronic payment credit service, and carry out the innovation of technology and service modes with security certificates. We should also improve the E-commerce service industrial chain, and promote industrial organizations, professional training institutions and enterprises to carry out E-commerce talent training and post-ability training.

Fourth, we need to carry out international exchanges and cooperation. In recent years, we have actively participated in exchanges with the UN, the WTO and APEC, and we have established multilateral and bilateral exchanges. Regarding the developmental trend, foreign enterprises have expanded the Chinese market through E-commerce. It will be an inevitable trend for China's enterprises to apply E-commerce platforms to "go out". We will continue to promote international exchanges and cooperation via E-commerce, and we will encourage and support E-commerce enterprises to expand their overseas markets by setting up exhibition centers and overseas windows.

All guests, the State Council of the Party Central Committee pays great attention to E-commerce. The *Resolution of Several Key Issues of Comprehensively Deepening the Reform of the Central Committee of the Communist Party of China*, approved by the Third Plenary Session of the 18th Central Committee of the CPC has made requests for the development of E-commerce many times. The 2014 government work report also explicitly stressed the promotion of information exchanges and encourages the innovative development of E-commerce. Leaders of the State Council have made important instructions regarding E-commerce many times, making us clearly realize China's confidence and resolution in greatly developing E-commerce.

Ladies and gentlemen, under the correct leadership of the State Council of the Party Central Committee, let's join hands to firmly grasp the strategic period of opportunity for the field of E-commerce, take innovative developments as the impetus and deepening E-commerce application as the key to continuously increasing the level of the development of China's E-commerce, so as to jointly create a beautiful future for our E-commerce.

At last, I wish the conference complete success! Thank you!

# Speech by Cai Yudong, Deputy Director General of the Department of Electronic Commerce and Informatization of the Ministry of Commerce, at the 2014 China (Beijing) E–commerce Conference

Honorable leaders and all guests,

Good morning! I will now talk about the 2013 *China's E-commerce Report*.

This report continues sticking to the principles of being comprehensive, practical, authoritative and clear. Based on the actual situation of the development of China's E-commerce, through research and after several discussions and seeking the opinions of experts in different industries and fields, the report has finally been issued. The report summarizes and reflects China's E-commerce development in 2013 regarding five aspects, including the developmental environment of E-commerce in China, the evolutionary trend of the service industry, the application of various industries, and the status of the development of all the regions of China.

In 2013, China's E-commerce continued growing rapidly, and the E-commerce volume of trade broke through 10 trillion RMB, with a year-on-year growth of 26.8%, wherein online retail exceeded 1.85 trillion RMB, with a year-on-year growth of 41.2%. As a strategic emerging industry, E-commerce plays an important role in changing the economic growth modes, promoting industrial transformation and upgrading and advancing the modernization of circulation, becoming one of the main ways for China to boost its domestic demand, expand its consumptions and promote employment.

China's E-commerce development in 2013 showed the following 6 characteristics:

1. China became the largest online retail market in the world. In 2013, the users of online shopping reached 302 million people, and the online retail volume of trade exceeded 1.85 trillion RMB, equal to 7.8% of the total retail of consumer goods.

2. E-commerce plays an obvious role in stimulating the domestic demand and promoting employment. On the one hand, online retail expanded to all corners of China, making E-commerce's role in stimulating the domestic demand increasingly obvious; on the other hand, the development of E-commerce strongly promotes employment and entrepreneurship:

up to 9.62 million people have chosen to start business through an online store.

3. Technological innovation became an important impetus to maintain the rapid growth of E-commerce. The application of Mobile Internet, big data, cloud computing and other new-generation technologies has become a new hot spot of the development of E-commerce. E-commerce business models are innovated continuously.

4. The integrated development of E-commerce and traditional industries promotes industrial transformation and upgrading. Traditional retailers have sped up their transformation to the Internet, becoming important forces of online retail. E-commerce further promoted the increase in the level of logistics and distribution. Internet Finance has begun to force traditional finance to carry out innovative developments.

5. E-commerce market competition is more and more fierce, and both the enterprise service ability and industrial concentration have been increased. The year 2013 was an active year for Chinese Internet investments, mergers and acquisitions. The leading position of major E-commerce enterprises was further consolidated. Industrial concentration increased gradually.

6. The management and the construction of the service system of cross-border E-commerce has made great progress. As the Ministry of Commerce has issued related policies of cross-border E-commerce together with other ministries and commissions, cross-border E-commerce is coming to a new developmental stage. Currently, China's E-commerce development is attracting worldwide attention and its scale has made a breakthrough, but it is still at a primary stage of development as a whole and there are many factors hindering a sound and sustainable development of the industry. Next, we will, according to the requirements of deepening the circulation system reform and building a law-based marketing environment, improve the law system, gradually solve the problems in network safety, consumer protection and other aspects of the development of China's E-commerce and guide the sustainable development of E-commerce. You are welcome to criticize and correct the report.

Thank you!

# Speech by Sun Yao, Deputy Director of the Beijing Municipal Commission of Commerce, at the 2014 China (Beijing) E-commerce Conference

Distinguished leaders, guests, ladies and gentlemen,

Good morning! As one of the key components of the CIFTIS, the 2014 China (Beijing) E-commerce Conference is officially opened. We are pleased to invite the world-wide industrial representatives and representatives from the governments of 31 provinces, autonomous regions and municipalities, and more than 500 enterprises to demonstrate the achievements made by the development of E-commerce and share their valuable experience. At this moment, on behalf of the sponsor, Beijing Municipal Commission of Commerce, I give sincere thanks for your concern for and support of the China (Beijing) E-commerce Conference and warmly welcome your arrival.

In recent years, under the guidance of the Ministry of Commerce, the competent ministries and departments, the concern and leadership of the municipal government, the leadership of Beijing City, the E-commerce of the city has been further developed and has become the leading industry.

First, the online retail sales are leading in the nationwide and the leading role of top enterprises is obvious. In the first quarter of this year, the amount of online retail sales of the city was 25.49 billion RMB, with a year-on-year growth of 38%, and the total of social consumables of the city has increased by 12.1%.

Second, infrastructures are perfect and the service covers all of China. More than 6 million households can access the optical fiber service in Beijing City. The wireless communication network coverage of the City is 97.92%, with 439,000 websites, ranking the top of the cities in China. The City has 8 E-commerce dealer certification organizations and 53 payment organizations, the top in China, and the E-commerce supporting system of Beijing City is the leader in China.

Third, the mutual support of conventional enterprises and E-commerce enterprises boosts the combined online and offline development. Under the prerequisite of the rapid development of online shopping, with the help of the B2C platform, the enterprise entities seek new space for development. The conventional retail enterprises use mobile phone WeChat-Shop to

Part III    Summary of Speeches at the Summit High-level Forum

perform online and offline marketing, and Wangfujing Department Store and Shopin are interfaced with WeChat payment to activate the online and offline service system. Quanjude is expanding network sales. Maliandao Tea Website, Elong and others featuring service platforms add vigor to the manufacturing enterprises, such as Eye Care, Qumei and Boloni. The conventional enterprises expand their advantages with the help of online and offline sales channels.

Fourth, there are aggregation and demonstration effects. The application system of the E-commerce industrial chain is beginning to take shape; it has cultivated 2 national E-commerce demonstration bases and 4 E-commerce featuring buildings. There are 12 model enterprises of E-commerce certified by the Ministry of Commerce, the top for quantity, in China. E-commerce has shaped a full industrial chain system with a complete category of E-commerce and outstanding advantageous projects. At present, based on the establishment of the Beijing E-commerce Development Zone, Daxing District and Beijing Economic and Technological Development Zone gather together more than 20 enterprises, including JD. COM and Jiuxian.com, and more than 1,000 enterprises involving related services of electronic technology. The Tongzhou Service Park includes 34 enterprises involving E-commerce; the industrial feature becomes evident.

We have adopted the following measures in building new advantages of the E-commerce industry:

The first measure is to perfect the policy guarantee. Beijing issued the *Opinions on Promoting a Healthy Development of Electronic Commerce*. It clarifies a series of objectives and proposes 26 tasks, such as developing the online sales, boosting the electronic commerce, the cross-border E-commerce and building an efficient E-commerce system, and builds the E-commerce processing mechanism led by the Ministry of Commerce and composed of 21 departments. Reinforce the linking and jointly optimize the E-commerce developmental environment.

The second is to advance the trial of E-commerce. The Municipal Commission of Commerce, together with the Beijing Administration for Industry and Commerce (BAIC) and the Beijing Local Taxation Bureau, is encouraging the trial. On April 27, 2013, the first Chinese E-commerce invoice was born at JD.COM. It marked the stage of success of the trial in electronic invoicing, and made breakthroughs in optimizing the developmental environment of E-commerce. At present, four enterprises, including JD.COM, Xiaomi Online and Happigo, are entitled to issue electronic invoices. The electronic invoice saves energy effectively. After the electronic invoice was fully issued, 500 million pieces of invoices are saved each year. Based on the calculation that each ton of paper consumes 3.6 cubic meters of wood, JD.COM can save almost 1,100 cubic meters of it. The promotion and application of electronic invoices will bring evident economic and social benefits.

The third measure is to open up a platform service for cross-border E-commerce communication information and encourage the cross-border E-commerce trial. As for the cross-border E-commerce trial, the city establishes a mechanism with the deputy mayor in charge, as the director, and made up of 9 departments involving commerce, development and customs. In September of this year, the Municipal Commission of Commerce, Customs and other departments opened the cross-border E-commerce communication platform in Beijing City, which realizes supervisory linking and information sharing among the departments. Up until now, the platform has shipped more than 10,000 orders, covering over 120 countries and regions.

The fourth measure is to explore the cultivation of the E-commerce platform. This measure includes holding the China (Beijing) E-commerce Conference publicizing the achievements of the development of China's E-commerce, establishing a platform for domestic and overseas enterprises and experts to share experiences and achievements and promoting online shopping. It also includes guiding the industrial associations to perform consumption promotion programs; the enterprises reached online sales of 49.125 billion RMB in 2013.

The fifth measure is to promote the application of an E-commerce cross-platform. This should fully yield the function of E-commerce to promote the upgrading and transformation of E-commerce, and expand the application of E-commerce into endowment, housekeeping and community services.

The sixth measure is to promote the construction of a logistics system of E-commerce. By establishing delivery points at communities and colleges, supported by information-based management platforms, this will make it possible to integrate the delivery requirements and re- sources at the logistics end, and realize information standardization, delivery in regions and the centralization of service. This measure also includes advancing the centralized develop- ment of logistic delivery for E-commerce, shaping E-commerce featuring a warehousing ag- gregation area to the south of Beijing City and assessing the logistics base, effectively manag- ing the warehousing pressure of E-commerce enterprises and reducing the costs of logistics.

As an emerging industry, E-commerce is becoming a non-core program of the capital and has a great potential for promoting the upgrading of conventional industries and the restructuring of industries as well as improving the quality of the residents' services industry. We will improve the developmental environment of E-commerce, so as to create sound conditions for domestic and overseas E-commerce enterprises. Finally, I wish the conference complete success and I hope that all of you will work and have a wonderful stay in Beijing.

# Speech by Lv Jijian, Deputy Director General of the Department of Trade in Services and Commercial Services of the Ministry of Commerce, at the Language Service and Globalization Forum

Distinguished Director Wang, Director Guo, Director Long, all guests, ladies and gentlemen,

Good morning! I am delighted to see you attending the Language Service and Globalization Forum during CIFTIS, and I would like to extend my warmest welcome to all guests present on behalf of the Department of Trade in Services and Commercial Services of the Ministry of Commerce.

Nowadays, the world is witnessing a deeper development of economic globalization, extensive exchanges in science and technology culture and constant breakthroughs in information technology, which promote the fast development of the language service industry and make the language service industry present an informatization and industrialization trend. In the scenario of globalization, developing the language service industry is the inevitable way for China, as the largest developing country in the world, to achieve the rise to a great power. It is conducive to: speeding up the transformation of the economic development mode, and realizing a more eco-friendly and sustainable economic growth characterized by job creation; strengthening the national capacity for cultural transmission and information usage, and dramatically improving its national soft power; increasing the facilitation level of trade and investment, as well as the level of the open economy. The Chinese language service industry started at the preliminary stage of reform and opening-up, developed after the establishment of a market economy and expanded after joining the WTO. Now, it has entered the preliminary industrialization stage, and is characterized by scale expansion; it has accelerated the process of marketization and the pace of "going out", and enhanced its technology innovation capacity. In the meanwhile, the Chinese language service industry has also suffered from weak international competitiveness, irregular market competition, and unsatisfactory industrial policies, which have a negative strain on its sustainable development. The Ministry of Commerce is willing to cooperate with relevant departments to support the Translators Association of China so that they can guide language service enterprises to grasp the

ORT ON MAJOR VIEWS AT THE 3RD CHINA BEIJING INTERNATIONAL FAIR FOR TRADE IN SERVICES

opportunity and expand both their foreign and domestic markets, thus jointly promoting the sound and fast development of the Chinese language service industry and trade in services.

First of all, the industrial development status of the language service industry has increased. We will further oblige relevant departments to define the status of the language service industry in national economic sectors, lay down political measures that facilitate the development of the language service industry, support the language service industry development planning formulated by the industrial association, and further improve the statistical system of the language service industry.

Second, the language service enterprises are supported in order to improve their international competitiveness. We will utilize special funds in service outsourcing and in the cultural industry to provide financial support for the exportation of translation services and the significant technological innovation project in language services, so as to promote the incorporation of the translation service into governmental procurement projects and further normalize the procurement process and quality control.

Last but not least, language service enterprises are encouraged to strengthen international exchanges and cooperation. We will support the industrial association to actively participate in the formulation of international industry standards and specifications, and support the construction of a "commercial operation-based" language service public platform to expand the depth and width of international cooperation.

Ladies and gentlemen, the Translators Association of China held the Bridge High-level Forum of the Language Service Industry Trade Globalization at the 2nd CIFTIS. This is the first time for the language service to be involved in the trade in services synthesis exhibition, which not only makes a good start for improving the specialized level of language services, but it also opens a window on the world for the Chinese language service development. I believe that this year's Language Service and Globalization Forum will bring more opportunities and benefits to all of you.

May the forum be a complete success, thank you!

III Summary of Speeches at the Summit High-level Forum

# Speech by Long Guoqiang, Party Member of the Development Research Center of the State Council, Director of the General Office and Well-known Economist, at the Language Service and Globalization Forum

Distinguished Director Wang, Director Lv, Chairman Guo, Chairman Huang, ladies and gentlemen,

I am very honored to attend the service and globalization forum. Language service is an emerging industry and a new service industry First of all, I am not familiar with it, but now I realize that it is an important force in globalization.

Today, the topic of my speech is "opportunities and challenges in cross-border bilateral investment". In fact, language service is a background. As we all know, globalization creates important opportunities for global direct investment. Since the 1990s, global cross-border investment has been developing rapidly. Before the outbreak of the financial crisis, global cross-border investment reached 2 trillion USD. However, every great financial crisis has a negative impact on global cross-border investment. In 2011, the bursting of bubbles of American IT led to a rapid decline in global cross-border investment. However, two or three years later, it had a rapid rebound and rose to its highest in 2007.

In 2008, the subprime crisis occurred in the USA and evolved into the European sovereign debt crisis, which affected global direct investment again. Cross-border investment continued to decline for two consecutive years, and in the past three years, it has enjoyed a modest rebound. With the recovery of the global economy, cross-border investments are advancing in twists and turns and have now reached about 1.3 trillion USD.

In the process, we can see a prominent phenomenon, that is, China is suddenly rising as an emerging great power in foreign investment. In 2003, China's foreign investment was only 2.85 billion USD, but it was up to 90.1 billion USD last year, meaning that Chinese foreign investments had increased by 30 times in ten years. Therefore, China is one of the most important foreign investment countries in the world.

Before that, China was a developing country that absorbed the largest foreign direct investment. On a global scale, China has ranked among the top five, only second to the USA in the absorption of foreign direct investment, in the past couple of years. Today, China is a great power in the utilization of foreign investments, as well as an emerging great power in foreign investments. Hence, China is playing an increasingly important role in global cross-border investment.

Just like China, the global direct investment pattern is also undergoing a new change. The developing countries, as a whole, are becoming more and more important in global direct investment. In 2012, the developing countries exceeded the developed economies in foreign direct investment for the first time in history, which was also a historical change.

In such a scenario, let us consider the new opportunities and challenges faced by global cross-border investments. It can be said that the opportunities go hand in hand with the challenges. There are a great many opportunities, as there are challenges.

First of all, the recovery of the developed economies and the industrialization of the emerging economies have given a powerful impetus to global cross-border direct investments. As I have just mentioned, every financial crisis exerts a negative impact on global direct investments. Recently, with the recovery of the economy, the advanced economies, such as the American economy, have shown a marked improvement, and the European financial situation tends to be stable. As a result, the recovery of the advanced economies is providing a new impetus to cross-border investments in the current year. In the meanwhile, in the course of the promotion of industrization and urbanization, the emerging countries and economies are in urgent need of cross-border investments, which creates a great many opportunities to help the emerging economies absorb global direct investments.

Second, the liberalization of trade investment creates new opportunities for cross-border investments. Trade and investment depend on two factors. The first factor is the progress of technology, such as the progress of communication technology or shipping technology. The process of technology is conducive to the development of trade, which will surely lead to the optimization of the division of labor, accompanied by global cross-border direct investments.

The other factor is institutions. In many cases, institutions are always an obstacle. Therefore, the liberalization of trade investment is actually a process of continuously removing obstacles that hinder global trade and investment.

Before the founding of the WTO, the main platform for the liberalization of trade investments was that of the multilateral organizations. The first step was trade liberalization, and then tariff reduction, non-tariff barrier elimination, and then the formulation of an investment agreement related to trade. Over the past decades, a critical phenomenon has appeared, that is, regional cooperation and Free Trade Agreements (FTAs). Hundreds of new FTAs have appeared, and a great number of new agreements have been concluded among different countries in trade liberalization and investment liberalization through consultation.

Besides, an increasing number of countries are negotiating bilateral investment treaties, which involves both the opening-up and the protection of foreign investments. Apart from investment treaties, countries are negotiating agreements for the avoidance of double taxation. For a transnational company, the lack of such an agreement means taxation in both the host country and the home country, which is not conducive to cross-border investments.

Over the previous decades, the number of bilateral investment treaties (BITs) in bilateral investment agreements and the agreements for the avoidance of double taxation increased rapidly. Currently, China and the USA are negotiating a bilateral investment treaty (BIT). Until now, China has negotiated 128 BITs, so why we should we specifically talk about the negotiation between China and the USA concerning their bilateral investment treaty? It is because that Sino-US investment treaty contains a crucial part which involves the Chinese system for the management of foreign investments. That treaty requires China to establish a system for managing its "national treatment of the right of admission and its negative list" concerning foreign direct investments, which is fundamentally different from its previous system for managing foreign capital. In order to adapt to the new progress in bilateral investments, about 70 countries are adopting a system for managing their "national treatment of the right of admission and their negative lists". Therefore, the management mode of "national treatment concerning the right of admission and the negative list" has been applied in the Shanghai Pilot Free Trade Zone, established last year, in preparation for the further promotion of investment liberalization.

With the progress in Sino-US investment treaty negotiations, we may also negotiate with central Europe regarding the Sino-US investment treaty, which will have a profound impact on the Chinese system of managing foreign investments.

In the meanwhile, the international community is exploring a multilateral investment treaty in order to reach an agreement. The change of these systems will strongly promote global cross-border direct investments.

Third, there has been a great change in foreign investment policies in most countries over the previous decades, from vigilance and limitation to approbation. Each year, every country in the world amends its laws and regulations relevant to foreign direct investments. About 80% of the amended laws and regulations aim at making foreign investment policies more open to foreign direct investors, and only a few enhance limitations on and management of foreign investments in some fields. Therefore, on the whole, many countries are adjusting their policies, especially since the outbreak of financial risk; many countries have a strong need of foreign investments in order to get out of trouble. The favorable foreign investment policies create new opportunities for global investors.

Fourth, the new technological revolution is dynamic. Since the outbreak of the financial crisis, what we have been discussing is how the developed countries can manage to get out of this crisis. On the one hand, the developed countries need to give financial support to financial institutions and stabilize the financial market through financial policies. On the other hand, a new technological revolution is required in order to help countries overcome the economic crisis, which is more important. In such a case, we will see industry and governments work together to promote a new technological revolution. Sometimes, this is called the "third industrial revolution", which may not be the right term, but it does reflect the fact that we are in an active period of research and development of new technologies.

Such an active period has brought about a great number of cross-border investment opportunities; for example, the developing countries hope to go to the developed countries to acquire technology, while enterprises from the developed countries may need to go to the emerging market to seek better opportunities to develop their markets. Therefore, the reform of technology and the adjustment of industries will impel a re-layout of global industries, which will actually be driven by cross-border investments.

Apart from the aforesaid four important opportunities, China is also facing some special favorable strategic opportunities.

The first favorable opportunity is low-cost overseas acquisitions since the outbreak of the financial crisis. Chinese enterprises are in a period of rapid internationalization, during which a great many Chinese enterprises have started to set foot on the international market. They want to get the opportunity to enter the international market through exportation. Now, with the requirement of industrial upgrading, enterprises pay more attention to technological innovation, brands and to the channel of international marketing, and some enterprises even hope to acquire natural resources and energy from overseas through investments. The outbreak of the financial crisis, especially the impact of the financial crisis on major advanced economies, has resulted in a dramatic decline in the market value of a great many enterprises. Due to the tight fund chain, enterprises are willing to look for new investors. Therefore, a strategic opportunity is created for the foreign investment of Chinese enterprises to acquire technology, brands and international marketing channels through investments.

The second opportunity is China's vast foreign exchange reserve, which lays a solid foundation for Chinese enterprises to make foreign investments. For a long time in the past, Chinese policies on foreign investments were limitation-oriented, which caused a shortage of foreign exchange, and further led to a change in the whole macro policy and foreign investment policy. Now, the Chinese government is considering how to make full use of the huge foreign exchange reserve, that amounts to 4 trillion USD, and preserve or increase its value. The Chinese government is putting forward the strategy of "going out" in order to drive Chinese enterprises to utilize the valuable foreign exchange resources better through foreign investments, which will further promote the corresponding adjustment of foreign investment policies.

The Third Plenary Session document and the Shanghai Pilot Free Trade Zone test have specially proposed to promote reforms of the Chinese foreign investment system, relax the control and enhance the services, revealing that the government can promote and help enterprises to better realize foreign investments.

There is another vital opportunity, that is, the change in the Chinese comparative advantage. In the past three decades, China has participated in international competition by relying on a low-cost labor force. Today, with the development of the economy, the level of per capita income has increased. At the beginning of the reform and the opening-up, per capita GDP was only 148 USD, but now it has reached over 6,700 USD. As a result, many traditional, low value-added and labor-intensive industries have gradually lost international competitiveness, so much so that many enterprises need to seek new low-cost production bases, which happens in most countries in the world. The conversion of the comparative advantage will promote industrial transfer. Some Chinese enterprises have started to transfer traditional industrial activities to low-cost countries such as, South Asia and Africa, which, in fact, also contributes to foreign investments.

Finally, the upgrading of the Chinese opening-up strategies also brings a series of opportunities. Xi Jinping, General Secretary, is putting forward the Silk Road Economic Zone and the 21st Century Maritime Silk Road, which is known as the strategic economic conception of "The Belt and Road". China is negotiating with many countries concerning the FTA, such as the Sino-U.S. BIT and the Sino-African cooperation, as mentioned before. The further adjustment and improvement of such regional cooperation strategies also encourages the Chinese enterprises to go out.

For China, apart from a great many new strategies concerning "going out", there are also many strategies for further absorption of foreign investment. On many occasions and stages in the past, we had often heard of propaganda jeopardizing China. Since the outbreak of the financial crisis, many people have said that the transnational countries would go back to America. The Obama administration is implementing the reindustrialization strategy which actually refers to the revitalization of the manufacturing industry rather than re-manufacturing or backflow of the manufacturing industry as hyped by media.

On the contrary, Chinese foreign direct investments enjoyed a steady growth while global cross-border investments dramatically declined due to the financial crisis. In the eyes of most people, Chinese foreign direct investments seem to have dropped compared with the notable surge in the couple of years since joining the WTO. However, on a global scale, Chinese foreign direct investments show a steady growth trend while global cross-border investments have declined.

Why is the case? According to a survey on hundreds of transnational companies conducted after the outbreak of the financial crisis through a list of questions such as how China is seen, how the Chinese investment environment is seen and what adjustment will be made on the Chinese investment strategy, we find that the status of China is becoming more important in future strategies of transnational companies. It is due to the fact that, since the outbreak of the financial crisis, the Chinese economy has come out smelling like a rose and is promising, making China's market more attractive.

We can see that China, as the world's second largest economy and importing country, owns the world's second largest market. In the meanwhile, it has the advantage of low costs as a developing country. Across the world, the country that has a large domestic market tends to be a high-income country without low costs, and a low-cost country and a developing country do not have a large domestic market in spite of a large population, just like India or China in the past. China has a potentially large market, which will be expanding continuously with the development of its economy. China owns both a large domestic market and a low-cost advantage, which is unique in the world. Such a unique advantage makes transnational companies optimistic about Chinese prospects, so that they are speeding up the transfer of their advanced manufacturing industries and high-end service industries, including some important research & development activities, to China.

For example, IBM employs five or six thousand R&D engineers in China, and Novartis, a Swiss pharmaceutical enterprise, once made an investment of 1 billion USD in the Shanghai Research and Development Center to act as a research and development center. Therefore, the integrated advantage of a vast market and low costs creates a significant opportunity to worldwide investors. That is why Chinese investments have steadily increased while global cross-border investments have dropped.

Another important issue is the adjustment of the Chinese economic structure. The Chinese government has been emphasizing the fact that we need to change the development mode and speed up the adjustment of our industrial structure to create more new development opportunities, which is an important issue to assimilate foreign investors. The reason why investors come to China is that they want to not only occupy the Chinese market, but also leverage the strength brought by over 7 million college graduates each year, which was unheard-of before. More than a decade ago, the annual college enrollment was 1.08 million but now it reaches more than 7 million. Therefore, the upgrading of the industrial structure, as well as the upgrading of the demand structure brought by the increase in income, will urge worldwide investors to speed up their industrial transfer to China.

What needs to be specially stressed is the new round of deepening the all-round reforms

Part III  Summary of Speeches at the Summit High-level Forum

and expanding the opening-up decided by the Third Plenary Session of the 18th Central Committee of the CPC, so as to provide foreign investors with new opportunities. In the new round of the opening-up, the opening-up of the service industry is the focus. The State Council decided to open 18 sectors in 6 fields in the Shanghai Pilot Free Trade Zone and carry out the management mode of the negative list, and it also planned to further shorten the negative list in the future. Hence, deepening all-round reforms and expanding the opening-up means that China is promoting trade liberalization, trade facilitation, investment liberalization and investment facilitation in essence, which will create new opportunities for foreign investors.

Of course, opportunities are always accompanied by challenges. Worldwide investments are facing challenges, the same is true for Chinese foreign investments.

The first challenge is the geopolitical risks. On the whole, the global pattern is steady, and peace and development are the main trend in the world today. However, local confrontations constantly occur without any sign, which leads to many risks for enterprises. Let me take the example of Ukraine. Two years ago, I went to Ukraine to carry out a survey. Many enterprises are interested in Ukraine because Ukraine is abundant in natural resources, in black soil, and has a strong attraction for agricultural investment, science and technological capability. However, over the past few months, political unrest has broken out in Ukraine, which will surely affect the international investors. Another example is the riot that occurred in Vietnam a few weeks ago; it was not only against China but also against many foreign investors, which surely creates many risks.

Chinese enterprises have been rapidly developing in the last ten years. As many enterprises have no experience in overseas investments, they are unconsciously setting foot in risky countries and regions. Therefore, it is really a great challenge for Chinese enterprises to prevent geopolitical risks such as political unrest and nationalization.

The second challenge is that the turbulence of bilateral relations also affects bilateral investments. For instance, the Japanese government has achieved the nationalization of the Diaoyu Islands without the permission of the Chinese government, which exerts a huge impact on the relationship between China and Japan. Political relations will directly affect bilateral investment relations and trade relations. As a consequence, either the Japanese investments in China or the Chinese investments in Japan will be greatly affected.

The third challenge is that enterprises, especially Chinese enterprises, have an insufficient capacity for foreign investments. Although thousands of enterprises conduct foreign investment activities, leading to a huge flow of investments, the experience in and the capacity for foreign investments by Chinese enterprises are still inadequate. New capacities are required in both cross-border investments and global operations, such as the risk-coping capacity and the ability to cope relationships with the host country. The most important capacity is communication competence, which involves the language service. We have been emphasizing the need for interdisciplinary talents who not only can speak the language of the host country, but they also know how to carry out global operations. In fact, however, cultivating and developing such talents are anything but easy. The increasing cross-border investments lead to a strong demand on the language service industry. Specialized language services help all cross-border investment enterprises, including Chinese foreign investment enterprises, to interact better with the host country and trade partners regarding language, to better understand and respect each other in regards to culture, thus allowing Chinese enterprises to go out and the host country to achieve mutual benefits and win-win results. Therefore, the language service industry is indispensable for Chinese enterprises to go out to enhance their capacity for foreign investments and globalization.

I believe the discussion about the language service industry and globalization during the forum is of great significance. I hope the friends in the industry can provide assistance to Chinese enterprises in making foreign investments go on more smoothly and in addition, help them take advantage of the new opportunities offered to foreign investments by Chinese enterprises in order to promote the development of the Chinese language service industry.

That is all, thank you!

# Speech by Guo Xiaoyong, First Vice President of the Translators Association of China, at the Language Service and Globalization Forum

Distinguished Vice Director Lv Jijian, Director Long Guoqiang, Mr. Hans, Mr. Andrew, all guests and friends,

Good morning! Welcome to Beijing to attend the 3rd CIFTIS Language Service and Globalization Forum. I would like to take this opportunity to extend my sincere gratitude to the Department of Trade in Services and Commercial Services of the Ministry of Commerce and the CIFTIS organizing committee on behalf of the Translators Association of China. It is their energetic support that makes us open a distinctive language service platform on the grand stage of the CIFTIS.

We are not boasting. Language service is a special module in CIFTIS. People are familiar with the translation service. However, when it comes to the concept of language service, most people may not fully understand it. It is not strange, because the concept of language service was first proposed in the world ten years ago and officially proposed in China four years ago, when the first session of the China International Language Service Industry Conference was held by the Translators Association of China in 2010.

Why do we propose the concept of language service? First of all, the rapid development of informatization and globalization endows translation & interpreting with new connotations and denotations. Today, the language service is far more than a simple interpretation and translation. It has expanded and formed an initial industry chain including translation & interpreting services, localization services, language asset management (such as language technique and tool R&D terminology), globalization and localization consulting services and new services (such as the education and training service). The CIFTIS provides the emerging industry of language service with the first unique domestic centralized displaying platform.

Furthermore, language service is an indispensable and important service within the CIFTIS. Language service not only produces enormous values in itself, but it also drives the development of all the service industries, so that it is an important economic force in trade globalization. The introduction of language services into the CIFTIS provides a vital and convenient service and platform to institutions and enterprises that need language services; this is a significant measure to promote the connection of supply and demand. Besides, it is conducive to improving the international level of the CIFTIS.

Last but not least, the module of language services, enjoys a high level of internationalization, which is manifested in the organizational structure of the forum. The forum is hosted by the Translators Association of China in cooperation with world-famous industrial associations and globalization and localization associations of business consulting institutions, etc. Leaders from over ten transnational enterprises in the USA, Germany, Italy, Norway and Japan have come from afar to attend the forum to create exchanges and to communicate, which fully demonstrates that the CIFTIS drives the development of international trade in services. Here, I want to take this opportunity to express my heartfelt thanks to three cooperative partners on behalf of the CIFTIS for their active cooperation and support in terms of the publicity of CIFTIS and the planning of the forum.

The CIFTIS has been held just three times. The language service and the exhibition activities are just a prologue. We are willing to work with the CIFTIS organizing committee to grow together in order to be able to continue to establish a high-end international professional bridge for the supply and demand of language services , thus making language services play its supporting role in trade globalization better.

May the forum be a complete success. The Translators Association of China, as one of the organizers of the 3rd CIFTIS, hopes that the CIFTIS will be able to achieve great accomplishments. Thank you!

# Speech by Dong Baoqing, Deputy Director General of the Department of the Promotion of Informatization of the Ministry of Industry and Information Technology, at the 2014 Internet Financial Risk Control and Regulation Trend Conference

I'm glad to attend this conference. I would like to extend my warm congratulations to the conference and to the Zhongguancun Internet Finance Institute for its inauguration and founding. The process and pace of the integration and innovation of informatization and finance have been accelerated. It is widely recognized that the year 2013 was the first year of Internet finance, indicating that our informatization is continuously driving and leading the innovation of finance. We can say that Internet finance has been good experimentation and realization.

The year 2013 was the first year of Internet finance due to four reasons. ① Finance is open and is continuously being marketized, from the marketization of loan rates to quasi-marketization of deposit rates, the foreign exchange rate fluctuates, private enterprises and foreign-funded enterprises have entered the financial industry. ② The rapid development of information technology and its popularization have laid a good social foundation. ③ The essence of the financial industry is united at a philosophical level with that of the information industry, because they are both dealing with symbols, which can be called symbolic finance. Naturally, there is feasibility in the integration and innovation of both of them. ④ It is a result of the joint efforts of Internet entrepreneurs, the Internet industry and financiers, especially Internet entrepreneurs. The promotion of the application of the Internet to finance has a history of more than 10 years. It seems that an important push in the first year of Internet finance last year was mainly by the Internet industry, so some Internet entrepreneurs say that, "our understanding of finance far surpasses the financial understanding of the Internet."

In my opinion, informatization, especially information technology represented by the Internet, does not change the essence of finance, but it changes the business model and the type of finance as well as idea of the thinking behind it, the methods, processes and other aspects involved in it as well. The essence of finance is still to serve the real economy and create value, to better play the capital role of currency and financial funding and to create new value. Risk control is the key to finance. With the priority of safety production, there would be no sound development of finance without good risk control. Informatization plays a very important driving and leading role in all walks of life. Particularly, the innovation of finance has started or is undergoing at least the following three stages.

Stage 1 is a broad application of information technology in finance, i.e. a stage of driving financial electronization. This stage mainly opens up the processing capacity and generates the innovation of finance. We are now in a stage of informatization or a stage of integrated development of informatization and Internet finance. Cross-industry fusion and cross-industry marketing occur: E-commerce enterprises are engaged in finance, and financial enterprises are engaged in E-commerce, with the online sales of capital, insurance, and financial products. Cross-industry fusion is being carried out. In Stage 2, financing continuously extends and expands to network space, and even forms a situation of moving the entire network forward with entire-network channels and entire-network marketing. For example, YuEBao is an important representative product at this stage. Stage 3 is the most important stage, a stage of leading financial innovation by informatization. With informatization, P2P, crowdfunding and online financing are all prospective directions for future development, but such experimentation is immature in the business model and is under experimentation and development. Online supply chain finance is also starting. Online supply chain finance is more realistic than P2P and crowdfunding as a form of finance, because it is an important carrier to closely combine the real economy of financial industrial services under the conditions of informatization.

There are so many appearance and exploration. We should see through the appearance to perceive the essence, to master some essential laws in driving industrial innovation by informatization. The most important change is that the background for and the space of our thinking in the development of various industries were only the realistic world and realistic space in the past, but our current economic activities have expanded from physical space to network space, or the integration of network space and physical space. With people's wisdom and brain space, some watchwords like "wisdom × × ×" have been formed. I think this constitutes a very important background for development. For instance, we used to think only with our left cerebral hemisphere, but now we have to use the right one at the same time. In other words, we should think about problems using both levels of the brain. From a philosophical perspective, we should see the essence of change behind the appearance. Integration and coordination of business space are very important analytical methods. We will carry out topic discussions on finance, financial innovation and Internet finance regulation at this point.

An important principle is that we must carry out financial innovation and strengthen regulations at the same time. Regulation is a must. Globally, financial innovation is always like dancing with shackles, so we should organically unify innovation and the strengthening of regulations. Carry out innovative development with cautious and subtle attitudes, and deal with the consistence of physical space and network space regulation. Any business is essentially consistent in physical space and network space without substantial changes, so I do not agree that informatization and the Internet overturn finance. They are consistent in essence, but we must consider the inconsistency in the method of technical processing. Corresponding regulation policies should essentially be consistent with the matching of different technical characteristics.

We should give full consideration to the functional orientation of competition in finance and cross-industry finance and the statistical problems, so that the role of informatization in the integration of the Internet industry and finance can be better driven. Of course, the most important thing is to adopt a method and way of thinking for informatization in order to complete the regulations regarding cross-industry finance. Within the scenario of Internet of Everything, people's ability to master and process information has improved to a certain degree. Information asymmetry is a source of risks, so the ability to process information eliminates information asymmetry to a great extent; this allows for better control and a reduction of risks. I really feel that informatization has brought unprecedented opportunities and a bright prospect to the innovation of finance. This is the end of my speech. I wish the conference a complete success. Thank you!

# Speech by Li Zhigang, Deputy Director of the Beijing Municipal Bureau of Financial Work, at the 2014 Internet Financial Risk Control and Regulation Trend Conference

Everyone has different thoughts as to how to understand the Internet and finance, and so does everyone here. Experts, scholars and practitioners have different views regarding finance, Internet finance and financial Internet. In my opinion, Internet finance is only a supplement to traditional finance, and although it impacts traditional finance, it cannot replace it or overturn it. We may have different understandings of the essence of finance from different angles and at different levels, but I think finance involves, first of all, operating and controlling risks, and the second essence is that finance must have integrity. We have talked about a series of problems, including the necessity for us to overturn traditional finance with Internet thinking. What is Internet thinking? Is the Internet a platform, a tool or a thinking model? The answer is unclear. So, I agree that financial management departments, including the People's Bank of China, should assume a cautious and responsible attitude towards Internet finance.

The basic reason why fast-changing products during the development of Internet finance are popular with people is that our modern financial system has not fully met people's needs nor those of the real economy, and the existing financial system has a low coverage. Internet finance makes up the deficiency of traditional finance to a certain extent, so that our traditional financial institutions find that the market does not belong to one enterprise anymore, and the potential customer base is huge. However, in return, Internet finance enterprises use people's saving deposits as financial institutions' deposits to negotiate prices with financial institutions, and to gain a margin of interest between the rate of the interbank market of financial institutions and people's current saving deposit rate. Whether the funds are really invested in the real economy and whether they are important directions for China's support are worth thinking about.

The Party Central Committee and financial management departments of the State Council pay great attention to the development of finance and to the risks of finance, and affirm that finance should support society, but our "babies" do not really exploit the advantages of their products for financial development, so there is a rumor that "the mother (the People's Bank of China) is angry". Why is that? We hope that the real economy can be really implemented

Part III  Summary of Speeches at the Summit High-level Forum

when an industry develops, and we do not hope to distort the fictitious economy or cause it to go out of regulation, causing the risks to affect the financial system and increase the unstable factors of finance.

Based on this, I'm not sure what Internet thinking is. Undoubtedly, the Internet is a very effective platform for financial institutions to promote and develop business, and also a tool that brings convenience to our life. Financial institutions can carry out business on the Internet and Internet enterprises can also carry out financial business using the Internet platform. I think we should clearly realize that finance is a licensed industry and not everyone can be engaged in finance. I'm glad to attend the conference because the People's Government of Haidian District, the Haidian District Financial Service Committee and the Beijing Haidian District Commission of Commerce, including the Haidian District Financial Research Institute to be established, have paid great attention to the potential damages caused by financial Internet risks. When supporting the development of the Internet finance industry, we hope it will operate positively, truly serve the real economy and make a beneficial supplement to traditional finance; and we also hope it will not be damaged during the development of the Internet financial system, or that consumers and people are damaged. We hope that Internet finance will not have any negative effects on the safety and the stability of the entire financial field in case of risks.

The market supports Internet development with a cautious attitude, and supports Internet enterprises in carrying out finance using the Internet platform within the regulation framework of financial laws and regulations, really applying our financial service to the real economy, with no fictitious economy and financial disintermediation.

I hope you will criticize and correct me in case you find my ideas wrong. Thank you!

Today's theme is "Internet Financial Risk Control and Regulation Trend". I would like to talk about two views: Internet financial risks and regulation on Internet financial risks.

At the beginning of 2013, the Internet was just beautiful scenery, but after it had developed for more than one year, Internet finance influenced our traditional finance to a certain extent, attracting the general attention of financial regulatory departments, social media and some social public investors; moreover, it is becoming a hot topic. In the past year, Internet finance developed rapidly, on a surprising scale. In my opinion, there are two aspects of the rapid development of Internet finance. One is of course a positive aspect. Internet finance is an important tool that benefits finance, solving difficulties in financing for small and medium-sized enterprises to a great extent. The other is that Internet financial risks are increasingly obvious. Due to the essence of Internet finance, from its current operation model, some non-financial enterprises or enterprises without financial qualifications can enter the financial field by virtue of Internet tools, which is a financial transaction and a financial service with no restrictions or standards.

During this process, risks are mainly reflected in three aspects.

Risk 1. If the scale is expanded to a certain extent, it will squeeze traditional finance, affecting the capital flow of the entire society. Of course, if Internet finance rapidly develops on a standardized basis and the industry is steady with experience accumulated as a whole, it may indeed reasonably squeeze traditional finance after 10 or 20 years, and promote the self-reform and structural adjustment of traditional finance. These are all reasonable preconditions. But now the problem is that China's Internet finance appears to have an explosive growth over a short time span, and this brings about rapid expansion with no standards or restrictions; and the regular financial system is impacted, which I think should be worthy of attention. Besides, Internet finance does not compete with existing financial institutions on a fair competition platform, because it is not regulated by financial institutions, which is unfair to a certain extent. So, the first risk is that Internet finance rapidly expands with no standards, and this will cause systematic risks after reaching a certain scale of expansion.

Risk 2. Due to short operation and less experience in operation, existing Internet finance has a weak ability to control risks. A considerable number of enterprises have bad management due to weak abilities to control risks. More seriously, enterprises with pyramid sales or illegal financing enter this field by virtue of Internet finance, and their purpose is not legal operation; and they will develop into financial enterprises with centennial development, but money encirclement as well, which greatly infringes consumers' interests.

Risk 3. Since current Internet finance has no regulation or standards, most operating activities are not transparent, nor are there operation models, operation data and fund flow, so social supervision is lost, making the social public unable to screen business. This is also a big risk.

This is my first view. The development of Internet finance has a positive function and also potential risks, so it is time to standardize the market and construct a regulation framework. The second view is the future trend of the regulation of Internet finance. Regulation of Internet finance is immature all over the world, and there is no successful model. The USA regulates P2P as a fund and incorporates it into the Securities and Exchange Commission. This regulation model controls financial risks to a certain extent but it also greatly restrains industrial development. This method causes the failure of a large number of enterprises, so the USA's regulation method may not be a reasonable and effective model. China is exploring an Internet regulation model which needs the joint participation of the entire society.

From my personal perspective, the regulation of the risks involved in Internet finance should have several basic principles:

Principle 1. We should tell the category of the risks involved in Internet finance. Current Internet finance has many models. Risk regulation is different for the characteristics of the different models and risks, so a unified regulation standard and regulation model cannot be established for Internet finance, and this is not realistic. We should introduce regulation methods and policies according to the different models, especially the industry with the most prominent risk currently, e.g. P2P.

Principle 2. Regulations regarding Internet finance should be a product of combining self-disciplining regulations with other-disciplining regulations. Since Internet finance is extremely different from traditional finance in terms of its technological base, its operational mode, and its operational concept, we cannot mechanically apply the model of regulation of traditional financial institutions. I advocate strengthening a self-disciplining kind of regulation on Internet finance in the early stages, but few "black sheep" cannot be restricted without other-disciplining regulations, which is also not conducive to the survival and development of good enterprises which hope to become powerful for a long period of time.

Principle 3. Internet finance originates in Europe and America, but Internet finance has developed steadily in Europe and America so far, with no explosive growth as there has been in China. A major reason is that the financial service industry in Europe and America is quite well-developed, the financial market is mature, there is much less financial regulation than in China's financial field, so there are few voids in financial services; moreover, financial service is good. China's Internet finance has lots of voids in its financial service, so there are lots of operational platforms and opportunities for our Internet finance. If we just block Internet finance but do not dredge the existing regular financial system, shadow banking problems, including Internet finance, will not be solved. Therefore, on the one hand, we should standardize Internet finance; on the other hand, we should strengthen the reform of the traditional financial field so as to eliminate unnecessary administrative regulations, which would thus enable our financial institutions to provide better financial services for consumers and enterprises in a freer market environment.

The focus of regulation on Internet finance is as follows: ① Establish behavioral standards. It is not to set a rigid access threshold, but to establish and improve industrial standards of Internet financial enterprises. ② Risk management method, i.e. how to control risks for Internet financial enterprises. ③ Investment regulation. Many P2P companies only guarantee a yield rate of 12% to consumers but do not mention any risks. This indicates that they do not consider the ability of consumers to perceive risks, which will greatly damage vulnerable groups who are not familiar with financial knowledge and have no anti-risk capability, and this also makes the entire society unstable. So, consumer protection should be guaranteed. ④ Statistics of Internet financial business and information transparency. This should be specified by a regulatory framework. It is worth discussing whether it is necessary or not for financial regulatory departments to regulate the regulatory framework. We can also refer to regulation models of small loan companies: on the one hand, establish a macro top-level designed financial regulatory framework; on the other hand, the local government regulates Internet finance to a certain extent. Of course, my views may be immature, so they are only for reference. Thank you!

# Speech by Gu Wenzhong, Standing Deputy Secretary General of China Association of Trade in Services at the Investment and Financing Forum of Trade in Services and Modern Service Industry

Distinguished leaders and guests,

Good morning! Welcome to attending the investment and financing forum of CIFTIS, and far-sighted personages from corporate, academic and political circles to discuss on how to be capable of continuous evolvement in the rapidly changing business competition. The so-called evolution is the fundamental cause for the existence of any species; the requirements on the evolution by business are more urgent. As the saying goes, sail against current, fall behind. In my opinion, the flatter and regenerated business competition like sailing against current, and business will end if not evolved. We hold the opinion that evolution is the industrial advantage obtained from enterprises on a long-term basis and also the reformation and innovation capability in the Internet era in global competition. Undoubtedly, if only you obtain more than others and change quicker than others, you can find the way to innovate and keep a sustainable competitive strength.

This forum is divided into 3 parts: how to run enterprise in the Internet era, edge and security of financial innovation, and ten years' strategic transformation of transnational companies in China. All the guests can share their opinions as they will, discuss their practice and reflection in the respective field and bring brainstorms to us, and we will have wisdom in challenging more severe competitions. May the forum be a complete success.

# Speech by Huang Hai, Director of Domestic Trade Expert Commission of Ministry of Commerce, Former Assistant Minister of Ministry of Commerce at the Investment and Financing Forum of Trade in Services and Modern Service Industry

Distinguished guests and friends,

Good morning! I ever took the First Vice President of China Association of Trade in Services for a long time. For the State Council approved a pawn trade association, I will be the president. The pawn trade is a part of investment and financing, and I am so pleased to share with you.

For the development of trade in services and service industry is a new stage of modern social development, in a global view, service orientation of the industrial structure, industrial activities and industrial organizations is the trend, and the service industry has become a key engine for the economic growth regardless of the developed countries or emerging countries and the most important core competitiveness. Concerning China, with the optimization of economic structure in the past few years, the service industry has developed rapidly. In 2013, the proportion of value added of service industry in China reached 46.1%, exceeding the manufacturing industry for the first time. The service industry has become the one with the most contribution of the three major industries in China, and the increasing is a milestone. Besides, the total import-export volume of service industry in China almost reached 540 billion USD, increasing by 14.7% compared with the last year, and the growth rate has been much higher than that of goods trade. All of you know that the growth rate of goods trade in the last year was more than 10%, which is large.

In the first quarter of this year, the service industry has continued to play the role of engine and stabilizer for the economic development. The value added and growth rate of the service industry are still higher than those of the secondary industry, and the proportion of the service industry in GDP accounts for 49% the service industry solves the issue of employment to a large extent. On a long-term basis, we hold the opinion that the employment will be a problem if the growth rate of GDP is less than 8%. In fact, the growth rate is less than 8%, but the employment goes well and the newly added employment is still increasing, which is greatly due to the service industry. Besides, the use of foreign capital by the service industry is still increasing rapidly, with a growth rate up to 20.6%. The service industry has become one of the fields with the fastest growth in utilizing the foreign investment. Investments on real estate include the service industry. More analyses will be made after the removal of the real estate industry. Since this year, the total import-export volume of the service industry has reached 138.8 billion USD, and the growth rate is more than 10% than that of goods trade. The proportion of trade in services to foreign trade is increasing, accounting for 12.8%.

Although we have made progress in the service industry and trade in services, we have a long way to go compared with the developed countries. First, the total volume of trade in services, including the modern service industry, is not enough, and the proportion in GDP this year is only 49%, far from that of the developed countries, as high as 70%–80%. Besides, our structure of service industry is laggard; of the traditional service industry, the labor-intensive service industry still accounts for a significant proportion. Although the emerging industry is developing rapidly, the proportion is still low. Meanwhile, there are many problems in the management of the service industry, including trade in services, which should be improved. In addition, the opening of the service industry is not enough, and market orientation is not enough. The theme of the conference falls in the field of investment and financing. At present, there are many restricting factors for the development of the service industry.

So I suppose that the Third Plenary Session of the 18th Central Committee of CPC will make the decision on all-round deepening and reform. I think that we will face a significant reform in investment and financing, in particular the investment and financing system and the management system of the service industry, business mode, products of investment and financing of the service industry. I think that it cannot meet the actual development requirements. May the forum be a success. Wish the Chinese service industry and trade in services contribute more to the development of China and the world. Thank you!

# Speech by Gu Shengzu, Member of the Standing Committee of the National People's Congress, the Deputy Director Member of the Financial Committee of the National People's Congress and the Vice President of the China National Democratic Construction Association, at the Investment and Financing Forum of Trade in Services and the Modern Service Industry

Ladies and gentlemen,

Good morning! The subject of my speech is *Six Opportunities for Rebuilding the New Pattern of Reform*. The CIFTIS in the past years has had different subjects. At the forum of CIFTIS, the subject for the investment is *Rebuild the Strength of Reform*. One key issue is how to seize the strength of overriding and rebuild the market after transformation. I think that there are six development opportunities for rebuilding the reform: The first is population urbanization; the second is the economic service orientation; the third is the development of low-carbon orientation; the fourth is the high-end industry; the fifth is the enterprise informationization; the main issue of informationization is the Internet financing; the sixth is business internationalization.

We see opportunities and challenges. Our enterprises are faced with the difficulty of financing: It's difficult and expensive; the difficulty of employment: It's hard to hire and retain employees for enterprises, and enterprises cannot afford employment; the difficulty of profitability: The cost and tax are high; the difficulty of investment: There are no orders from market and no space from investment; the difficulty of innovation: Enterprises have no willing, do not dare to, are not capable of and don't know how to innovate.

Our economy will be transformed in pains, and such a kind of pain will be summarized into 4 aspects: The first is to remove the production capacity of manufacturing industry, which faces an excessive production capacity; the second is to remove leverage of finance, but the leverage ratio is very high for government and corporate debt; the third is to remove the foam of real estate; the fourth is to remove the pollution of environment. This is the opportunity and transformation that I have just mentioned, as well as challenges.

First, let's take a look at the opportunities from urbanization. Looking into the next 20 years, the urbanization in China will increase from 50% to 70%, namely, 1% increased each year. The service industry will increase from 43% to 61%, 18 percent points, almost 1 percent point each year. However, the urbanization rate is only 30% according to the registered household population, less than 50%. The proportion of service industry is only more than 40%, over 70% in the developed countries, so the proportion of China's service industry is 10 percent points lower than that of countries with the equal economic development; we have many disadvantages in the service industry. As a Ph.D in Economics, Prime Minister Li Keqiang has his own opinions. He thinks that urbanization is a great potential for domestic demand, the service industry is the largest container for employment, and reform is the greatest bonus for development.

Urbanization drives upgrading consumption, and brings business opportunities in respect of energy, telecommunication, medical treatment, culture, media and electrical equipment. Urbanization drives consumption in food, clothes, housing, traveling and daily use, in particular housing and traveling. Urbanization drives requirements on investment and financing. At present, we need an eco-friendly development, in particular in Beijing. The biggest problem is to treat the diseases of the city. On one side, it becomes challenges; on the other side, it brings opportunities for eco-friendly development and eco-friendly industry.

According to forecast by the National Development Bank, in the following 3 years, the requirements for urbanization investments in China will be 25 trillion RMB. According to forecast by the Ministry of Finance, the investment and financing requirements by urbanization, by 2020, will be 42 trillion RMB. So we need diverse financing modes, including the innovation of Internet finance.

We have performed survey and research in more than 10 provinces and cities, and the results show that urbanization will bring investment opportunities to private capital.

The first is the service orientation. This is the theme of CIFTIS, namely the service orientation of the economy or the great development of service industry. Let's take a look at the proportion of service industry in Beijing, from 70% in 2006 to 77% today; the service industry keeps a high growth rate in investment. Last year, the investment on the manufacturing industry was low but it benefited from the growth of investment on the service industry. The increasing rate of investment on fixed assets from service industry in Beijing is high, in which the financial industry has also developed rapidly.

The second is low-carbon emissions. This is crucial for Beijing. Beijing is very affected by fog, so the most important thing is to reduce emissions. The deep cause of emissions is the extensive industrialization and the out-of-balance urbanization. The greatest pollution source in Beijing is the emissions from the tail gas of automobiles, many vehicles and people, so we must change the urbanization and industrialization mode if we are resolute to realize the goal of low-carbon emissions.

The third is high-end orientation. Our glorious achievements are made by low-cost competitive edges: low cost, low price, low profit, low-end market and low technology. We create GDP with high energy consumption, high material consumption, high emissions and high pollution, but we cannot create high-end profit; we have produced a great number of products but we cannot successfully create brands; we have created a lot of employment but cannot increase the income of the people. That's why we need to transit from a low-end economy to a medium and high-end economy.

The fourth is low-price industrialization. The industry has exchanged: low-price labor force and low cost, which is costly. The conference on economy proposes to restructure the industry, the fundamental philosophy of which is innovation. The innovation is not unique in China. The innovation and transformation is a world-class challenge and a world-class topic. Europe proposes to launch the 3rd industrial revolution, the U.S. proposes re-industrialization, China proposes seven strategic emerging industries.

The fifth is informationization and Internet financing which I will expound in detail. The enterprise informationization is divided into two aspects: The first is changing the traditional industry with information technology; the second is the industrialization of information technology, and the combination of information technology with other industries, such as E-commerce. The Internet has changed the newspapers, films, music, telecommunications and aviation, the next is finance. The Internet finance is the finance-oriented Internet and the Internet-oriented finance. The financing cost and the time cost of Internet finance are low and the transaction is convenient. In terms of function and influence of the Internet, we witness the popularity and the tolerance of the Internet, featuring popular finance and grassroots finance. The Internet finance is the direct transaction, removing links, cross-border operations, removing edges. With the advantages of big data and cloud computing platforms, the Internet finance is efficient. It promotes the transformation of the traditional finance, and the "Catfish effect" may be produced in the financial reform. Let's take a look at the achievements made by Ali Loan. It has addressed the needs of 700,000 small and micro-sized enterprises, with loans over 190 billion RMB, with a bad debt ratio of only 0.9%. The maximum annualized interest rate reaches 12%, the cost of each loan is only 2.3 yuan (the bank handling charge is about 2,000 yuan), and the Internet loan can be finished in several days. The Internet finance is not a territory out of laws. It should be guided according to situations and standardized in the development. Risks should be managed and opportunities utilized. I proposed six suggestions for supervision over the Internet finance, including categorized supervision, linking coordination, supervising over the negative list, standardizing products, and maintaining a fair competitive market order, etc.

The sixth is the operation internationalization. Based on optimistic forecast, by the year 2020, China will contribute more than 1 trillion USD as foreign direct investment to the world's economy China is transiting from the traditional large commodity export country to the large country for foreign investments. Transnational M&A has become a highlight of overseas investments. According to the speech by Vice Premier Wang Yang for CIFTIS, this is an era of service economy. He pointed out that the proportion of service industry has increased to over 50% of foreign capital in China. More than 70% of foreign-funded enterprises in Beijing are engaged in modern service industry. In the process of utilizing the foreign capital, the service industry takes up more than 80%, and trade in services has been shaped in Beijing, with a total amount of over 100 billion USD, more than 20% in local trade and more than 20% in China's foreign service trade. The two 20% show the theme of CIFTIS. We can see the standing of Beijing in trade in services.

In summary, we face six opportunities in building the new pattern of economic development: population urbanization, economic service orientation, development with low-carbon emissions, high-end industry, enterprise informationization and operation internationalization. The largest disadvantage for the Chinese economy is service industry and urbanization, which also bring opportunities. Therefore, the trade in services defined by CIFTIS is a good topic.

That's all for my speech! Thank you!

# Speech by Jiang Chaofeng, President of the China Supply Chain Financial Service League, at the Supply Chain Financial Development and Innovation Workshop

First of all, I would like to say something about supply chain finance. What is supply chain finance? What is the essence of supply chain finance? Its essence is to apply the philosophy and methods of supply chain management to providing financial service activities to the relevant associated enterprises. A theorist can use complicated language to describe supply chain finance, but in the case of business operations, we can describe supply chain finance as follows.

The main model of supply chain finance is to identify the upstream and downstream enterprises of the core enterprise as the service objects on the precondition of a true transaction so as to provide financial services in all procedures related to purchase, production and sales. As each enterprise has its own supply chain, a huge supply chain network appears. Therefore, the different enterprises are now prefixed with different product names. We all have our product and this product is actually a service product given a different name or title, but its essence is supply chain finance, namely providing a financial service on the supply chain. President Chen of the China Construction Bank gives his definition of this, but it was the definition given a year before. Supply chain finance means that the financial enterprises and logistics enterprises can search for and identify the core enterprises in the supply chain and provide the financing facilities to the upstream and downstream enterprises. E-commerce and logistics enterprises have huge groups of customers, and banks can strengthen joint venture cooperation with these enterprises, thus easily entering into a certain industry or field in order to obtain the resources of massive customers at a comparatively lower cost with financial trade services as the starting point, while at the same time, strengthening customer maintenance, tapping and satisfying the customers with large-sum loans, cross-market financing, wealth management and other derivative financial demands. This is the concept put forward by President Chen in 2012 when he talked about the operation of supply chain finance, so I think his idea is quite classic.

Next, we are going to talk about the development of supply chain finance. The integration of the supply chain finance and logistics industry is the first feature. Finance and logistics are the trading intermediary, which was first advanced by us. Actually, finance and logistics belong to the same service sector, and both of them are the intermediary. Finance is the intermediary for payment and actually the capital intermediary. However, logistics is the intermediary for goods delivery. So the innovation of the financial business of the supply chain mainly comes from the innovation of the financial products. It has a series of products just like order financing, policy financing, e-commerce financing, financial logistics, collateral management, bonded warehouse, factoring warehouse, trade financing and account receivable pledge financing, etc. Each bank may launch twenty or thirty products with different names. However, they have a common, but a most essential thing, namely providing financial service to all enterprises in the supply chain. What roles do the logistics enterprises play here? Actually they play a role in promoting the delivery of the goods, so logistics enterprises will guarantee the existence and delivery of the goods.

The second feature is the integration of finance and logistics into e-commerce. At a seminar organized by the Ministry of Industry and Information Technology, I gave a speech, which won the favor of all the participants at the meeting. I pointed out why e-commerce was so popular and that it was due to two supports, respectively Finance and Logistics, and I also pointed out that e-commerce cannot survive without these two things. So, we shall study them. Almost all e-commerce companies provide a financing platform while providing a trading platform to conduct a pledge loan to both buyers and sellers. All major banks and joint-equity banks launch a sub-service to cater to e-commerce business. A characteristic feature of current e-commerce is online trading and online financing as well as offline settlement and delivery or online payment; these three features represent a good summary of the core of e-commerce.

Now let us take a close look at e-commerce; it will weaken the traditional trading models with its six major features for subverting our trading models. First, trade will not be restricted by time and space; second, it can shorten trading procedures; third, fragmentation of orders reflects real needs; fourth, fast transaction requires fast delivery. We often say our trade, particularly e-trading, can be completed within a second. However, the delivery of the goods still requires a tricycle, vans or trucks to get the goods to the consumers so, fast trade now requires fast delivery; fifth, e-commerce provides small enterprises with a sales market since today's small enterprises do not rely on large enterprises for their market and can sell their own products. In particular, some OEM plants can sell their products without depending on the large brands for online sales. They can obtain a profit ratio of 50% at the price 80% lower than the market price. Sixth, e-commerce's cost and sales price are much lower.

Now look at big data. Some features of supply chain finance under big data have the following three characteristics: First of all is speed. The fast speed of transact requires the delivery speed to be as fast as possible. The second is flow, which is standardized and information-based with transparent regulations and platform, so supply chain finance does not need to depend on the core enterprises to develop its business. The third is integration, including the integration of the manufacturing industry, trade industry, financial industry, logistics industry and the market. Supply chain finance can exert some impact on the logistics industry, that is our business models are changing with fast response and fast sorting out; small quantity, more batches for delivery, visualized and network demands affect the scale, layout and structure, etc., of the logistics facilities.

The third is Internet financing, which is highly favored by every one of us. Last year it was quite popular and we constantly discussed it. What does it mean? My definition of it is "the completion of the financial activities by using Internet technology"; and this is the essence of it regardless of its complicated contents. The financial service breaks the limitation of time and space and greatly cuts down the costs through big data and micro-loans, all of which are features of Internet financing. Its data are used to support the relevant business. What is its importance? As a full-time deputy president of the banking association put it in a single sentence: keeping the banking service throughout the night. Just like the example given by them, the daily deposit capital in YEBao (a balance value-added service by Alipay) is 20 billion RMB. Now all e-commerce platforms are concerned about this and play with the funds, and then build themselves into a quasi-banking institution. However, attention should be paid to its precondition so that the supplier may postpone and extend the period for collecting the amount of the goods. Some agree with payment within 7 days while others agree with payment within 14 days. Some industries require the collection of the amount of the goods within 3 or 4 days. So Internet financing is not the only owner of YEBao or Alibaba. Actually, our financial institutions have been promoting the Internet finance for a long time. The website business of the Industrial and Commercial Bank and the China Construction Bank accounts for 78% of the total business, with 6,500 transactions each second, on the average. The web-page is actually Internet financing. How is the supply chain finance going this year? The credit system will be subject to severe tests, as there are the excessive production capacity, the false credit demand, the lack of an investment channel for the residents' savings, and excessive profit pursuit in the face of the crisis.

This year Shanghai's steel trade event had a strong impact, and the financial institutions suffered impacts from various sides. Actually, the banks suffered the maximum loss from Shanghai's steel trade event. The current impact on the banks was financial disintermediation, as mentioned above, without the bank serving as the intermediary; the competition is intensifying so that Internet financing and YEBao and the relevant payment models have gained a strong momentum for development, thus exerting a reversal pressure on the banks for reform. A responsible person from a bank in the economic and developmental zone told me that there are 19 banks with more than 110 business outlets within the development zone, so we can say there are more banks than hotels. The competition is becoming intensely fiercer, so whoever can create core competitiveness will win.

What is the new risk? The new risk is the fraudulence of joint guarantee. Actually, joint guarantee was mentioned in the *Guarantee Law*, promulgated in 1995. The enterprises conducted the joint guarantee in 1995, but in the end, the good-faith enterprises have to pay for the fly-by-night enterprises. This model is now promoted from south to north in China. Yesterday, I heard of it in Northeast China where people also have joint guarantee involving 10 enterprises. Shanxi also has a joint guarantee involving 10 enterprises, so can the joint guarantee be used by banks as well? They cannot use it, but banks will suffer a lot as it can add risks.

Here are some new problems. Where does the credit of the e-commerce dealers come from? The registered capital for an e-commerce provider is 200 million or 300 million RMB or so, but everyone trusts it and then deposit 500 billion RMB. What do we trust in this respect? It is the provider's credibility. When the e-commerce provider accumulates funds up to 1 trillion RMB, 2 trillion RMB, even 5 trillion RMB, we are likely to have more confidence in it. However, if a risk appears at this moment, it will be totally out of control. So e-commerce dealers must maintain their creditworthiness without doing anything wrong. In the past, there have been more than 10 cases of e-commerce dealers who have run off with the money since 1996, so we think we are ready to maintain vigilance. The current loan guarantee is mainly involved with the credit guarantee and in-kind guarantee. There is nothing new about in-kind guarantee; pledge of movables and real estate mortgage is another model.

Second, we will talk about how big data can affect the supply chain. In the current situation, the impact of the big data has become quite clear. How can it exert impacts? There are several points: First, it can accurately judge the direction and the quantity of the demand. The enterprises on the supply chain share a closer connection and a closer relationship. The change in the terminal consumption quantity naturally brings about changes in all upstream procedures, and big data can help us in judging the usual practice of a series of changes. Yesterday, I talked about it with some comrades and we concluded that big data is just like a spider web. The spider can immediately feel any kind of movement on the web. Therefore, the inevitable trend is to reduce the intermediate links. Due to the order fragmentation of bulk goods in circulation, the wholesale enterprises will decrease in number, which is a typical example. In addition, trade logistics integration is another trend. The logistics service is an integral part of trade as well as the source of the new profit of the value-added industries. Just as the daily product e-commerce dealers promote fast development, the bulk goods e-commerce dealers can promote the development of production logistics.

The second benefit is to conduct a credit evaluation of the target customers. With the consent of the customers, the lender may use big data and judge a series of data related to the customers' financial data, production data, water and electricity consumption, salary level, order quantity and cash flow, assets and liabilities, investment preference, success rate, technical level, R&D investments, product cycle, etc., If there are formula and standards after the judgment, the data shall immediately become the judging indicators. We can complete a loan business within three minutes, particularly a small amount loan. However, I also have an idea: it is risky to merely read the financial statements and transaction data, as the relevant data may be false. If we use big data to keep pace with the specific situation, it will be truly reliable as it cannot be totally manipulated by others.

The third benefit is to use big data for risk analysis, warning and control. The advantage of big data is that you can conduct the analysis of the market trend and price fluctuation to give a warning as soon as possible. The industrial risk is the biggest one. In case of industrial decline, most industrial enterprises will remain in a depressing state. Thus, if we can control more procedures involved in this way, we can give a warning earlier and we can effectively reduce the risks. If you are late in discovering a risk or even accept the satisfactory offer from others, it may cause greater loss, so big data will exert a positive impact on us.

Fourth, it can help us provide accurate financial services and logistics service in collecting the information related to the loan time, duration, scale, purpose, flow, warehousing, transport and commissioned purchase, etc., so as to have the the granting of an accurate loan.

So, according to our judgment, 2014 will be a year with big changes in the logistics industry. First, as the online settlement and delivery are faster and more convenient, the producers may obtain the information of a safety inventory according to the big data, and deliver the goods to all warehouses in advance for the ready goods delivery. So now, the warehousing network is more important than at any other time. We are all talking about the newbie, but what on earth is the newbie plan? The newbie plan actually means: after the online click trading, the goods ordered by you can be delivered to you within 8 hours. How can this task be fulfilled? If the manufacturer is in Harbin and its customer is in Guangzhou, how can he or it deal with the order? What he needs to do is forecast the specific demand quantity of this product in each region via big data, store up the goods in advance and then arrange for distribution and delivery. Second, the traders and manufacturers will increase their fund demand according to the increase in the inventory, so they have to turn to the financial sector to increase financing, and the demand for supply chain financial management will increase accordingly. Third, the market segmentation of the express delivery industry will be completed and will enter the fine management phase in the next step. So my goal is to optimize the nodes, and the first-level node scale should be larger to accommodate a full load. With the community-based destination nodes, we can solve the "Last Kilometer" problems.

The conditions for the application of big data: The authenticity of the basic data. If we use big data, the authenticity of the data must be guaranteed, particularly the basic data and the local GDP. Currently, the data related to the throughput capacity, investment, freight, warehousing facilities and investment amount are somewhat falsified, and the total local GPD exceeds the national GDP. Duplicating the computation of the container weight for the throughput capacity, the connected enterprises mutually issue invoices to increase the sales turnover, etc., so we have distorted data. Second, data should be collected to form the indicators. Actually, data is as dry as a chip and we are surrounded by data every day. However, can we use the data? If the data cannot form indicators, it is useless. After they are formed into the data, we find that data have life. Fresh indicators can exert a significant guiding effect. Third, different data systems are interconnected. Under the market conditions, data represents the resources and products. Interest division makes an information-isolated island possible. Such a condition even appears where public information is monopolized by the relevant departments for their own benefit so that the department data, the industrial data, the enterprise data and the international data are mutually separated and the big data cannot give full scope to its basic roles. Fourth, it is necessary to accumulate the accurate parameters. We should promote the analysis of the relevant data and form our business parameters. The basic parameters are extremely important, particularly the critical parameters. What is a critical parameter? It means that the parameter is likely to change. We don't know the specific data about the warehousing area of the national enterprises, but the storage capacity has increased year by year at a growth rate of more than 30% for five consecutive years. Thus far, it has increased by more than 30% this year. So we would like to ask what the parameters are. Actually, parameters are the base line made by the carpenter, anything outside the base line will be planed off before we make the necessary things. Now, we are in urgent need of the data, but they are not available. Fifth, advanced data application concept.

If data are objective, the use of data is closed to the awareness and judgment of the people. The concept of advanced data application can bring the roles played by data into their fullest play, so we can draw our conclusions as required.

The fourth problem is related to the trend of supply chain finance. First, it develops toward a credit guarantee, but physical guarantee is now less and less and it follows the trend of the credit guarantee. Second, if it is oriented toward a physical guarantee, it requires the cooperation among logistics enterprises and guarantee enterprises. I have fewer chances to analyze the ins and outs of the Shanghai Steel Trade Event. Last time, General Manager Xiao suggested that if anyone could conduct a meticulous and direct analysis of the Shanghai Steel

Trade Event, it would be an attractive and readable paper. It is so indeed, but we do not have much time to do this. We can only say that the 2008 financial crisis is the reason for the bubble. A brake was suddenly put on a fast-growing fund supply, yet with a view to extending the project and reducing the loss, enterprises had to borrow usurious loans. Our project is halfway in progress, but if we are in short of funds, this project will be totally gone. I have to borrow money even at the interest rate of 20% or 40%, which adds to our capital cost. In 2011, when Minister Chen Demin asked us to attend a seminar, three of our enterprises reported their work to Minister Chen. He was surprised at the interest rate of the loan interest, roughly at 24% for small and medium-size enterprises. It was really 24%, so usurious loans are very popular as the best operation model; therefore, people on the market cheated bank loans against a pledge. When the bank loans are further compressed, the upper chain breaks and all the participants are on the alert to collect favorable evidence, but they conceal it and refuse to report it to the authorities. When the situation becomes more looser, all of the participants delay taking actions, and departments do not take any action under the accountability system with the bureaucratic working style and the approaching limitation of legal proceedings, so we have an outbreak cluster of lawsuits.

The third problem is about the construction of the cooperation platform for e-commerce, finance and logistics, all of which are integrated into a whole, virtually inseparable. Now there is a trend that three of them jointly build a cooperation platform. So we can say that both the buyers and the sellers can apply for loans through the e-commerce platform. The lenders are the financial institutions and they are now the e-commerce platform. The e-commerce dealers can accumulate a lot of funds through the commissioned collection of the amount of goods and also provide financing to customers by using the time difference of the collection and payment without the occupying cost as the main profit source. It is the innovation demand for the combination of big data analysis with the financial service in order to provide the customers with a guarantee-free bank credit by offering a higher trade credit. The e-commerce platform is the collector of big data. The integration of the trade platform with the logistics system, the integration with the payment system, the integration with the trade financing system can all ensure the authenticity and reliability of the trade resources as well as the good faith and reliable trade actions for unified information flow, fund flow, logistics and e-commerce. This platform has six major fundamental functions. My friends engaged in e-commerce business told me that if we want to have a functional platform for all of us, the six major functions are absolutely necessary. First, the information consulting function; second, the trading function; third, the financing credit function; fourth, the logistics service function; fifth, the customer management function; sixth, the security guarantee function. I have read through the design solutions of 89 e-commerce platforms, including the exchange-based platforms, the platforms built by manufacturers, the platforms built by traders, the platforms built by IT enterprises, and I have found that the platforms built by e-commerce dealers with different backgrounds in the four fields are quite different, but quite interesting.

Roughly speaking, there are as many trading models for bulk commodities. I do not want to say any more about it as all of us are quite familiar with it, particularly the bidding and transaction matchmaking, but the latter is outdated; however, someone designed it that way. Nevertheless, I would like to introduce something to you, which is very important. If you are involved with E-commerce financing, you will take into account these factors. First, you must have online financing product. What is the name of this product? You may call it "Bao or something else", but you must have a name for it, so that everyone can quickly find it. Second, you will have the financing management software and a supervisor in charge of the goods. Some say there is no need for the supervision over the online sales, but actually everything should be under supervision, so we should have a supervision office, a goods location, an area, a contract list, the total amount and the discount, etc. Therefore, the credit system is something worthy of greater efforts on the part of management. Your balance sheet and your legal person materials shall be saved here, so I can provide them to the very person in need of them. This is your actual credit. However, it is not so easy; as a matter of fact, it is necessary to show the production, operational and financial conditions of this enterprise, so, in any case, this constitutes a defect. Fourth, it is necessary to strengthen cooperation and reduce suspicion. Financial logistics is faced with a greater difficulty. What are the banks concerned about? What are the enterprises concerned about? What are the investors concerned about? The three participants need funds and need to serve the funds. If we can properly coordinate with these interest relationships, this business can be upgraded for our benefit though we just said it dropped by 50%, yet we can actually see its initial recovery.

This speech is a summary of my understanding of the above-mentioned aspects. If we hope that supply chain finance can develop into a safer environment, we should first change the evaluation system and mechanism without cramming down of loans, nor do we take a drastic measure to deal with a situation. It goes without saying that we will pay attention to another point: big data. Third, we will build a supply network system and look a little further towards building a supply chain network.

That is all of my speech. Thank you!

# Speech by Wan Lianpo, Deputy Director General of the Department of Trade in Services and Commercial Services of the Ministry of Commerce, at the Traditional Chinese Medicine Theme Day Launching Ceremony and the Traditional Chinese Medicine Trade in Services Investment & Financing Conference

Respected Deputy Director General Yu Wenming, and all guests,

Good morning! I am very delighted to attend the Traditional Chinese Medicine Theme Day Launching Ceremony during the 3rd CIFTIS. Please allow me to extend my warmest congratulations on the successful holding of a series of traditional Chinese medicine activities on behalf of the Department of Trade in Services and Commercial Services of the Ministry of Commerce.

Nowadays, the international transfer of the service industry has become the new trend of in economic globalization, and trade in services trade has become a new impetus to boost global economic growth. Since entering the new century, the global service industry and trade have enjoyed a strong momentum for of development. Up to now, the ratio of the service industry in the world economic aggregate has reached 70%. For developed economies, the ratio is even up to around 80% around. What's more, the ratio of service exports in world trade exports is approximately 20%. To develop trade in services trade has become an important measure for all countries that want to improve their international payments situation and increase their status in the international division of labor. In the field of trade in services, international competition is more intense, and the development of global trade in services presents the new feature of a "synchronous advance in scale expansion and structure adjustment". From 1980 to 2013, world service exportation climbed to about 4.6 trillion USD, with an increase of 12 times, and the ratio of world trade exportation increased to 1/5 from 1/7. In 2013, the total export-import volume was 9 trillion USD, a rise of 6.1% over the previous year, of which the export volume was 4.6 trillion USD, with a year-on-year increase of 6%.

Our trade in services has made tremendous progress, with its main characteristics as follows:

The first characteristic is rapid expansion of the scale of trade in services and a constant increase in international status. We started collecting statistical data regarding trade in services in 1982. The total export-import volume was 4.4 billion USD in 1982, and it climbed to 539.6 billion USD in 2013, 123 times as much as that in 1982, which hit the record. In 2013, our service exports and imports were ranked 5th and 2nd respectively in the world.

The second characteristic is the fast development of the emerging trade in services and the steady development of traditional trade in services. In the past three years, new trade in services, such as computers, information services, insurance and financial consulting, has been developing rapidly at an annual growth rate of 16.2%, which leads to an increasing rise in competitive advantage. Besides, traditional trade in services, such as transport, tourism and architecture, is also developing steadily, with its scale advantage constantly enhanced.

The third characteristic is the small ratio of service exports, leading to a long-term trade in services trade deficit. In terms of in total volume of trade in services trade, there is still a great gap between our country and large trading countries. The ratio of Chinese service exports in the total export volume of commodities and services is small; in 2013, the ratio was 20.2% in the world, but only 8.7% in China. The industry of traditional Chinese medicine makes up an important part of China's excellent culture and is the treasure of Chinese cultural heritage; containing rich philosophical thoughts and humanistic spirits, it is a healthy national healthy industry with completely independent intellectual property rights, so that it deserves high attention by the Chinese government. The *12th Five-Year Plan Outline for the Development of Trade in Services* jointly released by 34 departments, including the Ministry of Commerce, defines the development goal of traditional Chinese medicine trade in services, and the *Opinions on the Promotion of Traditional Chinese Medicine Trade in Services*, jointly released by 14 departments, including the Ministry of Commerce, clearly points out developmental direction of traditional Chinese medicine trade in services during the next stage; this is of practical significance in optimizing the structure of foreign trade, accelerating the development of foreign cultural trade and fostering new export advantages with Chinese characteristics. In the coming days, the Ministry of Commerce and the State Administration of Traditional Chinese Medicine of the People's Republic of China will cooperate with relevant departments in order to perfectly complete work on the following four aspects.

Firstly, a good developmental environment is should be created to enhance the application and protection of intellectual property in the field of traditional Chinese medicine, and unremitting efforts are should be made to innovate protection protective measures and means based on the actual developmental conditions of traditional medicine. Enterprises are should be encouraged to carry out work of protect transnational intellectual property. A system of integrity for traditional enterprises within the field of Chinese medicine trade in services trade enterprise integrity system should be established and improved, the construction of enterprise credit technology collection and credit rating should be accelerated, and a market environment for fair competition should be safeguarded.

Second, a promotional policy and system should be improved. The *Opinions on the Promotion of Traditional Chinese Medicine Trade in Services* should be thoroughly implemented, enterprises in the field of traditional Chinese medicine trade in services need to be encouraged to set up and improve an overseas marketing network, and eligible enterprises should take the lead to go outside.

Third, the public information service, as well as the construction of a public platform for traditional Chinese medicine trade in services, should be improved. A statistical system of traditional Chinese medicine trade in services should be established and improved. Besides, by relying on marketization consulting services, information exchanges and resource sharing can be gradually achieved between government organs and consulting companies.

Lastly, the role of system and mechanism should be fully played. The trade in services trans-departmental contact mechanism and industrial management department need to play their roles to intensify macro planning and guidance, and coordinate so as to solve institutional problems in traditional Chinese medicine trade in services. Besides, the multilateral and bilateral relations of our country with other countries are used to promote the entrance of the traditional Chinese medicine trade in services into the foreign market.

Distinguished guests, the Ministry of Commerce really expect hopes that all of you present can will be able to seize the opportunity faced by the development of the traditional Chinese medicine trade in services trade to speed for speeding up the pace of showing traditional Chinese medicine to the world, which; this is not only the an important part of the development of Chinese trade in services, but also a great contribution of the Chinese nation to all human beings. We are fully confident in the development of traditional Chinese medicine trade in services. Thank you!

# Speech by Yuan Yaming, Deputy President of the Chinese Medical Doctor's Association, at the First International Pension Service Industry Fair

Distinguished leaders and guests,

Good morning! In order to express several opinions on strengthening the development of the pension service industry and several opinions on promoting the development of the health care industry of the State Council, improve the level of our pension service, achieve cross-industry cooperation of medical treatment, pensions, real estate and finance, and to promote the development of China's pension undertaking, the International Pension Service Industry Promotion Conference, held by the Chinese Medical Doctor's Association, officially opens today. On behalf of the Chinese Medical Doctor's Association and the conference organization, I want to extend a warm welcome and a sincere thanks to all the leaders, guests, experts and scholars, and friends in the media attending the conference. The theme of the conference is medical pension administration triggers global resources to invest in China's pension service industry. The conference is aimed at providing opportunities for developers, operators, investors and local governments to explore China's flourishing pension market, to set up a platform to determine strategies and contribute cooperation, to show the excellent foreign management and operation institutions in China, to set up a pension information platform, to exchange intelligent pension construction schemes, and to promote pension industrial park projects and projects for the approval of government funds that are full of business opportunities, striving to hold a grand meeting in the field of pension services. The promotional conference is supported by the Organizing Committee of CIFTIS, the National Health and Family Planning Commission, the Ministry of Civil Affairs, the National Working Commission on Aging and other units as well as CCTV, BTV, Xinhua News Agency, China Pension Health News and other main media. Leaders of related ministries and commissions will share their precious experience, focus on the promotion of 5 projects, organize funds in the amount of 30 billion RMB for pension services, and promote the development of the pension service industry in the form of industrial alliances. The pension industry is a traditional industry and also an emerging industry, and insurance and medical treatment are always important contents of the development of the pension service industry. Reform of public hospitals, and especially China officially published several opinions on accelerating the

173

development of social hospitals in 2014, will play a more positive promotional role in medical treatment closely related to pensions, especially for institutions with a combination of medical treatment resources and pension resources. The Meeting of the Political Bureau of the Central Committee held on April 25 mentioned many points related to health and the pension industry, specifying basic services and taking market orientation for middle and high-end market, which will be a strategic opportunity for social capital.

The Chinese Medical Doctor's Association is an industrial organization of Chinese doctors. We will actively support developmental strategies of China's health-care industry, and we believe that China's pension service industry will develop better with your active participation and enthusiastic support.

Finally, I wish the promotional conference a complete success. Thank you!

# Speech by Zhu Yong, Deputy Director of the National Working Commission on Aging, at the First International Pension Services Industry Fair

All guests, ladies and gentlemen,

Good morning! I'm pleased to attend the pension services industry promotional conference of the 3rd CIFTIS. I, on behalf of the National Working Commission on Aging, want to extend my warm congratulations to the conference and a sincere thanks to all the sectors of society who care for the problem of aging and have supported work regarding aging for a long time.

Today's theme is the development of the pension services industry. I think the theme is good. Under the situation of the rapid development of the aging of the population, actively promoting the development of the pension services industry is an important response to China's current situation concerning aging and it is also important in the promotion of a sound development of the economy and of society. So, I would like to take this opportunity to talk about my views regarding the development of the pension services industry.

First, we should correctly understand the status and policy environment of China's population aging. China has entered a stage of rapid development regarding the aging of its population. The population over 60 years old had reached 202 million by the end of last year, accounting for 14.9% of the total population. According to our prediction, that part of the population will exceed 300 million by 2025, 400 million by 2033, and will reach its peak of 487 million by 2053. It can be said that China will face a very serious problem of population aging in the next 40 years. On the one hand, the aging population is increasing, and in particular, it is estimated that it will increase by 10 million elderly people each year for the next20years; such a growth rate and scale are unprecedented domestically and internationally; on the other hand, with a sharp increase of the elderly in the proportion of the population, the burden of providing for the aged is becoming increasingly heavier. One third of the population will be elderly in the future, which will basically be a situation in which China will find itself with huge potential demands for pension services. Under this situation, China has to pay great attention to the development of the pension services industry. Since the "12th Five-Year Plan", China has revised its *Law on Protection of Rights and Interests of Seniors of the People's Republic of China,* and has published a series of documents, such as the "12th Five-Year" plan for aging undertaking, the *Construction and Planning of the Social Pension Services System* and the *Several Opinions on Accelerating the Development of the Pension Services Industry,* providing support and guarantee for the development of the pension services industry in terms of legal construction, planning, guidance and policy formulation. In the meantime, the national finance is continuously increasing its related input, and is trying to promote the coordinated development of the aging undertaking industry. Related ministries and commissions further specify preferential policies in support of the development of the aging services industry, such as tax preference, reduction or exemption of taxes, financial subsidies and land supply. From 2013, China has incorporated the pension services industry and the health care industry into preferential fields of development of the life services industry and has encouraged local governments to explore effective modes to develop the pension services industry by combining actual situations. So, on the whole, rapidly-increasing market demands and a good policy environment provide a very rare opportunity for the development of the pension services industry.

Second, we should correctly understand the market demands for the pension services industry. We should realize that the development of this industry has opportunities and also challenges; in particular, we should treat the potential demands of the market rationally. Although the pension services market has huge potential demands and shows an increasing trend, potential demands cannot be converted to effective demands, and are currently limited. First of all, China has a large proportion of elderly in the population with low and middle incomes, which limits their consumption. By 2014, China had increased its basic pension standard of enterprises' retirees with a fluctuation of 10% for the following 10 years. Currently, the average standard pension of the retirees of China's enterprises is still lower than 2,500 RMB, so the income of the elderly needs to be raised. At the same time, unsound social security systems are an important reason for low income of the elderly. Security systems for the elderly in developed countries are multi-level, and old-age pensions are made up of national basic endowment insurance, supplementary endowment insurance and commercial endowment insurance, but in China, basic endowment insurance is the pillar, playing the main role. As other pillars, enterprise annuity, occupational annuity and commercial endowment insurance have a short guarantee period and account for a small proportion of the pension. Besides, China has not established a long-term mutually-beneficial insurance system, the loss of which greatly restricts the expansion of pension services demands for the elderly.

Next, our pension service consumption market is not standard, which limits the willingness of the elderly to consume. In recent years, the pension services industry has attracted more and more attention from party and governmental departments, that have established a series of regulations and standards. However, compared with the development of the pension services industry, the current standards and regulations are not perfect, and in particular, the market supervision mechanism is unsound and there is no system for safeguarding rights. Once consumption rights of the elderly have been violated, there is no way to complain, which puts a great limit on the possibility for the elderly to purchase a pension service.

Then, most elderly people are conservative in their concept of consumption. With China's economic and social development, the structure of residents' consumption has changed a lot. However, according to our survey, although the elderly's pattern, concept and behavior regarding consumption have changed, their consumption still focuses on daily expenses, and they are highly sensitive to prices. Therefore, in addition to the limited economic income of the elderly, their psychological idea of over-saving on themselves and being over-generous to their grandchildren is an important factor contributing to the low level of their consumption. Therefore, although the pension services market has huge potential demands, the problem that the effective demands of the market are small is emphasized. How to convert potential demands into effective demands requires a long developmental process. This is an important direction we should grasp in order to develop the pension services industry.

Third, we should correctly understand the future of the pension services industry. Discussion on the industrialization of pension services first needs to specify the connotation of pension services. Pension services have two meanings. In a broad sense, pension services refer to all the industrial organizations which provide products and services to meet the needs of the elderly, such as household management services, medical treatment, insurance, wealth management, leisure and entertainment, appliances for the elderly, their travelling, their education, culture, sports and their mental health. In a narrow sense, pension services mainly refer to such services provided to the elderly as daily care, health care and rehabilitation nursing. In whichever sense it is considered however, the pension services industry is not the concept of simply providing for the elderly. To be exact, the pension services industry is a comprehensive industry, characterized by a long industrial chain, high correlation and wide correlative fields.

Currently, enterprises are enthusiastic about investing in the pension industry, but in my opinion, we have misunderstandings regarding investments. Many enterprises unilaterally think that what the elderly need the most are luxurious residences and facilities. With this thinking, many of the early pension institutions lack five-star pension service operation modes although they have five-star infrastructures. These institutions have not formed effective profit models and most of them are in a state of deficit. Thus, when developing the pension services industry, we cannot simply consider that pension services mean building luxurious pension institutions or pension real estate, and we should pay more attention to services that the elderly need. The only thing that equipment technology can do is play a role and generate a certain effect in the services. We should focus on making the pension services work effectively with efficient management and good services.

Fourth, we should correctly understand and play the role of the market mechanism. We must fully realize that pension services have many specialties compared with other industries, and its marketization degree and profit pursuit should be properly limited and adjusted. However, in general, the pension services industry should possess at least the following 3 basic requirements:

1. For pension service investment by government, enterprises, individuals or non-profit organizations, management and operation costs should be able to be recovered in some way and these institutions should obtain reasonable profits through service charges, government subsidies, preferential policies and other methods, so that pension services can attract investments from various sources; otherwise, there would be no future in relying merely on the government for investments in the pension services industry. Of course, the development of the pension services industry should be limited in case there is no government support, but complete dependence on government investments is not sustainable and will damage the development of the pension services industry.

2. Rewards for personnel engaged in the pension services industry should be consistent with and even higher than other social service industries, and they should enjoy the same social status as the personnel of other social service industries. That is, the pension services industry should be a formal, professional and respectable profession, so that it can attract a large number of laborers to work in pension services, so as to develop professional education and training for those people working in the pension services industry; and this would improve the professional level of the pension services industry. Otherwise, it will cause a shortage of energy within this industry and give it a low professional level, which will be a hindrance and would limit the development of the pension services industry.

3. The price of pension services should be determined according to the supply-demand relationship of the market, or be paid according to the commodity exchange principle, and prices should be agreed on by both parties. The payment includes self-payment and government subsidies, so that pension service enterprises can obtain certain profits and are able to improve the quality and level of their services, thus the elderly can receive services which meet their needs and reach a professional level. Only by meeting these 3 basic requirements, can we form a developmental situation with win-win results for all sides and promote the sound development of the pension services industry.

Fifth, we should pay attention to relying on scientific and technological progress to promote the development of the pension services industry. In addition to such macroscopic aspects as system and mechanism, the development of the pension services industry has mainly three bottlenecks:

1. The scientific and technological level is low. Compared with other industries, the technological content of China's current pension services industry is low.

2. The professional degree is low. Practitioners basically have no high professional skills. There is a view in society that, a true heart and two hands can do pension services well, which is a misunderstanding in my opinion. The pension services industry is an industry with high professional degree.

3. We are short on professional talent. High-quality professional talents are few, and such reasons as working conditions and low salaries cause an outflow of most talent. To solve this problem, the National Working Commission on Aging proposed the concept of intelligent pensions in 2012, and plans to build 100 intelligent pension bases in China during the "12th Five-Year Plan" and the "13th Five-Year Plan". Meanwhile, we actively promote experimentation and practice of pension methods such as intelligent scientific and technological industrial parks for the elderly as well as intelligent pension experimental areas. We hope to be leaders in demonstrating how to create this kind of industry by establishing an incentive mechanism, so as to promote improvement in the scientific and technological level of China's pension services industry.

Friends, the development of the pension services industry is coming about in an era where there are also opportunities and challenges. I sincerely hope that the entire society can jointly cooperate in order to promote the sound development of the pension services industry and make more contributions to the well-being of the elderly. I wish the conference a complete success. Thank you!

# Speech by Zhu Zhongyi, Honorary Vice President of the China Real Estate Association and the Executive Director of the Elderly Settlement Committee, at the First International Pension Services Industry Fair

Director Zhu Yong has clearly talked about the macro situation just now, hoping for more coordination and cooperation with you. Just as leaders said earlier, the pension field has attracted much attention, including the attention of real estate enterprises. It is mainly because the industry regarding the elderly has a large market, great potential and many prospects. The macro policy environment is continuously improving, so it can be said that it has good prospects. However, under these circumstances, I think that enterprises should have a sense of responsibility and mission. On the one hand, our government should have perfect supporting policies; on the other hand, the enterprises should keep rational, and refine the market and the demands, noticing both potential demands and effective demands. I would like to talk about 4 issues from this point of view:

First, carefully carry out a market analysis for early-stage planning of the project. This is very important, because most real estate enterprises enter the industry dedicated to the elderly in the form of real estate basically. Objectively speaking, our society does not reach a consensus on the pension industry, but anyway we must have a pension infrastructure, including medical, rehabilitation and activity centers for the elderly, which is very important. In addition to the supporting facilities, we should also have numerous pension services. A community/residential district cannot be a pension service area if there are no pension service facilities and considerate pension service. Two problems should be identified: ① We should completely understand what China's pension policies involve, and which policies conform to our national situation. Whether model 9,064 or 9,073 is considered, most cases involve home-based care or community-based care for the elderly, under which circumstances, the primary task, according to the State Council, is to strengthen the planning and the construction of communities for the elderly. ② We should have excellent community care services for the elderly. Developmental enterprises should pay attention to this consideration when planning the development of new areas in the future. The Ministry of Housing and Urban-Rural

Development has issued a document involving the planning of the construction of pension service facilities; this document requires new residential areas to be equipped with pension service facilities. This objective needs the support of governmental policies. On-the-spot policies need the most attention.

Second, we should refine the market. Among the more than 200 million elderly people in China, more than 100 million live in rural areas. Most of the elderly living in cities choose home-based care or community-based care. Generally speaking, considering the number of families able to pay for the care of the elderly, the number of the elderly who truly hope to live their life outside of their homes or in a special pension service center is limited. Of course, the total number of these people may be large since China has a large population, but the market must be refined. Now, there are two problems regarding developmental enterprises: one is that the scale is large: the land area may be as large as 1,000 mu, 2,000 mu or 4,000 mu; the other problem is that the level is high: some pension service centers are luxurious, reaching a four-star or five-star category. However, the elderly do not go there to enjoy five-star hotels, but to have good pension services. Luxurious facilities are not practical for the elderly. In many foreign countries, the time limit of the housing property purchased by the aged is 30 years. Why is this? If the aged purchase their houses at the age of 60 or 70 years old, they will be 90 or 100 years old after 30 years, which is nearly the age limit of humans, and at that time the purchase of luxurious things by the elderly is of no practical significance; what they truly want to purchase is pension services. How to develop products suitable to the elderly is very important, and it requires market analysis. We are not thoughtful when making policies, but the Ministry of Land and Resources has recently introduced a policy regarding rules and regulations concerning land for pension service facilities. These have a narrow definition and refer to the land for pension service facilities, i.e. the land should be specifically used for housing facilities and sites where daily care and rehabilitation nursing services are provided for the elderly. Besides, there is a preference, i.e. rural construction land can be used for pension institutions, but only for units strictly dedicated to pension institutions. The land in vacant plants, schools and community buildings can only be preferential for non-profit pension service facilities. That is, the preferential policy specified in No. 35 document of the State Council regards non-profit institutions and pension institutions, but there is no preference for developmental enterprises including some policies on their land use. So, developmental enterprises should have a sense of responsibility and mission, keep rational and refine the targeted market and demands, and should not be without specific objectives. After entering the China Real Estate Association, I made two main suggestions: ① Formulate a plan for development. Excess real estate in China's third-tier and fourth-tier cities is due to housing purchase restrictions in first-tier cities during the years 2010 and 2011, which made large enterprises develop in third-tier and fourth-tier cities, leading to excessive development. Pension real estate must learn from this lesson. Any product has a problem of general rational structure and a problem involving the consumers' ability to pay, and this needs our consideration. ② Some experts say that, for the projects developed by developmental enterprises, constructors tend to be separate from operators. For example, the location of some pension service facilities is not convenient for their operation and management, so it would be better to negotiate with designers, operators and managers, in order to make the projects conform better to national standards. The latest construction standard is the construction and design specification for pension facilities implemented from May 1 this year. It is more important that pension bases are easy to operate and manage, or they will be difficult to use after the pension infrastructure has been completed.

Third, enterprises should deal with the relationship of construction with joint capital, operation and management. Referring to general practices overseas, pension institutions are completed with the cooperation of investors, constructors and operation and management units. In China, especially when developmental enterprises are involved, investors and developers are often the developmental enterprises, because developmental enterprises raise the funds. Large enterprises in China are often self-operated and self-managed, e.g. today's Sun City is operated by the investors themselves; however, many enterprises invite a third enterprise for the operation and management of the facility. Anyway, the relationship should be clearly established.

Fourth, we need to consider developmental modes. Currently, due to restrictions on land policies, developmental enterprises may choose to construct certain pension service facilities in some new residential areas, and hospitals in large residential areas. If there are pension services available, funds can be recovered for residential parts by adopting methods such as sales, membership and others; and cost can be recovered through operation and management services for the pension service facilities, so that continuous operation can be achieved. According to current policies, how to invest in the pension industry for non-profit institutions needs more research, because enterprises need to consider the problem of making a profit.

The Elderly Settlement Committee works under the guidance of the National Working Commission on Aging, and we cooperate continually with the China Silver Industry Association, including all meetings. We are launching the China Elderly Livability Pilot Project together with the China Silver Industry Association, and we have a very good team of experts. If you are interested in listing your project with our pilot demonstration project, please contact us.

Thank you!

# Speech by Wang Jun, Former Leader of the Discipline Inspection Group of the China National Tourism Administration of the Central Commission for Discipline Inspection, Honorary Deputy President of the China Tourism Association and President of the International Leisure Industry Association, at the Seminar on the Development of the Tourism Industry Regarding China's Ancient Towns

Ladies and gentlemen, all guests, good morning! I feel honored to be invited to attend China's Town Tourism Industry Development Conference and Project Promotion Conference. Currently, when developing a tourism economy, China should learn from some Western countries and developed countries regarding their theories, concepts and successful practices in the development of the leisure economy, which would be of great benefit to us. Our urbanization will create new thoughts and new ideas concerning these thoughts. According to our previous development status and basis, when stressing urbanization, we will bring some new thoughts and new methods of development to the departments that design our kind of tourism, to our real estate development departments and to our tourism industry. As we usually say, current real estate development is encountering difficulties and problems, which of course can be studied, analyzed and solved. Enterprises need to do research on real estate for tourism and pension development. Recently, I have found that many enterprises are carrying out research on how to develop and how to find a new way to revive these areas. Urbanization provides a window and a method for us, telling us to aim at urbanization. Development of a leisure tourism economy gives us some new enlightenment.

Of course, urbanization does not mean to make towns larger and wider. In my opinion, urbanization should be in line with the status of environmental resources and the characteristics of the towns; practical thinking that is most conductive to the status of economic and social development and to the overall objectives of the economic development should be adopted when planning and carrying out urbanization.

When I read the newspapers the day before yesterday, I saw that there is a town, governed by a prefect in the Zhejiang Province, which is to be built as a characteristic tourism town. This is good in Zhejiang Province, Jiangsu Province and many places in the suburbs of Beijing. So, urbanization includes 3 aspects. ① Urbanization shows our development objective. ② It also states that the process of urban development is not to create a modern city at one stroke. This process includes research on the characteristics of the towns, the environmental resources, population and culture, etc., so as to have a suitable process and trend of development. Accomplishment at one stroke often causes some problems, so you may have regrets after developing for a few years. ③ Urbanization indeed puts forward some new tasks and goals to enterprises and personnel engaged in tourism.

Hence, urbanization is an important and vivid issue, which should attract the attention of experts, entrepreneurs, and leaders in the tourism industry present and absent.

As time is limited, I'm not giving a lecture but mainly showing support for the conference, and expressing my own understanding of the meaning and task of the conference. Last, I wish the conference complete success and I hope everyone will return with fruitful results.

# Speech by He Guangye, President of the Asia–Pacific Tourism Organization, at the Seminar on the Development of the Tourism Industry for China's Ancient Towns

All leaders, guests, comrades and friends, good morning! The Dragon Boat Festival, a traditional festival in China, will be in two days' time. I would like to wish you a happy holiday and a happy family gathering! I'm glad you are attending today's grand meeting in such a busy schedule. I, on behalf of the Asia-Pacific Tourism Organization, want to extend a warm welcome and a heartfelt thanks to all guests!

With the arrival of summer in Beijing, the 3rd CIFTIS opens as scheduled. CIFTIS is a comprehensive international trade in services fair, whose most obvious characteristics are a large platform and high specifications. This is the first time that a forum regarding the tourism industry has been held at CIFTIS, which is of profound significance.

For the past few years, China's tourism industry has been developing steadily and rapidly, and now China has become a famous world tourism power. Currently, China has entered a new historical process of urbanization, which provides rare developmental opportunities and has an unprecedented impact on the development of China's tourism. Both the governmental departments for tourism and operators within tourism should conform to the strategic needs of urbanization. So, it is a rare opportunity to discuss these issues with you and carry out new research on new problems, new topics and on the new business of the development of tourism during urbanization; in this way we can achieve win-win results for the development of tourism. I wish the conference complete success and I also hope that you all enjoy yourselves in Beijing. Thank you!

# Speech by Fang Aiqing, Vice Minister of Commerce at the International Conference on China's Cultural Trade Development

Distinguished Vice President Li Wuwei, all guests, ladies and gentlemen,

Good afternoon! First of all, I, on behalf of the Ministry of Commerce of China and the organizing committee of the 3rd CIFTIS, would like to extend a welcome and thanks to all guests attending the International Conference on China's Cultural Trade Development!

Today, with the increasingly deepening mutual integration of world culture, economy, politics, science and technology, the cultural factors in economic and trade development are more and more important, so developing cultural trade is an important way to improve a country's cultural soft power. Cultural importation reflects the cultural tolerance and confidence of a country and a nation, while cultural exportation directly reflects the cultural influence of a country and a nation. Both reflect the hard power of cultural soft power and are a part of the make-up of culture. In the scenario of economic globalization, introducing the domestic market to the competition of the international market and making full use of the two markets will be conducive to encouraging China to achieve its historic aim of making the cultural industry be the national economy's pillar industry. Developing cultural trade is an important content for accelerating the transformation of the foreign trade development pattern. Cultural trade is characterized by less resource consumption, high added-value and more employment opportunities, especially the cultural value connotation, and it is a high-end field in international trade. Developing the cultural trade and expanding the cultural industry are conducive to optimizing the trade structure and pushing the development of related industries forward.

In recent years, China's foreign cultural trade has continuously developed, showing 4 characteristics: the first is that the scale has been in constant expansion. In 2013, the total import-export volume of China's cultural products reached 27.41 billion USD, including 25.13 billion USD for exports, 2.6 times that of 2006; the total import-export volume of cultural services was 9.56 billion USD, including 5.13 billion USD for exports, 3.2 times that of 2006. The second characteristic is that the structure has been gradually optimized. From 2001 to 2013, China's cultural service export increased by 26.3% on average, 7.2% higher than the average annual growth of cultural products. The proportion of cultural services in the total exportation of cultural products and cultural services rapidly increased from 9.1% to 17%. The third is that the new kind of cultural trade is developing vigorously. Currently, digitalized and networked technology is widely applied to the cultural industry. During this process, the cultural enterprises in new fields such as anime, games, film post-processing, and database service, are transforming the advantages of technology and cost into export competitiveness, enabling a rapid growth in the exportation of the cultural field with high technical requirements and mature industrialization conditions. The fourth characteristic is that the foreign investment objectives are increasingly diverse. In the past decade, China's cultural enterprises' investment objectives extended from constructing marketing channels to obtaining technology advantage, cost advantage and talent advantage, with a strong intention of expanding the industry chain upstream and downstream abroad. According to the statistics of the Ministry of Commerce, China's foreign direct investment in the culture, sports and entertainment industries rapidly increased from 760,000 USD in 2006 to 180 million USD in 2013. But compared with developed countries, China's foreign cultural trade is still at an initial stage for both scale and quality, which are mainly embodied in the following: cultural export enterprises have a small scale, the number of influential transnational cultural enterprises is small; there has been a deficit in trade in film and TV, publishing and commercial performance products for a long time, and policy environment supporting the development of cultural trade needs to be further optimized.

Ladies and gentlemen, in March 2014, the State Council officially issued the *Opinions on Accelerating Foreign Cultural Trade Development*, which comprehensively deployed the national foreign cultural trade work. This was an important measure for the development of the cultural industry, and for promoting Chinese culture to go out and improve its open economic level in the new era. We will firmly promote and implement all of the measures of the State Council, strengthen the policy guidance, optimize the market environment, expand the market subject, and improve the trade structure to further promote the development of foreign cultural trade.

1. Carry out the overall development to further play the role of developer of cultural trade in the going out strategy for Chinese culture. Chinese culture's going out cannot do without the mutual promotion and coordinated development of cultural exchanges, cultural communication and cultural trade. We will focus more on the role of enterprises and market operations in the going out strategy of Chinese culture, transforming it from sending out to selling out and from going out to going in, so as to promote cultural trade and investment cooperation to be important ways for Chinese culture to go out in the new era. In the meantime, we will enhance the government leadership and social participation, fully play the unique role of cultural exchanges and cultural communication, improve the levels of foreign

cultural exchanges and strengthen the building up of China's international communication capacity.

2. Deepen the reform to further simulate the enterprises' vitality on the cultural market. We will strongly promote reforms of the foreign investment system, revise the overseas investment management measures, simplify the overseas investment administrative licensing procedures including the cultural field, expand foreign investment cooperation in the cultural field, continue deepening the reforms of the foreign investment system, and promote the revision of the "three laws of foreign investment", to create a good environment for expanding the cultural opening-up. Recently, the Foreign Investment Project Approval Measures were officially issued, clearly pointing out that foreign investment has changed from full approval to limited approval. We will also implement more convenient Customs measures for the personnel of the enterprises when they go abroad on business.

3. Further optimize the export pattern of the foreign cultural trade. We will fully exploit the characteristics and advantages of cultural exportation in all regions, rely on the Shanghai Pilot Free Trade Zone and special Customs supervision zones, and establish cultural products and services export platforms, to form a cultural export pattern with the Yangtze River Delta, the Pearl River Delta and the Bohai Rim as the frontier and the vast central and western regions as the support. Meanwhile, we will make overall plans for various cultural trade promotion activities abroad, provide funds for qualified institutions and enterprises to hold cultural trade matching conferences, exhibitions and other activities, and promote the forming of a broad pattern of the international cultural market to consolidate the Chinese market, deepen the European and American markets and expand new markets.

4. Strengthen the efforts to further refine taxation and financial policies supporting the development of cultural trade. We will encourage and guide cultural enterprises to enhance innovation, provide support for cultural service exportation, overseas investments, marketing channel construction, market exploitation, public service platform construction, cultural trade talent training and other aspects ; implement zero tax rate or tax exemption for the exportation of cultural products and services encouraged by the country, support the integrated development of culture and technology, encourage enterprises to carry out technical innovation, promote cultural enterprises to actively utilize the advanced international technology, improve abilities in implementation, adoption and re-innovation, enhance financial services regarding credit, bonds, guarantees, insurance, foreign exchanges and other aspects, and greatly support cultural enterprises to go out.

5. Implement an effective connection to further improve the level of public services for enterprises to carry out trade investment activities. We will continue to enhance intellectual property protection in the cultural field to create a good environment for the healthy

development of domestic and foreign enterprises, and to strengthen the public information service of foreign cultural trade to provide foreign trade and investment information to cultural enterprises in order to exploit their international markets. Besides, we will promote the establishment of industrial intermediary organizations, focus on the development of exportation, industry self-regulation, international exchanges, talent training and other aspects, strengthen cultural trade statistics and publish unified data of cultural trade and foreign investment.

Ladies and gentlemen, Chinese culture is extensive and profound, with a long history which has made a unique contribution to human civilization, and it is a common spiritual treasure of the world. We'd like to raise the trade sail and start the cultural voyage so that we can make a contribution to cultural trade. I wish the conference complete success.

Thank you!

# Speech by Li Wuwei, " Father of China's Creative Industry" and Vice Chairman of the 11th CPPCC, at the International Conference on China's Cultural Trade Development

Distinguished guests, good afternoon!

Today I would like to talk about opportunities and challenges in Chinese enterprises' going out. Cultural prosperity is a strategic goal of development and this is a worldwide consensus, so all countries around the world are developing their cultures, and China is also developing its cultural products. In the scenario of economic globalization, as business subjects of the cultural industry, Chinese cultural enterprises are undertaking the mission of participating in and disseminating Chinese culture, and they are actively going abroad to enter the world market. The path for cultural enterprises to follow in going out has two aspects, namely, cultural trade and overseas investments. Cultural trade includes trade in cultural products and cultural trade in services; overseas investment includes direct investment and merger & acquisition. Overseas direct investment enables Chinese cultural enterprises to have subjects engaged in cultural business activities in the host country in order to disseminate Chinese culture more directly and more effectively.

The significance and responsibility of cultural enterprises' going out can be summarized in four points. First, this can accelerate the speed at which China's cultural enterprises can go out, which is conducive to disseminating Chinese culture and enhancing the world's understanding of China. Second, the acceleration of cultural enterprises' going out can promote the development of the cultural industry and quicken the pace of upgrading China's industrial structure. With low pollution and low consumption, cultural enterprises can also integrate into other industries so as to drive their development forward, thus driving the upgrading of the industrial structure. Third, the acceleration of cultural enterprises' going out can also improve China's soft power. Fourth, the acceleration of cultural enterprises' going out is conducive to increasing the demands for Chinese culture. Due to the increase in demands, industries will need to develop, thus increasing China's employment opportunities. The acceleration of cultural enterprises' going out can also improve the diathesis of our residents. The cultural enterprises' going out, through international exchanges and cooperation, can improve our innovation power and improve the innovation capacity of the enterprises in culture creation, so  it is conducive to increasing our overall cultural demands.

Next, we will talk about opportunities when cultural enterprises go out. China strongly supports cultural enterprises going out. On July 22, 2009, China issued the *Plan on Reinvigoration of the Cultural Industry*. With this favorable policy, in a short 4 years, from 2009 to 2012, foreign direct investment in China's culture, sports and entertainment industries increased by 10 times, from 17.96 million USD in 2009 to 196.34 million USD in 2012. In November 2012, General Secretary Hu Jintao stressed that, in the report of the 18th National Congress of the CPC, cultural innovation should be an important sector of self-improvement and self-development of the socialist system. In February 2014, Xi Jinping chaired the deliberation and approval of the *Implementation Plan on Deepening the Reform of the Cultural System*, which emphasized that the government should strengthen investments in the cultural industry and enhance financial support for Chinese cultural enterprises to go out.

The rise of China makes the world eager to get to know China and its culture in an unprecedented way. China's economic development ranks second in the world, and accordingly, culture should match the ranking. This year, a series of hits of Chinese TV plays in various countries and regions have confirmed this. According to the overseas broadcasting statistics of China's TV plays, many have entered the international market, such as *White Collar Apartment, New Shanghai Grand, Dwelling Narrowness, My Ugly Mother, Beautiful Daughter-in-Law Era, Jin Tailang's Happy Life, I am Special Forces, Empresses in the Palace, Treading on Thin Ice,* and *My Four Seasons.* It's not hard to see that the number of China's TV plays, broadcast overseas, has markedly increased since 2010, and the broadcasting range, which was limited to Asia, is now wider, expanding to such developed countries as the USA, Canada and Africa's friendly neighboring countries such as Tanzania. The popularity of *Beautiful Daughter-in-Law Era* in Africa triggers African people's advocating the image of a fashionable Chinese mother-in-law. The popularity of *I am Special Forces* in the USA presents a new appearance of Chinese soldiers, in the new era, to the USA. Although *My Four Seasons* has not been broadcast in the USA, it has already triggered a strong comparison of the Chinese and the Americans, between a Chinese uncle, acted by Yang Lixin, and an American uncle acted by Kevin Spacey in *House of Cards*.

There are quite advantageous resources for our cultural enterprises to go out, since China is one of the four ancient civilizations with a history of thousands of years, and China is also a multinational country with historic culture and ethnic diversity. Historic culture and ethnic diversity provide important resources and conditions for Chinese cultural enterprises to go out. The exploitation of these resources still needs to be innovative. According to the statistics of world cultural and natural heritages, China has obvious advantages in cultural enterprises' going out. By the end of 2011, China had ranked second in the world's cultural and natural heritage sites with 42 world cultural and natural heritage sites, indicating that China has good resource advantages and potentials to carry out the exportation of its cultural trade internationally. The specific ranking in number and proportion is as follows: Spain ranks first in the world, China second, Italy third, France fourth and Germany fifth. In terms of the number of national cultural heritage sites and natural heritage sites, Spain has 43 items, China 42, Italy 40, France 33 and Germany 32.

At present, China's economy is developing well, the foreign exchange reserve is rich, with the appreciation of the RMB, and service agencies are expanding, all of which support our cultural enterprises in their going out. As the largest foreign exchange reserve country in the world, China's huge foreign exchange reserve is a strong economic background for our cultural enterprises to go out; the appreciation of the RMB reduces the overseas investment cost of our cultural enterprises; our commercial service agencies are distributed globally and have gradually become mature and strong, providing trade guarantees for our cultural enterprises in their going out and reducing their trade cost and trade risk. Without the support of the international branches of the Bank of China, it would have been difficult for Wanda Real Estate's overseas to finance the merger and acquisition of the American AMC; the expansion of financial service agencies represented by China International Capital Corporation Limited (CICC) brings more professional and more efficient financial consultant services for overseas mergers and acquisitions of our cultural enterprises. With financial support, the Wanda Group achieved the merger and acquisition of AMC , a film platform.

There are many opportunities for our cultural enterprises to go out, accompanied by challenges. One of these challenges is that our cultural enterprises do not have sufficient experience in overseas direct investment. Chinese enterprises started to carry out direct investment abroad from the beginning of this century, so we have a short history to go out to the world, while the overseas direct investment of cultural enterprises has even a shorter history. In 2012, the acquisition of AMC by Wanda was the first trial for China's cultural enterprises. The merger started earlier, but it did notcome into the people's view until 2012. Overseas direct investment, especially in the form of merger and acquisition, is facing huge legal risks and investment risks. The acquisition in the USA may be disapproved or disagreed to, but it is now more convenient after some development of China's free trade zones. Legal risks are mainly trade risks due to the unfamiliarity with foreign laws; the greatest risk is the trade examination and the approval of risk. Almost all countries have set review procedures for cultural enterprises which want to merge and acquire local enterprises through overseas investments. Since culture belongs to ideology, it is difficult to define the examination and approval standards of foreign enterprises of countries with different ideologies, so there is much uncertainty for Chinese enterprises to get approval for their merging and acquiring of cultural enterprises overseas. The investment risks are mainly trade risks due to the inability to correctly judge the value of the subject matter of trade. As an intelligence-intensive industry, the value of cultural enterprises usually lies in the creativity of the staff, but it is difficult to accurately anticipate the sustainability of the staff's stability and creativity , which undoubtedly brings more trade risks to overseas mergers and acquisitions of cultural enterprises. In its first trial in merger and acquisition of overseas cultural enterprises, an important reason why Wanda chose the cinema operator AMC, as the subject matter of its merger and acquisition, is that AMC's core value lies in such tangible assets as cinema and film screen, which enables Wanda to more accurately estimate the company's value and continuously control its assets after the merger and acquisition. To merge and acquire a film production company which takes creativity of the screenwriter, director, actors, producer and other staff as the core, the difficulty in judging the value  and the continuous control will greatly increase. The acquisition of a production company is different from that of an exhibition company;  the latter is easy to estimate while the former is difficult to estimate.

Second, we do not have sufficient capacity for creative development in cultural resources. Although we have abundant cultural resources, the development of the cultural industry is still at an initial stage, and we do not have sufficient creativity to develop wonderful products with cultural resources to win the foreigners' praise. To successfully go out, cultural enterprises must strengthen their integrated development of technology and culture, so as to carry out creative development. Therefore, although we have lots of resources, the foreigners should take and develop them if we have no creative development. For example, the Americans are carrying out creative development with China's Hua Mulan story; the Americans also used China's panda and Chinese Kung Fu to create the film *Kung Fu Panda*. The two films have made a lot of money in China, so we must strengthen our creative development. During the development, we also need to combine technology, such as the 3D and the 4D. The West Lake of Hangzhou is world-famous. Songcheng Stock Corporation createda humane scenic spot in Hangzhou, and the show "Legend of Romance", during a large shopping festival, made the tourists at home and abroad feel the Chinese culture. In 2012, Hangzhou received more than 3 million foreign tourists, which is an important starting point for Chinese enterprises to go out and show  Chinese culture. Thus, Hangzhou utilizes and develops cultural resources. Taking historical allusions, myths and legends as the base point, Hangzhou integrates world dances, songs and acrobatic art and utilizes modern high-tech means to create a dreamy image, making the people feel a thousand years in one day. The "Legend of Romance" is now the theatrical performance with the most performance sessions and the greatest number of audiences in the world last year, and it is considered one of the three world-famous shows by the overseas media. Historically, we have many successfully-developed cases, such as the "Impression Liu

Sanjie", which was developed by using folk singing in the antiphonal style of the Zhuang nationality. In addition, the "Tianmen Fairy Fox" of Zhangjiajie adapts a historical legend, "Woodcutter Liu Hai", to a literary and artistic show. The "Show Shanghai to the World" is also successful.

We also need to promote creative cultural development and give full play to our advantages in cultural resources. A successful case is Shenzhen Huaqiang Holdings Limited which has built some theme parks by combining culture, such as Shenzhen OCT, Happy Valley and Fantawild Adventure Theme Park, which are all shown, with the combination of technology, as theme parks. Huaqiang is now going out to the world, and it has been invited by Iran and South Africa to build theme parks for them. Its development trend is similar to Disney's worldwide development. In addition to the two resources, mentioned earlier, developed by the USA , Korea and Japan also utilize our cultural resources in *Romance of Three Kingdoms* and *Journey to the West* to develop animation and games. We must have creativity to develop our own resources and try to develop by combining technology and culture to avoid the utilization of our resources by other countries.

Third, our cultural trade in services is underdeveloped. Our exportation of cultural products ranks first in the world, but our exportation of cultural services is low. We have a favorable balance in the exportation of cultural products and a deficit in the exportation of cultural services, and the deficit is severe. Comparing the overall condition of the import-export trade balance of China's cultural trade from 1997 to 2006, the data show that China's cultural trade develops rapidly, but our cultural trade in services has a small scale although the exportation of our cultural products ranks first a continuous deficit occurs together with an overall continuous expansion, which has become an important part of China's overall trade in services deficit. How to turn the scale of the severe deficit in trade in services is a challenge for China's cultural enterprises to go out.

Fourth, the overseas Chinese were the main consumer groups for cultural exportation in the past, lacking the support of international consumer groups. Due to language, the traditional culture and the difference in living habits, destination of our cultural exportation is mainly Hong Kong, Taiwan, Southeast Asia, the USA, Canada, Australia and Europe, which are the main areas gathering lots of ethnic Chinese. The overseas Chinese have a natural affinity with the local Chinese culture, so they can easily accept it. Take the book copyright as an example. In 2010, China exported a total of 3,600 book copyrights, and the first 5 destinations were Southeast Asia, Taiwan, Hong Kong, the USA and Canada; the exportation of book copyrights to the five regions accounted for about 67% of China's total exports. China's cultural export areas are narrow and concentrated, and the main consumer groups are the ethnic Chinese, lacking the support of wider international consumer groups. *Empresses in the Palace* is receiving a good response after it was first broadcast on the Chinese TV Station in the USA, and now is going to be broadcast on the English TV Station in the USA, after having been edited by an American team. This is just the beginning for Chinese TV series to go to international mainstream consumer groups, but China's cultural enterprises still have a long way to go to becoming international. Language is a problem. How to do translation work for our enterprises' going out? This needs our government's support. For example, the Korean government helps its enterprises translate Korean into the the language of various countries helps them export to those countries. That's why the Korean wave is popular.

Fifth, we lack internationally-influential brands. America's dominance in the world's cultural field was jointly created by its regional brands such as Hollywood and Broadway, enterprise brands such as Disney and Fox, role brands such as Snow White and Mickey Mouse and star brands such as Tom Cruise and Brad Pitt. Good brands for cultural exportation need both product brands and enterprise brands;  however, China currently lacks influential brands. China is still at a stage, in various international cultural exchange activities, where such folk-custom works as paper-cut, clay figurine, embroidery, red lantern and Terra-Cotta Warriors, as well as other unearthed cultural relics, play the leading role. We have few influential dramas, songs and dances as well as film and TV works abroad, very few influential cultural enterprises and stars abroad. The lack of brands makes it harder for China's cultural enterprises to go out. We need more star brands such as Jackie Chan and Jet Li to increase the international influence of Chinese films and help more enterprises to go out to the world.

Sixth, the short-time development of China's cultural industry and the separate management of segmented industries cause insufficient scales of cultural enterprises. At present, good public properties of culture are overemphasized while the industrial nature is ignored . In the past several decades, China's cultural industry has been operated as a cause, not as an industry, by the public institutions led by the government. The cultural industry is now at an initial stage, so the scales of cultural enterprises are generally small, lacking economies of scale. Minister Fang has just mentioned this problem. We lack large-scale enterprises. Since different administrative authorities manage different segmented industries, our main cultural business is concentrated on some industries, lacking synergy among segmented industries. Take the listed companies as an example. The listed companies in the same film and TV sector almost have no business overlap in the segmented industries, such as film & TV, advertising and publishing. For example, Huayi Brothers Media Group and Enlight Media, two listed companies, are not engaged in publishing business, and other listed companies in the advertising sector are also not engaged in film and TV business.

The lack of scale effect and synergy makes it difficult for China's cultural enterprises compete with US comprehensive media giants. Take Huayi Brothers and CBS as an example of the huge difference between our company and the same company in the US. The two companies have a very close profit growth rate and return on equity, but both asset size and main business  revenues of CBS are more than 60 times those of Huayi Brothers. In addition to the film and TV production company, CBS also has multiple operation businesses including advertising, publishing, broadcasting and TV stations. Enlight Media's main business revenue is 1.034 billion USD, Disney's is 42.2 billion USD, Time Warner's is 27.95 billion USD and China's Huayi Brothers is only 1.386 billion RMB.

Based on the opportunities and challenges, we will propose some countermeasures and suggestions for going out. First, enhance the originality of China's cultural enterprises. Second, accelerate the scientific and technological innovation of China's cultural enterprises, and combine cultural industry with technology, so as to attain our status in the world with scientific and technological innovation and cultural creativity. Third, accelerate the innovation of the cultural management system and change the government's cultural management function which was put forward in the Third Plenary Session of the 18th Central Committee of the CPC. Fourth, enhance the international marketing concept and try to create more cultural brands; we also need to accelerate the building up of brands. Fifth, give full play to the impetuses of the ethnic Chinese all over the world. The ethnic Chinese love Chinese culture, and they will help promote our culture overseas.

To revive China, a cultural renaissance is needed. As the second largest economy in the world, China's culture needs to match our economic development. Only when Chinese culture goes out to the world can there be a place for China in the world's cultural market competition, and China can be a cultural power and thus a powerful countryin the world.

Thank you!

# Speech by Liu Jun, Deputy Director General of the State Post Bureau, at the 2014 China Express Industry (International) Development Conference

Distinguished guests, friends, ladies and gentlemen,

Good morning! This is a get-together of the express staff. At this moment, we congratulate you on convoking the 2014 China Express Industry (International) Development Conference on behalf of the State Post Bureau, and give a sincere welcome and thanks to the attending leaders, guests and friends from enterprises and media.

The express industry is a key component of the modern service industry, and is strategically significant for boosting E-commerce, the development of the modern logistics industry, improving the manufacturing of industrial competition, promoting trade and investment, and driving economic growth forward. It plays a key role in the making of national economic restrictions, carrying out the transformation of the developmental mode and the promotion of social employment. In recent years, China's express industry has achieved a sound development, and processed 9.19 billion pieces of express mail in 2013, an increase of 43.5% on average in the past 5 years. The business scale ranks No. 2 in the world. Our maximum daily processing volume is more than 65 million pieces; the employees of the industry are more than 1 million and we provide services to more than 5,000 express consumers. According to the work report by the State Council this year, we need to intensify the reform of the circulation system, remove any gates barring a united nationwide market, reduce the costs of logistics and promote the development of logistics delivery, the express mail service and online shopping. The express industry was mentioned in the work report of the government for the first time, and this marks an improvement in the influences of the express industry on economic society and indicates the direction for the development of the express mail service in the future.

At present, the basic conditions of a long-term good development of Chinese economic society have not been changed. As a key component of the postal service industry, the main problem of the express industry is that the industry's developing capability and proficiency cannot meet the people's increasing demands nor adapt to the social and economic development. Meanwhile, we can see that, with the continuous advancement of the all-round expanding reforms, in particular the optimization and perfection of the comprehensive transportation and traffic system, the express industry will encounter many more opportunities for development. Our intrinsic power and innovation performance will be intensified day by day, and all the industry will enter a brand-new stage that is increasingly efficient.

Facing new situations and new mechanisms of development, the express industry, according to the general philosophy of focusing on reforms, promoting development and benefiting the people, and according to the developmental concept of safety fundamentals, development and service foremost, seizes on the strategy of transformation and upgrading, it keeps the momentum of positive development, works on quality, seeks benefits from service proficiency, stabilizes a base of safe operation and pushes an increase in the efficiency of the industry. The State Post Bureau is encouraging the programs of establishing an express industry in the western area and in rural areas, of combining the development of "bring-in" and "going global"; moreover, it actively promotes the development of a link between the express industry and the manufacturing industry, it continues to reinforce its support of online shopping, solves bottlenecks of the express industry, issues a series of policies in industry security supervision, the building up of a credit system, the implementation of service standards, building a mechanism of self-discipline and professional talent training. All of the above are core issues to be discussed at the conference.

Against such a background, the 2014 China Express Industry(International)Development Conference was convened to determine the theme of "A Credit Service and Combined Development so as to Share the Future". With the platform of CIFTIS, it is able to unite developmental resources, gather industrial developmental wisdom, discuss hot issues, keys and trends for the development of the express industry strategically and globally, advance strategic cooperation in express service, inspire non-exhaustive power of sustainable development of reform and innovation, build enterprising values and an industrial culture, and advance the modern, international and market-oriented development of the express industry.

This conference is solemn, simple and fruitful, and the issues under discussion include integrating the development of the express industry, online shopping, the financial industry and the manufacturing industry, corporate management, brand-building and service quality enhancement, the application of information technology to the express industry and a strategy for internationalized development, etc. These issues approach industrial demands, focus on the developmental frontier, and have been actively called upon by express enterprises, experts, scholars and related industries. A key agenda is included in the conference. That is to obtain strategic cooperation. Compared with the conference last year, the signing coverage is wider, the contents are richer, there are more diverse forms and the amount of those signing in has broken the limit.

I hope that the signing parties will be able to take advantage of the opportunities for cooperation and realize the great objective of win-win development. I also believe that the successful convening of the conference and supporting activities will expand the developmental space for express service, create brand value, and continuously enhance the quality of the service. All of you are expected to make efforts to demonstrate the surprising achievements attained by the express industry, look forward to the future, move forward in the exploration of new areas for cooperation, bring more resources to use in the express industry, realize a rapid, healthy and safe development and contribute to building a well-off society. To conclude, may the 2014 China Express Industry (International) Development Conference be a complete success. Thank you!

# Speech by Li Huide, First Vice President and Secretary–General of the China Express Association, at the 2014 China Express Industry (International) Development Conference

Distinguished guests, friends, ladies and gentlemen,

Good morning! The 2014 China Express Industry(International)Development Conference was solemnly opened. As the sponsor of this conference, on behalf of the China Express Association, I'd like to extend my sincere greetings and sincere thanks to the attending guests, delegates and friends from the media circle.

This conference specially invites leaders of the National Development and Reform Commission, the Ministry of Commerce, the Ministry of Public Security, the Ministry of State Security, the Ministry of Transport, the General Administration of Customs, the Civil Aviation Administration of China, the National Railway Administration, and the All-China Federation of Industry & Commerce. It is also supported by the State Post Bureau and the Secretary of the Party Committee, Director Ma. the Deputy Director Liu Jun gave the opening speech to welcome the arrival of all guests.

As a key component of the 3rd CIFTIS, the China Express Industry (International) Development Conference has been convened for two sessions. With the theme of "Credit Service and Combined Development to Share the Future", the conference invites competent government bodies, industrial research institutes, financial service institutes, electronic business platforms and well-known domestic and overseas express enterprises, experts and scholars to express their opinions on the new subject of the development of the express industry in their own fields. This conference discusses hot issues such as how the express industry keeps a foothold on credit in order to tackle the service requirements of the express industry, how to promote the coordinated development of the express industry, E-commerce and the manufacturing industry, how to share the future and combined development of local express enterprises and the capital market and participating in international competition.

As Deputy Director Liu Jun has just pointed out, the CPC Central Committee and the State Council give sufficient confirmation and positive encouragement to the express industry. The State Post Bureau proposes a macroscopic plan for industrial development under the new situations, and directs the future of the industry. With innovation as the driving force and reform as the engine, how to accelerate the reform of the express industry, upgrade the industry, improve the industrial competitive force and make the express service system perfect in future years will be the main rhythm of the industrial development.

The industrial conference not only leads the development of the industry, but it also brings opportunities for cooperation to the express industry and industries of the upper and the lower reaches. The signing ceremony of the express industry which will be held in the afternoon will push the conference to a climax. Leaders of the State Post Bureau and the People's Government of Beijing Municipality will witness the signing ceremony. The projects to be signed involve the strategic cooperation among the China Express Association and aviation, electronics, commerce and other industrial associations, and the overall cooperation between express enterprises and E-commerce platforms; the value of the signed projects is worthy of expectations. The industrial conference and the signing ceremony will increase the scientific development of the express industry, reinforce the communication with industrial management, research institutes, finance, the manufacturing industry, and it will also encourage enterprises to focus on progress in science and technology, on scientific management and on standard operations. I believe that China's express industry can seize the prime opportunity period for the overall intensification of reforms and economic globalization and realize a great leap forward in the development of the express industry.

Today, we are significantly discussing the theme of "credit service and combined development to share in the future of the Chinese express industry". By calling the conference, we are reinforcing the foundation, planning on a long-term basis, and building the top express services with our efforts. Thank you to the leaders attending the conference. Thank you all!

# Speech by Wang Feng, Director General of the Market Supervision Department of the State Post Bureau, at the 2014 China Express Industry (International) Development Conference

Distinguished leaders, guests, ladies and gentlemen,

Good morning! First, I'd like to congratulate the organizers on calling the 2014 China Express Industry (International) Development Conference and extend thanks to all circles for your care, help and support of the express industry. Now, I will give a speech with the theme of "Credit Service and Combined Development to Share the Future".

An American author, Thomas Loren Friedman, wrote in the work *The World is Flat*, that in an era of globalization, in a world that is conveniently and closely interconnected due to information technology, worldwide market of labor and products is shared; modern communication technology solves the issue of information exchanges and the modern financial system makes it possible for the funds to circulate worldwide. The developed express network transfers objects fast, consumers can buy commodities from any place without leaving home and dealers can sell commodities to every corner of the world without a distribution channel. The manufacturer can allocate production according to resources, change the traditional mode of production and minimize the costs. The express industry is changing our production and life, potentially. In the past 3 years, the Chinese express industry has maintained an annual growth of 10%, and the business volume and income increased by 2 times and 1.5 times, respectively. The business volume in 2013 reached 9.2 billion pieces, an increase of 62% compared with the previous year, and the business income was 144.2 billion RMB, an increase of 37% compared with the previous year. At present, the daily average processing capacity is more than 30 million pieces, the maximum daily processing capacity reaches 65 million pieces, and the employees are more than 10 million. The layout, made up of various ownerships, such as state-owned, private and foreign capital, has been formed.

The satisfaction of the express service in 2013 was 72.7 points, 1 point greater than that in 2012, having achieved an increase for five consecutive years. In the second half of the year 2013, the express service process in key areas was 58.18 hours, having improved for four consecutive years. The industry transmits values of credit service and transmits its positive energy. In the past year, the environment of industrial development was optimized, the

*Management for Express Service Market* was revised and the *Express Service Code* was listed in the legislation plan of the State Council. We are striving for a policy to change business tax into value-added tax, and jointly release a guide to advance the development of express services and the manufacturing industry, to promote the industry in combination with the industrial chain, the supply chain and the service chain of production and consumption. We would also like to jointly release a guide to and industrial standards for reinforcing and improving city delivery, to solve the bottleneck of the "last kilometer" of delivery.

The leaders of the CPC Central Committee and the State Council attach great importance to the development of the express industry. Prime Minister Li Keqiang praised the express staff and said that the express industry was related to national livelihood. He also said: "You are carrying commodities, passing the ideas of friends and relatives to others, and delivering the warmth of the Spring Festival and happiness to thousands of households. The express industry was the Black horse of the Chinese economy. I hope you speed up and achieve success. While the express industry is developing rapidly, the quality of the services is low, and the proficiency of the development and the safety issues are evident, which will have an impact on the long-term development of the express industry."

The first issue is the quality of the services; the most serious issue is the complaint by consumers about delays in the delivery and delivery service, accounting for over 80% of the valid complaints. Some enterprises only focus on front-end service but ignore the post service. The express industry does not match individualized demands well, the quality of the regional service fluctuates and overall development is affected.

The second issue is the low level of development, which is a major problem that the industry faces. With the global competition, the level of "going global" is very low. The enterprises focus on eastern areas and urban areas, and the express service covering Western China and the rural areas has a long way to go. Low-level, low-price and homogeneous competition are serious; there is a long way to a clear market segment, a perfect system of service and a developed product system with a rich value-added business.

The third is the channel and security issue. The employers do not focus much attention on security issues and their investments on these issues are insufficient, thus incurring information disclosure on the customers, bad positioning of safety supervision and a lot of hidden problems regarding safety. Compared with the scale which has continuously increased, the pressure from security supervision has increased day after day.

As for problems in development, we will improve the proficiency of development and promote sustainable, healthy and safe development. We will:

1. Improve the express service for online shopping, drive the enterprises to invest in the transportation network, distribution centers, operation networks and other infrastructures,

Part III   Summary of Speeches at the Summit High-level Forum

encourage the enterprises to develop diverse and individualized product systems, and provide cash on delivery, goods verification and other value-added services. Establish a mechanism for coordination, and push information sharing and standard interfacing forward.

2. Drive the express service to better serve the cross-border exportation of E-commerce retail and push the General Office of the State Council to implement the *Opinions on Policy Supporting Cross-border Exportation of E-commerce Retail*, encourage and support key domestic express enterprises to expand their overseas markets, establish a cross-border network by cooperating and M&A (Mergers and Acquisitions), cooperate with the Ministry of Commerce and the General Administration of Customs, etc. to do research and improve the development of E-commerce and express services, make the environment of the cross-border E-commerce customs clearance perfect, and boost the development of online shopping.

3. Push forward the coordinated development of express services and the manufacturing industry, intensify the support for the logistics of the manufacturing industry by express services, establish warehousing and distribution centers at the bases and at the industrial parks of the manufacturing industry, accelerate the construction of warehousing and distribution, encourage manufacturers to rely on express enterprises to perform comprehensively integrate and distribute deliveries, and lead the express enterprises to establish long-term strategic and cooperative relations with large manufacturers.

4. Kick off the program of the express industry in rural areas and westward expansion, encourage express enterprises to set up bases in rural areas, extend the network, and facilitate the farmers to enjoy the online shopping service. After having taken traffic location and business trends into account, accelerate the construction of the Western China express network, promote the upgrading of the consumption environment in the western areas, coordinate with local governments to boost the construction of the Taobao (online shopping) village and make the channels towards the east smooth for agricultural by-products with local characteristics.

5. Push forward the last 1-km of express service. Commercial authorities carry out demonstration projects for joint development in both the node city of the express service and the E-commerce demonstration area; also drive the express enterprises to carry out delivery service modes with commercial organizations, convenience service facilities, community service organizations, authorities and school administrations and a third party's cooperative enterprises to explore new service modes. Reinforce and improve a guide on the management of urban delivery, solve the traffic and stop problematic issues of delivery.

6. Encourage the innovation of the express service and the progress of science and technology, prepare the development index regarding the express industry, and establish a comprehensive assessment system reflecting the development of the industry. Carry out

standardization, automation and informatization construction, accelerate the converting and applying of express achievements, apply green gas emission and measurement standards for the express service, and issue technical requirements on the non-motor elements of express services.

7. Optimize economic license flow of express services, establish green channels for business, implement registration management rules, establish registration authorities, simplify registration procedures, and apply registration for terminal service networks.

8. Intensify the supervision of the express service, start the construction of the credit system, and establish a credit rating mechanism subject to indexes such as service commitment fulfillment, service standard performance, legal operations and safety management. Reinforce corporate self-discipline and social supervision, continue to perform satisfaction surveys and testing, increase the strength of the publicity of results, boost the system operation of complaint information, fully make the function of the complaint system to protect the consumers' rights and interests and improve the quality of the industrial service.

9. Speed up the building of talent teams. Continue to manage the employee's training and appraisal of occupational skills, improve the quality of the staff and increase the ratio of qualification-bearing, drive some enterprises with these conditions to apply the system of working with certificates, carry out the construction of express websites, provide convenience for the staff, continue to exercise the talent training program, encourage colleges to offer specialty courses of study in the field of express services and urgently train the required talents.

10. Concentrate on guaranteeing the development of security within the industry. Reinforce the security duties of shippers, enterprises and postal administration, prepare standards and codes for the safety production equipment of the postal industry, and boost the enterprises to improve safety, make the mechanisms of joint operation perfect, intensify security prevention in key areas and key channels, reinforce measures of security inspection in special areas, implement the management code of personal information security and guarantee information security.

That's the end of my speech! May the 2014 China Express Industry (International) Development Conference be a complete success. Thank you!

# Speech by Cao Jiachang, Deputy Director General of the Department of Western Asian and African Affairs of the Ministry of Commerce, at the 2014 China Express Industry (International) Development Conference

Distinguished guests, friends and participating delegates,

Good morning! I am very pleased to attend the 2014 China Express Industry (International) Development Conference. First, I'd like to extend my warm congratulations to the Conference on behalf of the Department of Western Asian and African Affairs of the Ministry of Commerce, express my sincere thanks to the sponsor of the conference. I believe that the conference plays a positive role in improving service awareness and the proficiency of the express industry in China by accelerating, transforming, upgrading, expanding the internationalized developmental space and participating in international competition.

Since 2013, the world's economy has been showing a poor recovery and the international market demand is low; the prime time of foreign trade since China's entry into the WTO will never come back and the situation is very complicated. In 2013, although China became the largest trading country in the world, the total import-export volume reached 4.16 trillion USD, with a rate of increase of only 7.6%, the lowest in the past 30 years. Against the background of a poor rate of growth for foreign trade, the cross-border E-commerce business developed rapidly, becoming the field with the fastest growth in importation and exportation. The figures show that, till the end of 2013, there were more than 20 enterprises engaging in the online import and export business, and the annual amount of cross-border E-commerce transactions reached 3.3 trillion RMB. In the past 5 years, the annual average rate of increase has been 31%, an increase from 4% to 12% of China's total imports.

In the year 2014, the recovery of the world's economy improved, the increase became impressive, but it was still risky, and international competition was fiercer. Although China's foreign trade has increased stably, it still faces many difficulties and challenges. In the first quarter of 2014, the total import-export volume, and the exports diminished, which had never happened in the past 30 years or since the reform and the opening-up. Such a poor performance shows that the complicated situation of foreign trade cannot be underestimated.

For this reason, the Ministry of Commerce and other competent authorities, will make efforts to ensure the stable growth of imports and exports; they will release policies that are aimed at stabilizing the growth of foreign trade; they will further improve convenience trade, and build a more relaxed environment for foreign trade enterprises. Meanwhile, the export growth points should be analyzed, including pushing cross-border E-commerce and other emerging business forms forward, encouraging enterprises to increase investments in technological innovation, exploring overseas markets with cross-border E-commerce and expanding trade related to China.

Present delegates, since the year 2013, the Ministry of Commerce and the National Development and Reform Commission have released the *Opinions on Policy Supporting Cross-border E-commerce Retail Export*, and the Notice on Building an E-commerce Model City in Dongguan and other 29 cities. The General Administration of Customs has also reformed the supervision of the customs clearance mode and increased the support and guarantee of science and technology, so as to speed up the sharing of information between electronic port platforms and E-commerce dealers. The release of these advantageous policies will create a sound environment for the further development of cross-border E-commerce in China.

The logistics industry is an accelerator promoting national economic development, and it is vital for optimizing resource allocation, adjusting the economic structure, improving the investment environment, increasing the comprehensive national strength, the corporate competitiveness and realizing sustainable economic development. As for the cross-border E-commerce business, with the increasing scale of the market and the development of express services, it will provide a new round of upgrading that will lead to further development.

To present delegates, in the past half century, China and Africa have established a comprehensive strategic partnership, and their economic and trade cooperation represents the satisfying achievements obtained under the framework of the Forum on China-Africa Cooperation (FOCAC). The amount of Sino-Africa bilateral trade reached a record high of 210.2 billion USD in 2013. Resource-based products and characteristic products of Africa, including coffee, were sold in China. Although China is far away from Africa, with the continuous development of bilateral economic and trade cooperation, there is great potential and opportunities for cooperation in cross-border E-commerce and cross-border logistics, with these aspects:

First, high-speed growth of the total amount of trade. In the year 2000, the Sino-Africa trade stepped into a milestone of 10 billion USD. Afterwards, the Sino-Africa trade grew fast, and we almost became Africa's largest bilateral trading partner. Since 2009, China has become Africa's largest trading partner for five consecutive years, and the Sino-Africa trade in 2013 was 210 billion USD. Our exports to Africa were 92.8 billion USD, which was contributed by the express industry and cross-border business. Regarding Sino-Africa trade, South Africa, Angola, Nigeria, Egypt and Albania are the most important partners for us and they are also our key export markets.

Second, E-commerce-based trade structure. In the 1980s and 1990s, the commodities exported to Africa by China included light industrial goods, food and chemical products. Since the year 2000, the exportation of machinery and electronic products, etc. has been increasing, accounting for 50% ; the exportation of textiles accounts for 20% . The importation and exportation of these consumables are processed by E-commerce operations.

Third, Africa's infrastructures have been modernized. The African government pays great attention to the construction of infrastructures, and the international society also focuses on the improvement of African infrastructures. Supported by China's technology and funds, Chinese enterprises undertake the building of housing, bridges, railways, airports, hospitals and a series of projects that contribute to the improvement of infrastructures in African countries. Traffic and communication in South Africa, Nigeria, Egypt and Kenya can meet hardware conditions for the rapid development of E-commerce business.

Fourth, convenient trade policy. The African government attaches great importance to the improvement of trade and investment policies, hoping to develop the manufacturing industry by expanding trade and importing foreign trade, in order to increase the export capacity and expand local employment. African countries have made outstanding achievements in regional integration. The East African Community (EAC), the Southern African Development Community (SADC), and the Economic Community of West African States (ECOWAS) have played active roles in economic development. China follows the principle of mutual benefits, carries out trade with the African countries according to WTO rules, and has signed bilateral trade protocols with 46 countries. Chinese enterprises have built six economic and trade cooperation parks in five African countries, actively participating in the construction of railways, highways, aviation networks as well as the construction andoperation of key coastal harbors to provide advantageous conditions for carrying out cooperation on Sino-Africa bilateral logistics.

To leaders and attending delegates, since the beginning of the new century, Sino-Africa trade relations have begun the best period for all-round development. The bilateral political relations are close, economic and trade relations are developing continuously, and cooperation in all fields is fruitful. In the year 2013, Chinese President Xi Jinping visited Africa for the first time after taking office. Prime Minister Li Keqiang also visited Africa in May, 2014. At present, the development of China and Africa is proceeding step by step and is complementary, so cooperation is promising. As the sector in charge of Sino-Africa economic and trade cooperation in China, the Department of Western Asian and African Affairs of the Ministry of Commerce is willing to provide more support for cooperation on cross-border E-commerce and logistics for China and the African countries.

Finally, may the conference be a complete success. Thank you!

# Speech by Fang Zhipeng, Deputy General Manager of the China Postal Express & Logistics Company Limited, at the 2014 China Express Industry (International) Development Conference

Distinguished leaders and guests,

Hello, everyone! On behalf of China Postal Express & Logistics, I will make a presentation here to talk about how to build the comprehensive service platform of cross-border E-Commerce and how China Postal Express & Logistics provides an integrated logistics solution. The previous leaders have made presentations from a macroscopic point of view, while my speech concerns the operational plan from a microscopic point of view.

I. Current situations of the cross-border E-commerce market. In recent years, the appreciation of the Renminbi (the Chinese currency) has caused a drop in foreign trade, and the economic crises in Europe and America, trade frictions, etc. have resulted in a slow development of mass export trade. However, with the development of Internet technology and the boosting of E-commerce platforms, the development of online trade and marketing and the maturity of online payment, have enhanced the social requirements of cross-border E-commerce. Currently, the bottleneck is the solution of logistics.

In 2013, there were 200,000 dealers engaging in cross-border E-commerce and 5,000 platform enterprises, with a total volume of 3.1 trillion RMB and an annual growth of over 30%. However, the growth of imports and exports has fallen in the last few years, 7.5% for 2011, 9.6% for 2012 and 12.1% for 2013; cross-border E-commerce is keeping a growth rate of approximately 30%. The import and export structure of cross-border E-commerce is out-of-balance, dominant in exports, with 2.7 trillion RMB of exports in 2013, accounting for 88.2%, and imports accounting for 11.8%. More than 50% of exports by cross-border E-commerce dealers is shipped by China Postal Express & Logistics, which has become the main channel for exportation. In the year 2013, the import volume was over 70 billion RMB, an increase of 1.7% compared with the previous year; the packages imported via China Postal Express & Logistics in April, 2014 reached 2 million pieces, increasing by 110% compared with the previous year.

II. How does China Postal Express & Logistics build the comprehensive postal platform for cross-border E-commerce service? In the year 2013, the authorities released policies that actively encourage and support the development of cross-border E-commerce. These measures show that China wants to add cross-border E-commerce as a powerful supplement of its mass trade and form a new trading channel. In summary, at present, there are 2 kinds of export modes and 2 kinds of import modes for cross-border E-commerce. The first mode is general export, the commodity is exported through postal customs clearance, postal commercial customs clearance and social commercial customs clearance. The second mode is bonded export, the export from special regions. There are 2 kinds of import, the first is general import, namely the goods consolidation import mode; the second is bonded import, namely the stock import mode.

China Postal Express & Logistics builds up the concept of an export platform for cross-border E-commerce. There are 4 channels in the export platform layer; the first channel is the postal channel, the second channel is the express package center of the postal channel, the third channel is the cross-border E-commerce park and the fourth channel is the bonded zone. The one below the channels is China Postal Express & Logistics which is a product system for all channels. The top layer is the comprehensive postal cross-border E-commerce service platform; the governmental supervision authorities should carry out the internetworking of express services. It builds the export platform of cross-border E-commerce, the entire platform is in the process of becoming operational, and some channels have been developed. We have a powerful capacity for warehouse processing. Concerning the construction of the import platform, the top layer is made up of business clients, the middle layer includes 4 main channels which are in charge of the imported product design, and the bottom one is the postal service platform with interconnected data.

III. How can we provide an integrated logistics solution? We have the following advantages in the integrated logistics solution. First, logistics service tailoring; second, a powerful system of supply chain management; third, information system support, especially close cooperation with the largest international cross-border E-commerce platform, EV, by which we have obtained a lot of practical experience on powerful information system interfacing; fourth, well-developed, perfect supporting resources to enter bonded zones and parks.

As for the export integrated logistics solution, we develop online interfacing of the E-commerce network information system, with professional customer service teams which track the entire course. Customs clearance includes postal customs, postal commercial customs, B2C general export, B2B2C bonded import, sea, land and air transport, overseas warehousing and distribution system, pickup, departure, packing and combining services. Value-added service, logistics insurance, customs clearance alarm and other integrated supply chain solutions are used to provide customers with tailoring plans and they can be combined at random. Reversely, it is an integrated import logistics solution.

The overseas warehouses of China Postal Express & Logistics have been distributed around the USA, and will be distributed on the east and west coasts of the USA, in the U.K., Australia and Japan during the second half of 2014 and in the Middle East and Russia in the near future. Why should we have overseas warehouses? They mainly provide overseas sales for cross-border E-commerce dealers, so that the delivery time will be reduced by 5 to 10 days, and the seller's sales and sales price will be increased; thus it is easier to become the prime seller. This is the profile of the main imported products, postal EMS, postal international packages, business express mail, urgently required imported products and stock imported products.

The above is an introduction to the export and import cross-border E-commerce platforms built by China Postal Express & Logistics, an integrated logistics solution relying on the two platforms, and several competitive products for import and export. We hope to cooperate with all circles of society, in particular the cross-border E-commerce platform and related sellers to make joint efforts for the development of Chinese cross-border E-commerce. Thank you!

# Speech by Li Dongqi, Vice President of SF Express, at the 2014 China Express Industry (International) Development Conference

Distinguished leaders and guests,

Hello, everybody! On behalf of SF Express, please allow me to extend my thanks to the leaders and friends who are helping the development of SF; the subject I will talk about today is: SF makes life brilliant.

To adapt to the external market environment and changes of customers' requirements, SF has made a series of strategic transformations based on the philosophy of "market oriented and customer centered". At this moment, I'd like to share the transition of SF from traditional B2B to B2C, some achievements and plans of the transformation the complete supply chain. In order to provide customers with diverse services, SF adheres to improve the service quality and benefits with the application of science and technology, and focus on the environmental protection and social undertaking while innovating and developing the complete supply chain.

We plan to optimize the SF logistics service, including domestic express service, regardless of local city, in-province and out of province, so as the package will be delivered on the same day of shipping and will be exempted from freight if not delivered on time. A special discount is granted for special needs, under which the price is economical and time effectiveness is still stable and reliable. We will launch these products based on customers' requirements to diversify the options and standardize services, so as various customers will have SF services with high standards and high requirements.

As for products with special operation processes, SF Te'an (Highly Secured Express Service) is launched, featuring high-quality, full-track monitoring, specially-assigned persons in charge of service and one hundred percent security guarantee; this service is designed for high-valued goods, such as jewelry. The service that guarantees security in delivering, transporting and collection, which is our preferred choice, the preferred choice for carrying valuables, and the service process has become the standard in the industry and keeps the leading position.

SF is developing towards carrying heavy objects, and is launching an economical logistics service for large-sized pieces or heavy objects called Logistics Cargo Service. The packing and operation of large-sized packages is complicated, transportation difficult and consignment

Part III  Summary of Speeches at the Summit High–level Forum

expensive, hence SF Logistics Cargo Service solves difficulties for customers. Its advantage is a high cost performance, as well as the security and stability of time effectiveness. We have perfected our international network, activated the express service in the U.S., Japan, Korea, Singapore, Malaysia, Thailand, Vietnam, Australia, Hong Kong, Macau and Taiwan, and expanded the market and improved the service quality. We are leading in China and pursue: the international standard enterprise; meanwhile, we are expanding our service coverage and improving the service quality and time effectiveness.

As for the E-commerce market, we have reorganized our product and launched the "Discount Series" to meet the requirements of intermediate and high-end customers with high-quality service, and this is our market positioning. The launch of the "Discount Series" is aimed at applying the market philosophy of "market-oriented and customer-centered" with differentiated services according to requirements of the E-commerce market. For all consumers, SF always sticks to leading service and does not involve any price war, provides the market with differentiated services, reorganizes the internal process and the service process, and optimizes internally based on customers' specific requirements. Based on E-commerce requirements, on time effectiveness and security, the operation processes are different from the traditional express service. We optimize these markets internally, save costs and give feedback results to customers, and launch the "Discount Series".

The E-commerce industrial park is the new business to be greatly developed, and it is a measure for strategic transformations. With the strong operation capability of SF, we provide one-stop services for E-commerce enterprises through a close cooperation with local governments, including warehousing, office setting, logistics, financing, sales, agency operations and all-bearing services such as photographing, training and other services for E-commerce dealers, similar to the incubation parks, and provide the most rational E-commerce industrial park services. The SF E-commerce industrial park features on building the supply chain solution of E-commerce enterprises, links the supply industrial chain of E-commerce enterprise by integrating E-commerce supporting resources, removes the bottleneck for the development of small and medium-sized enterprises (SMEs), and facilitates SMEs to gather resources for core competitive strength; SF provides full industrial chain services for agency operations.

SF has some advantages in developing E-commerce industrial parks. The first is the scale advantage; the layout will be completed in more than 50 Chinese cities in the following 5–8 years, and a nationwide E-commerce service system will be established to meet the new demands of E-commerce dealers and enterprises; the second is service advantage; most services of the industrial park is provided by SF, with a united standard and a great stability. The third is the logistics service; SF has set up logistics allocation and transfer centers in some industrial parks to increase logistics and the circulation rate.

A hot issue has been recently discussed, that is SF Heike. Since May, we have opened several hundreds of stores in China, and Heike stores are new measures for O2O strategic transformation used for meeting the customers' requirements, E-commerce dealers' requirements and community services. SF Heike is the directly operated stores of SF; it provides online and offline dealers with community-based O2O services, assists dealers in improving their brand reputation and sales volume and provides customers with flexible, convenient and smart community consumption experience. These services include some online shopping, such as showcases, publicity, advertisements and GIP reservations. When customers are not certain satisfied with the commodity, they can reserve and try the commodity, and then pay it; so this service is of great importance. Besides, it also includes convenience service, financial after-sales service and logistics service. In the future, there will be more than ten thousands of Heike stores to provide online and offline O2O service and community value-added service with a united image and standard services and provide dealers and customers with brand-new services in the Internet era. I believe that these Heike stores will approach the leaders and guests very soon; I hope you all to experience it. Your valuable opinions are appreciated, so that we can perfect and walk closer to life, provide more convenient O2O experience and bring the best service to dealers and consumers.

Tomorrow is a significant day for SF. May 31 is the 2nd anniversary for SF B2C food website (sfbest.com). In recent days, a lot of activities have been held for the SF-best anniversary; I hope you can visit the website to enjoy the discounts and high-quality services during the celebration. SF-best, the global gourmet online shopping mall created by SF on May 31, 2012, collects gourmet from more than 60 countries, including imported foods and those directly taken from the place of origin, operated in B2C and C2B; litchi and blueberry are very popular; we deliver directly from the place of origin. We always attach great importance to quality and safety, and provide rich commodity recommendation and logistics support. Now, SF-best is the second E-commerce dealer with qualification of food import and export in China. SF-best has 3 multi-functional warehouses in North China, East China and South China; each warehouse has 5 divisions, with span up to 90 degrees to satisfy the storage requirements of full-category of commodity. Soon, we will open other two warehouses in Central China and Southeast China and expand the coverage of commodity with temperature control to a larger scope. Products of SF-best are delivered by SF Express, and are delivered to users within 24 hours from places of origin. At present, SF Express is building food industry logistics solutions.

SF financial services include two aspects, the first is the financial service itself and the second is the financial logistics service. The financial service is Shunyin, which provides

Part III  Summary of Speeches at the Summit High-level Forum

professional customers, E-commerce enterprises and industry with 3-in-1 integrated solution by combing logistics, information flow and fund flow, and with fund and brand support, including supply chain finance. We have a professional financial insurance service team, an advanced information management system for research and development, and provide customers with professional, individualized and differentiated services supported by the Company's resource platform.

The customization market is the brand-new strategy trend in the business of SF. Supported by public praise, brand image and operation performance in the express field, we provide the opportunity of customized logistics and give some good trials for future key professional solutions, such as automobile parts and medicine. The automobile parts mainly serves motor factories and parts manufacturers, provides dealers with professional solutions, customized solutions, special logistics services, optimized parts, warehousing and parts integration, parts packing, design and manufacturing, value-added services, exclusive customer services, and, besides, it provides customers with full-course high-quality service of automobile parts. It mainly relies on the fruitful logistics network and vehicle resources. The perfect information system established by SF, provides special customization for some industries, satisfies the automobile parts' requirements on safety and cost and helps customers to improve their core competitive strength. In terms of medicine service, SF tries to launch the temperature control trunk line transportation of medicine, with a professional feature and temperature control, plus medicine inspection and registration. The full course is open and visible.

In terms of information, SF's future is based on the present information. SF spares no efforts in building an information system. Today, SF activates a membership system, customer APP, SMS, self-order & inquiry, We-chat service, etc. for clients, and provides other consultation services. I hope you all experience and give some opinions on improvement. SF exercises the duty of environmental protection, launches eco-friendly logistics by following the express service greenhouse gas measurement of the National Standard Committee, and reduces the influences on environment in express operations, including the packing material optimization, the vehicle, the transfer link reconstruction, the energy conservation of daily office work, the reduced energy consumption and the carbon dioxide emissions. In terms of operation, SF launches paperless office work, takes eco-friendly service into account, saves paper and packing materials and make them more eco-friendly. We have established some SF share platforms to encourage the staff to transfer personal idle objects to others. In terms of social responsibility, SF adheres to help others in a low-key principle. Since 2003, SF has invested nearly 90 million RMB on public welfare and it will continue.

By following the philosophy of "market-oriented and customer-centered", our mission is

216

to satisfy the customers' requirements based on innovation, and realize and create value for customers. Facing great challenges, SF will make progress with customers from a new start and make life more brilliant. Finally, may the forum be a success. Thank you!

# Speech by Curtis Rousseau, Vice President of the Information Technology of UPS Asia Pacific at the 2014 China Express Industry (International) Development Conference

Thank you very much for giving me a chance to make a speech on behalf of UPS. I will share more environment-friendly and sustainable business practice with data. First, I will briefly introduce UPS's engaging in an environmentally sustainable development, and how to realize more environment-friendly, sustainable and cost-effective objectives with data. Then I will put forward some suggestions to the government for encouragement of more environment-friendly and sustainable trade practices.

More than one hundred years ago, UPS started to provide package service in the U.S. With time flying by, we gradually expanded services all over the world. Today, UPS is a global leader in package service and supply chain solutions, provides services for 9.4 million customers in 200 countries. The trucks and planes of UPS carry 2% of global GDP. UPS entered Chinese market in 1988, and became the first wholly foreign-owned enterprise for express service from Sino-foreign joint venture. We have two operation centers in Shanghai and Shenzhen, own the most advanced medical and health care warehousing equipment in Shanghai and Hangzhou, develop business in more than 330 cities in China, have over 6,000 employees and 280 airline segments, and link China, America, Europe and Asia.

As for us, the most important thing is to develop in an eco-friendly and sustainable manner. In 2003, UPS released the *Report on Sustainable Development* for the first time, which covers the practice in every year. As the CFO said, we always realize the responsibility for environment and the contribution to environmental protection which also produces value. We do not only obtain a sound eco-friendly benefit but also realize sustainable development.

We can know our business by data analysis. We continuously adjust our operation by analyzing data, including vehicle performance and network construction, as well as planning the vehicle route. Data analysis produces great value to us. UPS drivers operate more than 96,000 vehicles, deliver 17 million packages every day and serve 9 million customers. If we save one kilometer, we can save 80 million USD each year. Our drivers also reduce the idling time of engines, for each cut down minute, we can save 515,000 USD. Based on the data of the year 2011, we cut down a mileage of 582 million kilometers and greatly reduced the idling time of the trucks.

How can we realize this? One reason is that we continuously perform operation and survey and exercise advanced analyzing. We know about our contribution to business and reduction of carbon emission through our conclusion and a third party's survey and research. Now we can use describable, diagnosable and predictable analyzing means to help us convert data into sound profitable measures.

The system acquiring express information is shortly called DIAD, from the preliminary electronic touch pad to the most advanced technology tools, DIAD can provide drivers with data and make them decide better and deliver orders more effectively. The DIAD system makes us provide customers with better services and perform commitments to customers. It also supports complicated engine planning forecast, forecasts some requirements in the future, creates daily delivery plan, helps us expand package quantity and improve services, thus benefits our profitability.

The other system is the onboard information service, as well as the DIAD system, through which vehicles and drivers can have better performances. We have 20 sensors and GPS. We can check whether the drivers fasten the safety belt, the drivers' speed, where the drivers' route is and whether they leave keys in the truck after parking, all of them can be sensed. Such an onboard information system makes better diagnosis. We make drivers fasten the safety belt with a ratio of 99.9%, the highest level in history for us.

We have a navigation system which makes us more innovative to satisfy the customers' and business requirements, and this is also an advanced data analysis tool. One UPS driver should complete the job quantity of 120 stations a day, the best route can be fixed with the software, and delivery will be faster. By using 250 million address data points and all kinds of relating software, and considering the consumers' transportation requirements, we can prepare proper map information and help them navigate better, reduce route and carbon emissions. The system helped us save 5.6 million liters of fuel in 2013 by using 100,000 routes in it; it can support more operation centers. We will bring benefits to every corner of North America, and will complete the deployment at the end of 2016.

Up to now, we are concerning on how to use data analysis and technology innovation to realize more effective operations, reduce cost, use of energy and carbon emissions. The environment sustainability is the most important investment, and the government also provides incentives to encourage the enterprises to have benefits from eco-friendly business. Many governments also provide subsidy for vehicles in replace of fuel-driven vehicles, and other subsidies to train staff and talents for data analyzing and increase investment efficiency. While focusing on data analysis, we make traffic more sustainable, and it is vital for data to be communicated across borders. Many participants, suppliers or consumers worldwide contribute to the quality of data.

Generally speaking, the government helps logistic companies to realize better fuel economic efficiency and environment sustainability, opens traffic domain and makes companies access to the shortest and most eco-friendly routes to yield multi-mode transportation. Here is an example, in the year 2015, ASEAN countries decided to reinforce the interconnection in ASEAN regions, link the route for trucks between Yunnan Province and Singapore. These traffic options created more fuel economic efficiency options for ASEAN countries, contributing much to fuel save in the transportation industry.

To realize the changes of the environment, the best way is cooperation among powerful companies. Many transnational companies engage in environment sustainability, the same in China and other countries in the world, and we hope that we can have the opportunity to share experience in joint operations. One organization cooperating with us is the Green Freight Asia (GFA), founded in 2013, a non-profitable organization in Asia; it provides eco-friendly transportation and traffic routes in the supply chain on behalf of carriers. We launch the eco-friendly transportation program, certify transportation enterprises that adopt eco-friendly fuel economic efficiency technology, and encourage them to take the desirable purchasing and eco-friendly purchasing into their business.

We hope more Chinese transportation enterprises can be qualified with our certification, and hope to cooperate with China Road Transport Association (CRTA) and its members in eco-friendly transportation, and realize the objective of a sustainable development of economy.

Thank you very much. Let's make the great efforts to reach the great goal of eco-friendly profits. Thank you!

# Speech by Li Jinqi, Director General of the Department of Electronic Commerce and Informatization of the Ministry of Commerce, at the Beijing Dialogues among Famous Entrepreneurs

All guests, ladies and gentlemen,

Good afternoon! I'm very pleased to attend today's Beijing Dialogues among Famous Entrepreneurs. I, on behalf of the Ministry of Commerce, would like to extend warm congratulations to the activity! The organizing committee of the CIFTIS and the People's Government of Haidian District, Beijing Municipality jointly hold these dialogues to talk about the mobile Internet, which will play a positive role in industrial cooperation within the mobile Internet field at home and abroad for promoting a wider application of China's mobile Internet.

With the rapid development of the Internet industry, the Internet is not limited to industry, but it is increasingly integrated into various aspects of production and life, and the resulting Internet economy is becoming a revolutionary force for change. E-commerce is the most prominent application of information technology and the Internet in the economic field. In recent years, China's E-commerce has developed rapidly and its influence on the national economy is increasingly prominent, playing a positive role in changing the economic growth pattern, adjusting the economic structure and improving economic efficiency, etc. Last year, China's total volume of E-commerce trade exceeded 10 trillion RMB, having quadrupled in 5 years. Up to 30,000 people have shopped online, and the number of mobile network users reached 440 million, with a year-on-year growth of 60% with the mobile trade volume exceeding 160 billion RMB. Online and offline accelerated integration, trans-boundary business, mobile E-business and Internet financing have caused heated debates and aroused extensive attention. The new government attaches great importance to informatization and the development of E-commerce; Prime Minister Li Keqiang and Vice-premier Wang Yang have given instructions with regard to these issues many times. In November of last year, the Ministry of Commerce issued the *Implementation Opinions on Promoting E-commerce Application*. The National E-commerce Conference was held last February, which system-

Part III  Summary of Speeches at the Summit
High-level Forum

atically studied the E-commerce developmental trend and focused on deploying this year's work. In terms of the promotion of E-commerce, we insist that being market-oriented and with enterprises as the main body, E-commerce's development should be regulated, and it should be developed with specifications; we should actively guide the standardization of E-commerce, and jointly promote the application of E-commerce, to solve the problems in the development process.

Our main work includes:

1. Strengthening the standard establishment of laws and regulations and creating a good environment. Carrying out E-commerce legislation carefully and thoroughly, actively promoting the revision of laws closely related to E-commerce, studying the formulation and introduction of third-party trade rules and regulations, and actively building the E-commerce statistic detection system and the E-commerce credit system.

2. Carrying out application promotion and encouraging practicing and trying beforehand. In the retail field, supporting network retail platforms to further expand coverage and innovative modes, and supporting the development of E-commerce by relying on offline resources to achieve online and offline resource complementation and application collaboration. In the area of foreign trade, breaking through the environment that is not suitable to the development of E-commerce foreign trade, and promoting the establishment of a series of supporting measures, such as basic network facilities, logistics, payment, supervision and credit construction. In terms of agricultural products, encouraging the docking of E-commerce and traditional agricultural products, driving the branding of agricultural products, promoting the circulation of agricultural products with information service, and encouraging support for E-commerce application in people's daily life. In terms of E-commerce pilot demonstrations, playing a leading role in E-commerce demonstration cities, demonstration bases and demonstration enterprises, and promoting the application of E-commerce innovation.

3. Improving E-commerce that supports the service environment. Establishing an E-commerce logistics system, promoting the construction of a logistics distribution system suitable to E-commerce development, promoting E-commerce payment, credit service and other supporting service enterprises, carrying out technological and service mode innovation, establishing and improving the E-commerce service industry chain and promoting industrial organizations, professional training agencies and enterprises to carry out E-commerce talent training and post-skill training.

4. Carrying out international exchanges and cooperation. The Chinese government will actively participate in the E-commerce work of the UN, the WTO and APEC, and it will promote E-commerce multilateral and bilateral exchange mechanisms. The expansion of

foreign E-commerce enterprises on the Chinese market and in the going-out of China's E-commerce will become a new trend. Next, the government will promote E-commerce exchanges and cooperation and will utilize E-commerce methods to expand its market at home and abroad.

China's E-commerce is facing a rare opportunity in this historical development with broad prospects for development. We believe that, through the promotion of innovation of this industry, markets and enterprises, relying on the innovative development of the Internet and information technology, E-commerce will continuously expand and spread throughout various fields, and the relevant service industry and supporting system will be more complete and perfect. Finally, I wish these dialogues complete success. Thank you!

# Speech by Zhang Zhikuan, Deputy Secretary General of the People's Government of Beijing Municipality, at the Beijing Dialogues among Famous Entrepreneurs

Honorable guests, ladies and gentlemen,

Good afternoon! I feel very honored to attend the Beijing Dialogues among Famous Entrepreneurs at the 3rd CIFTIS on the first day. I, on behalf of the People's Government of Beijing Municipality, want to extend the warmest welcome to all guests present! I wish the dialogue complete success!

The CIFTIS has invited merchants operators and guests from more than 100 countries and regions all over throughout the world. Full communication and exchange exchanges are being carried out at the fair, centering on "building a high-grade, high-precision and advanced economic structure and greatly promoting the development of international service trade in services development". The People's Government of Beijing Municipality has always attached much great importance to E-commerce, and has successively printed and distributed the *Opinion on Promoting the Healthy Development of E-commerce* and the *Implementation Plan on Recommending Beijing's Cross-border E-commerce Development*, and it has made specific deployments regarding the recommendation for cross-border E-commerce development. Beijing Municipality was approved as an E-commerce City in 2011, the Economic and Technological Development Zone of Daxing District, the First-batch National E-commerce Demonstration Base in 2012, and 12 enterprises including JD.COM were awarded the title of 2013 –2014 E-commerce Demonstration Enterprise by the Ministry of Commerce in 2013, ranking the first in China in terms of number. On June 27, 2013, the first electronic invoice was created in Beijing, marking new progress in the developmental environment of Beijing's E-commerce field, becoming a new engine leading the standard E-commerce development, which is of great significance for the promotion of China's E-commerce to be in line with international standards.

In recent years, a new situation has appeared in Beijing's E-commerce development. On the premise that China's traditional foreign trade growth is slowing down, cross-border E-commerce is suddenly rising. In 2013, Beijing Customs totally supervised the importation and exportation of nearly 100 million pieces of international mail and over 300 million cross-border E-commerce parcels; its platform has such functions as commodity notification, data sharing, customs clearance and supervision. This is another important measure of Beijing's E-commerce development.

In the future, Beijing Municipality will continuously concentrate on building innovation centers for science and technology, on making full use of its advantages in information, talent and industry management practices in developing E-commerce, promoting and leading E-commerce innovation, greatly developing mobile E-commerce, supporting the innovation mode of E-commerce and continuing to play a leading and demonstrative role in E-commerce in China.

Finally, I hope that entrepreneurs will bring new contributions to the development of E-commerce throughout this dialogue in order to promote the development of E-commerce at a higher level. Thank you!

# Speech by Paul Misener, Vice President of Amazon at the Beijing Dialogues among Famous Entrepreneurs

Good day! Thank you very much to all government leaders and friends for inviting me to give a speech on behalf of Amazon today! Thank you for holding this grand meeting and building this platform. Today's topic is of significance, showing the attention that the People's Government of Beijing Municipality and the Ministry of Commerce give to E-commerce. I feel greatly honored to participate in these dialogues. Twenty years ago, when I first came to Beijing, I was invited by the government to discuss HD-TV. Ten years ago, I led the delegation from Amazon to discuss cooperation with Beijing Century Joyo Information Technology Co., Ltd. We have celebrated the 10th anniversary of Amazon's entry into China this year. Getting older, I am an old friend of Beijing's.

How does Amazon go global? Amazon now has operations in 13 countries and regions with over 200 million users, playing an important role in website customization for users. By understanding the local culture, tastes, currency and commodities, Amazon has been committed to website personalization and customization. Our goal is to provide the best user experience for customers in Spain, the USA and China. We focus on three points: one is that Amazon has rich product categories. Amazon provides more than 200 million products and is the website with the most product varieties of all online stores in China; the second is that Amazon pays great attention to convenience. Amazon is committed to making consumers find what they need more easily; the third is that Amazon forces product prices down as much as possible. Therefore, the range of choice, convenience and lower price are the reasons for Amazon's global success.

What's the difference in doing business in Brazil, the USA and other countries? There is certainly a difference, but there are far more similarities than differences. Consumers all over the world avoid trivial choices and hope to get the lowest price, the most convenient choice and the richest product category. We are using the current technology to provide these services for consumers.

Amazon has three businesses in China. The first is a traditional retail business. Both for domestic and international business, retail business has a simple start: first, purchase some goods from the wholesaler and store them in the warehouse, and then sell the goods by retail.

In this way, this is not innovative, but the key factor is our online operation. We have 13 warehouses in China with an area of 800,000 m², providing 200 million different products. Goods provided by Amazon are stored in the warehouses.

The second is third-party sales business for small business operators, providing a platform for other operators to conduct online sales. Media critics and investors could not understand this view when it was put forward at the beginning. They thought that, sales on the same platform with other sellers might cause losses due to lower prices. Why did we insist? Consumers like to make a choice among different sellers and are able to compare their prices. For sellers, it is attractive for both buyers and sellers that such a national website can be used to sell products and services all over China. Our platform has millions of middle-and-small-scale sellers all over the world, with a growth of 150% last year. The growth in number is remarkable.

The third is the handheld electronic reading device. In addition to tablet computers, which can be used to enjoy pictures and videos conveniently, people can read books with a handheld electronic reading device. This device is popular with consumers due to high demand and low price. Over 400 publishing houses and 70,000 users in China are using this platform. At the same time, meeting the Chinese consumers' needs, we sell China's products, especially cultural products, and to the world, through this platform, such as books published in China, books written by Chinese authors and books published by Chinese publishing houses. Amazon.com of the USA has Chinese bookstores which have sold more than 200,000 kinds of Chinese books, with an expectation for growth in number. There are two reasons for this: one is that we hope that the customers in other countries, such as the USA, will have more opportunities to contact China's cultural products, such as books, music and videos, although Amazon is currently focusing on book sales; the other is that Amazon has 13 websites around the world, which is a good chance for Chinese authors and publishers to go to the world and come into contact with consumers and readers worldwide. Now, we are beginning to translate books written by Chinese authors to benefit Western customers and readers as well as Chinese authors and publishers.

Amazon is committed to developing business with continuous growth in Beijing. We hope to have a chance to cooperate with other entrepreneurs and we also hope to continue maintaining close cooperative relations with friends of the People's Government of Beijing Municipality and the Ministry of Commerce. It may be difficult, to some extent, to discuss long-term plans in China, which has a 5,000-year-long history of civilization, but Amazon, which has developed into a global company in 20 years, also has a 10-year-long history in China. We have much confidence in its development, we will maintain close cooperative relations and focus on long-term development. Thank you!

# Speech by Tong Daochi, Assistant Minister of Commerce, at the WTO and China–Beijing International Forum

Distinguished President Sun, Ambassador Yi, all friends and guests,

Good afternoon! First of all, I would like to extend congratulations to the 3rd CIFTIS. President Sun has just mentioned trade in services which is the theme of the CIFTIS, and also a highlighted theme. During the CIFTIS, the China Society for World Trade Organization Studies (CWTO), chaired by President Sun, and the Beijing International Service Trade Center, jointly hosted the WTO and China: Beijing International Forum. Today, I feel honored to attend the forum and I want to talk about some personal views on behalf of the Ministry of Commerce.

Since the beginning of the new century, the global service industry and trade in services have been developing strongly, becoming important driving forces for balanced and sustainable global development and an important way for all countries, all over the world, to participate in the global economy. Since the reform and the opening-up, especially since joining the WTO, China has been promoting the opening-up of the service industry in an orderly way. As a Secretary-General of the WTO, Ambassador Yi attaches great importance to the development of the WTO. Ambassador Sun was the first ambassador of the WTO. Both spare no efforts at promoting the opening-up of the service industry. China is promoting the opening-up of this industry in an orderly way; the scale of trade in services is expanding rapidly and China's international status is rising consciously: China's total volume of service industry trade broke through 100 billion USD in 2003 for the first time, 200 billion USD in 2007 and 300 billion USD in 2008, with a multiple growth. In 2013, in spite of the circumstances of the profound adjustment of the global economic pattern, economic slowdown, a severe external situation and various declines in imports and exports for all countries, China's total volume of trade in services reached 539.6 billion USD, ranking third in the world, wherein the total volume of service exports reached 210 billion USD, with a growth of 10% compared to that of last year, achieving a double-digit growth for the first time since 2001. Of course, we not only stress the growth rate, but we also pay attention to the constant optimization of the service industry trade structure; at the same time, steadily developing the traditional service industries, such as tourism and construction, we also focus on the

Part Ⅲ   Summary of Speeches at the Summit High–level Forum

transformation and upgrading of the service industry; we are also starting such modern service industries as computers, finance and consulting; we have service outsourcing centers now, all of which represent steps in the transformation and upgrading of the service industry. The development of this industry plays an important role in accelerating the transformation of China's economic development mode and adjusting its economic structure.

I also want to emphasize that, although China's service industry is developing rapidly, it actually started late. Traditionally, China is mainly a country with trade in goods, so trade in services is still an emerging industry and a developing industry. In terms of total number, China's total volume of trade in services is only half that of the USA. Trade in services accounts for 11.5% of China's total import and export trade, which is nearly half that of the global average of 20%. Therefore, trade in services in China has much room for development.

Compared with other BRICS countries, Brazil's service industry accounts for 1/4 of its import and export trade. We still have a big gap with that. Besides, we also mention that China is a country with a favorable balance of trade, but the balance is mainly reflected in trade in goods. China is a deficit country in terms of trade in services—China's trade in services deficit in 2013 was up to 118.4 billion USD, with a year-on-year growth of 32%. It may not be bad that China has a large amount of imports within its trade in services. In fact, it is good for promoting the development of global trade, increasing imports (a direction for the development of China's foreign trade) and achieving equality of imports and exports. China's imported service industry mainly focuses on the high-end service industry, because China has major deficiencies in such high-end service industries as finance, computers and consulting, of which we import a lot. Hence, China needs to improve the structure of its service industry and, at the same time, maintain the advantages of its traditional service industry, that is, carry out the transformation and upgrading of its service industry. We need to, when focusing on labor-intensive service industry exports, increase technology- and knowledge-intensive service industry exports. As we all know, the pattern of the world's trade competition is now dramatically changing; the competition is transforming from traditional trade in goods to trade in services, and trade in services has become a focus for the competition among the emerging markets and great powers. Some mature markets have basically already transformed from trade in goods to trade in services, so most emerging markets are transforming in this direction. According to the latest research on the global value chain, issued by the United Nations Conference on Trade and Development (UNCTAD), service departments have contributed about half of the global export value-added. Therefore, a vigorous development of trade in services is of significance for China in order to comprehensively deepen its reforms, accelerate the transformation of its economic developmental mode, improve the international competitiveness of its industrial chain, comprehensively participate in global value chain cooperation, increase the employment of college students and create an upgraded economy.

The APEC Meeting of Trade Ministers that just ended in Qingdao issued a report on the global value chain, which is an important result in the area of trade in services.

With the promotion of the "12th Five-Year Plan", China takes the global adjustment of the industrial structure and the acceleration of the transfer of the service industry as an opportunity and it takes the promotion of the development of the service industry as a strategic focus of the optimizing and upgrading of the industrial structure; China then insists on an orderly promotion of the opening-up of its service industry and actively creates a policy environment in favor of the development of trade in order to promote the rapid development of its trade. In order to further improve the trade in services management mechanism, the State Council has issued the *Opinions on Accelerating the Service Industry,* the *Implementation Opinions on Several Policy Measures for Accelerating Service Industry Development,* the *12th Five-Year Plan for Service Industry Development,* the *12th Five-Year Plan Outline for Service Industry Development* and other supporting policies for trade in services. The Beijing Municipal Commission of Commerce is expanding its platform for the promotion of trade in services. The CIFTIS is the first comprehensive trade in services international exhibition in the world.

The Third Plenary Session of the 18th Central Committee of the CPC put forward a call to comprehensively deepen the reforms. In terms of deepening the reforms, especially deepening the trade system reform, China greatly promotes transformation and upgrading. We have considerable responsibility for promoting trade transformation, and this mission is great. I will talk about issues concerning how China will promote the development and innovation of its service industry in the following aspects:

First, it will comprehensively promote the innovation of the trade in services policy, discuss and formulate the feasibility of regulations on service import-export management, and make a guidance catalogue of the key service export fields in order to provide help for such supportive polices as fiscal, tax revenue and finance. China will also promote the introduction of fiscal taxation and financial supportive policies, the establishment of special funds for trade in services, innovate the financial supportive policies, develop the financial products according to the characteristics of trade in services, deepen the cooperation with banks and insurance companies, support the construction of key projects concerning trade in services, actively promote the convenience of trade in services, and enhance the international exchange of staff mobility, mutual recognition of the professional qualification and formulation of industrial standards. As is known to all, a big difference between trade in services and trade in goods is staff mobility, which is related to the formulation of qualifications and standards, and requires further internationalization with improved exchanges. Meanwhile, the service industry is at a

Part III Summary of Speeches at the Summit High-level Forum

stage of transformation and upgrading, and needs the help of supporting policies, especially the support of the financial industry.

Second, China will promote the sustainable development of the service field. We will innovate the trade in services development platform and continue improving the trade in services promotion system to make a contribution to both China's and global development; there will be a focus on trade in services' positive role as a social stabilizer; China will also actively deepen international cooperation, encourage technological innovation, increase the employment of knowledge-based talents, and strengthen such fields as brands, information, messages, talent and intellectual property, so as to lay a solid foundation for the rapid development of trade in services. Trade in services has contributed a lot to China's employment, especially regarding the employment of college students, as I mentioned earlier. In this respect, trade in services is of great significance for social stability and for the solving of employment problems, especially the employment of knowledge-based talents. So, we will strengthen our support for laying a solid foundation for the development of China's service industry.

Third, China will continuously promote the opening-up to the outside of the area of trade in services. According to the national strategy of further promoting the economic opening-up, we will further promote the opening-up of the trade in services field and stably expand the opening-up of such fields as finance, logistics, energy saving and environmental protection. These fields are not open enough, and the service industry is in a stage of rapid development, so next we will promote the opening-up of such aspects as finance, telecommunications and environmental protection, encourage foreign operators to invest in professional design, software development and other knowledge-intensive service industry fields to expand the service supply, stimulate development vitality within the service industry, improve policy measures, encourage the flourishing of global technology, R&D, service and other features of innovation in China, encourage enterprises at home and abroad to jointly carry out technology R&D, promote the industrialization of scientific and technological results and improve the quality and level of service innovation. The opening-up is important for the development of China's service industry, so we cannot develop the service industry domestically, since the mature experience of the developed markets that have developed their service industries can be borrowed by us for reference. Therefore, we hope that all our friends in the business circle present will work together to take a new step in the opening-up of the service industry and in international cooperation.

This forum is not big, but Ambassador Yi, Deputy Secretary-General of the WTO, President Sun and leaders of the Beijing Municipal Commission of Commerce and lots of entrepreneurs are present. I hope that we will share our experiences and build a consensus through this platform. As a member of the Ministry of Commerce, I'm willing to strengthen the dialogue and increase the mutual trust within the international society to jointly promote continuous coordination and balanced development of international trade including trade in services.

At last, I wish the forum complete success. Thank you!

# Speech by Yi Xiaozhun, Deputy Secretary–General of the WTO, at the WTO and China–Beijing International Forum

I'm very happy to come back to China today! This is the first time that I have participated in such an important meeting in Beijing after taking office at the WTO. I would like to talk to you in Chinese, but Chinese is not the working language of the WTO, so I will give my speech in English. To facilitate your understanding, I've made a PPT presentation in Chinese, hoping for your forgiveness.

I'm glad to come back to attend the CIFTIS in Beijing again. This year's theme is very suitable to the occasion. The global economy is now experiencing an unprecedented transformation, and the core of the transformational trend is the transition to a service-oriented economy. The service industry supports all phases in the production process, such as R&D, design, engineering, finance, transportation, distribution and marketing. In short, the value added and innovation we can obtain would be very limited without the service industry. I would like to talk about the reasons why I think the service industry is particularly important to China's future development regarding the following five aspects.

First, China's trade in services has achieved a great leap forward in its development, which is mainly because China has completely fulfilled its commitments and has promoted reforms in big strides after joining the WTO. After joining the WTO in 2001, China has gradually become the absolute largest exporter of trade in goods and the fifth largest exporter of trade in services in the world. If we consider EU countries as a whole, China would be the third largest exporter of trade in services in the world. China's achievements in the manufacturing industry are remarkable, but the development of China's service industry is rarely known by people. In fact, China's achievements in the development of its trade in services are also prominent. The service industry's exports have been rapidly increasing, reaching 11% annually from 2002 to 2013; at present, service exports, based on a balance of payments, has reached 207 billion USD. Before 2001, when China had not yet joined the WTO, China's service exports ranked 12th, accounting for 2.2% of the world's proportion; in 2013, China ranked 5th in the world, accounting for 4.5%. China, surpassing Germany, became the second largest service importer in 2013, with service imports reaching 329 billion USD, accounting for 7.6% of global imports.

In today's economic mode characterized by a global value chain, service imports play an important role in promoting economic growth and improving competitiveness. For example, such service industries as logistics and transportation have become a binder that connects manufacturers. Other service industries, such as R&D, communications, finance, design and marketing, are all key elements in the manufacturing industry. By virtue of import-related services, China's producers can not only integrate into the global value chain, but they can also get access to the world's leading technological and managerial skills, so as to improve China's economic competitiveness.

China's rapid development, to a great extent, can be attributed to the complete fulfillment of its commitments and to its promotion of policy reform and adjustments after joining the WTO. When China joined the WTO in 2001, it made a commitment to open up the service industry which is more extensive and more significant than that of most developing countries. I believe this is a key factor that has influenced the faster development that it has had compared to many developing countries.

Next, I want to introduce China's performance in trade of some of its specific service departments. Constructional engineering, computer and transportation services perform most prominently in China's trade in services, and undoubtedly they have made substantial progress compared with their conditions before China joined the WTO in 2001. In constructional engineering, China's ranking has improved from its previous 10th ranking to its 2nd in the world today, with its trade accounting for 10.2% of the global proportion. China's ranking in computer and information services has improved from 16th to 5th in the world. In transportation services, China's ranking has improved from the previous 20th position to today's 7th, accounting for 4.2% of global trade. This significant development mainly benefits from remarkable achievements in China's average annual growth rate of 26% in ocean transportation services, from 2001 to 2012.

If we put all of the commercial services together and exclude transportation and tourism, which are classified in other services statistically, China's service exportation, ranking 18th previously, ranks 5th in the world currently, accounting for 4.8% of global trade. Telecommunications, express, audio-visual, finance and other commercial services are all classified in the category of rapid growth.

It is worth celebrating the remarkable achievements of the development of China's trade in services. As a Chinese person, I feel proud of my country. China's development in commercial services shows that the mode of promoting development by the reform and the opening-up is very successful and wise. However, in the meantime, we should also notice that, although the opening-up of the market promotes substantial development of China's service industry, we still need further reforms. China's success in the manufacturing industry is more prominent than in its service industry.

According to the commitment in trade in goods when joining the WTO, China has gradually diminished the applied tax rate from 42% in 1992 to 8.7% in 2013. Calculated with the trade-weighted method, the more accurate current applied tax rate is only 4%, which is the lowest among all large developing countries and emerging economies. China's bold opening-up in the manufacturing industry brings a robust growth of our manufacturing industry. Compared with trade in goods, China has more protection on the service industry, especially in finance, telecommunications, professional services and digital trade. According to the trade in services restrictiveness index (STRI) of the World Bank and the OECD, China's restrictiveness on trade in services is much higher than the average of developed countries and also higher than many developing countries, such as Brazil and Mexico. Of course, STRI is generalized, and many factors in calculating the index need further careful research, but this index still indicates that China's service industry urgently needs a new round of liberalization to improve its competitiveness after its development for a period of a dozen years.

In order to improve its status in the global value chain, China takes the service industry as a strategic priority field for economic development. In this way, we must realize that promoting the opening-up of the market is the only way to improve the efficiency and competitiveness of the service industry. If China wants to copy our great achievements in the manufacturing industry, it must further open up the market of the service industry. This means we need to further intensify reforms to facilitate and promote trade and investment in the service industry. After China joined the WTO, the liberalization of trade improved the competitiveness of the service industry. The departments with the least limitations develop the fastest in China.

Third, to further strengthen the manufacturing industry, China needs to improve its status in the global value chain, which requires a greater service industry. China's economy is gradually integrating into the global supply chain. By joining the global value chain, China has developed a manufacturing industry with a huge scale, providing employment and income and helping a large part of the population shed poverty. However, we often hear complaints from the Chinese that China's manufacturing industry is large but not strong. The true cause of this is the service industry lags behind in its development, which has become a bottleneck for China's status of improvement in the value chain. People always say that, China's manufacturing industry needs to develop forward along the Smiling Curve to gain more value added, that is, expand to such fields as design, innovation, R&D, patent, brand, marketing, software, logistics, transportation, after-sales services and maintenance, financial management, accounting and consulting. These service departments have contributed about 90% of the value added. If they cannot develop together, the manufacturing industry can only increase in quantity, but not improve in quality, which is not sustainable.

For a car exported by Germany, half of its value is reflected in services related to the finished goods. All countries realize that the service industry is an important factor, because it can decide the success of international competitiveness, including competitiveness of trade in goods. Improving China's status in the value chain is the key to continuing to maintain China's competitiveness. Since the global value chain is easy to transfer and it will look for suppliers and countries that are more competitive regarding costs and benefits, some people are able to achieve low value added with lower costs, but it is more difficult to replace professional and knowledge-intensive services.

Fourth, trade policies can play an important role, by avoiding the middle-income trap. The middle-income trap refers to a situation that a developing country can no longer be a low-cost producer but it is difficult for it to become a developed economy; this is an extremely urgent challenge for China. According to recent research on the developmental situation of the global manufacturing industry carried out by the Boston Consulting Group (BCG), four factors have a great influence on manufacturing costs, including salaries, labor productivity, energy costs and the exchange rate. Compared with the USA, China has only a slight advantage, and the gap between the two countries is quickly being narrowed. Manufacturing costs in Mexico are obviously lower than those in China, and such a trend has made about 300 companies transfer their manufacturing plants from China or other regions in Asia back to the USA. China has no choice regarding the increasing manufacturing costs but to carry out an economic transformation from the low-cost manufacturing industry to the high value-added service industry.

New data show the participation in the global value chain, involving both direct service exports and proportion of service value added in the exportation of goods. In terms of the contribution of direct and indirect value added of China's service industry to total exports, China now lags behind the developmental goal of economic servitization. Data show that, although China's service industry exports gain an increase, its contribution to the global value chain has not significantly improved and has been keeping the same since 1995, accounting for 5% in 2008, compared with the average of 15.6% for developed countries and the average of 10.3% for developing countries. The proportion of the value added of China's domestic service industry in total exports is also very low, accounting for 18.5%, compared with the average of 37.3% for the developed countries and the average of 23.1% for the developing countries. So, it can be said that China used to be and is now an exporter of the manufacturing industry.

In 2013, the proportion of the service industry in China's GDP increased to 46%, exceeding the manufacturing industry for the first time, but still lower than 73.6% for OECD countries. The Chinese government emphasizes that we should carry out economic transformation as soon as possible and that China's economic growth mode should focus on the transformation of the developing manufacturing industry, to expanding and improving the service industry, which is the key to avoiding the middle-income trap for China. We believe that, trade policies can play an important role in this process and gradually cancelling the trade in services restrictive measures is necessary in order to improve the competitiveness of the service industry.

China's recent Shanghai Pilot Free Trade Zone demonstration project follows such development. This is a measure that has come at just the right time, which can assess the impact of important policy changes, especially the impact on the opening-up of the market. Current policy measures under test include managing foreign investments in the form of a negative list and further opening up a series of service departments, including banking, insurance, constructional engineering, logistics, education, medical treatment and E-commerce. Experience in these aspects is extremely important, because we hope to apply the experience obtained in the Shanghai Pilot Free Trade Zone to other places in China.

Fifth, China needs to obtain foreseeable rules and market access, which can be available by supporting a multilateral trade system. Another key factor needing consideration is China's overseas direct investments, since almost 67% of overseas direct investments is in trade in services. China's overseas investments with a rapid growth are concentrated in transportation, storage, distribution, finance and commercial fields, and such services usually support China's other overseas service activities. China can diversify its strategies, increase its service exports through overseas investments, and guarantee that these activities can be supported by a related commitment of the WTO. China should try to participate in the WTO's General Agreement on Trade in Services (GATS), and use it to guarantee its interests.

The WTO is the only platform for negotiations regarding multilateral rules and market access, including rules governing trade in services and market access. The same as other WTO agreements, GATS provides foreseeable and non-discriminatory channels for China to enter other markets, and can comprehensively protect a rule-based multilateral system. GATS encourages more transparent and non-discriminatory competition, and such obligations are consistent with China's domestic reform. The success in the multilateral negotiation process for trade in services might be able to guarantee China's development and growth in the next 10–20 years. The world also hopes that China will play a more important and more constructive role in the WTO.

Finally, I wish the forum complete success. Thank you!

# Speech by Song Jianming, Deputy Director of the Beijing Municipal Commission of Commerce, at the WTO and China–Beijing International Forum

Distinguished President Sun Zhenyu, Deputy Secretary-General Yi Xiaozhun, President Ricardo Melendes-ortiz, Director General Zhou Liujun, ladies and gentlemen,

Good afternoon! During this beautiful early summer, we are experiencing the WTO and China Beijing International Forum. I, on behalf of the Beijing Municipal Commission of Commerce, want to extend a warm congratulation to the forum.

Currently, the world economy has entered a service economy era, and the development of the service industry and trade in services has become an important engine for promoting a sustainable development of the global economy. Focus on global trade competition is making a transformation from trade in goods to trade in services, and innovation has become one of the main sources for increasing the value. Therefore, a strong promotion of the service industry and the innovation of the development of trade in services is an important way to transform and upgrade the modern service industry and the traditional industry and improve international competitiveness.

Taking the innovation of trade in services and industrial structure upgrading as the subject, this forum discusses the beginning of the transformation of the government's function, industrial upgrading and innovation and other frontier topics, which thus conforms to the new trend in international economic development and plays an important role in promoting the global service industry and the development of trade in services.

In recent years, Beijing Municipality has been committed to transforming the economic developmental mode and greatly developing the service industry and trade in services. In 2013, Beijing's total amount of the service industry reached 1.95 trillion RMB, accounting for 76.9%, about 31% higher than the national average, wherein the productive service industry achieved an increment of 981.2 billion RMB, accounting for over 50% of the GDP. Trade in services continued keeping ahead in China, and the total trade volume was 110 billion USD, with a year-on-year growth of more than 20%, accounting for 1/5 of the national proportion and more than 1% of the global proportion. Export growth in communications, insurance, finance, computer and information technology services all exceeded 50%.

In the future, Beijing will focus on developing the ecological service industry and the cultural creativity industry so as to form a new developmental pattern of scientific and technological innovation and cultural innovation, and to make a positive contribution to China's and the world's service industry and trade in services.

Finally, I wish the forum complete success and I wish all leaders and guests good work and best health. Thank you!

# Speech by Zhou Liujun, Director General of the Department of Trade in Services and Commercial Services of the Ministry of Commerce, at the WTO and China–Beijing International Forum

Distinguished President Sun Zhenyu, Deputy Secretary-General Yi Xiaozhun, all guests, ladies and gentlemen,

Good afternoon! I'm very glad to attend the WTO and China- Beijing International Forum activity. This morning, the Opening Ceremony and the Summit Forum of the 3rd CIFTIS were held at the China National Convention Center. Guests present at the summit delivered wonderful speeches on the role of trade in services in the global value chain. Comrade Wang Yang, Vice Premier of the State Council attaches a special importance to the CIFTIS and the summit and he sent a written address to the meeting, explicitly releasing signals, on behalf of the Chinese government, that we should accelerate the opening-up of the service industry, further promote the development of trade in services and the service industry and move China's economy forward along the road towards healthy development through transformation and upgrading. This increases the participants' confidence in the meeting, and we are greatly encouraged.

In Part Ⅰ of today's forum, several major guests made wonderful speeches. Particularly, Deputy Secretary-General Yi Xiaozhun inspected the development of China's trade in services as seen against the background of a global service economy; he also stated that China should further expand the opening-up of its service industry under the multilateral trade pattern to win a new impetus for the development of China's trade in services and to make a due contribution to the whole formation and improvement of the global value chain so that we can successfully go forward from a large trading country to a strong trading country, which deeply inspired us.

The speech delivered by Comrade Tong Daochi, Assistant Minister of Commerce, further expounded how to make the development of trade in services and the service industry, as specified by the central government, as a strategic mission under open conditions and to promote reforms and development through the opening-up; he also stated that we should accelerate ideological changes and policy innovation with real movement forward, indicating the directions for our future work. So, we can see, from speeches by guests in Part Ⅰ, that this forum is of great significance, with deep insight into the development of the situation and definitive judgment on the tendency and future directions.

The WTO and China: Beijing International Forum has been held three times, becoming a brand project of the CIFTIS. I, on behalf of the Department of Trade in Services and Commercial Services of the Ministry of Commerce, would like to extend a sincere thanks to all guests for their support of the 3rd CIFTIS and a warm congratulation to the successful hosting of the WTO and China: Beijing International Forum.

At present, the world economy has entered an era of a service economy. The proportion of the service industry in the global economy is nearly 70%, and that of the main developed economies is up to about 80%. With the continuous development of economic globalization, the economic integration of all countries has further deepened; the international division of labor and cooperation is increasingly extending from the traditional manufacturing sector to such a high-end sector as the productive service industry; and the international transfer of the service industry related to the manufacturing industry has become more and more important. The proportion of transnational investments in the current service departments in global investment is nearly 2/3, which drives a continuous and rapid development of trade in services and also triggers a new round of global economic restructuring and upgrading. In recent years, global offshore service outsourcing has rapidly developed, and foreign direct investment in the service industry has quickly expanded. The transnational corporations are accelerating the transfer of such productive service industries as R&D, consulting and information to the developing countries; the global service industry chain of transnational corporations as its main body has formed quickly, and the globalization of the service industry is continuously accelerating its development. Trade in services has become an important content of international trade, and particularly, the Department of Trade in Services and Commercial Services of the Ministry of Commerce is a young department established in 2006; and it has witnessed the rapid development of China's trade in services and service industry in the past few years.

The developed countries are now taking a leading position in trade in services, and the developing countries are also accelerating the development, transformation and upgrading of their service industries through the transfer of the service industry. In the era of a service economy, trade in services has become a new impetus for economic growth and a new focus of competition among the great powers. According to recent data released by the WTO, in the 2013 scenario where the total volume of global trade in goods declined, trade in services still maintained a steady growth: the total service import-export volume was nearly 9 trillion USD with a year-on-year growth of 6.1%, with an increase in growth rate of 4.1% compared with the same period of the previous year. Trade in services gives an outstanding contribution to the value added of foreign trade. Compared with the exportation of goods, the additional value of the exportation of services is higher. According to the results of research on the global value chain issued by the UNCTAD, trade in services only accounts for about 1/5 of global trade, service departments contribute for about half of the global export value-added. In the future, the competition in world trade will be more reflected in the competition in trade in services, and every country will take the development of trade in services as an important means to enhance the overall competitiveness of the industrial chain and improve their value-added ability in the international value chain, so competition in the field of trade in services will be increasingly fierce.

The opening-up is an effective way to promote the development of the service industry, and it is also a core power for promoting the development of trade in services. China made an extensive commitment to trade in services openness when joining the WTO. Among over 160 service departments classified by the WTO, China promised to open up 100 departments, involving 9 service categories including commercial service, telecommunications, distribution, construction, education, the environment, finance, tourism and transportation, wherein 54 departments allow wholly foreign-owned businesses, 23 allow foreign shareholding; there are basically no geographical restrictions and quantitative restrictions. According to the commitment, China's various service departments have cleaned up and rectified laws, regulations, policies and rules regarding the service industry on a large scale, standardizing further permissions and qualification requirements as well as procedures within the service industry and initially establishing an open and orderly service market system and an open economic system, basically conforming to the rules established by the WTO.

With the acceleration of the openness of the service industry, the actual inflow of foreign investments to China's service industry is achieving a substantial growth, and trade in services is realizing rapid development: in 2001, the actual inflow of foreign investments to the service industry was 11.23 billion USD, accounting for less than 25% of the actual total inflow of foreign investments; in 2013, the actual inflow of foreign investments in the service industry was 61.45 billion USD, accounting for 52.3% of the actual total inflow of foreign investments, with an average annual growth of 15.2%, with a growth rate over 7% higher than the average of the actual inflow of foreign investments.

In 2001, China's service import-export volume was only 71.9 billion USD, exceeding 100 billion USD in 2003 for the first time, exceeding 300 billion USD in 2008 and reaching 539.64 billion USD in 2013, with an average annual increase of 18.3% since joining the WTO. The proportion of China's trade in services in global trade has increased from 2.2% in the initial period after joining the WTO to 6% in 2013 and went from 13th to 3rd in the world rankings. The gradual opening-up of the service industry not only creates conditions for the actual inflow of foreign investments to the service industry, but it also provides an inexhaustible motivational force for the development of trade in services.

Currently, the scale of the actual inflow of foreign investments to China's service industry has exceeded that of the manufacturing industry for 3 years in a row, and foreign direct investments have gradually accumulated in the service industry. Trade in services is rapidly developing, the total service import-export volume ranks 3rd in the world, and the service industry is playing a more and more important role in China's opening-up.

We notice that, in spite of a good momentum of development in the attraction of foreign investments to China's trade in services and service industry, many problems exist, such as an irrational structure. For example, the structure of attracting foreign investments to the service industry is irrational as the foreign direct investments concentrate upon real estate and other high-profit industries. Since the technological gap of China's service enterprises and transnational corporations is much bigger than that for the manufacturing industry, the service industry has a limited technological capacity for absorption; most local productive service industries are suppressed at the low side of the industrial chain, and radiation and driving effects of foreign investments on domestic investments are not significant enough. The driving effects of foreign investments in the service industry on China's service exports are insufficient; the industrial structure of trade in services is irrational, the proportion of its high value-added is small. Trade in services has been in a state of deficit for a long time and the scale of the deficit is getting bigger. Gradually expanding lots of restrictions on the development of the service industry, actively expanding the inside and outside opening-up of the service industry, promoting reforms and development through the opening-up, cultivating and expanding the domestic service industry are important ideas for China to act upon in order to accelerate the transformation and upgrading of its service industry as well as the development of trade in services.

Ladies and gentlemen, China is now in a key stage of deepening its reform of the economic system and transforming its economic growth mode. The Third Plenary Session of the 18th Central Committee of the CPC proposed the building of an open economic system and accelerating the cultivation of new advantages in leading the competition in international economic cooperation. It explicitly pointed out that we should unify laws and regulations regarding domestic and foreign investments, keep foreign investment policies stable, transparent and predictable, promote an orderly opening-up of such fields in the service industry as finance, education, culture and medical treatment, and lift restrictions on access for foreign investments in such fields in the service industry as raising the young and providing for the elderly, architectural design, accounting and auditing, commercial logistics and E-commerce. This is also the overall scheme of opening up the service industry at a future stage. We will promptly implement and actively and reliably promote the policies, so as to further promote a continuous and healthy development of China's service industry and trade in services.

First, focus on improving environments for investment, enhance the international competitiveness for attracting foreign investments in the field of trade in services, study international investment rules, common practices and experience, actively check the various laws and regulations against the development of the service industry, further improve policies regarding laws and regulations of foreign investments in the field of trade in services, deepen the reform of the foreign investment management system, insist on law-based administration, continuously enhance the level of public services and the level of governmental regulations, get the approval of the foreign investments online service system and formatting, improve the efficiency of the administration, increase the transparency of the administration, enhance service awareness, strengthen the intellectual property protection and law enforcement, safeguard the legal rights and interests of domestic and foreign investors according to the law, and further create a good environment for attracting high-level service industry investments.

Second, actively and reliably guide the orientation of foreign investments, optimize the industrial structure of the service industry, further encourage the orientation of energy conservation and environmental protection, new energy, the modern service industry and other fields of foreign investments, encourage transnational corporations to set up regional headquarters, fortune centers, shared service centers, operations centers and other institutions, guide foreign-owned enterprises to develop new business forms within the service industry by relying on cloud computing, the Internet of Things and other emerging technologies, steadily expand the opening of such service departments as medical and endowment institutions, increase the absorption of employment through foreign investments and promote the role of domestic consumption. Actively utilize foreign investments to develop professional skill-training, improve the quality of the labor force, actively promote practicing and testing beforehand in such areas as the Shenzhen Qianhai Modern Service Industry Demonstration Area, the Zhuhai Hengqin New Area, the Guangzhou Nansha New Area, and the Fujian Pingtan Comprehensive Test Area as breakthroughs of the opening-up of the service industry, effectively utilize domestic and foreign capital markets and support listings at home and abroad of qualified foreign-invested enterprises.

Third, play the role of a window to the Shanghai Pilot Free Trade Zone, and promote the reform of the management system. The establishment of the Shanghai Pilot Free Trade Zone is a major initiative of the PCC to promote the reform and the opening-up in a new situation, marking the fact that China's promotion of reforms through the opening-up has entered a new stage of innovative opening-up. In the new historical period, the key to China's opening-up is innovation in systems and mechanisms. The meaning of establishing the Shanghai Pilot Free

Trade Zone is to explore new ways to comprehensively deepen reforms, expand the opening-up and accumulate new experience. The core of the Shanghai Pilot Free Trade Zone is institutional innovation, not creating policy depressions.

The essence of institutional innovation is to accelerate the transformation of the government's function, expand the opening-up fields, promote the transformation of the trade development mode, deepen the opening up and innovation of the financial fields and improve the institutional guarantee of the legal fields. According to the methods of practicing and testing beforehand, controllable risks, promotion by step and gradual improvement combine the expansion of the opening up and the system reforms as well as the cultivational function and policy innovation, to form a basic institutional framework connecting the common rules of international investment trade, and actively creating a market environment with equal access.

Fourth, improve the supporting system of trade in services policy, and focus on expanding the scale of trade in services. Assistant Minister Tong Daochi has made a clear speech about this, so I will ignore this issue here.

Fifth, improve the international influence and power of discourse of China's trade in services. We should actively participate in negotiations on relevant international rules of the WTO and other institutions, accelerate the realization of cooperation between the international rules and industrial development, and pay positive attention to the progress made during negotiations regarding the trade in services agreement. Jointly promote the process of trade in services liberalization and convenience within the WTO multilateral framework, discuss and negotiate with relevant countries and regions on high-level trade in services arrangements, realize an equal and reciprocal opening-up, promote transparency of the administrative examination and approval of the global service industry and promote the convergence of industrial technical standards in order to create a more favorable external policy environment for the development of trade in services.

Further opening-up of the service industry and further improvement in the developmental environment will certainly create new opportunities and space for the trade in services development. We will firmly promote reforms and the opening-up, seize opportunities, explore and innovate, stick to the policies of equal importance of imports and exports as well as of bringing-in and going-out, insist on taking the developing service industry and trade in services as a strategic focus for the optimization and upgrading of the economic structure, make efforts to expand the scale of trade in services, optimize the structure of trade in services, and improve the international competitiveness of service exports in order to make our due contribution to cultivating new advantages in the competition of international economic cooperation and in improving the global value chain.

Thank you!

# Speech by Lu Zhongyuan, Member of the National Committee of the CPPCC and Former Deputy Director of the Development Research Center of the State Council, at the WTO and China–Beijing International Forum

Thanks for inviting me to attend the forum! I want to talk about new opportunities and space brought about by China's economic transition to the development and opening-up of the service industry.

As everybody knows, China's economic development has slowed down, but it is interesting to notice that when the economic growth slowed down below 8% for two consecutive years, China's new employment did not diminish, but increased to 3.6 million and 4.1 million people, respectively. It was just the service industry that caused that. The service industry exceeded the proportion of the secondary industry in the GDP for the first time last year, reaching 46%. According to our prediction, by the end of the "12th Five-Year Plan" in 2015, it will be out of the question that the output proportion of China's service industry will reach 47% of the GDP. But we need to consider that employment in the service industry has a very low proportion in the national economy, so it has a bright prospect and a huge potential. The service industry has become a new impetus for China's economic growth and a new support for economic transition, as well as the main channel for the growth of employment in China. Please rest assured that it does not matter if China's economic growth cannot reach 7.5%. I believe 7.0%–7.5% is healthy, because China has had a new source of impetus and a new channel for employment. This is an important support because of which we are not worrying about a slow-down in the growth of China's economy. This is affirmative for myself.

Next, the service industry still has vigorous vitality. According to my recent research, the business activity index of the service industry, for consecutive years, has been higher than the purchasing managers index (PMI) of the manufacturing industry, normally 5%–10%. Even when the manufacturing industry is depressed and lower than 50%, the service industry is still 3%–4% higher than the manufacturing industry. Therefore, this further indicates that China's economic growth impetus is obtaining new sources, and the channel for China's employment is changing substantially, which is a new situation in China's economic transition, requiring our a great amount of attention. In case of inadequate attention, we could fall into the traditional set pattern of maintaining growth rate, focusing on growth speed and adding investment. So, I will first release a message that China's trade in services has much room for development. I would like to briefly introduce it by discussing 4 aspects.

First, the service industry has a good prospect for development in China, but it does not have enough policy resources, so its vitality has not been fully played. In order to further reinforce the vitality of the service industry, the State Council has lately issued special policies encouraging the development of the productive service industry. Please notice that, when mentioning trade in services, we mainly research foreign trade and import-export of trade in services. The policies of the State Council on developing the domestic productive service industry are important. They encourage us to develop business consulting, R&D design, marketing services, law, accounting and others, expanding our domestic market and undertaking ability, undoubtedly. Therefore, this creates a better policy environment in which we can expand the introduction of the service industry and undertake service industry outsourcing.

Second, we will further take the road towards market-oriented reform, further open restrictions on relevant fields, and encourage the entry of private capital and foreign capital; our reform direction is to reduce the positive list of the "encouraged" category and transform it into a negative list. We only publish the "prohibited" and the "restricted" categories reducing them as much as possible; we publish the government's power list reducing them as much as possible. In the area of the power list, in my opinion, we should highlight this: "It is prohibited without lawful authorization." The government cannot increase new administrative approval items at will. For the market subject, the message released by the negative list is that "it is free without lawful prohibition". These two cannot be mixed. For the market subject, "it is free without lawful prohibition", but for the government, on the contrary, "it is prohibited without lawful authorization". This reform of the way of thinking needs our careful investigation so as to enlarge the space of for market allocation resources. We rarely encountered such new opportunities and challenges in the past, and our related enterprises, government and professional circles should pay attention to this change, which brings about unprecedentedly important system conditions for the development of trade in services.

Third, we open up to the outside. China encourages private investment and enterprise investment. Administrative approval should be further reduced, and the opening-up of the area of services should be further enlarged. The Third Plenary Session of the 18th Central Committee of the CPC explicitly states that we should open finance, education, accounting and other related service fields in an orderly manner, further open up policies regarding the raising the young and providing for the elderly, and, with an unprecedented speed, we need to open up the related areas in trade in services which have not had enough opening-up in the past.

Fourth, another opportunity is that we need to further expand the regional opening-up and cooperation, and we should propose the Maritime Silk Road and the Silk Road economic belt. In addition, I notice that we have signed free trade agreements with Switzerland and other developed European countries, which will play an important role in allowing China's enterprises to experience and toughen up in their regional environment of opening-up and cooperation and to enlarge our trade in services import/export situation. At the same time, we welcome our partners in the regional cooperation and welcome more and more countries and regions who signed free trade agreements to enter the Chinese market, so as to jointly achieve win-win results with China's enterprises.

Thank you!

# Speech by Hong Xiaodong, Deputy Director General of the Department of WTO Affairs of the Ministry of Commerce, at the WTO and China–Beijing International Forum

Distinguished Ambassador Sun, Secretary-General Yi and all guests,

Good afternoon! I'm delighted to attend the forum and make a speech about the topic. There are two important factors for the rapid development of global trade in services in the last 20 years: one is economic globalization, that is, the continuous deepening of opening-up and liberalization; the other one is the wide application of information technology for trade in services, which enables the costs of telecommunications to diminish and the Internet to rapidly develop, further making service tradability increase continuously. Therefore, the promotion of information technology and the reduction of telecommunication costs have a much greater role in trade in services, especially for Mode 1 and Mode 2.

Under these two factors, global trade in services is rapidly developing and the market is continuously opening up. Let's look at three important data: first, the proportion of the service industry in the global economy is nearly 70%; second, stock in transnational investments accounts for 60%; third, services have contributed nearly 50% to the global export value-added. So, from the above data, it can be seen that services and their investments are of great significance to global trade and economy.

Let's take a look at another piece of data: trade in services only accounts for a little bit more than 20% of global trade. It is 23% if I remember correctly. Let's look at the Chinese data: in 2013, the total amount of China's trade in services was 540 billion USD, accounting for less than 13% of China's trade in goods, lower than the 23% mentioned before. This involves the service industry opening-up, Mode 3 and statistical problems. I'm not stressing that trade in services accounts for a small proportion of global trade, but that trade in services has a great potential and room from another point of view. We are also continuing to explore how to make the importance of services in economic investments become embodied in trade.

When mentioning 13% as China's proportion, from my recognition, we are not stressing that it is a low proportion, but that China's trade in services has a lot of room for further development. The first issue today is how to transform the potential with much room into realistic trade benefits. First, I would like to talk about several of our current conditions, and then look for future measures from the point of view of "making the market play a decisive role" by combining it with today's important theme. We have the following favorable conditions:

First, we have a strong internal impetus. First of all, the increasing level of incomes has created large demands for service consumption in China, thus bringing about many service transactions and trade opportunities. The higher the resident income consumption level of a country is, the larger the service demands for information, services, accounting, consulting and law. Therefore, the continuous increase in China's GDP and per capita GDP has created a large amount of opportunities for demands regarding the service industry. In 2012, the disposable income of China's urban residents reached 25,000 RMB, but only 7,700 RMB in 2002. In the meantime, we have observed a change in residents' consumption, that is, people's consumption focuses more on children's education, medical treatment and tourism. Please take a look at the following data: in 2012, the amount of China's tourism service importation broke through 150 billion RMB, ranking first in various services. The first internal impetus is that we have a great potential. The consumption by China's residents has broken through a point, and after this, we will have huge demands for services and services will play a more and more important role in the national economy. That is because another important channel is that China promotes its economy through consumption, besides through investments. So, in my opinion, the increasing level of incomes is a driving factor in China, and this will also provide huge market and investment opportunities for the world. The second internal impetus is that China is the first manufacturing power in the world, and we all know that many services are related to the manufacturing industry, such as R&D, consulting and professional services. Meanwhile, China is also the first goods power, and the import/export of goods also requires plenty of services, such as transportation, insurance, communications and finance. This can also be seen from China's Balance of International Payments. China's biggest deficit item is transportation. There is also a deficit in China's insurance, which provides a huge space for us. China's service enterprises should take full use of the advantages and market opportunities brought about by China as the first manufacturing power and the first power in trade in goods. China has a great development potential in this aspect. The third internal impetus is that China has obvious advantages in the quality and cost of human resources. China has obvious advantages in college students and professional personnel. The personnel include professional service personnel such as lawyers, accountants and engineers, as well as programmers and software engineers engaged in bulk service outsourcing. We should further expand the advantages we have in knowledge-intensive service exportation and service outsourcing; the advantages have been shown: the amount of China's contracting was up to more than 60 billion USD in 2012. Against the background of the rapid development of Internet information technology, the division of service labor should be further refined. I believe that China can create more opportunities by virtue of its advantage regarding human resources. The above factors are China's internal driving forces.

Second, we have a favorable external environment. China is now a WTO member and multilateral trade is China's largest plateform. Besides, China has its free trade zone strategies: China has signed a series of free trade zone agreements. We will conduct continuous upgrading, e.g. China's "10+1" has been negotiated successfully, and we are now preparing an upgraded version to talk about the China-Korea free trade zone and the China-Australia free trade zone. These multilateral and bilateral agreements will provide a better international environment for the liberalization of China's trade in services. This will create a better environment for exportation and will solve domestic demands for service importation. A trade system combining multilateral trade with bilateral trade provides favorable external conditions for China's development.

Third, we have a good policy environment. The government attaches great importance to the development of the service industry. The "12th Five-Year Plan" explicitly proposed to further emancipate our minds, deepen reforms and enlarge the opening-up, take the promotion of service development as an important breakthrough to adjust the economic structure, take marketization, industrialization, socialization and internationalization as directions and this will accelerate the development of the service industry. Thus, this good policy environment, including the relaxing of market access and the strengthening of post-supervision, has laid a foundation for the development of the future service industry.

With a good foundation, I would like to, in combination with the latest theme, talk about how to play the role of market to stimulate internal vitality and promote development through further opening-up of the service industry.

The first way is through competition. Practice in reform and opening-up for more than 30 years has proved that China's development must be continuously promoted by opening up. Some people may think participating in international competition will lose market shares. But in my view, the opening-up may cause local enterprises to lose some market shares in the short run, but new management and technology can be brought about and a new system of competition can be introduced through competition. More importantly, practice has also proved that the market has been enlarged. So in the long run, the opening-up will definitely achieve win-win results as a whole. Take insurance for an example. China's insurance just began to develop when China joined the WTO; we were worried about introducing foreign investments and the opening-up to foreign investments, but we concluded, afterwards, that foreign investments might take up a part of the cake but the cake is much bigger than in the past. At that time, China's insurance participation was low, but with the entry of foreign-invested insurance companies, the raising of insurance awareness, as well as the introduction of the concept of insurance and new methods of insurance sales, China's insurance totally realized a premium income of 1.72 trillion RMB in 2013, 8 times that when China joined the WTO. The enlarging of the "cake", of course, is attributed to our own developmental factors, but the competition factor also plays a certain role. The cake was enlarged by 8 times, and foreign investments cut a piece. How much is the piece? Foreign investment in life insurance is lingering over 5%. Therefore, competition brings about new management, concepts and modes as well as new products and services, from which the consumers will undoubtedly benefit. Actually, besides cases of foreign investment opening-up, domestic competition will also bring benefits to consumers: now, we can contact friends through WeChat for free, saving telephone charges. So, consumers can get continuous benefits from continuous competition.

The second way is to make the market play an important role. Besides competition, there is the problem of understanding: the market. How to understand the market? In my opinion, making the market play a role does not mean focusing on the domestic market, since the domestic market and the international market cannot be separated. If we make the market play a role and close the door to competition on China's market and not take this market as an international market, the market plays a role in closing the market, which cannot show an open environment. The market is made up of factors. Whether for capital or labor force, or foreign investment access in Mode 3 in the future, the market with mobile factors should be a full integration of the domestic market and the foreign market. Thus, we have a clear understanding in this sense: We should firmly promote the understanding of it based on competition and market integration, and firmly promote relevant reforms and opening-up. I have two specific ideas about this: The first is to change the opening-up by opening up. Under the current circumstances, either we pay "entry fees" for joining the WTO, or we are qualified for a WTO member, we were open unilaterally at that time; now, whether for multilateral negotiations or free trade zone negotiations, we should be based on the requirements of the development of the domestic industry, we should accelerate the opening-up of the service industry and promote mutual market opening-up with more economic trade partners, so as to create a good external environment for the development of our domestic service industry. The second is to promote reforms by opening up. Further clear unreasonable restrictions on further opening-up and development of the service industry, create a fair internal market environment, promote the innovation of the system of the domestic service industry, fully stimulate the developmental vitality of the domestic service industry and cultivate core competitiveness. This is to firmly promote the work through changing the opening-up by opening up and through promoting reforms by opening up.

Next there are the questions asked in the previous sector. From our point of view, the Shanghai Pilot Free Trade Zone is a pilot project of practicing and trying beforehand, promoting reforms and opening-up. The Shanghai Pilot Free Trade Zone explicitly proposes to enlarge the zone. In my opinion, the opening up of the service industry is of the maximum effect and on most measures in the Shanghai Pilot Free Trade Zone, which enlarges the opening up of six fields including finance, shipping, commerce and trade, professional services, cultural services and social services. The Shanghai Pilot Free Trade Zone is a reflection of the transformation of the function of China's government: On the one hand, to adopt the method of the negative list, which has a more direct opening, a stronger opening stability and predictability and is more favorable to attract foreign investors and service operators compared with the positive list; on the other hand, the innovation of the financial management system will further promote the orderly and free mobility of international and domestic factors as well as an efficient configuration of resources, conducive to a deep integration of the market. The last point is also important. In addition to domestic demands, a good policy environment, the promotion of reforms and opening-up, China should also actively participate in global trade in services negotiations by using an external impetus. As is known to all, the Doha Round of negotiations were launched in 2001 and have been unsolved for 13 years. However, the 9th Ministerial Meeting of the WTO, held on the island of Bali, successfully achieved an early harvest, covering trade facilitations and some topics regarding agricultural cooperation development. Although the achievements may be a part and even a small part compared with package programs, they bring confidence. The multilateral system can be something, it brings hope to people. The Post-Bali Trade Agenda can go on; all members were sitting at the table to negotiate the Post-Bali Trade Agenda. There is no doubt that trade in services is an important part of the Post-Bali Trade Agenda. It can be said that Bali's early harvest brings about new opportunities to reinitiate the negotiations of trade in services and even to initiate the entire Post-Bali negotiations. At present, it can be said that it is time for us to promote multilateral services.

China is a firm supporter of and an important contributor to the multilateral trade system. A sound development of the multilateral trade system is conducive for China to fully use multilateral rules and to create a fair, transparent and predictable external environment for us to comprehensively build up a moderately prosperous society.

This needs a domestic industrial circle, including our department, to carefully analyze our advantages and disadvantages in the negotiations. On the one hand, the whole competitiveness of our trade in services is weaker than that of developed countries; on the other hand, we are facing the integration of two markets, the further opening up and promoting of domestic reforms by opening-up. We have two purposes to finally participate in multilateral trade: One is to realize the fair, transparent and predictable environment mentioned before; the other is to really make our domestic service industry play the market role through the opening-up, enabling more integration of the domestic market. Of course, integration cannot be completed in one day. The opening-up makes our domestic service industry have a stronger developmental impetus. Actually, in the past 13 years, after China joined the WTO, WTO research results prove that the more open, the more rapidly the economic entity develops. We want to achieve this objective, and multilateral trade is our main channel. Of course, I heard other methods earlier, but we would like to try different channels to promote trade liberalization.

Last of all, I want to say that, as long as we have a suitable policy, actively participating in multilateral trade in services negotiations and integrating internal impetuses and external resources, I believe that China's service industry will develop more rapidly in the future.

Thank you!

# Speech by Abdel–Hamid Mamdouh, Director General of the Trade in Services Division of the WTO, at the WTO and China–Beijing International Forum

Ladies and gentlemen,

Good afternoon! A big thank you to the organizer, especially President Sun, for giving me the chance to deliver this speech. I have witnessed the development of the CIFTIS and this is the third time that I have attended it. I feel honored to attend this grand meeting every year and see its development over the past years.

CIFTIS may be the most important grand meeting, because it is related to trade in services. Trade in services is also discussed at different forums. This grand meeting focuses on trade in services, and I think it will gain more and more attention. Undoubtedly, my discussion is from the point of view of the WTO, and brilliant speeches by other speakers provide many essential analyses. I would like to talk about a different view, that is, discuss topics concerning trade in services that are current to the WTO from that organization's point of view. Also, we think that China should pay attention to some policy challenges.

First, in terms of the service agenda of the WTO, we have some suitable discussions on service liberalization, such as finance in 1997, and discussions on communication services. The members which joined the WTO after its establishment, such as China, have made important commitments and have achieved many economic reforms. In 2000, we started a discussion, i.e. making agriculture enter the Doha Development Agenda (DDA Round). The negotiations of the DDA Round have been going on for 13 years, which is the age of a teenager. Now, with many changes, the actual service industry has changed in the past 20 years, and the WTO also wants to promote the development of trade in services. The liberalization of Trade in services has made great progress unilaterally, and such change was discussed during the governmental function when we had the GATS discussion earlier, which included me and my country, Egypt. Currently, we have achieved liberalization to a large extent, and are developing in an organic way, because we need to establish a competitive service market.

Second, trade in services is of strategic significance and plays an important role. The current service industry decides the economic competitiveness, and a more developed, reliable and effective service industry can promote economic development. Sometimes, I don't want you to repeat my country's case-Egypt. The service industry is important to the manufacturing industry, and also to agriculture. We can see that, without a good service industry as support, agriculture will not achieve a good development. As we all know, Egypt ranks fifth in vegetable planting. But why is such an advantage in planting not reflected, accordingly, in Egypt's exportation? This is because vegetable planting is one aspect, and putting it on the market for sales is another aspect. There are a series of services, such as picking, packaging, financing, transportation, freezing and distribution, as well as a series of sectors such as insurance. Failure to provide such services causes a 30%–40% waste of vegetables.

In the meantime, this is also important from the point of view of policy. Service is getting more and more important, and so is social welfare. Service is not only involved in the economy, but also in efficiency and in social welfare. The level of services decides the level of social welfare.

In the past 20 years, another development has been that of the global supply chain and the value chain. With the cross-border feature, it implements cross-border transactions and localization absorption in terms of enhancing efficiency and productivity. Today, the supply chain is not only relying on technology, but also on some processes. New processes are developing and changing, but many operations are still using old and traditional technology.

How should we respond to this? What actions should we take for some multilateral activities? For many regional, bilateral and multilateral cooperations, some WTO members and EU members are carrying out negotiations on trade in services agreements, which is unusual. Since other rounds of negotiations did not continue, the members chose another way, but TISA is not the best way. TISA can achieve effective short-term objectives, but for the long-term strategic objectives, it's better to have negotiations on trade in services agreements within the WTO framework. The first reason is country coverage. These countries want to have a bilateral trade system and want more participants. If we take a look at Norway's distribution of the service industry within the country, we can see that it has established an EEA with EU countries, which is a European area agreement, and the remaining 30% of trade in services is conducted with non-TISA trade members. So, the long-term effect of multilateral negotiations is our pursuit. Multilateral rules are some specification standards. Looking at the issue from business circles, the best way to develop regulatory standards and cooperation is through multilateral systems. Since different regulatory standards on the market increase the costs of the enterprise operation, we need to homogenize such ideology and coordinate the enterprise operation. The second reason is implementation. We need to find out a long-term feasible solution to dispute resolutions. We hope to establish a fully comprehensive global project, including trade in services negotiations.

Now, let's focus on policy. How can we achieve greater integration of the global value chain, the supply chain, innovation, the efforts of the Chinese government and the world economy? We want to develop a framework to classify the things, so that we can take actions better. We mainly focus on 4 issues: The first is the development of the enterprise. Business circles are continuing to develop, but policy-makers do not catch up with the pace of the development of enterprises. New enterprises are innovating the processes, increasing the vitality of the market; they have deeper understandings compared with the policy-makers. Therefore, enterprises are catching up with and surpassing the policy-makers' actions. The second is our understanding. If we do not understand enterprise development, we cannot make polices in Step 2. Policy-making, especially in developed countries, still follows a traditional method where the connection between upstream and downstream service departments cannot be seen. The global supply chain has a series of different services, such as multi-level policy-making, but we have a way to coordinate them. So, when China's "12th Five-Year Plan" suggested adding some coordination factors into the policy vision for the first time, it did not suggest specially making policies for individual departments such as transportation and communication. We have made great progress in technical cooperation, and more countries are open, but policy-making is still isolated, which is also reflected in the developed countries. Thus, how we realize more coordinated developments in policy-making and how we plan policy-making as a whole to realize coordinated developments for a series of policies, such as investments, is important. The third issue is regulation. Policy-making is to build a vision. It is a difficult challenge to establish laws and regulations and to implement policies, because modern rule-making is complicated. Meanwhile, we should also think about the type of law framework to be developed and the way to implement regulatory systems. The fourth issue is international cooperation. From the point of view of law, how can we coordinate our agreement systems and the regional agreements as well as the systems and their law systems, and how can we achieve the integration of regulatory systems and the international cooperation framework? How can we achieve policy coordination? I think it is a huge challenge. We are focusing on how to use the global value chain to discuss and negotiate in Geneva. Why are there no such acts? The reason is that we lack international cooperation. We must understand policy coordination, so that the global value chain with seamless connections can be provided, but it has not happened. So, this is a challenge we need to solve.

I feel quite honored to come here, not only because I am a member of the grand meeting, but also because I can see that the Chinese government takes policy-making very seriously.

Thank you very much!

# Speech by Qian Fangli, Director of the China Service Outsourcing Research Center, at the International Conference of China Service Outsourcing Talent Cultivation

Distinguished guests, ladies and gentlemen,

Good morning. I am very delighted to have the opportunity to discuss with you about the development of service outsourcing of talents. The topic of my report is the construction of a system for the development of talent service outsourcing under the new situation.

First of all, let's review the development of the service outsourcing industry.

Ⅰ. The status of the development of service outsourcing.

From 2011 to 2013, the amount of signed contracts and the amount of those carried out increased at the annual rate of 40%.

Ⅱ. Pattern of the Chinese service outsourcing industry:

The service outsourcing industry has been rapidly developing in 4 municipalities, 28 provinces and 115 cities. Until 2014, there were over 160 service outsourcing parks, 2,500 enterprises and 5.5 million service personnel, showing that the pattern of the Chinese service outsourcing industry had basically formed.

Ⅲ. The condition of the development of substantial offshore contracts:

Regarding substantial offshore contracts, the top five industries in the first quarter of 2014 were the information service industry, the manufacturing industry, engineering design & inspection, financial insurance, and retail & wholesale, of which the information service industry enjoyed the largest proportion, that is, 50.9%, and engineering design & inspection enjoyed the fastest growth rate, that is, 723%.

From the boom index of Chinese service outsourcing, the leading index and the lagging index in the entire Chinese service outsourcing area were 99.1% and 106.6% respectively in April 2014. The former rose by 3.91% over March, revealing the fact that service outsourcing is in good conditions at present, and the latter fell by 14.32%, showing the downward trend in January 2014. This further showed the lag of industrial indexes.

In terms of the index of entrepreneur expectations and that of the enterprises' Comprehensive production and management climate, they were 143.3% and 139.0% respectively in the first quarter, which had dropped slightly with respect to before, but they were still in good conditions on the whole.

Secondly, let's take a look at the new situation facing the service outsourcing industry.

I . A new round of technological innovation is springing up. A group of technologies are rapidly developing, such as "Big Data, Cloud Computing, Platformization and Mobilization". IDC predicts that big data technology and service market scale will reach 32.4 billion USD in 2017, with an annual composition growth rate of 27%. As set out in the report of the Internet Society of China, the economic scale of the Chinese mobile internet was 108.3 billion RMB in 2013, accounting for 18% of the total internet economy scale. Hence, the mobile internet is the crucial driving force for the development of the internet.

The rapid development of technologies leads to a notable surge of information. By reference to materials, we predict that figures and data in the coming ten years will have a 44-fold increase, and that 80% of the global data will be non-structural data. Such non-structural data are alive, fragmented and original, and need to be further explored and analyzed; moreover, these data can bring some huge commercial opportunities to service outsourcing enterprises. It is the typical feature of the new type of service outsourcing business. We have made a simple analysis of new business types. The emergence of 3D printing technology, mobile internet and the Internet of Things, as well as the development of big data and industry convergence, creates many new businesses, such as product sampling services, field intelligent design, space information services, etc.

II . The emphasis on industry is enhanced. In order to guarantee an increase, expand its domestic demand, adjust its structure and promote employment, developing service outsourcing is a strategic need for China. The Third Plenary Session of the 18th Central Committee of the CPC, the Report of Premier Li Keqiang on the Work of the Government and the Executive Meeting of the State Council all have proposed to develop trade in services and outsourcing so as to make service outsourcing a significant means of transformation development. The Third Plenary Session of the 18th Central Committee of the CPC has specially pointed out that the government should enhance the procurement of public service.

III . The pace of transformation and upgrading is quickened. After years of development, competition among enterprises is growing, and in the meanwhile, enterprises are also facing some problems such as appreciation of the RMB, RMB cost raise, purchaser's premium rigorousness, which make enterprises pay more and more attention to transformation and upgrading. Transformation and upgrading mean that an enterprise constantly improves its capability of independent innovation through improving its technologies so as to provide overall solutions, integrate industry chain upstream and downstream, deepen industry application and expand market development, thus continuously increasing the level of the value chain of enterprises.

Finally, let's turn to the status quo of talent development, bottlenecks and how to construct a scientific system for talent development.

Ⅰ. Development status: The number of service outsourcing personnel with a bachelor's degree or above reached 3.27 million as of April 2014, accounting for 66.6% of all service outsourcing personnel. This figure is relatively high.

Ⅱ. The main bottleneck for talent development.

1. There is a shortage of interdisciplinary talents: A general employee who needs to do a good job should possess the following six occupational qualities according to the capacity competence model, that is, skill, knowledge, social role, self-image, characteristics and motivation. In general, the first two qualities can be shown clearly, but the remaining are potential capacities, like the part of the iceberg that is hidden under the surface. Anyone who wants to be competent for a job must possess these six capacities. Based on the capacity competence model, we can see that our talent cultivation still focuses on single skill and knowledge education and lacks the cultivation in value, communication skills and professional ethics, resulting in the shortage of interdisciplinary talents who not only possess professional knowledge in multi-fields but who also meet service outsourcing work requirements.

2. There is a shortage of leading talents with an international vision: According to our questionnaire, about 73% of the enterprises believe that the lack of talents is the main problem in the process of enterprise development, and nearly 50% of the enterprises believe it is hard to recruit mid-to-high-end talents successfully. Talent shortage is the most serious problem, followed by the rise in costs and financing difficulty. At present, the per-capita production value of our service outsourcing personnel is lower than 20,000 USD. The lack of high-end talent will directly result in a lack of a driving force for industry improvement, further affecting the transformation and upgrading of enterprises.

3. The system for talent development remains to be improved. Various regions have carried out many beneficial experimentations and attempts at cultivating service outsourcing talents, and they have obtained a good amount of successful experience. Here, I provide a simple list of attempts and training conditions in some cities. But so far, a national system for talent development has not be formed yet, including systems for a talent standard, talent evaluation and talent cultivation.

Ⅲ. Construction of a scientific system of talent development.

1. To improve the system of a talent standard: A system of talent development consists of systems of talent standards, talent evaluation and talent cultivation. Based on the theory of the capacity competence model, the improvement in the cultivation of different types of talents in service outsourcing needs to be speeded up; and in the meanwhile, it is necessary to study the required characteristics of the talents in the industry, regularly release a directory of

badly-needed talents based on the professional development emphasis in the new phase and work especially on the following three aspects: The establishment of a primary talent cultivation standard, of a mid-to-high-end talent cultivation standard and of a leading talent cultivation standard.

2. To set up a professional and effective talent evaluation system: A talent evaluation system supports the dynamic monitoring of talent conditions by the government, the cultivation and selection of an enterprise's external exchange talent and internal backup talent, and employee capacity and self-improvement. Therefore, a service outsourcing talent system should be jointly built up by professional institutions, industrial associations and enterprises, which can conform to the new requirements on service outsourcing talents within the new situation.

3. To construct a talent cultivation system: The first step is to improve the training mode, and then combine internal cultivation and external cultivation, which means the establishment of cooperation between colleges and enterprises so as to connect college talent cultivation and the actual needs of the enterprises. In the meanwhile, new training content needs to be created, and a complete course system such as an ITO training course should be established to conform to the different post-talent requirements.

4. To develop a training mechanism: The national industrial association sets up a national-level service outsourcing talent cultivation framework first, and various regions establish promotional institutions led by industrial associations or leading enterprises. Besides, a talent cultivation carrier focusing on colleges and specialized training institutions is required.

To sum up, talent development is a complicated system, including a talent standard subsystem, a talent evaluation subsystem and a talent cultivation subsystem which should work together. A scientific system of talent development is the only way that will lead to the construction of a new highland of service outsourcing. Thank you!

# Speech by Ren Hongbin, Party Secretary and Vice Director of the Academy of International Trade and Economic Cooperation of the Ministry of Commerce, at the China Service Outsourcing Talent Cultivation International Conference

I want to share my opinions with you about the construction of the service outsourcing supply chain. Just now, Director Qian made a comprehensive review on the development of the service outsourcing industry. Here, I want to show you the conditions regarding the following three aspects. The service outsourcing industry has played an increasingly important role in the development of the national economy and society, which has the following three features:

The first is that service outsourcing has brought new growth to our national economy. According to 2013 data, the offshore and onshore scale of the Chinese service outsourcing industry was 1.7 trillion RMB, equal to 2.97% of the GDP, leading to an economic growth of 0.8 percentage points, which fully demonstrates that the service outsourcing industry is not a small business but it is an industry that supports the development of a national economy.

The second is that the service outsourcing industry has become a system that facilitates the employment of graduates or of the Chinese or of urban residents. As was just mentioned by Director Qian, the yearly increase of employment in service outsourcing was 1.065 million in 2003, equal to 80.1% of the urban employment. Two-thirds of the new employees are graduates with a college degree or above. Therefore, the service outsourcing industry creates a great number of employment opportunities for graduates.

The third is that service outsourcing has become a significant means for Chinese economic transformation, especially the transformation of foreign trade. Since the outbreak of the financial crisis, the growth of our trade in goods trade has been relatively slow, with a growth rate of not more than 10%. On the contrary, the annual growth rate of trade in services has been very fast. Since the implementation of the "12th Five-Year Plan", our international outsourcing service has developed at the growth rate of over 45%. In recent years, owing to the decline of foreign demand and the downturn of the domestic economy, which has caused a change in the structure of the outsourcing services, such as ITO, BPO and KTO, the overall development of the outsourcing service industry has declined. Last year, offshore outsourcing was 4.541 billion USD, an increase of 35%. However, our outsourcing service industry has kept a growth rate of over 40% since the implementation of the "12th Five-Year Plan".

According to measurements and calculations, the turnover of the international service outsourcing business came to 21.6% of service exports in 2013, with a growth rate 3.3 times as large as the service export growth rate. Service outsourcing is not only the extension of the industrial, supply and value chains, but it is also a significant support for management. Besides, it is an important means for improving the international competitiveness of Chinese manufacturing, and an important measure for guiding the development of trade in services, for improving the structure of trade in services and for correcting the trade in services deficit. Below are three features of service outsourcing. I will express my opinions on talent construction.

I. The status and problem of talent supply. At present, a group of universities and colleges throughout the country have launched a course relevant to service outsourcing. Besides, a series of service outsourcing talent training bases and social training institutions have been established in various regions, which provide crucial support for the development of our service outsourcing industry. Service outsourcing is an important part of outsourcing, and a sustainable supply of talent is the major bottleneck of this service. Now, service outsourcing has the following problems.

First, service outsourcing shows a wide gap in demand regarding four aspects.

1. There is a shortage of high-end talent, especially industry-leading talent, high-level technical talent, management talent and international marketing talent who can lead large technical teams to undertake complicated outsourcing business orders.

2. Total service outsourcing is insufficient. On the one hand, although the number of college graduates is over 7 million each year, only a few of them are engaged in service outsourcing work. The cultivation of talent at colleges is is not closely related to the actual requirements of enterprises. On the other hand, professional training institutions normally provide short-term training, causing the trainee to fail to meet enterprise requirements in actual operation and application. Furthermore, training within the enterprise is a good training mode which can produce a good effect, but it is costly. Most enterprises prefer to recruit experienced employees rather than spend a great amount of money on cultivating service outsourcing employees.

3. Service outsourcing personnel are weak in capacity, which shows in their foreign language skills and in their single technical skills. Interdisciplinary talent is lacking.

4. There is a high mobility of service outsourcing talents. It is the result of ① low income, ② rise in costs, ③ boring work (since service outsourcing personnel are mostly youngsters, and

data processing, software and call centers are located in remote areas, life is drab and youngsters are reluctant to stay there for a long time), ④ prevalent poaching among enterprises.

Second, the effectiveness of the supply of service outsourcing talent remains to be improved.

1. Institutions of higher education and advanced training institutions fail to make full use of their resources. Nowadays, college education is unable to meet the developmental needs of the service outsourcing industry. Universities directly under the Ministry of Education impose restrictions on curriculum in conformity to the provisions established by the Ministry of Education, further resulting in restrictions on setting up independent specialties. Consequently, "985" and "211" universities are incapable of cultivating undergraduates according to service outsourcing requirements, so much so that graduates will not be able to undertake service outsourcing work. Moreover, vocational colleges and social training institutions focus on the cultivation of general low-end talent rather than interdisciplinary talent. As a consequence, there is a serious shortage of mid-to-high-end talents. The No. 33 document of the State Council has specially established that more efforts need to be made towards providing financial support to and cultivating mid-to-high-end talents.

2. Education is divorced from the needs of enterprises. Undergraduates need to be trained for three months before engaging in work.

3. There is a serious lack of faculty, especially regarding practical experience.

4. There is a lack of a training standard and a system of certification.

5. National financial support remains to be enhanced. Service outsourcing training institutions are designed to improve the abilities of service outsourcing talents. It is the main channel for the delivery of service outsourcing talents. Currently, the public subsidy for each trainee is 500 RMB, which is far from enough, because training expenses generally reach 6,000 RMB generally.

Third, service outsourcing suffers the problem of building up a service outsourcing talent supply chain.

A "Four-in-one" talent supply chain combining the government, enterprises, colleges and training institutions should be set up.

(1) The government cooperates with service outsourcing industry associations and enterprises at all levels in order to establish a market-oriented talent cultivation and management mechanism that can realize the sound development of service outsourcing manpower.

(2) A talent cultivation mechanism and platform should be established, and a complete set of scientific systems should be formulated for talent requirements.

(3) Colleges actively should adjust the structure of their subjects and their course settings, and increase their educational input.

(4) The cooperation among the government, enterprises, colleges and social training institutions should be strengthened to enhance a smooth, market-oriented system.

1. The introduction and cultivation of senior service outsourcing talent should be enhanced, mainly at the micro level, especially in enterprises. In the current year, the focus of work is to define the high-end talent standard. Other work includes the establishment and improvement of stock equity and the performance allocation incentive mechanism, the expansion of autonomy in team management, experimentation in cultivating high-level talents and the construction of an inclusive enterprise culture in an attempt at retaining talents, promoting high-end talents to further study and work abroad and creating promotional channels for them. What's more, national and local subsidies should be made available, and the problem of people's livelihood, such as housing, children education and household registration, should be resolved properly.

2. The training for mid-to-high-end talents should be enhanced. As I have mentioned, the governmental subsidy is 500 RMB, but training expenses are 6,000 RMB. The support from second-level governments may make it possible to increase governmental subsidies to 1,000 RMB at a proportion of 1:1 between the local government and the central government. Service outsourcing enterprises may grant proper allowances to intern students and new employees who receive training.

3. The mode of cooperation between colleges and enterprises should be innovated.

(1) The autonomy of colleges in course design should be expanded. Colleges should be encouraged to launch various specialized courses on the basis of the developmental need of domestic industries.

(2) The university credit transfer system should be actively carried out. The internship of a student in an enterprise should be converted into credit in order to encourage students to participate in enterprise training practice, promote direct employment after graduation, and directly enter the service outsourcing enterprise without the need for training.

(3) The cooperation between colleges and service outsourcing enterprises should be energetically promoted. A service outsourcing internship should be included in the college teaching system so as to meet talent demands.

4. Practical training of service outsourcing should be launched.

(1) Service outsourcing enterprises are encouraged to set up practice bases and they should be supported in their recruitment of undergraduates. Relevant enterprise business should be included in college course so that graduates will be able to obtain employment upon graduation.

(2) The training mechanism of the service outsourcing park should play its role fully.

(3) World-famous outsourcing enterprises are encouraged to set up service outsourcing talent training bases.

Ⅱ. Great efforts should be made to create new ways to improve the quality of training.

1. Professional training institutions, standards for qualification certification and market access should be made available as soon as possible.

2. Foreign institutions are introduced.

3. The level of domestic training institutions should be improved.

4. The construction of a service outsourcing public platform should be enhanced.

(1) A service outsourcing talent website and database should be established, a service outsourcing recruitment fair, forum and authoritative conferences need to be held regularly, and the establishment of communication, exchanges and a mechanism for cooperation among enterprises, colleges and training institutions should be promoted. In my opinion, the conference is a good information service exchange platform. Shortly before, the Academy of International Trade and Economic Cooperation of the Ministry of Commerce founded a service outsourcing journal, which is a unique national journal regarding the domestic service. We want to further propagandize service outsourcing through this journal in order to strengthen the understanding of service outsourcing and to enhance the cultivation of service outsourcing talents. Besides, I hope all of you present will pay attention to the journal and share your opinions regarding the journal so that we can promote the development of our national service outsourcing industry.

(2) Leading service outsourcing enterprises and transnational companies should be encouraged to set up training centers and create a normative service training platform.

(3) Social institutions should play their role.

(4) An attempt should be made to establish an outsourcing integrity system that will create an environment of orderly competition within the service outsourcing talent market and promote a reasonable flow of service outsourcing talents. The development of service outsourcing is inseparable from governmental support. I hope governments at all levels can strengthen the organization, the planning, the management and the propaganda work of service outsourcing.

Finally, may the conference be a complete success, thank you!

# Part IV

## Summary of the Speeches on Theme Days and Special Activities

# Speech by Fang Aiqing, Vice Minister of Commerce, on Beijing Theme Day

Distinguished Deputy Mayor Cheng Hong, all guests, ladies and gentlemen,

Good morning! Today is the last day of the 3rd CIFTIS which has lasted for 5 days. This year's CIFTIS continues to be brilliant with active negotiations and fruitful results. I'm delighted to gather with you on Beijing Theme Day. First of all, I, on behalf of the Ministry of Commerce, want to extend congratulations to Beijing Theme Day activity!

CIFTIS is a comprehensive global trade in services fair jointly established by the Ministry of Commerce and the People's Government of Beijing Municipality. After a three-year cultivation, CIFTIS has become an important window on the opening up of China's service industry and an important platform for strengthening international exchanges regarding trade in services. The People's Government of Beijing Municipality has done a lot of work and has made strenuous efforts to establish, cultivate and develop CIFTIS. I, on behalf of the Ministry of Commerce, would like to take this opportunity to extend a heartfelt thanks to all the personnel engaged in CIFTIS work!

At present, as the world economy slowly recovers, the service industry is becoming a new engine and a new impetus to drive that recovery. With the thorough development of economic globalization, the international division of labor and coordination extend from the traditional manufacturing sector to the productive service industry and other high-end sectors, triggering a new round of adjustment and upgrading of the global economic structure and stimulating the continuous and rapid development of trade in services.

The "12th Five-Year Plan" is a key transition for China to push the service economy forward, and it is also an important strategic opportunity to greatly develop trade in services. In 2013, the value-added of China's service industry accounted for 46.1% of the GDP, exceeding industry for the first time, becoming a leading industry in the national economy. China's trade in services volume reached 539.6 billion USD, ranking third in the world. The Chinese government will greatly develop the service industry and trade in services as an important way to change its methods of economic development as well as an important means for creating an upgraded economy, for further establishing a strategic orientation of trade in services, and for taking this as a strategic focus of economic development.

Beijing is the center of the innovation of China's politics, culture, international exchanges, science and technology. With rich scientific and technological resources, high-end talent agglomeration and development of the productive service industry, Beijing has unique advantages to developing the service industry and trade in services:

The first advantage is its solid industrial foundation. In 2013, Beijing's service industry accounted for 77% of the GDP, ranking first among China's provinces and cities; the service industry economy rapidly increased, and the utilization of foreign investments in the service industry exceeded 70%, the first to form a service-oriented economic development pattern in China; the total volume of service imports and exports exceeded 100 billion USD, accounting for 20% of China's total amount; basically it formed a pattern with the development of high value-added trade in services such as communications, insurance, finance, computer and information services.

The second advantage is its good environment for development. In terms of policy environment, the People's Government of Beijing Municipality pays great attention to the development of trade in services, it relies on the construction of the Shijingshan national service industry comprehensive pilot reform and the Zhongguancun modern service industry pilot reform; it also improves its policies regarding the development of the service industry and of trade in services, and it has hosted theme day activities during the CIFTIS for three successive years; in terms of market environment, the degree of the opening up of the market for Beijing's service industry ranks first in China, and the headquarters and the R&D institutions of 714 transnational corporations have been established in Beijing.

The third advantage is its perfect promotional system. Beijing has built 6 city-level service outsourcing parks, including more than 10 public service platforms such as the professionalization of the biological foundation. At the 3rd CIFTIS, Beijing also established a platform for enterprises to negotiate and cooperate in several fields, including financial services and E-commerce.

Ladies and gentlemen, today we are witnessing the results of the development of Beijing's trade in services. I believe that we will promote comprehensive services, including Beijing services, so that we can go out to the world better and more quickly with our joint efforts. Finally, I wish the Beijing Theme Day activity complete success and I hope that everyone will return home with fruitful results. Thank you!

# Speech by Cheng Hong, Deputy Mayor of Beijing Municipality, on Beijing Theme Day

Distinguished Vice Minister Fang Aiqing, President Bruno, all guests and friends in the media,

Good morning! I'm glad to get together with you during the Beijing Theme Day activity again. First of all, I, on behalf of the People's Government of Beijing Municipality, want to extend a warm welcome again to all our guests and friends in the media attending the Beijing Theme Day activity, a sincere thanks to the Ministry of Commerce for their support of Beijing and of CIFTIS, and a lofty respect to the insiders for their important contributions to the development of Beijing's service industry and trade in services!

It is June 1st today, a day with vitality, growth and hope. On such a day, we feel pleased and delighted to review the development of Beijing's service industry and trade in services over the past few years. I would like to take this opportunity to talk about 3 points in order to share with you the joy of seeing the growth of Beijing's service industry and trade in services.

The first point is the rapid growth of the scale. Looking back on the development of Beijing's service industry and trade in services during the past 10 years, we can see that the service industry is developing in Beijing. Since 2004, the value-added of Beijing's service industry has increased from 0.34 trillion RMB to 1.5 trillion RMB last year, with a three-and-a-half-fold increase within 10 years. During this process, with the growth of the service industry, trade in services has developed more quickly. The volume of trade in services increased from 23.57 billion USD in 2004 to 110 billion USD last year, with an increase of 4.7 times within 10 years. Beijing's trade in services accounts for 20% of China's trade in services, and 1.2% of the global trade in services, from which we can see the competitiveness and the growth of Beijing's service industry and trade in services.

The second point I would like to share with you is the acceleration of structural upgrading. The acceleration of structural upgrading can be described with three figures, i.e. "20%", "40%" and "60%". Service accounts for 20% of Beijing's foreign trade. The proportion has increased by about 10% in the past 10 years and at a high level in China, because service accounts for about 10% of China's foreign trade in services. Service accounts for 40% of Beijing's foreign trade. Beijing's emerging trade in services field accounts for 60% of trade in services. From "40%" and "60%", we can see that Beijing has a strong competitiveness and growth in the field of trade in services, which shows a flourishing trend in an emerging field.

The third point is the remarkable effect on trade in services. I will not repeat the role of trade in services in economic development and in the expansion of the scale of foreign trade; I would like to talk about the unique role of trade in services in cities by looking at the following 3 aspects:

1. Trade in services promotes an increase in employment. Trade in services is closely related to our production and our lives. In recent years, trade in services has provided a lot of unprecedented employment opportunities in Beijing's development. For example, thousands of people in northern mountain villages who used to be peasants are receiving overseas tourists locally. They actually make money from trade in services and explore their own careers at new employment posts. Furthermore, more than 100 thousand college graduates in Beijing are providing information services for many countries and regions all over the world through service outsourcing. These cases show that trade in services has created a lot of new space for promoting an improvement in employment opportunities.

2. Trade in services promotes an improvement in the quality of services for life in the city. In recent years, Beijing has been attracting more and more overseas investors. Now, an accumulated capital of 70 billion USD has been directly invested in Beijing successively, with more than 80% going into the service industry, including the productive service industry and the life services industry. In the productive service industry, the development of trade in services provides many new choices for residents. For example, in their daily lives, residents can consume in thousands of chain stores, comprehensive stores, specialty stores, brand stores and other places with a richer market and more life choices; people can enjoy lots of imported films in their spare time so as to feel regional culture and foreign culture; parents can keep close communication with overseas children through the international communication service; on overseas business trips or leisure travel, numerous overseas airlines are available; trade in services is in our lives. For the past few years, the strengthening of trade in services has enabled residents to enjoy more diversified and far better services, making a unique contribution to the improvement of the quality of life in our city. In particular, according to the strategic orientation towards the acceleration of building up and developing Beijing to be a world-class livable city, it is important to strengthen trade in services and provide an environment with more high-quality living conditions.

3. Trade in services stimulates China's culture and technology to go out, thus improving China's influence throughout the world. In the past several years, especially by virtue of CIFTIS, a large number of projects are going overseas. Up to now, Beijing has carried out trade in services with more than 200 countries and regions, and over 1,000 enterprises have gone out to carry out operation and management activities overseas. Beijing service has spread all over the world, forming a true vision of "Beijing Service, Global Sharing". For instance,

StarTimes, a private trade in services enterprise, has carried out the construction of a digital television and communications network in Africa, so common African families can watch *Beautiful Daughter-in-Law Era*, a popular Chinese TV show, which is a good cultural exchange. In the meantime, the famous brand Tongrentang has opened 64 pharmacies in 16 countries and regions, enabling overseas Chinese and local residents in more than 40 countries and regions to enjoy the unique service of traditional Chinese medicine. In the following Beijing Theme Day activity, lots of enterprises and entrepreneurs will share with us how they are exploring the international market overseas with China's culture and technology and even China's standards.

Therefore, the unique promotional role of trade in services regarding the 3 aspects makes us feel that trade in services is all around us and brings many wonderful wishes to our city's future.

All guests and friends, we gather together in CIFTIS to write a new chapter of Beijing services. For 3 years, through CIFTIS, we have fully felt the beautiful future and the huge opportunities of the service industry and trade in services, and we have obtained business opportunities, cooperation and friendship. Looking forward to the future, Beijing will base its strategic orientation on the function of the new city, in accordance with General Secretary Xi Jinping's requirements, it will firmly concentrate on the objective of the Wudu Construction, stick to the equal development of productive services and life services, make every effort to accelerate the development of the service industry and trade in services, and promote the accelerated development of Beijing's trade in services by continuously innovating its service system; by better utilizing international and domestic markets, it will accelerate the development of trade in services so that it can write a new chapter of "the accelerated development of the service industry and of trade in services, the accelerated upgrading of the foreign trade structure". At last, I sincerely wish the Beijing Theme Day activity complete success. Thank you!

# Speech by Lu Yan, Director of Beijing Municipal Commission of Commerce on Beijing Theme Day

Respected Deputy Mayor Cheng Hong, distinguished guests, ladies and gentlemen,

Good morning! On the Beijing Theme Day, the fruitful achievements of CIFTIS have been shown to us in an all-round way from multiple points of view. Together, we have jointly witnessed the brilliant process of its development, we have felt the booming vitality of its development and we have described its great developmental vision, where the vitality, charm, ability and potential of CIFTIS have been fully displayed.

First, settle in Beijing, get a broad view of the world. Its notable success in the service industry and trade in services shows the vitality of Beijing to the world. Beijing takes the lead in achieving the service-dominated economic pattern in China and has made impressive achievements with rapid development in the service industry and in trade in services. In 2013, the value added of the service industry of Beijing was 1.5 trillion RMB, accounting for 76.9% of Beijing's GDP, 3% higher than the national GDP; the import-export volume of trade in services broke through 110 billion USD, accounting for 1.2% in the world, keeping ahead in China. From January to March 2014, the total import-export volume of Beijing's trade in services exceeded 40 billion USD, with a year-on-year growth of 54%, showing a good momentum of development.

Second, improve people's livelihood and serve the public. Quick and convenient high-end services show Beijing's charm to the world. On June 27, 2013, the first electronic invoice on mainland China was born in Beijing and up to 2.8 million electronic invoices were issued in the same year; in 2013, credit card use was 6.79 billion RMB, with a growth of 164.2%; the amount of online receivables was 92.6 billion RMB, with a growth of 44.3%, accounting for 11.1% of total sales in the entire city, with a social consumption contribution of more than 40%. In the first four months of this year, enterprises on the wholesale market realized an online retail sales of 35.4 billion RMB, which is expected to exceed 100 billion RMB by the end of the year. Innovative service increases enterprise benefits, innovative consumption promotes consumption growth, and E-commerce facilitates citizens' lives, all of which fully displays the charm of Beijing, a livable city.

Third, look towards Beijing and go to the world. With a "bring-in and go-out" policy, the global extension of development strategies shows Beijing's ability to the world. Beijing has started business with over 20 countries and regions and more than one thousand service enterprises have achieved multinational operations. In 2013, mutual investments kept rising and the actual inflow of foreign investment was up to 8.52 billion RMB, with a growth of 6%, maintaining growth for 12 successive years. In the same year, the total import-export volume of the core cultural products of the whole city was 911 million USD, with a growth of 51%. Sixty enterprises and 37 projects were selected in 2013–2014 for the National Cultural Export Key Enterprise and Key Project, ranking the first in China in terms of number of both enterprises and projects.

Fourth, be open and practical and lead the upgrade. The quick improvement of the headquarters economic development level shows Beijing's potential to the world. Beijing introduces new headquarters policies to enable regional headquarters of foreign multinational corporations to compete with central enterprises, municipal state-owned enterprises and private enterprises in a fair way in Beijing. At present, 48 of the world's top 500 enterprises have set up headquarters in Beijing, ranking first in the world. Enterprise headquarters account for 0.4% of the city's units with about 25% of the employment, they create nearly half of the city's value added and they realize nearly 60% of income and tax revenue, becoming an important support for the economic development of the city.

Today, peers from Beijing's service industry and trade in services fields as well as those at home and abroad, in line with mutual trust and win-win cooperation, by virtue of the high-end service platform of the Beijing Theme DayActivity, have signed 29 cooperation project agreements with a volume of transaction of 13.85 billion USD, including 18 agreements for emerging industries such as computer and information service and culture and finance with a contract volume nearly 1.162 billion USD, accounting for 60% of the total number of agreements and over 80% of the total contract volume respectively, showing a sound momentum of development in the emerging high-end service industry. In addition to today's contract projects on Beijing Theme Day, Beijing enterprises have also achieved fruitful results in other sectors during the CIFTIS. At the 3rd CIFTIS, a total of 175 agreements have been signed, with the intentional contract volume up to 42.868 billion USD.

Dear guests and friends, the fruitful achievements shown in the Beijing Theme Day Activity are the result of our joint efforts. Today is Children's Day. Mayor Cheng just mentioned that this is a day full of hope for the future. In its third year, CIFTIS is just like a child and grows with everyone's care, concern and support. We look forward to responding again to the theme of "Beijing Service, Global Sharing" at the next CIFTIS, and we look forward to meeting you again at the next CIFTIS. Thank you!

# Speech by Lv Jijian, Deputy Director General of the Department of Trade in Services and Commercial Services of the Ministry of Commerce on Zhejiang Theme Day

Respected leaders, guests, ladies and gentlemen, and friends,

Good morning! I'm very pleased to receive the invitation from the Zhejiang Theme Day Activity of the 3rd CIFTIS. First, I, on behalf of the Department of Trade in Services and Commercial Services of the Ministry of Commerce, want to extend a warm welcome to all the guests attending the 3rd CIFTIS and warm congratulations to the Zhejiang Theme Day Activity!

Since the beginning of the new century, the global service industry and trade in services have developed immensely. The greatly developing service trade has become an important measure for all countries to adjust their economic structure and promote industrial transformation, turning into a growth impetus that is driving a new round of economic growth. The Chinese government pays great attention to the developing service trade, and actively promotes the development transformation mode of foreign trade. The report of the 18th National Congress of the Communist Party of China explicitly suggests developing trade in services and promoting the balanced development of foreign trade. In 2013, the total import-export volume of national service was 539.64 billion USD, an increase of 14.7% compared with the previous year, firmly ranking third in global import-export service, as well as fifth for exports and second for imports.

As a developed coastal province, Zhejiang actively promotes the development of trade in services, puts forward the developmental idea of "quantity expansion", and focuses on innovation in its legislation, policy, planning and statistics. Now, trade in services has become an important field for its opening-up and a new field for economic growth. Zhejiang is also at the forefront in development of the national trade in services.

The scale of Zhejiang's trade in services in 2013 ranked fourth in China, following Beijing, Shanghai and Guangdong. As an open economy-prosperous province, Zhejiang boasts a positive advantage in advanced manufacturing industry and a basis of modern service industry, possessing unique conditions to greatly develop its trade in services. We hope that Zhejiang Province will grasp the new opportunity of development in trade in services and continue strengthening new measures for its development, in order to make trade in services turn into a new engine for its economic growth. In the meantime, give full play to its demonstration effect to inject new power into the development of China's service trade.

With the theme of "Zhejiang's Service, Zhejiang's Future", the Zhejiang Theme Day Activity fully shows the important position and role of Zhejiang's trade in services in economic and social development. Enterprises participating in this activity concern the fields of culture, service outsourcing, tourism, education and other fields, showing that Zhejiang's service trade is characterized by many fields, which will play a positive role in propagandizing it.

Finally, I wish Zhejiang fruitful achievements at this CIFTIS and I hope that the Zhejiang Theme Day Activity is a complete success. Thank you!

REPORT ON MAJOR VIEWS AT THE 3RD CHINA BEIJING INTERNATIONAL FAIR FOR TRADE IN SERVICES

# Speech by Sun Chenghai, Director General of the Trade Development Bureau of the Ministry of Commerce at the Opening Ceremony and Theme Forum of the Hong Kong Theme Day

Distinguished President Fang Shunwen, Secretary General Ma Lin, all of the representatives from mainland and Hong Kong enterprises,

Good morning! I'm pleased to attend the opening ceremony of China (Hong Kong) International Fair for Trade in Services Hong Kong Theme Day, and I, on behalf of the Trade Development Bureau of the Ministry of Commerce, welcome your participation in the activity. As is known to all, CIFTIS is an important platform for the "bringing-in" and "going-out" of China's service industry, which strongly pushes forward the strengthening of communication and cooperation with the service industry for all countries; it also plays an irreplaceable role in service cooperation between Hong Kong and mainland China. Organizing the Hong Kong Theme Day Activity and building a bridge among the service industry, enterprises and experts from Hong Kong and enterprises from mainland China will certainly help bring the advantage of experience from Hong Kong's industries to support the transformation and upgrading of mainland enterprises and improve their international competitiveness, which is beneficial to promoting complementary advantages and common development for Hong Kong and mainland China!

I would like to extend my thanks to the Hong Kong Trade Development Council for meticulously organizing the Hong Kong high-end service industry representatives. We hope all Hong Kong experts and mainland enterprises will share their successful experience and innovative ideas in finance, accounting, law, trade, design, real estate management, medical treatment and other fields. We sincerely wish that, mainland industry and commerce and Hong Kong organizations, enterprises and friends engaged in related service industries will further enhance exchange and cooperation, seek beneficial development and achieve mutual benefits and win-win results by virtue of this platform, so as to jointly develop the market. The Trade Development Bureau of the Ministry of Commerce is the policy-making body of commerce. We need to do well both in the service industry and in trade in services. With increasingly close cooperation with Hong Kong, we have carried out a series of highly effective cooperative measures with the Hong Kong Trade Development Council regarding exhibition, training and

Part IV  Summary of the Speeches on Theme Days and Special Activities

other aspects. We would like to continue cooperating with the Hong Kong Trade Development Council and carry out efficient cooperation. At last, I wish the Hong Kong Theme Day Activity a complete success. Thank you!

# Speech by Ma Lin, Deputy Secretary General of the People's Government of the Beijing Municipality at the Opening Ceremony and Theme Forum of the Hong Kong Theme Day

Distinguished Vice President Fang Shunwen, Director General Sun Chenghai, ladies and gentlemen,

Good morning! I'm pleased to attend the China (Hong Kong) International Fair for Trade in Services Hong Kong Theme Day Activity, jointly organized by the China International Center for Economic and Technical Exchanges, the Trade Development Bureau of the Ministry of Commerce, and the Hong Kong Trade Development Council. I, on behalf of the People's Government of the Beijing Municipality, would like to extend a warm welcome to friends from Hong Kong and profound thanks to all friends from Hong Kong and mainland China for their long-standing contribution to Beijing's service trade!

CIFTIS is the first exchange platform for service trade units in the world, and it is also a fair with the largest scale of service trade and that covers the greatest number of fields in the world. CIFTIS has been held successfully twice, where some significant projects have been signed, bringing genuine benefits to enterprises. The 3rd CIFTIS is made up of exhibitions, forums and business negotiations, aiming at providing a chance for all countries and regions to show and introduce their service trade, and negotiate and exchange, so as to enhance the exchange and cooperation of enterprises and promote an accelerated development of the service trade. Since the "12th Five-Year Plan", Beijing has made new achievements in economic and social development. In 2013, Beijing's GDP was 1.95 trillion RMB, with the proportion of the service industry up to 76.9%, and the total volume of service trade exceeded 110 billion RMB, showing a solid developmental foundation and wide support. In the future, Beijing will insist on scientific and technical innovation to promote new development of the city, stimulate cultural benefits, improve the development of the high-end service industry by virtue of CIFTIS and accelerate the transformation of the mode of economic development.

As an important hub of the international service industry, Hong Kong has accumulated great advantages and a rich experience in the development of the service industry, and its advantages in talent and capital as well as professional service knowledge are remarkable. In 2013, Beijing enterprises directly invested 1,448 million USD in Hong Kong, accounting for

47% of total overseas direct investment of Beijing enterprises, showing that Hong Kong has become an important bridge for Beijing enterprises to "go out". In the meantime, you can see that, Hong Kong enterprises are involved in finance, accounting, law, market promotion, logistics, design, innovation technology, patent licensing and in other fields. We sincerely hope that the enterprises in Hong Kong and on mainland China will further enhance their exchange and cooperation in the service industry through the CIFTIS platform, in order to promote a higher level of their cooperation in services through their joint efforts. Finally, I wish the fair to be a complete success. Thank you!

# Speech by Sun Tong, Deputy Director General of the Department of Taiwan, Hong Kong and Macao Affairs of the Ministry of Commerce at the Hong Kong Theme Day Sub–forum

Respected Director Zhu Manling, Assistant Executive Ye Zeen, and friends from Hong Kong,

Good morning! I feel honored to attend this seminar today. All of the colleges and friends here will eagerly want to listen to the experiences of Hong Kong experts, so I will share with you my personal experience.

After developing for over 30 years since the reform and the opening-up, many Chinese enterprises have entered a stage of expanding internationalization. In this stage, it is certainly a very correct, as well as an optimal choice for us to "going out" by virtue of Hong Kong, so "going out" for Chinese enterprises in the next 5—10 years will become an important element in the field of our economy. Experts predict that China's overseas "going-out" fund may exceed 500 billion RMB in the next 5 years, which will be great favorable news to any economy. In this process, if our enterprises want to expand their international markets, intermediary professional services are necessary. As we all know, Hong Kong's professional services have developed with several obvious advantages: on the one hand, they are internationally compatible, they are familiar with international conventions and they have been closely cooperating with the international investment field for many years; on the other hand, after the reform and the opening-up, for more than 30 years, Hong Kong's experts have come to know the demands of mainland enterprises well and they utilize the culture of the mainland enterprises. Therefore, I think that using Hong Kong as a platform for "going out" is a very important way to cooperate with mainland enterprises during the next 5—10 years and even for a longer time.

Meanwhile, we think Hong Kong's intermediary service enterprises should also grasp the opportunity. I believe that very few governments will actively encourage their own enterprises to "going out" and help the enterprises explore the international market like the Chinese government. Hong Kong's enterprises should make use of the large-scale "going-out" trend in the next five years, and also take advantage of the convenience provided through government cooperation to Hong Kong's intermediary services. We combine these policies to create better conditions for enterprises in Hong Kong and on the mainland to explore the international market. We hope that everyone will reap benefits from speakers and that the cooperation will be better and better.

Thank you!

# Speech by Wu Kai, Director General of the State Intellectual Property Office of the International Cooperation Department and Director of the Hong Kong, Macao and Taiwan Office, at the Hong Kong Theme Day Sub–forum

Respected Mr. Wu Ziheng, mainland general representative of the Hong Kong Trade Development Council, honorable guests, ladies and gentlemen,

Good morning. I'm very pleased to attend the 3rd CIFTIS—the Hong Kong Theme Day Intellectual Property Sub-forum Activity. First, I want to extend my gratitude to the Hong Kong Trade Development Council for their kind invitation as well as their meticulous organization and preparation for this forum. With the theme of "Hong Kong: preferred platform to make your intellectual property business soar", this forum is strongly targeted and prospective.

As the Oriental Pearl of the South China Sea, Hong Kong is a hub of the international service industry, enjoying a high reputation in finance, trade, tourism, innovation and in other fields. By improving law formalities, Hong Kong has also achieved outstanding success in intellectual property work and established a good reputation. As the competent department of intellectual property on mainland China, the State Intellectual Property Office has been actively carrying out highly effective work in the field of intellectual property with the related intellectual property department of the Hong Kong Special Administrative Region since its return. In particular, both sides, through a series of efficient and impressive activities, have gathered more positive energy in enhancing comprehensive strength and improving competitiveness for the mainland and for Hong Kong in recent years. In terms of Hong Kong intellectual property trade, both sides have introduced it many times through such platforms as the Chinese Mainland, Hong Kong, and Macao Intellectual Property Seminar and the Business of the IP Asia Forum. It is gratifying that we can exchange experiences with all of you regarding this theme again today, during the Hong Kong Theme Day Activity.

Mr. Leung Chun Ying, Chief Executive of the Hong Kong Special Administrative Region (HKSAR), officially suggests forming a working group composed of government, industry and other sectors in order to research and promote the overall strategy of making Hong Kong an intellectual property trade center. For more than a year, under the leadership of the HKSAR Government, the work of making Hong Kong an intellectual property trade center has been soundly carried out. It is gratifying that the Asia IP Exchange, founded and managed by the Hong Kong Trade Development Council, has become a famous intellectual property deal center in the industry, possessing more than 25,000 intellectual property items available for transaction, with contents covering patents, copyrights, trademarks and appearance design. In the meantime, the Hong Kong Trade Development Council has signed an agreement with the World Intellectual Property Organization to jointly promote green science and technology innovation and the transaction of related property rights. All of these achievements are remarkable.

Now, the mainland is further promoting scientific and technical progress and innovation. The Third Plenary Session of the 18th Central Committee of the CPC explicitly proposes intensifying the reform of the scientific and technical system and strengthening intellectual property application and protection, which also indicates the direction of mainland China's development of its intellectual property undertaking. We believe that improving the intellectual property system and promoting the capitalization and industrialization of scientific and technological achievements in the future will be common topics for enhancing the creative level and for promoting overall social and economic development for Hong Kong and for the mainland. In this way, cooperation between the two sides in the area of intellectual property will also be more widely extended.

Ladies and gentlemen, long-term efforts of all parties are required to build Hong Kong into one of Asia's leading intellectual property trade centers. Today's forum is a gathering of people from the intellectual property circle, and this gathering also signifies that industrial, commercial and academic circles will make concerted efforts and grasp opportunities in order to meet challenges with confidence and resolution. Looking into the future, the State Intellectual Property Office will do its work well, it will support the development of Hong Kong's intellectual property undertaking and make contributions so that Hong Kong will be able to better play its advantages and convenience and constantly consolidate its leading position in the intellectual property trade; and this Office will also contribute to the economic development and social prosperity of the two regions.

Finally, I wish the forum enormous success. Thank you!

# Speech by Fu Haiyan, Minister of the Prime Minister's Office of Singapore, Second Minister for the Environment and Water Resources and Second Minister for Foreign Affairs at the Hand in Hand with Singapore and Eyes on the World–Singapore Professional Service Promotional Conference

Honorable ladies and gentlemen,

Good morning! Today, I'm honored to attend the Singapore service industry seminar. China's service industry is now rapidly developing, and is expected to be an important highlight of China's economy in the next 5 –10 years. Last year, China's service industry accounted for 46.1% of the GDP, exceeding the manufacturing industry for the first time. In the last five years, China's service industry created 37 million employment opportunities.

Singapore has been maintaining close cooperation with China for a long time in many fields. Two flag projects jointly explored by Singapore and China are noteworthy, namely, China-Singapore Suzhou Industrial Park and Sino-Singapore Tianjin Eco-City. Singaporean enterprises have also participated in the urban construction and development projects of many provinces and cities in China, providing professional service and assistance for the development plans. Singaporean enterprises look forward to continuing to participate in urban construction projects in an active way, especially in the modern service industry advocated by all cities in economic transition.

China's flourishing economic development promotes Chinese enterprises to be more and more international, and China's trade contacts with the world and its overseas investments have also rapidly increased. Many Chinese enterprises have already "gone out" to actively expand their overseas business. Singapore has always been supporting China's strategy of "going out". Chinese enterprises are welcome in Singapore to march towards the ASEAN and global markets by taking Singapore as a springboard. Here, we want to use three "easy" elements to briefly introduce Singapore's investment environment and advantages, and to suggest how to assist Chinese enterprises in "going out" for those enterprises which do not know much about Singapore.

First, easy understanding. Singapore is similar to China in terms of language and culture, so it is easier for Singaporean enterprises and Chinese enterprises to understand and communicate with each other during cooperation, thus gaining more understanding in order to seek more comprehensive cooperation. In this way, economic and trade contacts and relations between Singapore and China can be continuously sustained and deepened to explore new areas for cooperation. Based on this, Singapore can build a bridge for Chinese enterprises to open regional and ASEAN markets.

Singapore is an important financial center and service hub in the ASEAN region. Singaporean enterprises are familiar with the ASEAN market and also have extensive experience in ASEAN business. ASEAN is an economic region with huge potentials and business opportunities, and a market and production base with a total population of 600 million. When the ASEAN Economic Community was established in 2015, the integrated construction made this region an important economic center of world economic development. Therefore, ASEAN is a market which cannot be ignored by Chinese enterprises.

Second, easy transportation. With a convenient geographical location, Singapore is a world-class sea and air transportation hub and is one of the busiest container terminals in the world. Changi Airport provides services for over 100 international airlines, covering more than 280 cities in about 60 countries and regions. A perfect transportation network is one of our advantages, which is conductive to cargo transport and communication among people.

A smooth flow of funds is very important for enterprises. Singapore is one of the important financial centers in Asia, able to provide strong support for RMB market growth and promotion of fund flow of trade activities between China and ASEAN. Three banks of Singapore have marched into China, and seven commercial banks of China have also set up branches in Singapore, with good achievements for both sides. Financial cooperation between China and Singapore has been significantly enhanced, and more development opportunities and business opportunities will be created in the future. Since officially launching the RMB clearing business in May 2013, the ICBC Singapore Branch has achieved strong growth. The daily average trade volume of the RMB foreign exchange in Singapore increased from 16 billion USD in March 2013 to 31 billion USD in December 2013, nearly doubling. Now, following Hong Kong, Singapore is the most competitive offshore RMB clearing center. Singapore's financial institutions constantly launch more RMB financial products and services, so as to meet the needs of Chinese enterprises in refinancing, investment and funds management. Chinese enterprises should make full use of these advantages to accumulate the strength for expanding their business in the Asia-Pacific Region and even around the world.

Third, easy business. Singapore has ranked first in the Ease of Doing Business of the

World Bank for 8 successive years, and is among the top three countries in terms of cross-border trade, investor protection, business starting, credit and loan getting and other aspects, which are key conditions to developing a knowledge economy. To encourage innovation, Singapore has established a perfect R&D ecosystem and a sound IP mechanism, that enjoy a good international reputation. Singapore promises to formulate complete rules and regulations to protect IP rights. In 2011–2012, the *Global Competitiveness Report*, issued by the World Economic Forum, reported that Singapore was the country with an optimum IP protection in Asia, ranking second in the world. Hence, more than 30 international corporations leading the biomedical science industry have chosen to set up regional headquarters here. In addition, over 4,500 companies provide various professional services, such as auditing, accounting and management consulting, market research, advertising, public relations, human capital services and legal services.

More than 2,000 years ago, China established trade with the world through its Maritime Silk Road, when Singapore was a trade hub of East Asia, Southeast Asia, India and the Middle East. As early as 700 years ago, Singapore had become a shipping and trade center, accumulating regional recognition. This long history has laid a foundation for trade cooperation between the two countries, providing a good platform for future development. We hope that Chinese enterprises will be able to understand the potentials of cooperation more and make more exchanges with Singaporean enterprises here, in order to discuss and jointly explore more opportunities for cooperation.

# Speech by Fang Aiqing, Vice Minister of Commerce at the Hand in Hand with Singapore and Eyes on the World–Singapore Professional Service Promotional Conference

Respected Minister Fu Haiyan, all guests, ladies and gentlemen,

Good morning! I'm very delighted to attend the 3rd CIFTIS Singapore Theme Day Activity. First of all, I, on behalf of the Ministry of Commerce of the People's Republic of China, want to extend congratulations for this activity!

The Chinese government pays great attention to developing friendly relations with Singapore. Since establishing diplomatic relations, senior government officials of the two countries have closely interacted; with rapidly developing economic and trade relations, the level of cooperation has continuously improved and interests have increasingly deepened. China and Singapore signed a Free Trade Agreement in 2008, which was the first free trade agreement signed by China with a developed country and it was also China's first free trade agreement covering trade in goods, trade in services, investments and other fields. Since the Agreement became effective, bilateral economic and trade relations have quickly developed. In 2013, the bilateral trade volume reached 75.9 billion USD; China became Singapore's largest trading partner for the first time, and the latter is also China's second largest trading partner in the ASEAN region. By the end of 2013, Singapore's accumulated direct investment in China had reached 66.5 billion USD and China's direct investment in Singapore had also reached 13.6 billion USD. In 2013, the total import-export volume of Sino-Singapore services reached 19.3 billion USD. Singapore was the sixth largest service trading partner and China's fourth largest service export destination. The volume of high value-added services such as computer and information services and consulting services was more than half of the total bilateral service trade volume. As bilateral economic and trade relations increasingly deepen, cooperation vectors of the two countries are increasingly enriched. Currently, five inter-governmental economic and trade cooperative mechanisms have been established, including JCBC and the China-Singapore Suzhou Industrial Park Joint Steering Council. On May 21, Xi Jinping, President of China, made a keynote speech at the 4th CICA Summit and pointed out that China would, together with all countries, accelerate the construction of the Silk Road Economic Belt and the 21st Maritime Silk Road, and further participate in regional cooperation. Singapore is an important country under the "One Belt, One Road" policy and is also China's largest service trading partner among the countries under this policy. China and Singapore have respective advantages in the area of trade in services, with strong complementarity. China is competitive in tourism services, construction services, computer and information services, and service outsourcing, while Singapore is relatively advantageous in financial services, communication services, medical care, professional services, environmental services and in other fields with a modern developed service industry. With huge cooperation space, the two countries signed the Memorandum of Understanding of the Service Trade Cooperation Promotion Working Group in October 2013. China will take this as a new starting point to enhance its pragmatic cooperation with Singapore in the area of trade in services and to promote bilateral cooperation in trade in services to reach a new level.

Ladies and gentlemen, in the era of the global value chain, as the adhesive for the manufacturing and service industries, trade in services will drive the products and services of all countries to integrate better into the global value chain. China will make developing its service industry as an upgraded strategic move to create China's economy, and it will make trade in services a strategic focus of its economic development. Enterprises involved in trade in services in both countries are welcome to make full use of the CIFTIS platform to strengthen communication and exchanges and to deepen pragmatic cooperation, so as to achieve mutual benefits and win-win results, as well as to jointly promote better and faster development of global trade in services.

At last, I hope enterprises and friends from Singapore will have a worthwhile trip and obtain information and business opportunities. I wish the CIFTIS Singapore Theme Day Activity enormous success.

Thank you!

Part IV Summary of the Speeches on Theme Days and Special Activities

# Speech by Zhang Wei, Vice Chairman of the China Council for the Promotion of International Trade at the Hand in Hand with Singapore and Eyes on the World–Singapore Professional Service Promotional Conference

Distinguished Minister, Fu Haiyan, Vice President, Fu Chun'an and Deputy Minister, Fang Aiqing, all guests, ladies and gentlemen,

Good morning! I'm pleased to attend today's "Hand in Hand with Singapore and Eyes on the World–Singapore Professional Service Promotional Conference". I, on behalf of the China Council for the Promotion of International Trade and the China Chamber of International Commerce, want to extend my sincere congratulations to the promotional conference and give a warm welcome to our friends from Singapore!

In recent years, China has maintained sound and healthy relations with the ASEAN region. In 2013, the total import-export volume between China and the ASEAN group was 443.6 billion USD, with a year-on-year growth of 10.9%, which was at the forefront of China's main trading partners. Chinese enterprises are accelerating their going out. Cooperation between China and the ASEAN has explored new fields, and the ASEAN region, represented by Singapore, is gradually becoming the main destination for the foreign investment of Chinese enterprises. By the end of 2013, the Chinese enterprises' total accumulated non-financial investment in the ASEAN countries was 29.31 billion USD. The ASEAN has become one of the regions with the fastest economic growth of foreign-invested enterprises. In the ASEAN countries, Singapore is the preferred investment destination of Chinese enterprises. Relying on its advantageous geographical location and perfect investment environment, Singapore has become the portal for Chinese enterprises to enter the ASEAN market. With increased internationalization, more and more Chinese enterprises realize that the proper use of professional investment service agencies is crucial to the efficiency and effectiveness of international operations. For many years, the China Council for the Promotion of International Trade, when supporting and promoting enterprises to go out, has been actively integrating Chinese and foreign financial institutions, law firms, accounting firms and other investment service agencies into participating in the process, and providing professional support and services for foreign investments by Chinese enterprises. As the financial, commercial and professional service center in the Asia-Pacific Region, Singapore has advantages because of its large number of professional service agencies, high-quality professional service staff and elaborately-divided professional services. As internalization of China's economy increases, the enterprises in both the manufacturing industry and the service industry, especially for many small and medium-sized enterprises, need to improve their abilities in upgrading and updating, R&D, design and market development of products, as well as their professional services in international law, consulting, accounting and other aspects, in order to go out and expand their overseas business. In this sense, China has a huge cooperation potential with Singapore in the area of professional services.

Today, the Singapore Delegation composed of many Singaporean professional service agencies present at the CIFTIS are holding this promotional conference in order to explain how to take advantage of these professional services to Chinese enterprises. Currently, China is actively promoting the construction of the Maritime Silk Road to expand pragmatic cooperation in various fields with the ASEAN countries. As the portal of the ASEAN region, Singapore will also play a very important role in this process. Singaporean professional service agencies can seek more cooperation opportunities in China. Finally, I hope that enterprises in both countries will obtain valuable results.

# Speech by Fu Chun'an, Head of the Singapore Delegation at the Hand in Hand with Singapore and Eyes on the World–Singapore Professional Service Promotional Conference

Respected Ms. Fu Haiyan, Minister of the Prime Minister's Office of Singapore, Second Minister for the Environment and Water Resources and Second Minister for Foreign Affairs, Mr. Zhang Wei, Standing Vice Chairman of the China Council for the Promotion of International Trade, Mr. Huang Rong, Vice President of the All-China Federation of Industry & Commerce, Mr. Luo Jialiang, Singapore's Ambassador to China, all guests, ladies and gentlemen,

I, on behalf of the members of the Comprehensive and Economic and Trade Delegation of the Singapore Business Federation, want to extend a sincere welcome and heartfelt thanks to your enthusiastic attendance and strong support! I came to China for business opportunities as early as 1981, and I have witnessed achievements and the process of China's rapid economic development as well as fruitful results of Sino-Singapore friendly cooperation in the last 33 years. Due to time constraints, I will briefly introduce Singapore's internationalization process and achievements and share with you why Singapore is an ideal platform for internationalization.

For 140 years, from 1819, when the British politician, Raffles, landed in Singapore, to 1959 when Singapore became a self-governing commonwealth, Singapore was colonized by Britain. Mr. Lee Kuan Yew became the first Prime Minister of Singapore in 1959 when Singapore had no industry and was very backward, with very little agriculture, bad security, and social unrest. It was difficult to solve the problems of survival of this small poor island country with a population of 2 million. In 1963, Singapore became a prefecture of Malaysia, hoping to share Malaysia's market, but Mr. Lee Kuan Yew continued to act as the Prime Minister of Singapore. However, it was found that the two countries had different policy principles, causing various contradictions. For example, Prime Minister Lee Kuan Yew advocated a Malaysia for Malaysians, but then the Prime Minister of Malaysia insisted on a Malaysian-oriented Malaysia. Because of this, Singapore declared its independence on August 9, 1965 to become the Republic of Singapore, and Mr. Lee Kuan Yew continued to act as the Prime Minister. Facing difficulties, the pioneer generation led by Lee Kuan Yew made great efforts at elaboration, successively made several plans with preferential development and gradually implemented the plans, for example, the government established the Construction Development Board in 1960, and made the plan of the "home ownership scheme". Now, 82% of the Singaporean residents are living in ancestral houses planned by the government, which are called public housing by our Chinese friends. 9.1% of the Singaporean residents are living in private houses, and about 8.6% of the Singaporean residents do not have their own houses. In the "house ownership scheme", Singapore is one of the most successful countries. The Singapore Economic Development Board, established in 1961, is responsible for formulating and implementing business and investment strategies and attracting investment, successfully introducing the world's top 500 enterprises and more than 7,000 international transnational corporations to settle in Singapore. The National Trades Union Congress, established in 1961, in addition to delivering benefits to people, gradually formed an "iron triangle" mechanism of labor, management and government to comprehensively eliminate vicious strikes, creating a stable society and an ideal investment environment in Singapore. We established the Industry Management Board in 1968 to encourage Singapore to march towards industrialization and overall employment. We established the Trade Development Board in 1981, making full use of Singapore's superior geographical location to further develop its transit trade. In order to meet the needs of economic globalization, the Trade Development Board was changed to the International Enterprise Singapore in 2004. The International Enterprise Singapore successfully assists Singapore to go out into the world and achieve the internationalization of Singaporean enterprises, fully exerting the strategy of "small country with a big mind". Besides, with the continuous improvements to the Central Provident Fund Board, its system has become a one-package service chain covering savings, housing, education, medical care and pensions, benefiting people.

Singapore is a small country, with a national territorial area of 716.8 square kilometers and a population of about 5.4 million, including 3.84 million Singaporeans and more than 1.5 million foreigners, with the Chinese accounting for 74.2%, Malaysian 13.3%, Indian 9.2% and others 3.3%. Singapore is a multi-racial and multi-religion country. To maintain racial and religious harmony and guarantee successful internationalization, Prime Minister Lee Kuan Yew and his team insist on bilingual education and declare that Chinese, Malay, and Hindi are Singapore's official languages, and that the official language and the language of business communication is internationally-used English. The language policy respecting various racial cultures and conforming to the international trend brings huge advantages to Singapore's internationalization and economic development, and makes incomparable contributions.

The reason why I specially introduced these main areas is to emphasize that Singapore's pioneer generation laid a solid foundation for Singapore in the first 10-15 years with the most

Part IV  Summary of the Speeches on Theme Days and Special Activities

difficulties, providing strong support for its healthy growth in the subsequent 40 years. Today's Singapore has the best harbor and the best aviation in the world, and is one of the most important financial centers in the world. We have no petroleum, but Singapore is the third largest refining center in the world. Singapore is also one of the countries with which it is easiest to do business and one of the most livable countries in the world. Today's Singapore is a country with multiple cultures, harmonious multiple races and multiple religions. Singapore has an efficient administrative system as well as a fair, just and open legal system; everything is institutionalized and easy to be accepted.

Singapore's success lies in the confidence accorded it from the international society. The world's top 500 enterprises and more than 7,000 international transnational corporations have brought a huge fund as well as cash management experience and technology to Singapore. Dear friends, we do not introduce Singapore's various advantages to show off, but to introduce more foreign businessmen to using Singapore as their preferred platform for internationalization, so we hope entrepreneurs present here will carefully consider making Singapore their preferred platform for their enterprises. The Singapore Business Federation has more than 20,000 enterprise members. We hope to sincerely cooperate with you and enhance the advantages in order to jointly create prosperity for all.

I, on behalf of the Singapore Business Federation, want to take this opportunity to extend a heartfelt thanks again for your support and to the leaders of the Ministry of Commerce, the China Council for the Promotion of International Trade and the Singapore Business Federation for their on-the-spot guidance. I wish you all good health, safety and happiness. Thank you!

# Speech by Chery Low, President of the China–Britain Business Council in China at the British Creative and Innovative Forum

Ladies and gentlemen,

Good afternoon! Today's theme is to show the most excellent British creativity and innovation and their creators. Britain leads creativity in all industries. Today, we will discuss how China and Britain are complementary to each other, and combine the advantages of each in various fields so as to achieve common development. Creativity and innovation are not just useful for designing beautiful products, but they can also be applied to the manufacturing industry, business dealings and daily work. Britain's creativity attracts the Chinese. As a country, China hopes to transform its industries from low-cost production to global brands with independent property rights, and from "Made in China" to "Created in China". Meanwhile, China's consumer demands are increasing; with the economic growth in China, young consumers are changing psychologically. China's consumer demands are dramatically changing the economic and social situation of China and of the world.

Cooperation between China and Britain in brands, products and services will promote the growth of consumption all over China. Britain keeps ahead of the world in design and innovation, and Britain's creativity source is its openness. We have a strong gifted working staff as well as advanced experience in technology and management. China can provide the market, manufacturing ability and investment capital for Britain, so Britain's professional technology and China's great objective will promote the development of the whole world.

I will briefly introduce Britain's creative industry. Britain's creative industry accounts for 5% of the British economy, and its growth rate is twice as much as that of Britain's economic growth. Such British industries as advertising, fashion, film, games, music and TV stay ahead of the world. The exports of Britain's creative industry reached 16 billion GBP in 2011, almost 8% of Britain's total service export. Britain also keeps developing the pioneer industries, such as the automobile and the aerospace industries. Britain's pioneer design and innovation can guarantee the survival of many traditional industries and also continue improving its strength; e.g. Seventeen of the top 20 auto parts manufacturers in the world are British, 6 of the world's top 10 Formula 1 teams are British and 13% of the global aerospace industry is British. With creativity and innovation, we have unique products and services. The China-Britain Business

Council has been helping enterprises explore business in China for the last 6 years. British innovators are impressed by the Chinese market, by Chinese aspirations, the Chinese entrepreneurial spirit, and the Chinese attitude of "anything is possible". Thank you!

# Speech by Sudhanshu Pandey, Director General of the Ministry of Commerce and Industry (India) at the Seminar entitled "India–China: New Opportunities of the Trade in Services Industry"

Good afternoon! Welcome, honorable Mr. Zhao Zhongyi, Executive Vice Chairman of the China Association of Trade in Services, Mr. Miao, guests, friends from India, and Mr. Vats, the CEO of Viacom18.

Actually, I'm very willing to share my thoughts with you. Trade in services is very important, because over 65% of the employment opportunities are from the trade in services industry. What are we expecting? What are we looking for? We hope to provide good job opportunities for the younger generations. Many new job opportunities are from trade in services, which is a very important factor.

About two centuries ago, India and China contributed approximately 25% of the GDP. Now, we have a long way to go, and this is a trip or a journey. We know that the best way for us to be successful in this journey is to stay together. Currently, India accounts for 3.3% of the global service industry, and China 10%. If the two countries join hands, we should consider our total population a proportion of the global population and our service and trade a proportion of global service and trade. You will understand what I am talking about if you compare the two proportions.

But actually, the service and trade of the two countries are less than 1 billion RMB, which means we have a great potential. Indians respect and admire China very much. When I was growing up, I liked reading Chinese novels, and sometimes I read some Chinese novels translated into English. My children buy Chinese toys, which are very popular on the Indian market.

Currently the younger generation loves music. Surrounded by IT and computers, they download music and use online translations in search engines such as Google, so language is not a barrier any longer. The barrier for my generation can be solved by modern technology and the Internet.

Today's India cherishes and values our relations with China. Trade in services is one of the important fields. We still have a long way to go. In my view, we have not really started, so our journey will be full of fun and achievements. Specifically, such service industries as health care, media and entertainment are involved. We will see many Bollywood stars and some Indian films, which will be fun. Although the programs are not translated into Chinese, I do not think that language is a barrier, just like music. Indian films can be seen in Latin American countries, Middle Eastern countries, Japan and Korea.

Britain has many doctors from India, who provide health care service. About one third of the scientists in the space agency are Indians in the USA and in other countries. With great potential, we have many in which to develop our cooperation. How should we cooperate? Language is not a problem anymore.

What is the next important thing for us? Our cooperation threshold is low, but our cooperation potential is great. We look forward to having meaningful discussions with China, so that the people in the two countries can benefit and both countries can achieve prosperity and power with sustainable growth. Thank you!

# Speech by Ashok K. Kantha, India's Ambassador to China, at the Seminar Entitled " India–China: New Opportunities of the Trade in Services Industry"

Mr. Zhao Zhongyi, Executive Vice Chairman of the China Association of Trade in Services, Mr. Yan and Mr. Miao, peers from various fields, ladies and gentlemen,

First of all, welcome to our seminar. We will discuss some issues regarding the improvement of Sino-India cooperation, such as the trade in services field. I want to extend particular thanks to the Ministry of Commerce of the PRC as well as the Ministry of Commerce and the Ministry of Trade and Industry of India for their efforts.

India and China are the two largest emerging economies in the world with the fastest growth, so there is no doubt that we have a lot of growth points of economy. At the same time, India just concluded its general election. The new government has been established, and the new prime minister took his post three days ago. India's new prime minister also pays special attention to developing the trade in services field, as well as how to carry out international cooperation in order to solve some problems. Undoubtedly, the service area will attract people's attention. I firmly believe that, as the largest developing country and an emerging economy, China will be an important sector for India's foreign cooperation.

In the past few days, the supreme leaders of the two countries have made a satisfactory example. We expect that the government and business circles in both countries will take a step forward to strengthen our economic cooperation, and if possible, to make overall and long-term progress.

We have a good basis for cooperation. In the past several decades, we have developed well in trade, for example in trade in goods. At present, China is India's largest trading partner. In spite of some problems between us, we have great opportunities for the potential development of trade, which conform to the overall trade and strategy of the two countries.

Now, in terms of trade in services, there is little cooperation between China and India. I'm glad to see that a large delegation from India, made up of 6 government departments, have come to attend our meetings regarding this area this year. They attended the CIFTIS, and we held a round-table conference this morning and communicated with the State-owned Assets Supervision and Administration Commission of the State Council. All this means there are

Part IV  Summary of the Speeches on Theme Days and Special Activities

bright prospects for the future, and we look forward to shaping these.

Referring to the economies of China and India, people might say that China is the world's factory and India is the world's office, but what do we see when looking forward, into the future? We see a convergence effect in both countries. For example, China is stressing the development of the service industry, particularly the area of trade in services. Industry is a key point for India, and in my view, it will be increasingly important with the establishment of the new government of India, especially the processing industry.

With globalization, opportunities in the area of trade in services are increasingly assuming strategic significance; for example, as we mentioned in the previous speech, making trade in services acquire a higher proportion of global trade can bring more high value-added products and employment opportunities, etc.

In the middle of last year, India's service industry accounted for one fifth of the FDI, becoming a very important part of the world's economy. We hope to further develop the service industry in the next years.

I would like to show you some figures obtained from a series of statistics. Our overall service industry of last year reached very high figures, mostly from IT. The next highest was our professional service industry. As I mentioned earlier, China has been playing an increasingly important role in the service industry, and its trade volume of the service industry last year reached 5 billion RMB. Of course, I think China and India are largely complementary, and particularly in the service industry, we can complement each other with our respective advantages. China is advantageous in tourism and transportation, while we have advantages in IT, media and health fields, so that both sides can mutually promote and complement each other. The two countries can not only complement but also cooperate with each other to provide more services for third-party countries.

We will focus on some fields this afternoon, in which India has its own unique advantages, such as IT or the service industry, media and entertainment. As we discussed this morning, many Indian IT companies have been in China for more than 10 years, and plenty of Chinese companies are developing internationally. I got some figures this morning, indicating that lots of Chinese companies have set up offices around the world to develop and achieve a globalization strategy. We expect, and I believe, that, as Indian IT companies continuously expand all over the world, these companies will have better development in China.

A number of Chinese state-owned enterprises choose to develop in India. After today's meeting, the State-owned Assets Supervision and Administration Commission of the State Council will carry out subsequent activities. I believe that, from our discussion this afternoon, we will obtain more results.

We will also discuss Sino-India tourism this afternoon. Last year, a large number of

Chinese traveled abroad, and India is certainly one of the tourist attractions for the Chinese. We will have related topics for all exchanges on tourism this afternoon, including exchanges with the Director General of the Indian Ministry of Tourism and the Vice Chairman of the CTS. Tourism will have a huge market for both India and China. We need to do some things to make it easier for Chinese and Indian tourists to travel in both countries. Of course, visas are not a big problem, but there is something else.

Moreover, India's health care industry is well developed. We have advantages in medical equipment, in the areas of tumors, cardiovascular and nervous systems, and we are considering making it possible for people to afford health care service. Our international medical treatment is developing faster and faster. China and India have same visions in the health care industry; both hope to provide competitive services for people. I believe the partnership of the two countries is the right choice. Of course, we need to jointly discuss some problems regarding access to the market with China.

Health care service is not just provided in the free trade zone of Shanghai, established last year. We are constantly expanding on the entire Chinese market.

In addition to the industries mentioned above, India and China will also cooperate regarding the media and entertainment, which is also one of our topics this afternoon. We have carried out a number of activities related to media and entertainment in 12 Chinese cities. For example, we will display Indian films and TV programs in 6 cities this year, either introducing some Indian animations or some video programs. We hope to enhance cooperation in these fields through a series of cooperation and display.

A Chinese leader in media and entertainment will go to India for to have an in-depth discussion next week. I would like to emphasize again that both China and India attach great importance to the economy, and the leaders of both sides have been very clear about this. Sino-India exchanges and cooperation will be further deepened at the next level.

We are willing to cooperate with Chinese friends and partners in various fields and discuss cooperation opportunities, including the fields mentioned earlier. This small step is very important and it will lead to a big step in the future. Thank you very much!

# Speech by Zhao Zhongyi, Executive Vice Chairman of the China Association of Trade in Services at the Seminar Entitled " India–China: New Opportunities of the Service Trade Industry"

Your Respected Excellency Ambassador, Mr. Pandey, ladies and gentlemen,

Good afternoon! I'm very delighted to attend today's India Theme Day to jointly discuss new opportunities for the development of trade in services with Chinese and Indian friends from all walks of life.

As is known, the year 2014 is the China-India Friendly Exchange Year. China and India are the two largest developing countries, with similar economic conditions and strong complementation. Both China and India are ancient civilizations with a long history and a splendid culture, a rich cultural and natural heritage as well as abundant tourism resources.

As we enter the 21st century, China's and India's social economies have substantially developed, people's living standard has generally been raised and the tourism industry has entered a new stage. More and more Chinese choose to travel abroad. In 2012, the number of Chinese outbound tourists was 83,182,000, with a year-on-year growth of 18.41%. China's outbound tourism market has exceeded Germany and the USA, becoming the largest outbound tourism market in the world. In terms of inbound tourism, the number of foreign tourists to China in the same year was 27,191,600, with an increase of 0.3% compared with last year. Asia is still the main tourist market, including Korea, Japan, Malaysia and Vietnam.

In 2012, the number of India's inbound tourists was 610,200, ranking 17th among all of the countries. In recent years, as China's traditional trade in services item, tourism's deficit has increased year by year. In the first 4 months of 2014, its deficit reached 30.1 billion USD. A big problem for China's tourism service is how to attract more foreign tourists to China, so as to realize a balance of trade.

India's unique culture attracts tourists from all over the world, so its tourism has developed, and occupies an important position in India's trade in services. In the process of expanding China-India economic and trade cooperation, tourism will play a crucial role.

In order to implement the proposal of the prime ministers of China and India, the Ministry of Commerce of the PRC and the Ministry of Industry and Commerce of India jointly established the Service Trade Work Promotion Group last year. Director General Pandey of the Ministry of Commerce and Industry (India) and Director General Zhou Liujun of the Department of Trade in Services and Commercial Services of the Ministry of Commerce of the PRC led the first working group meeting. This is a breakthrough measure to promote service trade cooperation between the two sides. As a representative of the China Association of Trade in Services, I had the honor to participate in the working group and attend the meeting. Founded in 2007, the China Association of Trade in Services is the only national association promoting trade in services in China, with its members covering major enterprises in 12 areas of trade in services in China.

The China Association of Trade in Services, by taking this opportunity, carries out related activities and promotional work with the corresponding agency in India in terms of trade in services promotion. It can be said that China and India are creating new opportunities of development in many fields within the trade in services industry, especially in IT, cultural media and tourism.

The agenda for me is to offer some opinions on tourism, but I have noticed that President Yu of the China Tourism Association is also present, so I will just show him my slight skill. There is a saying that the world's development depends on Asia and Asia's development depends on China and India. Tourism is an industrial entity. I would like to make several small suggestions regarding cooperation on tourism between China and India.

First, establish a long-term mechanism for tourism-related associations and agencies in the two countries, and jointly advocate important contents of the China-India Service Trade Promotion Working Group of the tourism service.

Second, increase propaganda about our respective advantageous tourism resources in the other country in order to make people in the two countries to better understand the respective social environments, historic cultures and tourism resources, and to eliminate all their negative concerns, so as to attract more foreign tourists.

Third, strengthen the integration of relevant cooperative and tourist supporting resources of travel agencies in the two countries, such as hotels, transportation, international flights, combine and increase the efficiency of cooperation in both countries regarding the tourism service and improve the quality of the service so as to make traveling easier.

I believe that, under the joint efforts of the governments, associations and enterprises in China and India, the cooperation between the two countries will be getting better and better in many fields of trade in services, especially in tourism. I wish the meeting a complete success. Thank you!

# Speech by Humberto Luiz Ribeiro Da Silva, Secretary General of the Department of Trade in Services of the Ministry of Development, Industry and Commerce of Brazil, at the China–Brazil Economic and Trade Cooperation and Development Vision Forum

Good morning! I would like to extend thanks to all distinguished guests present for your devotion to and concern about Brazil, especially to all ambassadors to Brazil, Brazil's Ambassador to Latin America, all Chinese guests interested in Brazil, Mr. President of the Brazil Services Unite Union, Mr. Zhi Weizhong organizing this meeting and Chen Duqing, China's former Ambassador to Brazil for providing warm help for our visit. I want to express thanks in three sentences.

First, I want to extend thanks. Thanks for the warm reception provided by the Chinese people. When we came to China once again yesterday, they warmly introduced China's business opportunities in the new era to me. We feel honored to be able to experience China and the Chinese people's enthusiasm. Signing the establishment of the Bank of Brazil's Shanghai Office on Tuesday is a move with a significant meaning, since this can accelerate the cooperation in financial services for both sides. Our cooperation has a huge potential, so today's theme day is for full exchanges in undertaking more developmental paths and more cooperation projects.

Our cooperation has developed in a good and profound direction. The Brazilian people are now in a joyous atmosphere; we are celebrating the advent of the FIFA World Cup. Ms. President, Dilma Rousseff, will receive the representatives of the BRICS countries. President Xi Jinping will also attend the BRICS meeting with his team. Business contacts between China and Brazil have developed immensely.

We felt very honored to have a conversation with Mr. Minister of Commerce of China yesterday, who provided some figures concerning bilateral trade, indicating a very small favorable balance of trade. The area of trade in services is now a highlight, and a strategic focus of China's economy and also a very important field of our economic services. Seventy percent of our economic source production value is related to the service industry. Our objective is to improve our enterprises' competitiveness in the service industry, and the international trade fair is being held for this purpose.

Therefore, we hope to strengthen learning and exchanges between the two countries. We have made a work plan and signed a letter of intent to establish a commerce and trade bridge between the two countries. Next week, we will sign more letters of intent. I hope the Brazilian entrepreneurs and the Chinese entrepreneurs will have a closer connection in order to establish a bridge of good projects, seeking joint cooperation. The FIFA World Cup also provides us a lot of good cooperation in various other fields.

China successfully hosted the Olympic Games in 2008, and we will host the FIFA World Cup in 2014 and the Olympic Games in 2016, so the cooperation of the two countries is very mature. We hope the leaders of both countries will further discuss both sports and services.

We mainly discussed technical cooperation at the meeting yesterday. With different styles, China and Brazil can be complementary. The Brazilian government has reached a consensus regarding banking business with China. The establishment of the Bank of Brazil's Shanghai Office is of great significance; it will be able to provide an efficient service for Chinese investors or foreign investors in terms of banking and financial information, in line with the vision of further international development.

We will strengthen the competitiveness of our banks. Like China, we have competition in many fields. We can build a way conforming to the current social development and cooperation in competition, so as to find a way suitable to our development. Mr. Fang, the Minister of Commerce introduced a team to us that will provide support.

Talking about the banking and service industries, we have taken a big step forward in logistics, culture, sports, tourism and other fields. Some visions of cooperation with China are very important. This is a very good platform, where we will be able to find out about and understand each other.

At last, I hope that, from this moment onwards, the developing countries, including China and Brazil, will establish strategic partner relationships and display different fusion mechanisms in the trade in services industry. Entrepreneurs, please do not overlook this opportunity and the government's support. We have a lot of cooperation opportunities. China's stable politics and economic development will promote all enterprises and other countries to cooperate in various fields. I wish you all a successful career. I hope you will achieve success at the CIFTIS.

# Speech by Luigi Nese, President of the Brazilian National Confederation of Services, at the China–Brazil Economic and Trade Cooperation and Development Vision Forum

Good day! I'm very delighted to make a speech at the 3rd CIFTIS. We attended the 1st CIFTIS here in 2012. In our view, today is very important, because all the guests and representatives from the various fields can provide some information about Brazil concerning all the areas of the service industry. Thanks to Mr. Humberto, Secretary General of the Ministry of Development, Industry and Commerce of Brazil, for his great support for Brazil's service industry. Thanks for your devotion to Brazil and for your support of Brazilian enterprises.

We have a long history in the service industry of enterprises. First of all, let's see our total output value. Brazil's economy increased by 3.1% in 2014. Particularly, the service industry accounted for 72% of the total output value, covering the service industry, banking industry, agriculture, industry and commercial fields.

We have different forms. Enterprise loans account for 34.2% and the information field accounts for 7.7% , indicating that Brazil has a huge information and network field. Transportation and logistics account for 15.4%. The warehousing industry is increasing each year. The total output value in 2014 was 304.8 billion RMB. Sao Paulo's proportion in the service field has reached 42.8%. Sao Paulo is a state with the largest service industry in Brazil.

I would again like to present our trade in services fields to be exported. Competitiveness can be driven in different ways and play a positive role.

It's a pity that only over 6 million people in the world know about Brazil's tourism resources, although Brazil is a big country with rich resources. The tourism industry only accounts for 0.1% of Brazil's GNI currently. I hope our Chinese friends will be able to get to know Brazil's tourism industry and our tourism facilities, and travel in Brazil in order to learn more about Brazil and its beautiful scenery.

Brazil has a negative growth in the rental, equipment and main industries, such as the shipbuilding industry and oil platform exploration, so we hope to have more cooperation opportunities in this aspect of services.

We have excellent teams in technology and banking. Our banking system is one of the most advanced in the world. We have an information-oriented and programmed organization for receiving customers. Economic growth further the banking industry as one of the industries that provides excellent worldwide services, so we will be able to provide great support in terms of banking, if required by Chinese entrepreneurs.

We also need increasing foreign investments in environmental protection. Foreign investments are increasing progressively. Total investments in 2013 were 64 billion USD. All foreign investments were distributed throughout different fields, mostly in industrial and agricultural buildings and 19.6% went into the service and banking industries.

China-Brazil trade transactions rank 8th, but we hope to have more cooperation in trade in services. Specifically, the service industry barely exists in our cooperation, so we hope more Brazilian enterprises will cooperate with China. China needs to increase cooperation opportunities in various cooperation fields by 60%. We hope Chinese enterprises will more actively do business in services, such as sports.

We can also provide some other services, such as high-end technical services. We can establish partner relationships in the fields of tourism, health, housing and transportation in order to attract more investments. With the continuous development of China's economy, we hope the two countries will have more cooperation in other fields, in addition to trade cooperation in raw materials.

Thanks again to Brazil's Ambassador and to the Secretary General of Brazil's Ministry of Development, Industry and Commerce for their arrival, showing the high value we hold in China. We hope to establish more cooperative relations with China, and we hope that the Brazil Services Unite Union will be able to provide more services. Thanks very much!

# Part Ⅴ

## Research on Hot Issues in the Fields of Trade in Services

# Analysis of the International Competitiveness of China's Trade in Services

## 1. Introduction

Service is regarded as a kind of economic activity, which is playing an increasingly significant role in the contribution of economic growth and employment in most countries. In recent years, 60%-80% of the gross domestic product (GDP) of developed countries is service, an average 50%-60% in developing countries. The world trade in services has accounted for about 20% of global trade. Since China's reform and opening up, China's trade in services has a greater development. The annual growth of trade in services is not only higher than the growth of the national economy, but also higher than the growth rate of domestic services, which plays an important role in promoting the development of the domestic service industry. With the development of economic globalization and trade liberalization, it is an inevitable trend that the development of trade in services should promote the development of China's new foreign trade. Meanwhile, the field of China's international trade in services is also gradually expanding, with the rapid development of communications, finance, insurance, technology trade, operation and management consultation, personnel training and other services. Through the development of trade in services, the introduction of foreign advanced management methods, technology and experience will play a positive role in China's modernization.

## 2. Analysis of the Competitiveness of China's Trade in Services

On the basis of the data obtained, this article establishes the index system including the Three Indexes to evaluate the international competitiveness of China's trade in services. This index system combines the relative number index with the absolute quantity index, which reflects on the import and export of the comparative advantage index, the export proportion of the revealed comparative advantage index and the market possession rate of the international market share index.

### 2.1    The International Market Share

The international market share (A) is the ratio of the amount of exports of a certain country's industries or products to the total exports on the world market. $A_{ij}=X_{ij}/X_{wj}$. Based on the comprehensive consideration of the overall size and strength of the country, the index can show the overall competitiveness of the country concisely.

Figure 1 shows that the share of China's trade in services on the international market is low, at present about 4.6%, but observing after nearly 20 years of development, the share of China's trade in services on the international market is showing an increasing trend year by year, and the ability to compete is gradually increasing, too. The share of China's trade in services on the international market increased from 0.7% in 1983 to 4.6% in 2014, an increase of more than 5 times, and it rose to second in the word in 2014. This fully reflects that the overall competitiveness of China's trade in services is improving in the twenty-first century.

Compared with other countries or regions in the world, the overall competitiveness of China's trade in services has also increased. As shown in Figure 2, in 14 countries and regions, in 2001, the possession rate of China's trade in services on the international market ranked ninth, far behind the leading positions of Britain, America, Japan and other developed economies. In 2010 it exceeded that of Japan; France and Germany, ranking fourth in the world, increased the gap with Italy, South Korea, Singapore and Hong Kong. In 2010, China was one of the two developing countries in the top 10 countries in the world for trade in services. The possession rate of trade in services on the international market made the fastest rise in 10 years, and the international market share increased 2.4 percentage points, but compared with America, Britain and Germany and other developed countries, a great distance still exists.

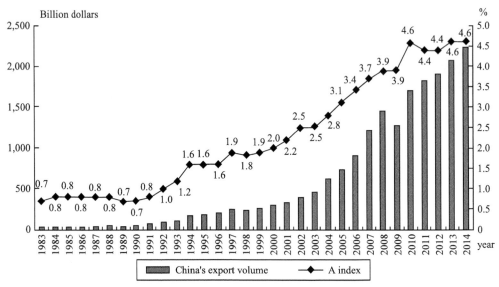

**Fig.1   China's trade in services export volume and A index from 1983 to 2014**

Data source: The WTO international trade statistics database.

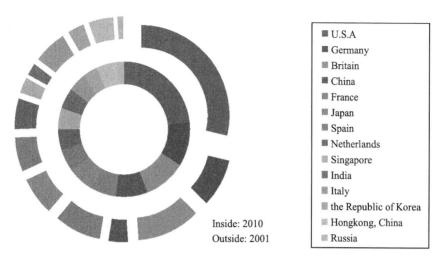

U.S.A
Germany
Britain
China
France
Japan
Spain
Netherlands
Singapore
India
Italy
the Republic of Korea
Hongkong, China
Russia

Inside: 2010
Outside: 2001

**Fig.2   A index comparison among China and some developed countries and the newly industrialized countries (regions)**

## 2.2   The Revealed Comparative Advantage Index

The Revealed Comparative Advantage(RCA)index shows that the comparative advantage of industry/product j in country i can be "demonstrated" by calculating the ratio of the export share of industry/product j in country i to the current world trade share of industry/product j in the total world trade. $RCA_{ij} = (X_{ij}/X_{it}) / (X_{wj}/ X_{wt})$.

If RCA is [2.5, $\infty$], it indicates that the export product j for country i has extremely strong international competitiveness.

If RCA is [1.25, 2.5), it indicates that the export product j for country i has a strong international competitiveness;

If RCA is [0.8, 1.25), it indicates that the export product j for country i has a less strong international competitiveness.;

If RCA is [0, 0.8), it indicates that the export product j for country i has a weak international competitiveness.

Although this index is a relative value, it can effectively eliminate the impact of the fluctuation of the total exports of a country and the worldwide exports on the comparability. Therefore, it can make a more accurate measure of a country in the current industry or the export product in the relative position of average world level as well as the trend of change in the time sequence.

From the point of view of a longitudinal comparison, from 2000 to 2014 the RCA index of China's trade in services was between 0.4 and 0.6, that is less than 0.8; this indicates that the whole of China's trade in services, without the international competitive advantage index, is obviously on the low side and the RCA index showed a downward trend ,demonstrating that in recent years, China's trade in services international competitiveness has gradually weakened

(Fig.3). It is because in the past ten years, China's trade in services exports accounted for the very low proportion of its total export commodities. In recent years it also showed a downward trend.

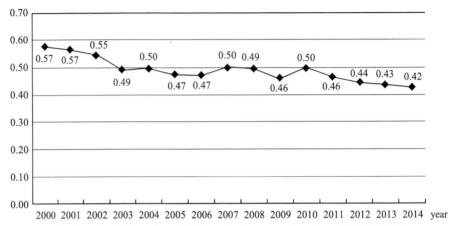

**Fig.3    The RCA index of China's trade in services from 2000 to 2014**

Data source: "China Statistical Yearbook", WTO.

Compared with the RCA index in the developed countries and Asian countries, the RCA index of the United States and the United Kingdom was between 1.25 and 2.5, showing an extremely strong international competitiveness. The RCA index of France was between 0.8 and 1.25, showing a strong international competitiveness as well, while Japan and South Korea lingered somewhat behind for some years; their RCA index was greater than 0.8, showing a relatively strong international competitiveness. Germany's RCA index was also relatively low, but higher than China's. Instead, India, in recent years, due to the development of its domestic IT industry and the rise of service outsourcing, has enhanced the international competitiveness of its trade in services. The 2010 RCA index was 1.72, showing an extremely strong international competitiveness (Table 1).

**Table 1    A comparison of the RCA index among China and some developed countries and the newly industrialized countries (regions)**

| Country year | China | The USA | Great Britain | Germany | France | Japan | Korea | India |
|---|---|---|---|---|---|---|---|---|
| 2001 | 0.64 | 1.38 | 1.55 | 0.66 | 1.04 | 0.75 | 0.81 | / |
| 2005 | 0.52 | 1.49 | 1.72 | 0.68 | 1.05 | 0.81 | 0.71 | / |
| 2010 | 0.55 | 1.47 | 1.89 | 0.79 | 1.08 | 0.78 | 0.76 | 1.72 |

Data source: The WTO International Trade Statistics Database.

## 2.3    The TC Index

The competitive advantage index (TC) is the ratio of the total net exports of certain industries or products of a country and the total amount of imports and exports. $TC_{ij} = (X_{ij} -$

$M_{ij}) / (X_{ij} + M_{ij})$.

The range of the index is [-1,1]; the competitiveness monotonically increases in this interval. The closer to 1 that TC value is, the greater the comparative advantage is, indicating a stronger international competitiveness of the industry/product in a country and vice versa.

The index excludes the impact of fluctuation of all macro-economic aspects, such as inflation. Therefore, the TC index is comparable in different periods.

As can be seen from the TC index, which is derived from Table 2, the overall TC index of China's trade in services has been negative. Trade in services has always had a trade deficit. The value of the TC index has no big ups and downs, but it shows a clear downward trend: the international competitiveness is weak and the competitive power drops. This explains that the imports from China's trade in services grew fast in the past decade.

For various industries involved in trade in services, governments and related sectors have put emphasis on the development of trade in services in recent years, which has greatly improved these industries' competitive index, indicating that their international competitiveness is gradually improving. Only the TC index of other business services has always been positive, which indicates a certain competitiveness. The trade competitiveness index has been in a negative state, which is traditionally due to the labor-intensive transport services. The competitiveness of the tourism industry, which is considered as the pillar industry of China's trade in services, has shown a weaker and weaker trend in recent years. The TC index has been negative and less competitive since 2010, because tourism consumption has increased year by year with the continuous improvement of the income of China's residents.

The TC value of some industries, such as building services, communication services, computer and information services and the advertising industry, was positive for most of the years. These industries mainly rely on the state monopoly policy and so the development of service outsourcing is gaining advantages. The trade competitiveness index is overwhelmingly negative in the field of trade in services with high added value such as finance, insurance, patent rights, consulting, films and videos. This indicates that the international competitiveness of China's capital- and technology-intensive trade in services is low. In particular, the TC index for patent royalties and licensing fees has been close to -1 for many years, which reflects that the industry is highly dependent on imports (Table 2).

Table 2    TC index of all areas of China's trade in services

| Items | 2000 | 2002 | 2004 | 2006 | 2008 | 2010 | 2012 | 2014 |
| --- | --- | --- | --- | --- | --- | --- | --- | --- |
| Transport | -0.48 | -0.41 | -0.34 | -0.24 | -0.13 | -0.30 | -0.38 | -0.43 |
| Tourism | 0.11 | 0.14 | 0.15 | 0.17 | 0.06 | -0.17 | -0.34 | -0.49 |
| Communication services | 0.70 | 0.08 | -0.11 | -0.02 | 0.02 | 0.03 | 0.04 | -0.12 |

Continued

| Items | 2000 | 2002 | 2004 | 2006 | 2008 | 2010 | 2012 | 2014 |
|---|---|---|---|---|---|---|---|---|
| Construction services | -0.25 | 0.13 | 0.05 | 0.15 | 0.41 | 0.48 | 0.54 | 0.52 |
| Insurance services | -0.92 | -0.88 | -0.88 | -0.88 | -0.80 | -0.80 | -0.72 | -0.66 |
| Financial services | -0.11 | -0.28 | -0.19 | -0.72 | -0.28 | -0.02 | -0.01 | -0.09 |
| Computer and information services | 0.15 | -0.28 | 0.13 | 0.26 | 0.33 | 0.51 | 0.58 | 0.37 |
| Patent royalties | -0.88 | -0.92 | -0.90 | -0.94 | -0.90 | -0.88 | -0.89 | -0.95 |
| Consultation | -0.29 | -0.34 | -0.2 | -0.03 | 0.15 | 0.20 | 0.25 | 0.24 |
| Advertising and publicity | 0.05 | -0.03 | 0.10 | 0.20 | 0.06 | 0.17 | 0.26 | 0.14 |
| Film and video | -0.54 | -0.53 | -0.62 | 0.08 | 0.24 | -0.51 | -0.62 | -0.67 |
| Other commercial services | 0.07 | 0.28 | 0.31 | 0.27 | 0.06 | 0.35 | 0.18 | 0.17 |
| Total | -0.08 | -0.08 | -0.07 | -0.05 | -0.10 | -0.06 | -0.38 | -0.43 |

Date source: China Trade in Services: http://tradeinservices.mofcom.gov.cn.

## 3. Problems Existing in China's Trade in Services

### 3.1 The first problem: The Development of Trade in Services Is Still Relatively Backward

China's trade in services has developed from the 1980s to the present; the total import and export volume has increased rapidly, the status of global trade in services has increased year by year, rising to fourth place among the top 25 in the world, but the level is still relatively backward compared with the level of development of worldwide trade in services; the overall competitiveness is weak. In 2010, China's trade in services accounted for only 5.1% of the world's trade in services. In 2014 it rose to 6.1%. In the same year, the United States' trade in services accounted for 12.1%, about 2 times as much as China's. Regarding the scale of imports and exports, China's trade in services has been in a state of deficit during the past twenty years. The total trade in services reached 604.36 billion dollars in 2014; it had expanded by 12.6 percent year-on-year. Of that total, the imports for trade in services reached 382.15 billion dollars, the exports reached 222.21 billion dollars, the trade deficit was 159.94 billion dollars.

However, from the other point of view, trade in services and trade in goods, two different means of trade, have a very close relationship. On the one hand, with the development of trade in goods, service industries such as finance, transportation, insurance emerge, which support the development of trade in goods; on the other hand, the development of trade in goods will increase the demand for trade in services and so it will drive the growth of trade in services forward. The induced effect among China's trade in goods and service has not yet fully played out; there is still much huge room for the development of both. It is estimated that the proportion of China's trade in services exports and trade in goods exports was 1:10.5 in 2014, far below the world average of 1:4.9, less than 1:2.3 of that of the United States.

## 3.2    The second problem: The Unreasonable Structure of Imports and Exports of Trade in Services, and the Fact that Traditional Services are the Main Project

Seen from the above analysis of the TC index, the competitive disadvantage of Chinese trade in services is very obvious in the financial, insurance, patents, consulting and most capital and technology-intensive industries, which is closely related to the unbalanced development in China's service industries and the unreasonable import and export structure of trade in services. The pillar of China's trade in services is the traditional service industries, such as tourism, transportation and other labor-intensive sectors, and resource endowments, such as traditional services, low value-added industries; these industries are gradually shrinking all over the world. In contrast, in the global trade in services in the thriving business service industries, such as finance, telecommunications, film, culture and consulting, China is still in the preliminary stage of development. It is in a weak link; it is basically in a trade deficit position, and has no export competitive advantage. In 2014, in the Chinese trade in services imports and exports, the international tourism trade reached 221 billion and 710 million US dollars, accounting for 36.7% of the total imports and exports within trade in services; the international transport trade reached 134 billion and 520 million US dollars, accounting for 22.3%; both accounted for 59%. And some emerging areas of trade in services, such as the telecommunication services, reached $4.11 billion, accounting for 0.7%. Film culture was lower, accounting for only 0.2%. On the other hand, the pace of development of the emerging areas of trade in services, such as the financial services was in good shape; their import and export volume reached $ 10.1 billion in 2014, an increase of 59.5% compared with 2013. The year-on-year growth rate in 2013 and 2012 reached 66.2% and 139.2%, respectively (Table 3).

**Table 3    The Imports and exports of China's trade in services in various industries in 2014**
**(UNIT: 0.1 Billion dollars)**

|  | Exports | Imports | Total | Trade Balance |
|---|---|---|---|---|
| Transport | 383 | 962.2 | 1,345.2 | -579.2 |
| Tourism | 569.1 | 1,648 | 2,217.1 | -1,078.9 |
| Communication services | 18.1 | 23 | 41.1 | -4.9 |
| Construction services | 154.2 | 49.3 | 203.5 | 104.9 |
| Insurance services | 45.6 | 225 | 270.6 | -179.4 |
| Financial services | 46 | 55 | 101 | -9 |
| Computer and information services | 183.6 | 85 | 268.6 | 98.6 |
| Patent royalties | 6.3 | 226 | 232.3 | -219.7 |
| Consultation | 429 | 263 | 692 | 166 |
| Advertising and publicity | 50 | 38 | 88 | 12 |
| Films and videos | 1.8 | 9 | 10.8 | -7.2 |
| Other commercial services | 335.4 | 238 | 573.4 | 97.4 |
| Total | 2,222.1 | 3,821.5 | 6,043.6 | -1,599.4 |

Data source: "China's Trade in Services Statistics 2015".

### 3.3 The third problem: The Industrial Base of the Development of China´s Trade in Services Is Still Weak

3.3.1 The GDP's Dependence on the Service Sector

The dependence of the GDP on the service industry refers to the value of the service industry in proportion to the GDP. The service industry is the foundation for the development of trade in services. Although the service industry in our country has obtained an unprecedented rapid development after the reform and the opening up and has become an important part of the national economy, the development of China's service industry lags behind that of other industries, and it lags far behind that in other countries too, especially in Europe, America, Japan and other developed countries, due to various reasons, such as a talent shortage, the lack of policy orientation, and inadequate attention paid to the development of the service industry for a long time. In 2009, the added value of China's service industry reached 14760 billion yuan, accounting for 43.4% of the national GDP, far less than the 78% in the United States, 70% in Japan, 73% in Germany and 78% in the UK in the same period. In 2015, China's service industry value accounted for 50.5% of the proportion of GDP, which

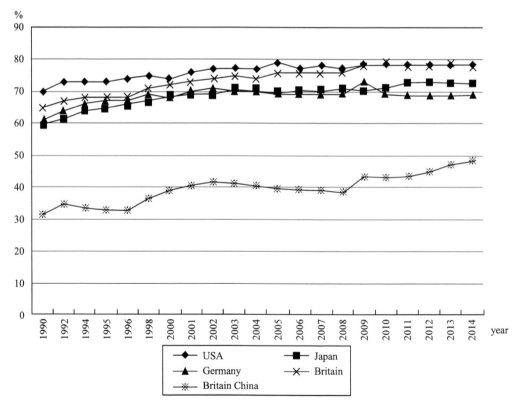

**Fig.4 Output value of developed countries and China's service industry accounted for the proportion of GDP**

Data sources: Chinese data from "China Statistical Yearbook"; other countries data from the United Nations Statistics website (http://unstats.un.org).

exceeded 50% for the first time, but still lower than the proportion of developed countries, and also that of the total global amount which is over 60%.

3.3.2　Dependence on export service

Dependence on export service refers to the proportion of export services in the total output value of services; generally it reflects the degree of internationalization of the services or the reliance on the international market. By calculation and analysis, China's dependence on export services over the past decade was extremely low, less than 0.01 since 2000, but the overall change during a period of 15 years showed a slight increase, reaching a peak of 0.077 in 2008, and then it showed a downward trend because of the 2009 world financial crisis. This indicated that China's dependence on export services is low, the opening up of the service industries is inadequate, and that the status of the service exports in the development of China's service economy is still relatively low (Fig.5).

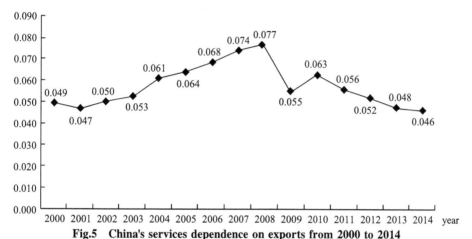

**Fig.5　China's services dependence on exports from 2000 to 2014**

Data sources: Data of the service industry output from the "China Statistical Yearbook", the service trade data is the same as that in the previous text.

## 3.4　The fourth problem: Inadequate Policies and Regulations, as There is Not Much Use of the GATS (General Agreement on Trade and Service)

In recent years, China has accelerated the legislation pace of trade in services; it has promulgated the "Maritime Law", the "Commercial Bank Law", the "Insurance Law", the "Advertising Law", the "Law Regarding Lawyers," the "Foreign Financial Institution Regulations" and a number of important laws and regulations involving trade in services, which play an important role in building a system of trade in services with unified open, orderly competition, standardized management, which is needed by a socialist market economy, and international rules. However, compared with developed countries, there is still a wide gap. Limited by the degree of openness and marketization, the legislation of China's trade in services is not perfect. There is a lack of appropriate laws and regulations in many areas; for some of the important service sectors there is no legislation or lack of supporting laws; some of the existing laws and regulations on services trade are vague and lack practical significance, resulting in the situation that no specific law can be referred to for the service sector, which has seriously hindered the development of China's trade in services. In addition, some laws and regulations have a certain gap in comparison with the rules of international trade. For example, telecommunications and tourism have a lack of relevant laws and regulations; and other related existing laws such as the "Intellectual Property Protection Act", "taxation", the "Company Law" do not have comprehensive legal support provisions. In addition, even if the degree of openness of trade in services has increased, particularly foreign operators of trade in services have continued to enter the domestic market, the domestic market still lacks a "Competition Law", an "Immigration Law" and other supporting laws.

In addition, the application of GATS in China's trade in services is mainly reflected in the relevant legislation. There is a discrepancy between the legislation of the rights and obligations of the foreign providers of trade in services and the principles of GATS, which leads to a dispute in international services. The supporting regulations of some service industries are not in conformity with the provisions relating to the trade in services in China's entry into the WTO. In GATS, four types of trade in services are defined; in addition to the commercial presence, there are very few relevant laws and regulations related to the other three kinds of service provisions. Thus, China's trade in services should improve its ability to use GATS.

### 3.5　The fifth problem: the Statistics System of Trade in Services Needs to Be Improved

For a long time, the statistics system of China's trade in services has been behind the developed countries; there are many details that need to be rebuilt and improved. Although, in 2007, the Ministry of Commerce and the National Bureau of Statistics, complying with international standards and combining with the development and characteristics of China's trade in services in recent years, jointly issued the "Statistics System of International Trade in Services" and amended it twice in 2010 and 2012 respectively, due to some flaws in the comprehensiveness, timeliness and accuracy of the data; however, it is still unable to meet the community demands for information regarding trade in services. At the same time, we still lack centralized management of the statistics of trade in services. Although the statistics of China's trade in services were prepared jointly by the Ministry of Commerce and the National Bureau of Statistics and an international reporting system for trade in services was also established, there are a large number of service trade enterprises with wide coverage, there is no relevant effective limit on laws and regulations, and the enterprises are not prone to declare their autonomy in this regard, resulting in the fact that a direct return recovery rate is not high and there are problems of poor data availability. Moreover, the service trade statistics system makes it difficult to clearly and correctly know the real development of China's trade in services, which also affects the development and introduction of relevant policies.

## 4. Policy Recommendations for Accelerating the Development of China's Trade in Services

Based on the above comprehensive analysis, China's international trade in services is still in the early stages of development, and there are still many problems to be solved. However, international experience shows that the development of trade in services to optimize the industrial structure, promote economic development, improve labor productivity and the level of employment, increases the competitiveness of the city and has a positive significance.

### 4.1    The Reform and Innovation of the Management System is Becoming a Strong Impetus to the Development of Trade in Services

At present, the outstanding contradiction in Chinese economic society is the growing demand for public services and goods and a serious shortage of effective supply; the reform of the social management system lags far behind, and it is difficult to meet the needs of economic and social development at the present stage.

As described above, the drawbacks of the system of trade in services is a key problem that restricts the development of trade in services; therefore, we must insist on intensifying the reform of institutional mechanisms, make innovations in the management mode of trade in services, and seek a breakthrough in the establishment of institutions. The inter-ministerial joint conference office of the development of trade in services of China's State Council should give full play to its own functions, jointly with the relevant departments, to strengthen macro guidance, plan and formulate unified policies of trade in services, relevant laws and regulations and strategic planning, and take on the work relating to inter-ministerial coordination. At the same time, we should identify and seize the key points of trade in services for development, actively promote the reform and the innovation of the management system of trade in services with the characteristics of "small government, big society".

First, in the next three years, in 10 provinces (municipalities), namely Tianjin, Shanghai, Hainan, Shenzhen, Hangzhou, Wuhan, Guangzhou, Chengdu, Suzhou, Weihai, and 5 national new districts, namely Harbin New District, Jiangbei New District, Liangjiang New District, Gui'an New District, West Ham New District, which launched pilot projects on innovation and development of trade in services, based on the motivation of intensifying the reform, expanding the opening up and encouraging innovation, we should actively promote the reform of institutional mechanisms conducive to the development of trade in services; we should focus on building a fair and competitive market environment, exploring promotion of mutual investments in the service areas, improving the policy supporting system of trade in services, accelerating the liberalization and facilitation of trade in services, thoroughly liberalizing the productivity in the service industry, launching pilot projects in pilot cities and new districts to form reproducible and applicable experiences. Within five years, we should have built an external agency of governmental management of the service industry and trade in services similar to that in mature market economy countries; the government, academia and representative enterprises of trade intermediary associations should jointly participate in the planning and formulating of the policies of the service industry and of trade in services. Within eight to ten years, central and local governments should create a "small government, big society" management system in trade in services.

Second, we should change the traditional concept of the development of foreign trade, so as to vigorously develop a unified way of thinking and understanding of trade in services, as expanded in the new stage for open economic developmental strategies. Of course, the emphasis on trade in services does not deny the necessity of trade in goods, and the coordinated development of the two is the direction and idea for the future adjustment of China's foreign trade policy.

Third, it is necessary to strengthen the training of the cadre team of trade in services, regularly organize department staff to participate in the related training regarding trade in services, and go to developed countries or regions to inspect, to learn advanced management concepts and improve the quality of work and the capacity for management. At the same time, we should improve the statistics system of China's international trade in services, and establish institutional arrangements which are conducive to the development of trade in services. For taxation, customs declarations, foreign exchanges and so on, we should adjust their policies according to the characteristics of the service industry and of trade in services, formulate the preferential policies for the development of trade in services according to the characteristics of the industry and the region, to avoid the situation of "one size fits all", and regularly evaluate the implementation of policies and timely adjust them. We should implement effective measures to facilitate the separation of the manufacturing industry from the service industry, converge industries and break the administrative technical monopoly in the service industry and market, and promote the professional development of the service industry and trade in services.

Fourth, we should give full play to the linking role of the service industry and the industry association of trade in services, and assist the competent authorities to carry out effective statistics and related management work. In addition, we should strengthen the coordination ability among departments to achieve resource sharing, and establish the inter-departmental coordination mechanism in order to communicate in a timely manner and effectively solve problems.

## 4.2    The Development of Trade in Services Needs to Deal with the Relationship of the Service Industry and Trade in Goods

The development of trade in services is necessarily closely linked to the service industry, particularly producer services, which can organically combine trade in services, t trade in goods and manufacturing to achieve coordinated development among them. Therefore, it is necessary to continue to promote the structural optimization and upgrading of the service industry , develop finance, insurance, logistics, information services, cultural and creative exhibitions and other production services, in order to lay a solid industrial foundation for trade in services. However, trade in services also needs, through imports, to introduce advanced foreign services, and use spillover effects to enhance the upgrading of the service industry, to continue to strengthen the international competitiveness of the service sector, and ultimately turn it into service exports. Of course, trade in services also needs to be closely coordinated with the goods trade, in order to be productive service industry, service outsourcing, cultural and creative industries as a major breakthrough in international trade in service, the establishment of mechanisms for the coordinated development of trade in goods and trade in services.

At the same time, we must fully affirm the real dividends of the development of service outsourcing. Objectively, the local governments consider service outsourcing as an important field in the development of trade in services. When talking about trade in services, the development of service outsourcing is essential. As a processing element of the trade in services industry, the biggest role of service outsourcing in promoting the development of trade in services is not only reflected in its current size and growth, but also in the training of future high-end talents in trade in services. Service outsourcing can increase employment, and improve people's livelihood, but its more far-reaching impact is on the cultivation of talents. Through undertaking service outsourcing, with the overflow of foreign advanced technology and experience, and engaging in outsourcing labor will digest and absorb the advanced technology, process and management experience, and will then become potential high-end talent in the field of China's trade in services.

## 4.3    Breaking the Monopoly of the Service industry, Expanding Foreign Exchanges and Cooperation

China's trade in services TC index of the previous analysis from 2000 to 2014 shows that the TC index of China's financial service and telecom service industry is positive and has enhanced competitiveness in some of the years in a 10-year period. It also shows that the competitive advantage may be obtained by the state monopoly, which has not only damaged the normal market order for fair competition, but has also led the service industry to be low in efficiency, have a lack of innovation and ineffective competition. Therefore, in the future, when the Chinese government formulates a developmental strategy for China's trade in services or releases relevant policies, it should aim at completely breaking up the monopoly, expand exchanges and cooperation with other countries, and promote technological innovation, institutional innovation, organizational innovation and innovation of manners and ways. With the gradual intensification of China's accession to the WTO, stronger and stronger competitors of the service industry will enter from countries with mature market economies, which has forced China to establish an open, equal, and standardized access system to its service industry, a fair and just environment for service industry market competition, and to break the monopoly of the industry, introduce a competition mechanism, and let the service companies into the market to create and improve China's service industry to participate in international competition.

### 4.4 Make the Legal System of Trade in Services Perfectly in Line with the WTO Rules

Learning from the advanced experience of developed countries in terms of trade in services legislation, in combination with the actual situation of China, China should: establish and perfect the systems of laws and regulations for trade in services, which are not only in line with the characteristics of China's foreign trade, but also in line with the WTO rules, and especially in line with the GATS standards; make the development of China's trade in services depend on laws and rules. It should be provided in the form of laws such as principles of service market access, taxation of trade in services, investment, preferential terms and so on, in order to increase the transparency of China's trade in services, so that trade in services achieves institutionalization and standardization. At the same time, China needs to develop suitable protection policies by correctly using the exception clause so as to protect the normal development of China's trade in services. Regarding the national sovereignty and security service departments, both the extent and scope of their protection should be clearly specified in the laws, to prevent the developed countries from taking advantage of the loopholes in the laws to retaliate on China.

(Jiang Lihua, School of Economics and Trade, Ningbo Institute of technology, Zhejiang University; Yu Lixin, Professor, Head of the International Economic, Trade and Finance Research Center, the Chinese Academy of Social Sciences)

# Research on the Path and Strategy of Integrating China's Trade in Services into the International Market

## 1.  Analysis of the Developmental Status of Trade in Services in China

The service industry refers to the tertiary industry plus the construction industry, which includes extremely wide contents. By definition of the *General Agreement for Trade in Services* (GATS), trade in services can be defined into four modes of services supply: ① services supplied from one country to another; ② consumers or firms making use of a service in another country; service provider; ③ a foreign company setting up subsidiaries or branches to provide services in another country; ④ individuals travelling from their own country to supply services in another. In the WTO, the trade in services is summarized as over 150 branch departments and 12 big departments. According to *GATS* reached during the Uruguay Round of GATT, the service sectors include the following contents: commercial services, computer information services, building and associated engineering services, distribution services, transport services, finance services, environment services, travelling services education services, medical services and so on. The world economy is gradually developing towards the service industry, which is in the leading position. The service industry, instead of the agriculture and manufacturing industries, in the national economy, has become a general trend, both in developed countries and developing countries. Thus, the opening up of the service industry not only represents the economic interest of developed countries, but also the symbol of global industrial progress.

### 1.1    The general status quo of the service industry in China

In the middle and later periods of the opening up, the service industry realized a great leap forward in its development in China. In the 1980s, the annual growth rate of the service industry in China reached 10.9%, two points higher than the GDP growth rate during that period. However, since the 1990s, the development of the service industry in China has slowed down and has shown a downswing, but the scale still maintains a high-speed growth. The total output value of the service industry in 1990 was 588.842 billion RMB. It increased to 1.61798 trillion RMB in 1994 with the speed increasing by 28.7%. Its proportion of the GDP increased by 2%. Since 1997, the proportion of the service industry has shown a steady growth. It reached 39.0% in 2000, a 7.5% increase on that of 1999. In the 21st century, the service industry in China is still maintaining a high-speed expansion. It increased by nearly 4% in 2000 compared to that in 1999; the growth rate in 2007 even reached 25.7% (Fig. 1). Owing to the impact of the global economic crisis, the speed of increase showed a downswing from 2008 to 2012, but the proportion of the service industry in China since the beginning of the 21st century still has shown a positive growth. The total output value in 2014 was 30.6739 trillion yuan, accounting for 48.2% of the GDP, higher than the secondary industry by 5.6%. The proportion of GDP of service industry jump over the second industry, marking the Chinese economy officially entered the "Service" of the ear.

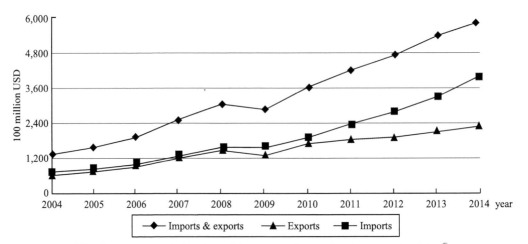

**Fig. 1   The general situation of imports and exports of services in China**①

Data source: Department of Trade in Services and Commerce and Trade in Services of the Ministry of Commerce.

### 1.2   The status quo of trade in services exports in China

1.2.1   The general status quo of trade in services exports in China

In 2013, in view of the complicated foreign and domestic situation and the pressure from the economic downturn, China optimized its trade in services structure positively and set about expanding the high value-added service export. The development of trade in services rose steadily. The annual trade in services scale hit a new record. The total exports and imports broke through 500 billion USD for the first time and continued to lead the world. In 2014, China's total export-import volume of trade in service reached 604.34 billion dollars, breaking the 600 billion dollars, an increase of 12.6% compared with 2013, which is much higher than

---

① Data source: The Department of Trade in Services and Commerce and Trade in Services of the Ministry of Commerce: *Imports and Exports of Services in China*, access website, http://data.mofcom.gov.cn/channel/includes/list.shtml?channel=mysj&visit=E.

the average level of global trade in services of 4.7%.

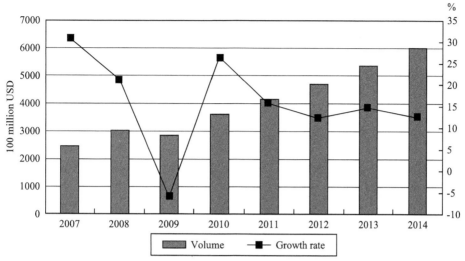

**Fig. 2    Total volume and growth rate of service exports and imports in China from 1991 to 2014**
Data source: The Ministry of Commerce

From the data in Fig. 2, it can be seen that, first of all, the proportion of total exports and imports of services in foreign trade is on the rise. In 2014, the increasing rate of exports and imports in consultation, computer and information services, financial services, exclusive rights royalties and loyalties is 19.9%, 17%, 66.2% and 16.7%, respectively. The rapid growth of high value-added service enhances capital-intensive and technology-intensive enterprises, promotes scientific and technological progress and optimizes the trade structure. Service exports realized a two-digit growth for the first time in those three years (Table 1).[①]

**Table 1    The export situation of Services in China from 2011 to 2014**

| Year \ Indicator | Amount of exports (0.1 billion USD) | Growth rate compared to the previous year |
|---|---|---|
| 2011 | 1821 | 7 |
| 2012 | 1904 | 4.6 |
| 2013 | 2106 | 10.6 |
| 2014 | 2222.1 | 7.6 |

Data source: China's Commerce Ministry

1.2.2    The status quo of trade in services in China according to industry

From Fig. 3, it can be seen that from 2004 to 2014, in the above five industries, the scale of exports of wholesale, retailing, leasing and commercial service industries is the largest and

---

① Data source: China Network of Industry Information (CNII), access website: http://www.chyxx.com/data/201402/228795.html.

it is growing swiftly and vigorously. The scale of exports for this industry shows an obvious decline in 2009. Afterwards, the overall scale of exports shows a steady growth trend; the overall scale of exports of computer services and the software industry shows a steady growth trend. Such trends reflect that since 2004, the international competitiveness of the Chinese information technology industry has strengthened constantly and that it has a great export potential; similar to information transmission, the computer service and software industry, the export level of the Chinese financial industry is also on the rise step by step and the speed of the growth of the scale of exports of the Chinese financial industry in the post-crisis era is more rapid.

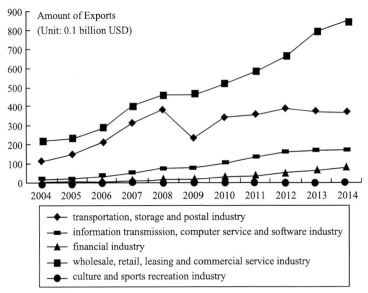

Fig. 3  **The changing trend of the scale of exports in different Chinese service industries from 2004 to 2014**[①]

1.2.3  Existing problems in the exportation of China's trade in services

First, the trade in services deficit has grown further. In 2013, China's trade in services deficit expanded to 118.46 billion USD, with a 32.1% of year-on-year growth. It reached 19.55 billion USD, 16.95 billion USD, 9.45 billion USD and 6.77 billion USD of trade surplus, respectively, in other commercial services such as, consultation, computer and information services and in the fields of building services, but it had a big trade deficit in the fields of tourism, transport services, exclusive rights royalties, loyalties and insurance services. The trade deficit amount was 76.92 billion USD, 56.68 billion USD, 20.15 billion USD and

---

① Hu Fei, "Impact of Foreign Direct Investments in the Service Industry on the Export of China's Trade in Services: Empirical Research Based on Industrial Panel Data", *Exploration of Economic Problems*, 2015 (6).

18.1 billion USD, respectively. [1] In 2014, China's deficit of service trade reached 159.93 billion dollars, and increase of 35%. Where the deficit of tourism trade was 107.89 billion dollars, a substantial increase of 40.3% from 2013, accounting for 67.5% of the deficit of total service trade, which was the trade deficit is the largest source of total deficit. Then the deficit of transportation services were 57.9 billion dollars, exclusive rights to royalites and license fees deficits were 21.97 billion dollars, a slight increase than in 2013. Insurance services deficit reached 17.94 billion dollars, slightly narrowed than in 2013.

Second, the regional development of trade in services is extremely unequal, and the export markets mainly focus on the developed countries and regions. Because of the particularity of trade in services, China's trade in services mainly concentrates on costal developed areas, Hong Kong and a few developed countries. In 2012, Hong Kong, the European Union (27 countries), the United States, the Association of Southeast Asian Nations and Japan were the first five trade in services partners of our country. The exports and imports of our country with the above-mentioned countries (regions) reached 310 billion USD, with a 7.6% of year-on-year growth. In 2014, there experienced a rapid growth of the amount of service outsourcing between China and the partners in the area of "the Belt and Road", the contract value and exercise amount of service outsourcing were 12.5 billion dollars and 9.84 billion dollars, an increase of 25.2% and 36.3%, respectively, which were much higher than the overall growth rate.[2]

Third, the development of trade in services centers over traditional trade in services. But the high value-added nwe services developed rapidly. China's trade in services mainly focuses on the traditional service industry. In recent years, the exportation of China's transport service has shown an increasing trend while the exportation of tourism services has declined slightly, bu the proportion is still big. In 2014, the imports and exports amount of three Chinese traditional services (tourism, transport services and construction services) reached 376.55 billion dollars, accounting for 62.6% of that of total trade in services.

---

[1] Lan Yucai, "Deficit Is Enlarged: the Current Situation of China's Trade in Services from Data", *China Business & Trade,* 2014 (10).

[2] Data source: BOP data from *Balance of International Payments of China* released by the State Administration of Foreign Exchange over the years.

**Table 2　The structure of China's trade in services exportation in 2007–2014　(1)**

Unit: 100 million USD

| Year | | Total | Transport services | Tourism | Communi-cation services | Construc-tion services | Insurance services | Financial services |
|---|---|---|---|---|---|---|---|---|
| 2007 | Amount (0.1 billion USD) | 1,216.5 | 313.2 | 372.3 | 11.7 | 53.8 | 9 | 2.3 |
| | Increasing rate over the previous year | 33.1 | 49.1 | 9.7 | 59.2 | 95.3 | 64.9 | 59 |
| | proportion | 100 | 25.7 | 30.6 | 1 | 4.4 | 0.7 | 0.2 |
| 2008 | Amount (0.1 billion USD) | 1,464.5 | 384.2 | 408.4 | 15.7 | 103.3 | 13.8 | 3.2 |
| | Increasing rate over the previous year | 20.4 | 22.6 | 9.7 | 33.7 | 92.1 | 53 | 36.7 |
| | proportion | 100 | 26.2 | 27.9 | 1.1 | 7.1 | 0.9 | 0.2 |
| 2009 | Amount (0.1 billion USD) | 1,286 | 235.7 | 396.8 | 12 | 94.6 | 16 | 4.4 |
| | Increasing rate over the previous year | -12.2 | -38.7 | -2.9 | -23.7 | -8.4 | 15.4 | 38.7 |
| | proportion | 100 | 18.3 | 30.9 | 0.9 | 7.4 | 1.2 | 0.3 |
| 2010 | Amount (0.1 billion USD) | 1,702.5 | 342.1 | 458.1 | 12.2 | 144.9 | 17.3 | 13.3 |
| | Increasing rate over the previous year | 32.4 | 45.2 | 15.5 | 1.8 | 53.2 | 8.2 | 204.6 |
| | proportion | 100 | 20.1 | 26.9 | 0.7 | 8.5 | 1 | 0.8 |
| 2011 | Amount (0.1 billion USD) | 1,820.9 | 355.7 | 484.6 | 17.3 | 147.2 | 30.2 | 8.5 |
| | Increasing rate over the previous year | 7 | 4 | 5.8 | 41.5 | 1.6 | 74.7 | -36.2 |
| | proportion | 100 | 19.5 | 26.6 | 0.9 | 8..1 | 1.7 | 0.5 |
| 2012 | Amount (0.1 billion USD) | 1,904.4 | 389.1 | 500.3 | 17.9 | 122.5 | 33.3 | 18.9 |
| | Increasing rate over the previous year | 4.6 | 9.4 | 3.2 | 3.7 | -16.8 | 10.3 | 122.5 |
| | proportion | 100 | 20.4 | 26.3 | 0.9 | 6.4 | 1.7 | 1 |
| 2013 | Amount (0.1 billion USD) | 2,105.9 | 376.5 | 516.6 | 16.7 | 106.6 | 40 | 29.2 |
| | Increasing rate over the previous year | 10.6 | -3.2 | 3.3 | -6.9 | -13 | 20 | 54.2 |
| | proportion | 100 | 17.9 | 24.5 | 0.8 | 5.1 | 1.9 | 1.4 |
| 2014 | Amount (0.1 billion USD) | 2,222.1 | 383.0 | 569.1 | 18.1 | 154.2 | 45.6 | 46.0 |
| | Increasing rate over the previous year | 7.6 | 1.7 | 10.2 | 8.9 | 44.6 | 14.1 | 57.8 |
| | proportion | 100 | 17.7 | 25.6 | 0.8 | 7.1 | 2.1 | 2.1 |

Continued

| Year | | Computer and information service | Exclusive right royalties and loyalties | Consultation | Advertising and publicity | Film and video | Other commercial services |
|---|---|---|---|---|---|---|---|
| 2007 | Amount (0.1 billion USD) | 43.4 | 3.4 | 115.8 | 19.1 | 3.2 | 269.1 |
| | Increasing rate over the previous year | 46.9 | 67.1 | 47.8 | 32.3 | 130.9 | 36.7 |
| | proportion | 3.6 | 0.3 | 9.5 | 1.6 | 0.3 | 22.1 |
| 2008 | Amount (0.1 billion USD) | 62.5 | 5.7 | 181.4 | 22 | 4.2 | 260.1 |
| | Increasing rate over the previous year | 43.9 | 66.7 | 56.7 | 15.2 | 32.2 | -3.4 |
| | proportion | 4.3 | 0.4 | 12.4 | 1.5 | 0.3 | 17.8 |
| 2009 | Amount (0.1 billion USD) | 65.1 | 4.3 | 186.2 | 23.1 | 1 | 246.9 |
| | Increasing rate over the previous year | 4.2 | -24.8 | 2.7 | 5 | -76.7 | -5.1 |
| | proportion | 5.1 | 0.3 | 14.5 | 1.8 | 0.1 | 19.2 |
| 2010 | Amount (0.1 billion USD) | 92.6 | 8.3 | 227.7 | 28.9 | 1.2 | 355.9 |
| | Increasing rate over the previous year | 42.1 | 93.4 | 22.3 | 24.8 | 26.4 | 44.1 |
| | proportion | 5.4 | 0.5 | 13.4 | 1.7 | 0.1 | 20.9 |
| 2011 | Amount (0.1 billion USD) | 121.8 | 7.4 | 283.9 | 40.2 | 1.2 | 322.8 |
| | Increasing rate over the previous year | 31.6 | -10.5 | 24.7 | 39.3 | -0.1 | -9.3 |
| | proportion | 6.7 | 0.4 | 15.6 | 2.2 | 0.1 | 17.7 |
| 2012 | Amount (0.1 billion USD) | 144.5 | 10.4 | 334.5 | 47.5 | 1.3 | 284.2 |
| | Increasing rate over the previous year | 18.6 | 40.1 | 17.8 | 18.2 | 5.9 | -12 |
| | proportion | 7.6 | 0.5 | 17.6 | 2.5 | 0.1 | 14.9 |
| 2013 | Amount (0.1 billion USD) | 154.3 | 8.9 | 405.4 | 49.1 | 1.5 | 401 |
| | Increasing rate over the previous year | 6.8 | -14.8 | 21.2 | 3.3 | 13.2 | 41.2 |
| | proportion | 7.3 | 0.4 | 19.3 | 2.3 | 0.1 | 19.1 |
| 2014 | Amount (0.1 billion USD) | 183.6 | 6.3 | 429.0 | 50.0 | 1.8 | 335.4 |
| | Increasing rate over the previous year | 19.0 | -29.4 | 5.8 | 1.9 | 22.3 | -7.1 |
| | proportion | 8.5 | 0.3 | 19.8 | 2.3 | 0.1 | 15.5 |

Data source: Data from 2007 to 2013 derive from *Statistics of China's Trade in Services in 2014*. Data in 2014 derive from *China's Trade in Services Situation in 2004* prepared by the Comprehensive Division of the Ministry of Commerce.

## 1.3　The current situation of the imports of China's trade in services

1.3.1　The current situation of the total imports of China's trade in services

According to the data table statistics of *China's Trade in Services in 2013* released by the Ministry of Commerce, the total amount of China's trade in services increased from 4.4 billion USD in 1982 to 470.6 billion USD in 2012, a 100 times' increase during 30 years with an annual growth rate of 16.85%. It can be seen from Table 3 that, due to the global financial crisis in 2009, the total amount of China's trade in services showed a decline for the first time,

Table 3　The total amount and imports of China's trade in services from 1982 to 2014

Unit: 100 million USD, %

| Year | Total exports and imports of services | | | Amount of service imports | | |
|---|---|---|---|---|---|---|
| | Amount | Year-on-year growth | Proportion in the world | Amount | Year-on-year growth | Proportion in the world |
| 1982 | 44 | - | 0.57 | 19 | - | 0.47 |
| 1983 | 43 | -2.27 | 0.58 | 18 | -5.26 | 0.47 |
| 1984 | 54 | 25.58 | 0.71 | 26 | 44.44 | 0.66 |
| 1985 | 52 | -3.7 | 0.66 | 23 | -11.54 | 0.57 |
| 1986 | 56 | 7.69 | 0.62 | 20 | -13.04 | 0.44 |
| 1987 | 65 | 16.07 | 0.6 | 23 | 15 | 0.42 |
| 1988 | 80 | 23.08 | 0.65 | 33 | 43.48 | 0.53 |
| 1989 | 81 | 1.25 | 0.6 | 36 | 9.098 | 0.53 |
| 1990 | 98 | 20.99 | 0.61 | 41 | 13.89 | 0.5 |
| 1991 | 108 | 10.2 | 0.64 | 39 | -4.88 | 0.46 |
| 1992 | 183 | 69.44 | 0.98 | 92 | 135.9 | 0.97 |
| 1993 | 226 | 23.5 | 1.19 | 116 | 26.09 | 1.21 |
| 1994 | 322 | 42.48 | 1.55 | 158 | 36.21 | 1.52 |
| 1995 | 430 | 33.54 | 1.83 | 246 | 55.7 | 2.08 |
| 1996 | 430 | 0 | 1.72 | 224 | -8.94 | 1.8 |
| 1997 | 522 | 21.4 | 2.02 | 277 | 23.77 | 2.17 |
| 1998 | 504 | -3.45 | 1.9 | 265 | -4.53 | 2.02 |
| 1999 | 572 | 13.49 | 2.07 | 310 | 16.99 | 2.27 |
| 2000 | 660 | 15.38 | 2.25 | 359 | 15.8 | 2.46 |
| 2001 | 719 | 8.99 | 2.43 | 390 | 8.85 | 2.65 |
| 2002 | 855 | 18.86 | 2.71 | 461 | 18.06 | 2.96 |
| 2003 | 1013 | 18.48 | 2.8 | 549 | 19.04 | 3.08 |
| 2004 | 1337 | 31.98 | 3.08 | 716 | 30.54 | 3.38 |
| 2005 | 1571 | 17.5 | 3.24 | 832 | 16.16 | 3.53 |
| 2006 | 1917 | 22.02 | 3.51 | 1003 | 20.62 | 3.8 |
| 2007 | 2509 | 30.88 | 3.86 | 1293 | 28.83 | 4.13 |
| 2008 | 3045 | 21.36 | 4.15 | 1580 | 22.24 | 4.47 |
| 2009 | 2867 | -5.843 | 4.46 | 1581 | 0.07 | 5.08 |
| 2010 | 3624 | 26.41 | 5.05 | 1922 | 21.55 | 5.48 |
| 2011 | 4191 | 15.64 | 5.2 | 2370 | 23.33 | 6.1 |
| 2012 | 4706 | 12.29 | 5.6 | 2801 | 18.2 | 6.8 |
| 2013 | 5396 | 14.7 | 6.0 | 3290 | 17.5 | 7.6 |
| 2014 | 6043.4 | 12.6 | 6.44 | 3821.3 | 15.8 | 8.1 |

Data source: data table Statistics of *China's Trade in Services in 2013* released by the Ministry of Commerce; from the situation of China's Trade in services in 2014 released by the Comprehensive Division of the Ministry of Commerce and the World Trade Organization's Website.)

but the proportion of the total amount of trade in services in the global amount increased from 4.2% to 4.4% and the service imports also showed a slight growth. The imports had slowdown, but a slightly increase in proportion of the global market of services trade, which was 0.5%.

Since China joined the WTO in 2001, both cargo trade and trade in services have shown a climax in the new round of growth. The total imports and exports of services increased from 85.5 billion USD in 2002 to 470.6 billion USD in 2012 increasing more than 5 times, with an annual growth rate of 16.8%. In 2009, the global financial crisis affected the development of China's trade in services, so the total amount of exports and imports of services showed a decline for the first time in the recent decade, with a decreasing rate of 5.8%. In the meantime, service imports rose steadily. They maintained the same level as that in 2008.[1] In 2010, the world economy's declining trend changed and the world economy obtained a slight growth, generally. The total amount of exports and imports of China's services was 362.4 billion USD with a growth rate of 26.4% over that in the previous year. The total amount of trade in services had broken through $ 600 billion with the proportion of global market accounting to 6.44%.

1.3.2    The current situation of China's trade in services according to industry

As shown in Table 4, imports of China's services focus on traditional trade in services, and modern trade in services is developing rapidly. In the traditional trade in services, tourism, transport and other commercial services always occupy the leading role, accounting for nearly 70% of the total amount of service imports. From 2002 to 2014, the proportion of imports of traditional service sectors was about 75.8%. The imports of modern service sectors showed a rapid growth: the proportion of imports of insurance, finance and consultation services grew rapidly, computer and information, patent loyalties and royalties maintained a stable level. This reflects the optimization of the structure of service imports to some extent.[2]

1.3.3    Existing problems in the importation of China's trade in services

First, the comparative advantage of China's traditional service sector, such as the transport sector, is gradually weakening. The deficit amount shows an increasing trend year by year. With the rapid growth of the cargo trade, the demand quantity of transport services increases constantly. China's transport sector, especially air transport, is far behind some large-scale transport corporations in Europe and the United States regarding quality and price.

---

①  Cai Hongbo, et.al, "Service Imports and Wage Difference: Empirical Test Based on Chinese Service Industry Enterprise Data", *International Trade Problems*, 2014 (11).

②  Li Jun, *Joint Investment Motivation, Structure and Performance of Transnational Risk Capital*, Degree Paper of University of International Business and Economics, 2013.

**Table 4    Industrial structure of China's service imports from 2002 to 2014**

Unit: %

| Sector \ year | 2007 | 2008 | 2009 | 2010 | 2011 | 2012 | 2013 | 2014 |
|---|---|---|---|---|---|---|---|---|
| transport | 33.5 | 31.9 | 29.5 | 32.9 | 33.9 | 30.6 | 28.7 | 25.2 |
| tourism | 23 | 22.9 | 27.6 | 28.6 | 30.6 | 36.4 | 39.1 | 43.1 |
| communications | 0.8 | 1 | 0.8 | 0.5 | 0.6 | 0.6 | 0.5 | 0.6 |
| building | 2.3 | 2.8 | 3.7 | 2.6 | 1.6 | 1.3 | 1.2 | 1.3 |
| insurance | 8.3 | 8.1 | 7.1 | 8.2 | 8.3 | 7.4 | 6.7 | 5.9 |
| finance | 0.4 | 0.4 | 0.4 | 0.7 | 0.3 | 0.7 | 1 | 1.4 |
| computer and information | 1.7 | 2 | 2 | 1.5 | 1.6 | 1.4 | 1.8 | 2.2 |
| patent loyalties and royalties | 6.3 | 6.5 | 7 | 6.8 | 6.2 | 6.3 | 6.4 | 5.9 |
| consultation | 8.4 | 8.6 | 8.5 | 7.9 | 7.8 | 7.1 | 7.2 | 6.9 |
| advertisement and publicity | 1 | 1.2 | 1.3 | 1.1 | 1.2 | 1 | 1 | 1 |
| film and video | 0.1 | 0.2 | 0.2 | 0.2 | 0.2 | 0.2 | 0.2 | 0.2 |
| other commercial services | 14.1 | 14.6 | 11.9 | 8.9 | 7.7 | 7 | 6.3 | 6.2 |

Data source: *Statistics of China's Trade in Services in 2013* released by the Ministry of Commerce and the *World Trade Report in 2010* released by the WTO.

Second, the demand of modern service products is growing rapidly, while the development of these industries in China is still at the primary stage. It cannot meet the increasing demand for services. Greatly developing the capital-intensive, technology-intensive and knowledge-intensive modern service industries is not only the demand of coping with the impact of the international service industry on China's service industry, but it also meets the developmental demand of China's service industry. Such phenomenon may certainly restrain the transformation of the international trade in services of our countries into technology-intensive and knowledge-intensive types.

## 2. Analysis of the Internationalized Level of China´s Trade in Service

### 2.1   Qualitative analysis of the internationalized level of China's trade in services

2.1.1   Definition of the concept of internationalization

With the development of global economic integration, the word "internationalization" has become the necessary trend of all kinds of countries in the world. No matter whether for small-size, medium-size or large-size enterprises or financial institutes such as banks, securities, insurances and so on, internationalization has become the necessary developmental trend in this century. About the concept of internationalization, there is no unified definition in China and foreign countries. For example, Reschauer, a well-known American scholar summarizes the generalized definition of internationalization as "Internationalization is an international phenomenon connecting the world as a community", while Beamish (1990) defines internationalization more accurately; he thinks that "internationalization is a process".[1]

2.1.2 The degree of internationalization of China's trade in services

Since the reform and the opening up, trade in services has grown fast in China, but after 1992, it has been in a deficit state and its absolute amount of deficit has enlarged constantly. The trade in services deficit in China from 2008 to 2014 reached 11.5 billion USD, 29.507 billion USD, 22 billion USD, 54.5 billion USD, 89.6 billion USD, 118.46 billion USD and 121.63 billion USD, respectively for each year. The largest deficit since the reform and the opening up appeared in 2014. China has become the first largest country in the world with a deficit in trade in services, especially concerning technical transactions in tourism, transport, royalty transfer, patents and so on.[2]

2.1.3 Setting the goal in the process of internationalization

2.1.3.1 Short-term goal in the process of internationalization

First, take the producer service industry as a breakthrough, mobilize the overall promotion of the service industry and boost the development of trade in services. The service industry has become the largest output sector in world economy, and the producer service industry has also become the sector with the fastest growth among the service industries. The producer service industry has an important role in modern economic growth. It is not only the result of economic growth, but it is also the important basic condition for modern economic growth. It promotes economic growth significantly. The industrial capacity of the service industry actually decides the competitiveness of trade in services.

Second, encourage domestic enterprises to contract international outsourcing service positively. China should apply its experience in manufacturing industry to the outsourcing service industry. Through the improvement of the institutional environment, make full use of the advantage of human capital to provide good value-added service for foreign-bidding enterprises; make full use of the constantly increasing scale of foreign capital in manufacturing in China, attract FDI, technology and knowledge to the service industry through associated relationships and interactive mechanisms; formulate policies and regulations to encourage the development of the outsourcing service industry, create a policy platform in order to develop the outsourcing service industry.

2.1.3.2 Medium-term goal in the process of internationalization

First, establish the system for the technological innovation of the modern service industry,

① Data source, *Internationalization of Chinese –funded Banks in the Condition of Financial Trade in Services Liberation,* access website: http://www.shfinancialnews.com/xww/2009jrb/node5019/node5036/node5040/userobject1ai 123743.html.

② Yao Zhanqi, "Promoting Organic and Interactive Development of Trade in Services and Cargo Trade", *China Business & Trade,* 2014 (10).

take the mutual support of the modern service industry as a platform and support the development of trade in services. Support the integration of the link in trade in services and the various resources, support the synergic interaction and the optimal reorganization of the information flow, capital flow, product logistics, political affairs flow and commercial flow. According to the characteristic that there are a majority of small and medium-size enterprises among China's trade in services enterprises, establish "flat" support of the service system and reduce the construction costs of the informatization of trade in services enterprises.[1]

Second, give play to the function of leading departments of the various service industries and relative associations. At present, some major service industry sectors and their directly subordinate public institutions have done a lot of work in promoting service exports. Therefore, these two subjects should be incorporated into the promotional system of trade in services and play a greater role in promoting trade in services in the service industry.[2]

2.1.3.3    Long-term goal in the process of internationalization

First, study and formulate a high-level national and regional plan for the development of trade in services in long-term. Study and formulate a plan in the eyes of the world as well as strategic thinking, and determine the fastest developmental goal during the "13th Five-year Plan" according to the fact that the scale of trade in services has obviously enlarged rapidly in recent years. Up to 2020, the total amount of exports and imports of China's trade in services is estimated to reach 1.2-1.5 trillion USD with an annual average growth rate of more than 20%. It makes the proportion of exports of trade in services, among the total exports of China's foreign trade, rise to above 25% and its proportion of the world's service exports will obviously increase. In the meantime, organize each region to study and formulate a developmental plan regarding the service industry in each region according to the major goal of the development of the national service industry in long-term.[3]

Second, study and formulate a guidance catalogue to develop trade in services. Speed up to make a detailed and better guidance catalogue; this will make it possible to develop trade in services according to the needs of the adjustment of the trading structure; it will also make it possible to: determine the priority of industrial development and support that direction, promote the constant optimization of the structure of trade in services through industrial guidance for trade in services, improve the level of the traditional labor-intensive trade in

---

① Zheng Jichang, Jiang Wenjie, "The Combination of Policies to Develop the Service Industry and to Develop Trade in Services in China", *Annual Meeting of China's International Trade Association and International Trade Development Forum*, 2008.

② Data source: Development Report on China's Trade in Services in 2008, access website: http://wenku.baidu. com/view/a02a62d8a58da0116c17490d.html.

③ Chen Wenling, "Policy Selection of China in Promoting the Development of Trade in Services", *Nanjing Social Science*, 2009 (3).

services with obvious competitive advantages such as transport, tourism and so on, and promote the continuous growth of widespread exportation.

2.1.4　The developmental trend of the internationalization of China's trade in services

Trade in services is China's major field of reforms and opening up and also a major breakthrough of speeding up the transformation of the mode of economic trade development. Especially since the convocation of the 18th National Congress of the CPC, the openness of the service industry and the development of trade in services has received a great amount of attention from the Party Central Committee and the State Council. The issuance of *Several Opinions on Speeding up the Development of Trade in Services by the State Council* has a profound historical background.

First, the service industry is entering a period of acceleration of reforms and opening up. At present, the emphasis of and key to the intensification of reforms in an all-around way lies in the service industry. Driving the reform of the service industry with opening up through expanding and intensifying its opening up has become a necessary choice for its reform, for the system mechanism of trade in services and for China's policy at present and in the future. Since the convocation of the 18th National Congress of the CPC, the government has sped up the pace of reforms and the opening up of the service industry through transforming its functions, streamlining the administration, instituting decentralization, promoting the establishment of domestic pilot free trade areas, and so on. Undoubtedly, since 2015, in the context of entering a new normality of the Chinese economy, the reform and the opening up of the service industry will enter a period of acceleration, thus a series of key and hard reform and opening up tasks will be carried out.

Second, the development of trade in services is entering a period of policy bonus. In recent years, the State Council has held Executive Meetings several times, specializing in studying the developmental problem of the service industry and trade in services. A series of policy documents in support of the development of the service industry and trade in services have been issued at these executive meetings. Especially after entering 2014, the State Council has issued plans, opinions, notices and so on, in order to intensively promote the development of the service industry, which involves more than 10 industries such as tourism, the pension services industry, the health service industry, the producer service industry, the insurance service industry, the shipping industry, the logistics industry, the sports industry, the science and technology service industry, service outsourcing, and so on. The State Council points out the key direction and trend of the relative fields for the development of the service industry and proposes some supporting measures in the areas of finance, taxation and trade. It can be said that the development of China's service industry and trade in services has entered the period of policy bonus. On January 16, 2015, the State Council released Opinions on

Promoting the Accelerated Development of the Service Outsourcing Industry (Guo Fa [2014] No. 67) to the public. It gives specific indications for the development of the service outsourcing industry in the future and proposes substantial policies in increasing the quantity of service outsourcing demonstration cities, establishing international service outsourcing industry guidance funds, the reduction or remission of taxes and so on.

### 2.2   Quantitative analysis of the level of internationalization of trade in services

2.2.1   The international market share of trade in services

From the internal trade in services, the result of the modified international market share according to the estimation of IMS-SSDVA is shown in Table 5. In 2014, the international market of wholesale and retailing, hotels and restaurants in China was lower only than that of the United States and Germany and higher than that in other countries (regions) of the sample. IMS-SSDVA of transport, storage and remote communication and commercial service industry was 1.94% and 1.77% respectively. Their international market shares were slow. The international market share of China's financial media industry was 0.20%, only higher than that of Taiwan and Russia, but lower than that of other countries (regions) of the sample.

**Table 5   The international market share of trade in services of each country (region) in 2014 according to detailed fields**[①]

Unit: %

| country (region) \ industry | wholesale and retailing hotels and restaurants | transport, storage and remote communications | financial media | commercial service |
|---|---|---|---|---|
| United States | 15.26 | 13.48 | 17.96 | 23.16 |
| United Kingdom | 1.79 | 4.83 | 23.18 | 12.98 |
| Germany | 8.8 | 6 | 5.72 | 8.59 |
| France | 6.2 | 5.83 | 1.51 | 4.84 |
| Japan | 3.94 | 6.75 | 0.8 | 0.88 |
| Italy | 2.35 | 3.95 | 3.26 | 3.59 |
| Canada | 1.31 | 1.91 | 1.13 | 2.57 |
| Spain | 0.77 | 4.99 | 3.73 | 6.4 |
| Australia | 0.81 | 2.23 | 0.49 | 0.92 |
| India | 1.57 | 1.25 | 1.21 | 6.7 |
| Brazil | 1 | 0.98 | 0.23 | 0.78 |
| Russia | 2.58 | 2.58 | 0.01 | 0.04 |
| South Africa | 0.65 | 0.43 | 0.22 | 0.05 |
| China | 7.15 | 1.94 | 0.2 | 1.77 |
| Hong Kong, China | 4.4 | 1.36 | 2.37 | 1.25 |
| Taiwan, China | 2.13 | 0.7 | 0.17 | 0.11 |

① Guojing, Liu Feifei, "Estimation of International Competitiveness of China's Service Industry: Research on Trade in Added Value", *World Economy Studies*, 2015 (2).

### 2.2.2    Revealed comparative advantage index of trade in services

According to the industry's classification (as is shown in Table 6), the RCA SSDVA index of China's wholesale and retailing, hotels and restaurants is 0.86%, lower than that of the United States, Germany, France, Russia and South Africa and higher than other countries (regions) in the sample, which means that it has stronger comparative disadvantages; the RCA SSDVA index of commercial service is only 0.21%, higher only to that of Russia, South Africa, Japan and Taiwan; the RCA SSDVA index of transport, storage, the remote communications industry and the financial media industry are 0.23% and 0.02%, respectively. Both of them are low in the sample countries (regions).

**Table 6    Revealed comparative advantage index of trade in services of each country (region) in 2014 according to detailed fields[①]**

| industry<br>country (region) | wholesale and retailing hotels and restaurants | transport, storage and remote communications | financial media | commercial service |
|---|---|---|---|---|
| United States | 1.23 | 1.08 | 1.44 | 1.86 |
| United Kingdom | 0.40 | 1.09 | 5.21 | 2.92 |
| Germany | 1.08 | 0.73 | 0.70 | 1.05 |
| France | 1.47 | 1.38 | 0.36 | 1.15 |
| Japan | 0.78 | 1.33 | 0.16 | 0.17 |
| Italy | 0.61 | 1.03 | 0.85 | 0.94 |
| Canada | 0.46 | 0.67 | 0.40 | 0.91 |
| Spain | 0.32 | 2.09 | 1.57 | 2.69 |
| Australia | 0.50 | 1.37 | 0.30 | 0.57 |
| India | 0.82 | 0.65 | 0.63 | 3.50 |
| Brazil | 0.65 | 0.64 | 0.15 | 0.51 |
| Russia | 0.87 | 0.87 | 0.00 | 0.01 |
| South Africa | 1.10 | 0.73 | 0.37 | 0.08 |
| China | 0.86 | 0.23 | 0.02 | 0.21 |
| Hong Kong, China | 6.88 | 2.13 | 3.70 | 1.95 |
| Taiwan, China | 1.68 | 0.55 | 0.13 | 0.08 |

### 2.2.3    Export potential of trade in services

In conclusion, the relative export potential of computers and information of China's trade in services shows a certain ascending trend, but there is still a greater difference between the potential of China's acquired exportation and that of the developed countries. Thus, it can be seen that China's computer and information trade in services is only a "great nation" of information services, rather than a "power" of information services. In order to build up trade in services, in view of the industrial level, China's scale of contracting overseas projects is

---

[①] Guojing, Liu Feifei, "Estimation of International Competitiveness of China's Service Industry: Research on Trade in Added Value", *World Economy Studies*, 2015 (2).

ex panding gradually, the market space is expanding constantly, the level of internation-alization is enhancing step by step and trade competitiveness is at a higher level. However, the building of trade in services in China still centers on labor-intensive industries. There is big gap between China and the developed countries. The expansion of export potential needs to be adjusted through the opening up, rational resource allocation and the enhancement of the industrial chain and the value chain. The international competitiveness of China's bank financial trade in services shows a slight rising trend, but it falls behind the other BRICS (Brazil, Russia, India, China, and South Africa) countries and the developed German and Japanese economic entities. Besides, it falls far behind the developed financial trade of the United States and the United Kingdom.

## 3. The Mode and Path of Integrating China's Trade in Services into the International Market

### 3.1  Analysis of the mode of integration of international market of China's trade in services

3.1.1  Cross-border supply

3.1.1.1  The concept of cross-border supply

Cross-border supply refers to a service provider from a country to provide services to consumers in the territory of another one. The mode emphasizes services not the providers and consumers stepping over the geographical boundaries between them, which functions a similar way to trade in goods.

3.1.1.2  Characteristics of cross-border supply

Firstly, cross-border supply transits services not providers, customers or their funds across the border. Therefore, the advantage of this mode is to save part of transaction costs without meeting for details of the trade in services. While it is deficient because there is not directly contact between the suppliers and buyers of the services, as well as the according regulatory systems have not been completed yet. Thus, the services quality cannot be well guaranteed, and the problems are difficult to be solved.

Secondly, the subject of cross-border supply is the services with the form of information, which support it strongly. So, the way to provide cross-border supply factors are mainly restricted by the rise of technology.

3.1.1.3  The direction of development of cross-border supply in the future

Innovative development pattern should be explored with new technology in China, such as cloud computing, big data, networking and mobile Internet. Chinese IT companies are competing layout of the areas in "the Belt and Road", in particular, actively expand market overseas. Take clouding computing as an example, different from traditional way of cross-border supply, the main distinction between them is that data are transited, stored and supplied through the internet, which are out of control and had no idea about the location to be kept. The services of solving data will become a new engine to promote the innovation of the model of trade in services and create a new cross-border network platform.

3.1.2    Consumption abroad

3.1.2.1    The concept of consumption abroad

Consumption abroad refers to a service provider of one nation that provides services for service consumers from any other member countries within the territory in order to gain a reward. Its characteristic is that the service consumers receive services in any other member country. For example, purchasing foreign luxury goods, patients seeing doctors abroad, overseas tourism, students and scholars studying abroad, and so on.

3.1.2.2    Characteristics of overseas consumption by Chinese consumers

First, the rapid growth of outbound traveling makes consumption abroad hot. At present, China has signed mutual visa abolition agreements with more than 90 countries and regions, 53 agreements to simplify visa procedures, with 39 countries, and China has won lateral landing visa treatment for Chinese citizens from 37 countries and regions. Driven by the good factor that the outbound travel visa policy is increasingly loose, the outbound travels of the Chinese keep growing in number. The Chinese outbound travels reached 109 million person-times in 2014. The Chinese tourists cover more than 150 countries and regions in the world. China has become an important tourist source country in the world and its contribution to the total number of global international tourists exceeds 10%. Tourism consumption covers eating, living, traffic, travel, shopping and recreation. The high growth in the number of outbound travels will certainly make consumption abroad hot. The *Investigation Report of the Chinese People's Desire for Outings in Spring Festival of 2015* released by Ctrip shows that 70% of mainland residents hope to spend the Spring Festival of 2015 travelling; outbound traveling will exceed domestic tourism for the first time and the passenger departure point has changed from first-tier cities to second-tier cities, third-tier cities and the western and middle areas.

Second, the difference between overseas prices and domestic prices generates the psychology of buying more, gaining more. The price of domestic imported high-end consumer goods is higher than abroad. Of which, the price of 20 brands of high-end consumer goods such as watches, bags, suitcases, dresses, wine and electronics is 45% higher than the price in Hong Kong, 51% higher than that in America and higher than that in France. The price of the products made in China of the same grade, the same quality and the same brand is higher than that abroad. Owing to the increasingly developed information technology and Internet shopping, the consumers easily get price information, and they are not willing to pay more for products made in China. There are two reasons for the high price difference: one is taxation. From the tax rate, it can be seen that the tax rate in the import link is higher; the tariff rate is usually 6.4%-25% while for high-end commodities the tax rate is 30%; from the way taxes are collected, it can be seen the tax included directly in the price of commodity is 4.17 times what it is in the United States, 3.76 times that in Japan, 2.33 times that in the European Union. Another reason is the skimming price strategy of foreign brand owners for China. Foreign brand owners expect to gain a high rate of profit in a short time, so the final retailing price is 2/3 or even higher than the cost of insurance and freight.[1]

3.1.2.3　Backflow reform of consumption abroad-Take tourism trade in services for example

Tourism trade in services refers to the activity that employees in the tourism industry of one nation (region) provide tourism services for tourism service consumers in other countries (regions) and get rewarded. It does not only include outbound travel of domestic tourists, namely international expenditure tourism, but it also includes inbound travel of foreign tourists, namely international incoming tourism. As per the classification provision of trade in services by the WTO trade in services Council, "tourism and its associated services include the following items: hotels and restaurants, services provided by travel agencies and travel operators, tourist guide services and other tourist services". For this, we can reform according to the following aspects.

First, make tourism regulations perfect and strengthen industrial management to promote exports of tourism service trade. Relevant departments of the government should strengthen tourist legislation, supplement, modify and improve the existing tourism service legislation according to WTO rules, establish a perfect tourism law system and normalize the tourist market behavior. Relevant departments of the government should strengthen the government's leading role in the development of the tourism trade, establish the "market leading, government leading" tourism developmental mode.[2] In the meantime, the government should enhance the quality of the service in tourism through industrial management and improve the environment for consumption by the tourist. In this way, we can lift the level of management, operation and global competition of Chinese tourist enterprises on the whole.

Second, strengthen the marketing force on tourism inbound of Chinese enterprises. On the one hand, from the perspective of the mental characteristics of tourists from different countries, adopt diversified marketing modes, reserve air tickets, train or bus tickets, hotel

---

① Zhao Ping, Sun Jiyong, "Analysis of Current Situation and Problem of Chinese Consumption Abroad", *International Trade*, 2015 (6).

② Hao suo, "Discussion of Government Behavior of the Chinese Tourism Industry Marketization Development", *Tourism Journal*, 2001 (16).

rooms, travel routes the introduction of scenic spots and other online services through the informatization of marketing instruments and tourism e-commerce so as to improve the efficiency and correctness of tourism services and constantly enlarge the passenger source market of the world.[①] On the other hand, strengthen the force of publicity and promotional features of tourism in western provinces and cities and expand the scope of tourism. In this way, we can break down the passenger flow in tourism-intensive areas as well as promoting new features of national cultural tourism products and attracting more passenger sources abroad.

### 3.1.3    Commercial presence

#### 3.1.3.1    The concept of commercial presence

Commercial presence is a kind of very important service provision method in GATS. The service provider of one member establishes commercial institutions (affiliated enterprises or branches) in the territory of other members and provides services for service consumers of its country and other members so as to gain rewards. The ways include the establishment of branches or agencies to offer services and so on. For example, the telecom company of one nation establishes a telecom operation agency abroad and participates in the competition of the telecom service market. This behavior belongs to "commercial existence".

#### 3.1.3.2    The characteristics of commercial presence

The characteristics of commercial presence is the service provider (individual, enterprise or an economic entity) that starts business abroad, and invests capital to establish joint ventures, cooperative ventures or solely-invested service enterprises (branches of banks, hotels, retailing stores, accounting firms, law firms and so on).

#### 3.1.3.3    The direction of reform and the development of commercial presence in the future

"The Belt and Road" strategy has entered the implementation phase, providing valuable opportunities and new trends for the commercial presence. The labor division of modern international production has deepened from different products to different work sequences of the same product. It can make full use of the advantage of the production factor of different countries. With the support of modern information and logistics technology, we should organize the global industrial chain and the production network through multinational corporations to realize global R&D, global production and global sales. If Chinese distribution enterprises or logistics trade in services want to gain the same global competitiveness as Western multinational corporations, they need to "go out" to develop, gain commercial presence and organize a global industrial chain, a production network and a storage network

---

① Victor Middleton, *Tourism Marketing*, translated by Xiang Ping, China Tourism Press, 2001.

led by themselves like the Western multinational corporations. The appearance of overseas warehouses is a reflection of optimizing resource advantages.[①] We need to utilize the factor advantages of different countries to make development in resource-intensive regions, products in regions with the lowest costs, marketing in regions with the largest market, financing in regions with the lowest interest rates, resource allocation and optimization around the world in order to gain commercial presence. This is also the highest state of internationalization.

### 3.1.4　Movement of natural persons

#### 3.1.4.1　The concept of movement of natural persons

The movement of natural persons means one member provides services after entering the territory of another member. Many service industries need employees with expertise and practical experience and all suppliers possessing international businesses will send working staff members with certain expertise and practical experience to the foreign market to provide services. Thus, the business will be carried out successfully. In order to normalize such movement, each member formulates various measures to protect the integrity of the boundary and guarantee that the natural person passes the boundary in an orderly fashion. However, these measures should not damage the other members' interests, acquired according to a specific promise.

#### 3.1.4.2　The major barriers owing to the movement of natural persons in China

First, the limitations of market access that the movement of a natural person may face in China. Educational training experience, qualification authentication and other access qualifications have become forms of common barriers that various host countries set up against the movement of the natural persons. In qualification authentication, host countries may increase the difficulty for access to the market by expanding the range of qualification conditions. They set up limitations in the type of work of the natural persons, the quantity of staff, the duration of the stay and other requirements. For example, they require that the immigrated service provider possess certain special education degree certificates, relative working experience, license, qualifications and so on to access work so as to limit the inflow of low and middle-level workers. In the meantime, the host countries discriminate against the immigrated service provider in terms of qualification and standards of authentication. Compared with the developed countries, China has greater differences in the educational system, qualifications and system of authentication. These differences make Chinese service providers have "different rewards but the same work" in host countries. That is to say, the Chinese service providers provide the same service but earn a lower income than the same

---

① Meng Yuming, "Formulation and Implementation of Chinese Enterprise 'Walking out' Development Strategy", *International Economic Cooperation*, 2012 (2).

level of labor in the host country.

Second, China's natural persons movement is limited by the visa system of the host country. After acquiring market access to the host country, the service provider needs to apply for a visa to enter the host country. At this time, the quota limitation for visas is also one of the major barriers that limit the natural persons movement. Quota limitation is not only against the quantity of overseas service providers, but it is also reflected in the time limit of visa issuance.

Third, national treatment discrimination of movement of China's natural persons. The discrimination treatment implemented by the host country also limits the movement of natural persons to a great extent. It is firstly reflected in the difference in wages and taxation between the foreign service provider and the host country service provider. For example, the Chinese service provider in the United States must pay American social guarantee fees and other taxes. They cannot enjoy the social welfare provided by the United States because of the short duration of their stay in the country. They only perform duties, but fail to get corresponding rights.

3.1.4.3    The direction of reform and development of the natural persons movement in China in the future

"The Belt and Road" strategy opened up a transportation link by "six economic corridors" with Eastern European markets, serving basic conditions to ensure objectively the free movement of skilled personnel to provide various service of to these countries. Through comparison of limitations on the mode of "natural persons movement" in the United States, the United Kingdom and Germany, it is known that these three countries are very strict with labor input. For example, the American Immigration Law/Labor Law and Labor Union have strict provisions on the access of construction workers and professional technicians, so for the foreign construction workers it is difficult to enter the United States. Therefore, in the face of international building service barriers, China can adopt the following measures: first, prepare a construction service standard template connected to the international building code according to the "Chinese standard" system, seek a system that corresponds to the "British Standard and American Code"; second, the expansion mode of the overseas market transforms from the "single contracting mode" to the "comprehensive commercial mode" and from contractor to investor and thus avoids barrier limitations through investments; third, take governmental procurement as a breakthrough, take investments and guarantee advantages as a bid to promote the application of the "Chinese Standard" to the market for construction services; fourth, strengthen cooperative exchanges with the top 10 companies of ENR and establish a consortium so as to better expand the market of developed countries.[1]

---

[1] Zhao Yurong, "Entry Norm for American Construction Market", *Shanghai Building Material*, 2006 (1).

### 3.2 Strategy and path of integrating China's trade in services into the international market

3.2.1    Export high-end trade in services in virtue of the "the Belt and Road" strategy

"The Belt and Road" is a trans-regional strategic concept with a global vision, stressing the creation of mutual benefits and a win-win "interest community" and "destiny community" with joint development and prospects with relevant countries. It needs to think of its strategic development prospects in a wider vision. We can export high-end trade in services in virtue of the "the Belt and Road" strategy in the following ways:

First, China constructs "the Belt and Road" together with the Central Asian and South Asian countries, Russia, the countries of the European Union jointly, and forms the big pattern of the development of economic integration of the Asia-European area. China, Central Asian and South Asian countries are collaborative good neighbors. They should construct "the Belt and Road" jointly through a creative cooperative mode. They should stick to friendship from generation to generation and be harmonious good neighbors. They should stick to mutual support and be sincere and mutually-trustworthy good friends. They should strengthen practical cooperation and be mutually beneficial and win-win good partners.

China and Russia should strengthen their cooperation within the frame of the United Nations, G20 (Group of Twenty Finance Ministers and Central Bank Governors), SCO (Shanghai Cooperation Organization), APEC (Asia-Pacific Economic Cooperation), BRICS (Brazil, Russia, India, China, South Africa), EAS (East Asia Summit) and CICA (Conference on Interaction and Confidence-Building measures in Asia) Summit, promote international political and economic order to develop in a more just and rational direction. Both parties should seek feasible meeting points on the Silk Road Economic Belt project and Eurasian Economic Union, promote cooperation in the fields of oil and gas, nuclear energy, power, high-speed railways, aviation, communication and finance and strengthen all-around infrastructures and connectivity constructions.

China and the EU countries (European Union countries) "should look on relations between China and Europe from a strategic perspective, combine their powers, markets and the civilizations of China and Europe, jointly create a partnership of peace, growth, reforms and civilization , inject new power into China-Europe cooperation and make contributions to world development and prospects".[①] China and the EU countries should be partners in peace and take the lead in walking along the path of peaceful development, be partners in growth, mutually provide development opportunities; be reform partners, learn from and support each

---

① Du Shangze, Xu Liqun, Liu Ge, Talks Between Xi Jinping and Fan Long Pei, President of European Council, *People's Daily*, 2014-04-01(1).

other, be civilized partners and provide each other with more nutrition for progress.

Second, the basis for cooperation between China and countries along "the Belt and Road" is solid. The basis for cooperation between China and SCO is solid, too. Within the frame of the SCO, each member country strengthens mutual trust and harmonious friendship and promotes effective cooperation of each member country in the fields of politics, economy and trade, science and technology, culture, energy, traffic, tourism, security and so on. "Silk Road: Road network of Chang'an-Tianshan Gallery" jointly declared by China, KZ (Kazakhstan) and Kyrgyzstan has been successfully selected in the world cultural heritage directory, which is the early-phase harvest of the construction of the Silk Road Economic Belt.

The basis for cooperation between China and ASEAN is solid. At present, China is the largest trading partner of ASEAN and ASEAN is China's third largest trading partner. China and ASEAN make up the largest free trade area of the developing countries in the world. China has signed cooperation documents such as the *Joint Declaration of a Peaceful and Prosperous Strategic Partnership between China and ASEAN, the Declaration on the Code of Conduct on the South China Sea, The Treaty of Amity and Cooperation in Southeast Asia* and so on with ASEAN, established dialogue-and-cooperation mechanisms such as the China-ASEAN Business Council, the China-ASEAN Expo, the China-ASEAN Business and Investment Summit and so on. In addition, they endeavor to build an upgraded version of the China-ASEAN free trade area.

The basis for cooperation between China and the Arab States is solid. China has made acquaintance and friends with the Arab States owing to the Silk Road. They are important partners in building "the Belt and Road". The Forum on China-Africa Cooperation has become the important platform for both parties to intensify their strategic cooperation on the basis of mutual benefits, win-win results and mutual respect. The Cooperation Forum has completed normalized and mechanized constructions, established more than 10 cooperation mechanisms, such as ministerial conferences, senior officials meetings, entrepreneur conferences and so on, and covers the cooperation of nearly all fields of politics, economy, culture and humanity.

3.2.2    Establishing regional economic cooperation areas on the basis of border ports

At present, economic globalization and regional economic integration have been increasingly intensified, and openness, cooperation and development have become the mainstream of the world nowadays. Owing to geographical proximity, cultural similarity and market structure complementation, the integrated regional economy can effectively reduce the transaction costs and default risks, expand the market share, form a scale economy, promote the flow of production factors, stimulate investment trading and thus improve the position of regional economy within the world economy. To speed up and strengthen the establishment of regional economic cooperation areas on the basis of border ports, we should set about from the following aspects:

First, strengthen the construction of hardware. Centering on services for the construction of international ports, build and improve supporting facilities to link each port, such as traffic, water and power, communications, hotels, storage and so on; enhance the level of urban construction management and make international ports play the window & platform role of foreign exchange.

Second, develop border trade and special industrial processing, expand the scale of exports and imports and enhance the proportion of foreign trade in the border regions. Relying on border ports, construct a batch of scaled commodity collections, a distribution market and a multinational logistics center.

Third, encourage the importation of resource commodities and the exportation of characteristic, high-quality and high value-added commodities. [1] Give play to geographical advantages along the borders, utilize the Free Trade Zone Agreement, the economic cooperation agreement between China and the neighboring countries and other economic cooperation frameworks between China and other multilateral and bilateral organizations, and build a bridge of economic and trade exchanges with the neighboring countries; actively explore and carefully promote a mode for a cross-border economic cooperation area.

3.2.3  Greatly expand producer trade in services

3.2.3.1  The function of the producer service industry

Expansion of the manufacturing industry and enhancement of its level are on the agenda for industrial centralization. There must be a series of conditions in order to attract manufacturing to one region, such as competitive product and industrial supporting capacity, a high-quality labor force, a good producer service system and a better environment for governmental public service. The above condition not only decides the enterprise's choice of which region to enter, but it also decides the cost of the manufacturing transactions in this region.

In the view of transaction cost, the development of the producer service industry has the following major functions regarding the development of the manufacturing industry:

(1) Reduce the transaction cost of the manufacturing industry. According to the theory of modern institutional economics, production in the manufacturing industry includes manufacturing cost and transaction cost. With the expansion of the scale of production and intensifying specialization, the cost of manufacturing is reduced greatly and manufacturing

[1] Data source: "12th Five-year Plan" in National Economic and Technical Development Zone and Border Economic Cooperation Zone (2011–2015) , access website: http://file.mofcom.gov.cn/article/gkml/201211/20121196423038.shtml.

efficiency will be improved, but the industrial revolution causes another phenomenon concerning production specialization, as does the refinement of the division of labor. The more particular the social division of labor is, the higher the transaction cost is. Nowadays, competition in the manufacturing industry is increasingly intensified, and the proportion of the transaction cost in the total cost of the enterprise is greater, while the reduction of the transaction cost depends a lot on the development of production services. The basic way to eliminate the increasing cost of the transaction is to greatly develop the producer service industry, especially modern logistics, financial insurance, legal services, accounting services, management consultation, advertisement services, technical intermediary services and so on.

(2) Provide urgently-needed intelligence services for the manufacturing industry. In the development of the modern economy, human capital and knowledge capital take an increasingly prominent role in the manufacturing industry. The process of human capital and knowledge capital getting access to the production process is carried out via vendors to use human capital and knowledge capital. The feasibility analysis of the enterprise investment project, capital operation, financing services, insurance services, product R&D, product design, technical engineering services, product market promotion, brand promotion, legal consultation, accounting services, information and technology services, management consultation and so on enter the production process of the enterprise. This speeds up the production specialization of the modern enterprise and improves the enterprise's productivity.

(3) Provide an urgently needed labor force for the manufacturing industry. Manufacturing enterprises need a large number of professional working staff, while vocational education training provides urgently needed technical workers. In addition, vocational training also provides senior professional workers for modern enterprises, such as training of bookkeepers and accountants, salespeople and marketing operators, modern shippers and logisticians, and customs declarers and so on.[1]

3.2.3.2　Strategy analysis on greatly expanding producer service trade

First, apply policy guidance to strengthen the importance of producer service trade. With the development of economic globalization, especially the constant deepening of the international division of labor and the constant upgrading of the adjustment of the world's industrial structure, China's international trading faces a new opportunity and a challenge. With reference to relevant data of developed countries, the growth of trade in services is the inevitable output of international trade developing to a certain stage. As an important part of trade in services, producer service trade faces a golden opportunity. However, for a long time,

---

[1] Du Xiuhong, "Impact Analysis of Producer Service Industry on the Development of Manufacturing Industry", *Jiangsu Commercial Forum*, 2007 (3).

the policy tradition of "stress manufacturing and weaken service" has existed in China, it restricts the development of China's trade in services to some extent, especially the development of producer service trade. Therefore, applying a policy guidance rationally and promoting the development of producer service trade in a strategic perspective has a certain significance on enhancing comprehensive international competitiveness.[1]

Second, normalize the operational mechanism of the producer service trade, shape the legal market environment. We should establish and improve a management system suitable for the fundamental realities of China and shape a good legal environment for the development of the producer service trade. On the one hand, by following the WTO principles so as to meet the the international practice and standards, we should clean up the legal provisions which are not adapted to the requirement of the development of the current producer service industry as soon as possible, formulate laws and regulations suitable for the national situation of China, normalize industrial rules and behavioral patterns, make the protection of the interests of the subject of trade in services be legalization, institutionalization and normalization, build a system of laws and regulations with a wide area of coverage and strong operability, and make the economic legal system of the socialist market perfect.[2] On the other hand, make foreign trade management system reform, break through multi-legislation and the situation of mutual contradiction caused by normalizing producer service industry by relying on regulation of administration and department and set up special service trade administration.[3]

Third, optimize the industrial structure of the producer service trade and carry out a specific analysis and rational positioning of each department. For structural optimization of China's producer service trade, we should concretely analyze it according to the specific situation. For the industrial structure, the traditional trade in services sector (such as transport services and commercial services) accounts for a great proportion of China's producer service trade. This sector possesses a certain number of comparative advantages. It should transform itself effectively on the premise of introducing the philosophy of advanced management and management mode, make full use of China's advantages regarding resources and labor force and build core competitiveness of each department; for newly-developing trade in services sectors, such as financial services, insurance services and other knowledge or capital-intensive industries, we need to broaden the market access, introduce a competitive mechanism, allow

[1] Liu Weizheng, *International Competitive Analysis of China's Producer Service Trade*, Degree Paper of University of International Business and Economics, 2012.

[2] Wang Suqin, Sun Yan, "Analysis of the development and Structure of China's Producer Service Trade", *Journal of Business Economics*, 2008 (11).

[3] Zhao Hui, "Considerations on the Guangxi Strengthening of Trade in Services with Vietnam in the Context of China-ASEAN Free Trade Area", *Journal of Nanning Vocational Technical Institute*, 2012 (1).

for a moderate inflow of foreign capital and folk capital and promote the development of market innovation and the enhancement of economic efficiency; for computer and information services, patent loyalties and royalties and other knowledge and technology-intensive industries, even if they do not have obvious comparative advantages, they should also be supported in consideration of their core functions in modern trade in services and on the basis of long-term international competition.

3.2.4  New activities within trade in services trade promote the service industry to "go out"

New types of trade in services refer to exceeding the traditional organizational mode, the business model and the operational mode to form a corresponding economic scale and form stable forms of trading. The development of new types of trade in services has significance for the "going out" of the service industry. Combined with China's current situation, it supports and guides the new types of trade in services and promotes the "going out" of the service industry from the institutional environment, the management system, associated industries, the service system, carrier construction and so on.

First, make the financial service system of the new type of trading perfect. Then, speed up the promotion of the use of offshore account. Allow more satisfactory multinational corporations to establish off-shore financial accounts, make the function of special accounts perfect, simplify the procedure for the settlement of exchanges and promote the convenience of collection. Second, strive for support of the national financial supervision department and allow for the implementation of financial business associated with financial innovation such as off-shore banks, off-shore insurance, future bonded delivery and so on, matched with off-shore trading in the pilot area. Third, strengthen the already-powerful support of e-payment to the new type of trading. On the basis of realizing the electronization of management services such as RMB cross-bank payment, cross-border payment and receipt, favorably develop the third party payment, encourage the development of various new types of payment channels such as internet payment, mobile payment and so on.[1] Fourth, strengthen the support for the new type of trading industry, grant certain loan securities and subsidy loan interest and encourage its innovative development according to the innovative result, the industrial schedule and fund requirement.

Second, make the cross-border e-commerce service system with the new type of trading perfect. Strengthen cooperation of cross-border e-commerce services and local enterprises. Establish stable partnerships with enterprises on the target market and strengthen enterprise

---

① Fan Xing: "Current Situation, Problems and Measures of the New Trade Industry", *Scientific Development*, 2013 (12).

cooperation and division of labor so as to understand and analyze the local commercial environment, the consumer's preference and so on. Improve the cooperative effect, enlarge the complementation of commodities and avoid vicious competition through cooperation and mutual exchange of enterprises. In the meantime, enhance the negotiation capability and the competitive advantages of cross-border e-commerce enterprises and increase the cooperation and exchange with network sale enterprises and logistics enterprises to seek greater room for development. In addition, Chinese enterprises should constantly explore new patterns of outsourcing. Enterprises can either outsource advertisement designs, cross-border logistics, management information system preparation or marketing publicity to the specialized service provider or establish straight overseas marketing channels and employ online store customer services on the target market to reduce the cost of building teams alone, avoid cognitive bias, be familiar with the shopping habits of the local market and meet the market requirements.[1]

Third, make the logistics service system of the new type of trading perfect. First, strengthen the building up of the supporting capacity of logistics for the new type of trading. Give play to the integration advantage of the electronic port platform, high-speed road, port and navigation EDI (Electronic Data Interchange) center, construct an integrated port logistics information platform, realize networking for major international port cities and enhance the speed of logistics circulation. Second, encourage to integrate and utilize the existing logistics distribution resource and support the construction of the cooperative service platform for logistics information and the joint distribution center. Third, encourage cooperation between the new type of trading enterprises and logistics enterprises, and promote full integration of the virtual trade network and the entity logistics network.[2]

(Yong Li, Post-Doctor, Shanghai University of Finance and Economics; Yu Lixin Researcher, the director of Foreign Economic and Trade International Financial Research Center of theChina Academy of Social Sciences)

---

[1] Xu Song, Zhang Yanyan, "Build Cross-border E-commerce into the New Passage of 'Made in China' Export", *Economic Review*, 2015 (2).

[2] Fan Xing: "Current Situation, Problems and Measures of the New Trading Industry", *Scientific Development*, 2013 (12).

# Strategic Research on Chinese Logistics Service Trade in International Competition

## 1. Current Internationalization and External Openness of Chinese Logistics Service Trade

### 1.1   General Internationalization Status of Chinese Logistics Industry

The logistics industry is an activity set organically integrating basic functions such as transport, storage, loading, handling, packing, distribution processing, distribution, information processing, etc. The logistics industry has two main features: first, it is compound type, namely, the logistics industry involves multiple processes, traffics and industries, even with need of inter-disciplinary talents; second, it is a productive service industry, which means that logistics industry provides service for production in primary, secondary and tertiary industries, and has the feature of service industry.

In recent years, Chinese logistics industry develops rapidly, and total costs of Chinese logistics industry increase from 2.91 Trillion CNY of 2004 to 10.57 Trillion CNY of 2014, with 13.7% average annual growth. Total Social Logistics Cost are 164.86 Trillion CNY in 2014 with 15.6% average annual growth in 2004-2014. It is obvious that, compared with manufacturing industry, the logistics service industry grows rapidly. From the view of components, total logistics costs are 152.10 Trillion CNY with 8.3% year-on-year growth for industrial products, 9.27 Trillion CNY with 2.1% year-on-year growth for imported goods,

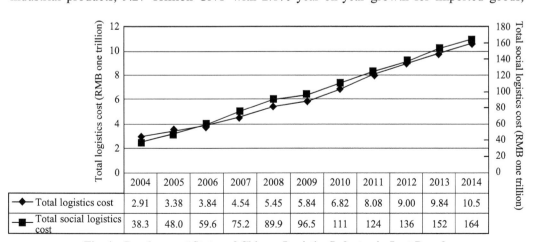

| | 2004 | 2005 | 2006 | 2007 | 2008 | 2009 | 2010 | 2011 | 2012 | 2013 | 2014 |
|---|---|---|---|---|---|---|---|---|---|---|---|
| Total logistics cost | 2.91 | 3.38 | 3.84 | 4.54 | 5.45 | 5.84 | 6.82 | 8.08 | 9.00 | 9.84 | 10.5 |
| Total social logistics cost | 38.3 | 48.0 | 59.6 | 75.2 | 89.9 | 96.5 | 111 | 124 | 136 | 152 | 164 |

**Fig. 1   Development Status of Chinese Logistics Industry in Last Decade**

353

653.1 Billion CNY with 14.1% year-on-year growth for renewable resources, 2.55 Trillion CNY with 4.1% year-on-year growth for agricultural products, and 285.8 Billion CNY with 32.9% year-on-year growth for goods for units and residents.

According to the data of State Statistics Bureau, the increase of Chinese logistics industry is 3.6628 Trillion CNY in 2014, with 9.5% year-on-year growth in comparable price. In 2014, the increase of logistics industry is 5.75% of GDP, and 12.09% of the increase of the service industry. In 2013, the increase of logistics industry is 3.34 Trillion CNY with 8.5% year-on-year growth in comparable price, and in 2013, the increase of logistics industry is 5.69% of GDP, and 11.95% of the increase of the service industry. The result shows that the rate of contribution of Chinese logistics industry to the service industry has increased by years, and Chinese logistics industry becomes more and more important for social and economic development. Chinese logistics industry still maintains higher growth rate and achieves 13% average annual growth in 2004-2014.

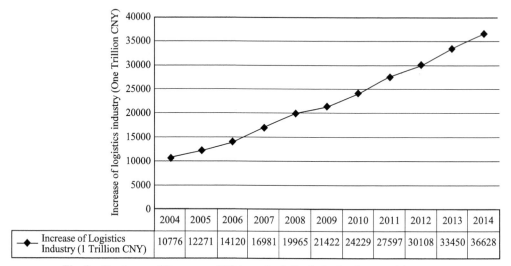

| | 2004 | 2005 | 2006 | 2007 | 2008 | 2009 | 2010 | 2011 | 2012 | 2013 | 2014 |
|---|---|---|---|---|---|---|---|---|---|---|---|
| Increase of Logistics Industry (1 Trillion CNY) | 10776 | 12271 | 14120 | 16981 | 19965 | 21422 | 24229 | 27597 | 30108 | 33450 | 36628 |

**Fig. 2    Tendency of Increase of Chinese logistics industry in recent ten years**

As shown in Fig. 3, the ratio of Chinese Total Social Logistics Cost to GDP generally has slow descending tendency. In 2005, Chinese Total Social Logistics Cost are 18.31% of GDP, and 16.99%, a staged low value in 2010, and continue to reduce in 2013 and 2014, and 16.61% of GDP in 2014, which is lowest over the years. According to the experience of developed countries, Total Social Logistics Cost are 10% of GDP, and so Chinese logistics costs are still a little higher presently although they decline. The high logistics costs, which can increase the incomes of logistics enterprises, from the view of economy, can increase the cost of production enterprises microcosmically and thus reduce the product competitiveness of the enterprises, and macroscopically affect the operating efficiency of national economy. Therefore, this is a challenge for the price of the logistics enterprises.

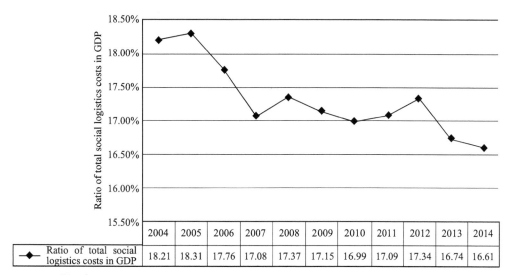

| Ratio of total social logistics costs in GDP | 2004 | 2005 | 2006 | 2007 | 2008 | 2009 | 2010 | 2011 | 2012 | 2013 | 2014 |
|---|---|---|---|---|---|---|---|---|---|---|---|
| | 18.21 | 18.31 | 17.76 | 17.08 | 17.37 | 17.15 | 16.99 | 17.09 | 17.34 | 16.74 | 16.61 |

**Fig. 3    Ratio of Chinese Total Social Logistics Cost to GDP in Recent Decade**

According to above, the logistics industry is an important industry in Chinese national economy, and the product transport process of more than 85% of industries is related to logistics. However, Chinese logistics industry has low quality development level, and more extensive development mode. The main problems are manifested in several aspects: First, high logistics cost and low efficiency. As shown in Fig. 3, Total Social Logistics Cost are 16.6% of GDP, and higher than that of other countries (including such developing countries as Brazil and India), and this means that there is expectation to reduce the logistics costs, and the logistics enterprises are forced to perform transformation. Second, there are serious barrier between higher and lower levels. System and mechanism barrier which hinder logistics industry development are not removed. The problems, such as high ratio of self-run logistics, small scale of logistics enterprise, difficulty in promotion of advanced technology and unification of logistics standard, round about transportation, etc., are serious; third, relatively lag infrastructure which cannot meet the development requirement of modern logistics. A comprehensive transportation system is not established with reasonable layout, unhindered connection, sufficient ability and high efficiency and conveyance, and construction of logistics park, and logistics technical equipment needs to be strengthened; logistics technology, talent training and logistics standard can also not meet the development requirement of the logistics industry, and the integration and intensification degree of the logistics service is not high. Four, policies and regulations are not perfect enough and market order is not normative enough. The issued policies needs to further implemented, the problems, such as arbitrary charging and arbitrary fining of the logistics enterprises, are serious in some regions. The construction of credit system is lagged, and the total quality of the employees of the logistics industry needs to be improved.

## 1.2 Current Development Status of Chinese Logistics Service Trade

According to above, although Chinese logistics industry develops rapidly in the last decade, the growth of Chinese logistics industry is driven mainly by domestic market. Once the growth rate of domestic total logistics costs is lower than the increase rate of new logistics enterprises (including domestic logistics enterprises and foreign-invested logistics enterprises), the operation performance of the logistics enterprises will decline. Therefore, the domestic logistics enterprises must go abroad, especially implements internationalization strategy in emerging market.

During the earlier stage of reform and opening-up, Chinese logistics industry develops slowly, and modern logistics rises till early twenty-first century. Except for COSCO which engages in shipping business (small scale), other business are not formally developed abroad. In recent years when the domestic logistics industry is mature, there are still problems such as relatively slow internationalization pace, small scale, single business mode. According to analysis, the specific causes include:

(1) Indefinite target. When foreign logistics enterprises establish a transnational corporation for domestic logistics business one after another, the internationalization process of Chinese logistics enterprises ceases to advance, and these enterprises consider that they are carefree as long as they occupy enough shares of domestic market, and they do not have overseas expansion power. Even if some enterprises try to "go out", such enterprises do not establish systematic and overall strategic planning.

(2) Unfamiliar with overseas market. When transnational business is done, the domestic logistics enterprises must understand all policies and business environments fully, including political environment, economic environment, business policies, etc. for example, tax policy, logistics clearance inspection, etc. At present, the logistics enterprises often do business lowly or are even forced to suspend the business due to no adequate talent and information;

(3) Weak international business mode. At present, during the transnational business, several globally top logistics companies often operate and supervise by a logistic network engineering system, and this means that logistic dynamic may be observed real time, and business flow is facilitated (Ling Chen, 2010; Xiaomei Sun, 2011). However, the domestic enterprises still use overseas agency mode in international logistics, rather than rely on modernized network, and so expertise is not strong and operation efficiency is low.

## 1.3 Measurement of Openness of Chinese Logistics Service Trade

### 1.3.1 Traditional measuring Method with industry data

How much is the internationalization degree of Chinese Logistics Service Trade statistically? At present, the statistical department does not perform the statistics for the international business of the logistic industry, mainly because relevant statistical accounting system and method are not established, and it is more difficult to perform statistics in reality. As relevant statistics (customs) is only the statistics of total logistic cost during international logistic process, rather than the cost of logistics enterprises (namely price), causing loss of the data on international data of the logistics service trade (enterprises). However, this does not represent that the internationalization level of the logistics industry cannot be measured, on the contrary, according to the logistics statistic data provided in China Logistics Yearbooks over the years, the openness of the logistics can be approximately estimated.

*China Logistics Yearbooks* over the years provides the macroscopic statistic data of the logistics industry, as shown in Table 1. It can be seen that, from 2004 to 2013, the ratio of the increase of the logistics industry to Total Social Logistics Cost trends to decline, and the decline range is not large, and 35% value-added rate are basically maintained. It is observed that the Ratio of Logistics Cost to Value has "U" trend, and the ratio of 2014 is almost equivalent to that of 2006 and the ratio is lowest in 2007-2009.

**Table 1    Operation Data of Chinese Logistics Industry of 2004–2014**

Unit: 100 Million CNY

| Year | Increase of Logistics Industry | Total Social Logistics Cost | Ratio of Increase | Total Social Logistics Cost | Ratio of Logistics Cost to Value |
|------|------|------|------|------|------|
| 2004 | 10776 | 29114 | 37.01% | 383829 | 7.59% |
| 2005 | 12271 | 33861 | 36.24% | 480583 | 7.05% |
| 2006 | 14120 | 38414 | 36.76% | 595976 | 6.45% |
| 2007 | 16981 | 45406 | 37.40% | 752283 | 6.04% |
| 2008 | 19965 | 54542 | 36.60% | 898978 | 6.07% |
| 2009 | 21422 | 58469 | 36.64% | 965503 | 6.06% |
| 2010 | 24229 | 68233 | 35.51% | 1110328 | 6.15% |
| 2011 | 27597 | 80857 | 34.13% | 1246898 | 6.48% |
| 2012 | 30108 | 90074 | 33.43% | 1369094 | 6.58% |
| 2013 | 33450 | 98451 | 33.98% | 1527909 | 6.44% |
| 2014 | 36628 | 105736 | 34.64% | 1648614 | 6.41% |

Data source: *China Logistics Yearbooks.*

Total Social Logistic Cost includes the total logistic costs of agricultural products, industrial products, imported goods, renewable resources, and goods for unit and residents, and the total logistic cost of the imported goods is the import volume of the total volume of import and export trade. However, considering the counterparty is a foreign enterprise in the international business of the logistics enterprises, the logistic service provided by the logistics enterprise for imported and exported goods are deemed to be the international business of the logistics enterprise. Therefore, the openness of the logistics industry may be calculated by the following formula:

Openness of Logistics Industry = Ratio of Logistics Cost to Value×(a × Volume of Export

+ b × Volume of Import) / Total Social Logistics Cost

Wherein, "a" is the ratio of the logistics enterprise's business volume in the volume of export trade, b is the ratio of the logistics enterprise's business amount in the volume of import trade. At present, there is not better method to determine "a" and "b". Generally, for export, the domestic enterprise would give preference to the domestic logistic enterprise, on the contrary, for import, the foreign enterprise would give preference to local logistics enterprises, therefore, a is not less than b theoretically. it can be assumed a+b=1, namely, the ratio of logistics cost for imported and exported goods are equal at home and abroad.

Table 2 shows the ratio of Total International Business Costs in Total Social Logistics Cost of the domestic logistics enterprises calculated with parameters a=0.6 and b=0.4, namely the openness of logistics industry (actually, due to small difference between Chinese volumes of export trade and import trade, when a is 0.5, 0.555, 0.6, 0.65 or 0.7, the change in openness is not obvious). It can be seen from the table that from 2004 to 2014, Chinese Total International Business Cost trends to rise progressively, but the openness declines. This result shows that Chinese logistics industry grows rapidly as a whole, but the income from international business is lower than the incomes from domestic business. On the other hand, from the view of coefficient, the openness of logistics industry is 8.16% in 2014, which is lower than the international business level of the international logistics enterprises. The income from international business of USA's top three logistic enterprises (UPS, FedEx Corp and Ryder System) is averagely 18% of their total business income.

### Table 2  Openness of Chinese logistics industry  (Method I)

Unit: 100 Million CNY

|      | Volume of Export | Volume of Import | Total Business Cost of Logistics Service Trade | Openness |
|------|------------------|------------------|-----------------------------------------------|----------|
| 2004 | 49103.30 | 46435.80 | 3643.62 | 12.52% |
| 2005 | 62648.10 | 54273.70 | 4178.05 | 12.34% |
| 2006 | 77597.20 | 63376.86 | 4634.94 | 12.07% |
| 2007 | 93563.60 | 73300.10 | 5158.05 | 11.36% |
| 2008 | 100394.94 | 79526.53 | 5584.63 | 10.24% |
| 2009 | 82029.69 | 68618.37 | 4642.70 | 7.94% |
| 2010 | 107022.84 | 94699.30 | 6273.98 | 9.19% |
| 2011 | 123240.60 | 113161.40 | 7730.24 | 9.56% |
| 2012 | 129359.25 | 114800.96 | 8127.56 | 9.02% |
| 2013 | 137131.43 | 121037.46 | 8421.28 | 8.55% |
| 2014 | 143900.00 | 120400.00 | 8626.37 | 8.16% |

Note: Total business cost of logistics service trade and openness shown above are calculated by a=0.6 and b=0.4.

### 1.3.2 Measuring Method with enterprise data

Above measuring method I for openness of logistics service trade is based on the estimate of Total Social Logistics Cost, that is to say, the ratio of the logistics cost incurred by the international logistics business in all logistics costs is estimated by overall macroscopic data, which is used as the openness. Compared with the results obtained by microcosmic data, these results have lower accuracy. Therefore, in this paper, the openness is estimated by more accurate microcosmic enterprise data.

When the openness of logistics industry is estimated by more accurate microcosmic enterprise data, the business income of Chinese listed logistics enterprises is used as benchmark data. Considering that the listed companies disclose their data in their annual reports according to sale areas, the openness may be estimated by the following formula.

Openness of Logistics Industry = Overseas Sales of Listed Company of Logistics Industry/ (Overseas Sales Income + Domestic Sales Income)

In this document, the classification standard for listed companies used in the Straight Flush stock Software is selected, and the listed companies of logistics and port shipping industries are selected as a sample, including 21 companies of the logistics industry, and 30 companies of the port shipping industry. Data period is 2004-2014.

**Table 3 Domestic and Overseas Sales Income of Listed Companies in 2004–2014**

Unit: 100 Million CNY

| Year | Listed Companies of Logistics Industry | | Listed Companies of Port Shipping Industry | |
|---|---|---|---|---|
| | Domestic Sales | Overseas Sales | Domestic Sales | Overseas Sales |
| 2004 | 1766185.13 | 488027.61 | 828798.3298 | 2286633.97 |
| 2005 | 1803623.314 | 562404.25 | 994781.1165 | 3185827.39 |
| 2006 | 2437618.471 | 589865.31 | 1162258.091 | 3392429.65 |
| 2007 | 2560317.081 | 947736.01 | 3101957.676 | 12505954.17 |
| 2008 | 2158632.823 | 438335.3857 | 5101428.953 | 13844634.2 |
| 2009 | 1247140.946 | 242576.0372 | 4476214.1 | 5372638.819 |
| 2010 | 3793363.25 | 316756.838 | 5942594.897 | 10370061.29 |
| 2011 | 5038267.146 | 527739.4354 | 13374757.28 | 8392178.467 |
| 2012 | 7302752.35 | 971435.7765 | 5482105.073 | 9060888.791 |
| 2013 | 8754138.533 | 1447148.589 | 14978154.48 | 8498661.414 |
| 2014 | 5668160.189 | 1471832.87 | 7577476.391 | 8667094.804 |
| Total | 42530199.23 | 8003858.111 | 63020526.38 | 85577002.96 |

Data source: the database of CCER.

According to the data shown in Table 3, the result, namely the openness of logistics service trade under the Method II, may be calculated, as shown in Table 4. According to Table 4, for the logistics industry (21 companies), the openness of logistics is about 10%-25%, which is closer to the openness shown in Table 2. The average of openness shown in Table 2 is

10.09%, and average of the openness of the logistics industry as shown in Table 4 is 15.84%, and their difference is only 5.75%. The port shipping industry has far higher openness than the logistic industry, and the average of 2004-2014 is 57.59%. However, as the company incomes of the port shipping industry is far more than these of the logistics industry, the superposed (mixed) openness of both is still higher, average is 46.99%.

**Table 4  Openness of Chinese Logistics Service Trade (Method II)**

| Year | Logistics Industry (21 Companies) | Port Shipping Industry (30 Companies) | Logistic Industry+Port Shipping Industry |
|---|---|---|---|
| 2004 | 21.65% | 73.40% | 51.67% |
| 2005 | 23.77% | 76.20% | 57.25% |
| 2006 | 19.48% | 74.48% | 52.52% |
| 2007 | 27.02% | 80.13% | 70.38% |
| 2008 | 16.88% | 73.07% | 66.30% |
| 2009 | 16.28% | 54.55% | 49.52% |
| 2010 | 7.71% | 63.57% | 52.33% |
| 2011 | 9.48% | 38.55% | 32.63% |
| 2012 | 11.74% | 62.30% | 43.97% |
| 2013 | 14.19% | 36.20% | 29.53% |
| 2014 | 20.61% | 53.35% | 43.36% |
| average | 15.84% | 57.59% | 46.99% |

Fig. 4 shows the tendency of the openness for three samples. According to the figure, it can be seen that the openness of the logistics industry is steadier in Recent Decade as a whole while the openness of the port shipping industry trends to fall. The unilateral openness to export of the port shipping industry reduces since 2008 due to impact of 2008 global financial crisis in which global trade fallen in 2008-2010, and appreciation of exchange rate after exchange rate reform in 2005, especially higher appreciation ratio since 2007. The

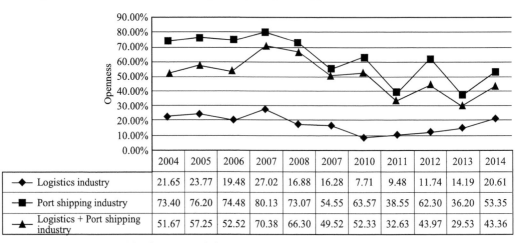

**Fig. 4  Trend of Openness of Logistics Service Trade**

appreciation of exchange rate causes the reduction of export trade and economic downturn, resulting in the international business of the logistics industry falling after rise.

1.3.3    How much is the openness of Chinese Logistics Service Trade on earth

The openness of logistics industry estimated by above Methods I and Methods II are significantly different. For Method I, the logistics cost of Chinese export and import is mainly considered, while for the Method II, the overseas sales income of the logistics enterprises is mainly considered. For example, for two magnates China Shipping Container Lines Co., Ltd. and China COSCO, the overseas (international) business incomes are 81.7% and 78.6% respectively in total incomes in 2014. Therefore, this paper considers that the openness calculated in the Method I may be inaccurate. First, the statistics of import and export trade data is mainly performed by the customhouse, but the total social logistic cost consists of two parts: Overseas logistic cost, which is mainly total amount of imported and exported goods, the statistics of which is performed by the customhouse and is more accurate, and domestic logistic cost, the statistics of which is performed by Statistical Bureau and China Federation of Logistics and Purchasing. Therefore, the statistical caliber of two parts may be different, and larger error exists. On the other hand, in import and export trade, port shipping mode is selected for goods logistics, and inland transport is selected rarely, and so the ratio of overseas business is very high, for example, CSCL and COSCO. Therefore, only from the view of the logistics enterprises, it is required to further verify the accuracy of the openness of logistics industry calculated in the Method I. Relatively, the openness calculated according to microcosmic enterprises is more reasonable and more accurate (Method II). However, according to the results shown in Table 4, for the domestic logistics enterprises, common logistics enterprises need to be differentiated from the port shipping enterprise, and the degree of internationalization is not high for the former (averagely 15.84%), and higher for the later (57.59%).

## 2. Evaluation and Analysis of International Competitiveness of Chinese Logistics Service Trade

### 2.1    Connotation of International Competitiveness of Chinese Logistics Service Trade

The industrial competitiveness generally refers to international competitiveness of the industry, and the competitive capacity of a country or a region in production efficiency, meeting market demand, making profit in same industry with comparison to other countries or regions. The comparison content of industrial competitiveness is industrial competitive advantages, and the competitive advantage is mainly embodied in the ability to implement market of product, enterprise and industry. Therefore, the essence of the industrial competitiveness is industrial comparative productiveness. The comparative productiveness is the comprehensive abilities of the enterprises or the industry to continuously make the products which the consumers are willing to accept in other more efficient mode than the competitor, and whereby obtain satisfactory economy benefit. The comparative scope of industrial competitiveness is the country or the region, and the industrial competitiveness is a regional concept.

Therefore, in a similar way, international competitiveness of a country in logistics service trade refers to the ability of the country's logistics service trade enterprise to strife for beneficial production condition and sale conditions and obtain maximum benefit in the competition under free and fair market condition. The productivity difference of the logistics industry may be caused by many factors, thereby influencing international competitiveness of the logistics industry, such as national economic development level, investment condition of logistics industry (infrastructure), market demand, governmental policies, etc. The change in the future openness of a region's logistics industry not only depends on the international trade level of the region, but also international competitiveness of the region's logistics industry (Lina Zhang, 2010; Liang Shen, 2014). Therefore, in the following of this paper, international competitiveness of logistics service trade is evaluated and measured, and the change trend of international competitiveness of Chinese logistics industry is calculated.

## 2.2 Evaluation method and appraisal system design for international competitiveness of logistics service trade international competitiveness

Many evaluation methods for industrial international competitiveness are available internationally. At present, the methods are approximately classified to five types: Index comprehensive evaluation method, Competition result evaluation method, Influence factor analysis method, Total factor productivity method and benchmarking method (Li Li et.al, 2007; Li Li and Donghui Xue, 2010). In this paper, the index comprehensive evaluation method is mainly used to measure international competitiveness of logistics industry. The steps mainly include the selection of reasonable factors impacting or deciding competitiveness for comprehensive consideration, finding suitable index corresponding to the factors, establishing scientific and systematic international competitiveness evaluation model, and obtaining final index for measuring international competitiveness of logistics industry by model calculation.

2.2.1 Design principle of industrial international competitiveness evaluation index

index selection is the key factor for comprehensive evaluation. For the index selection, scientificity and systematicness should be followed, that is to say, multiple principles will be used generally.

(1) Measurable nature. When the industrial competitiveness is evaluated in some

literature, the unalterable indices (objective indices) are used together with soft indices (subjective indices). The unalterable indices are a quantitative index, and the soft index is a qualitative index. This paper considers that although the soft indices may be used for quantization, relative to the quantitative index, its subjectivity is stronger. For international competitiveness of logistics industry, excessive soft indices may cause distortion of the elevation system. Therefore, the qualitative index is temporarily considered in this paper, that is to say, the measurable quantitative indices are selected for measuring.

(2) Relativity (comparability). The relativity means that the relative indices are generally selected for measuring rather than the absolute indices during index selection or index treatment. This is mainly for consideration of comparability of the countries. If the absolute indices are used, when the GDP of the country A is 100 Million USD, and the GDP of the country B is 5 Million USD, as the there is different level between two countries, the comparison of the absolute index always show the competitiveness of the country A is higher than that of the country B, and true comparability is lost basically. Therefore, measuring the competiveness by the relative index has higher comparability.

(3) Correlation: The correlation means the relative indices are selected for evaluation of the industrial international competitiveness rather than indices irrelevant to the competitiveness evaluation. Relative to other principle, this is crucial, and the index selection standard of the evaluation. The correlation is not measured by correlation coefficient and other quantitative analysis, but by subjective judgment, that is to say, the index represents the element for measuring international competitiveness of the logistics industry.

(4) Systematic hierarchy. The systematic hierarchy means that the index selection is based on the requirement of evaluation system and has hierarchy logicality. The indices should have hierarchical structure nature, for example, in the "diamond model" of Porter, it is considered that the industrial competitive edge depends on six factors: status of production factor, domestic demand condition, development degree of relevant industry and auxiliary industry, enterprise strategy, organization structure and horizontal competition, and governmental action and opportunity. The suitable indices are selected according to each of above 6 factors and finally combined into one index. Therefore, the whole elevation system may have 3-4 hierarchies.

(5) Availability. The index availability means that the data content of the selected indices are available and not imagined. For the logistics industry, a productive service industry in rapid development these years in China, systematization and generalization are not achieved for industrial statistics, causing many indices are incomplete, unspecific and inaccurate. In the system evaluation process, the index data may influence the evaluation result. Therefore, the statistical data of authoritative statistical department or statistical agency must be used, and

this is a foundation for establishment of the elevation system and the reliable guarantee for evaluation results.

2.2.2    Selection for evaluation indices for international competitiveness of logistics industry

The competitiveness of logistics industry relates to multiple aspect and various factors, and in this paper, the indices are selected for analysis from three accepts, such as the competitive strength of logistics industry, the competitive potential of logistics industry, and the competitive capacity of logistics industry by the common evaluation factor of international competitiveness, i.e. influence factor of logistics industry.

(1) Evaluation index for competitive strength of logistics service trade.

The competitive strength of logistics service trade mainly reflects the existing ability of the logistics industry to participate in competition. In this paper, the indices are selected for measuring from three aspects of logistics industry, such as industrial scale, human resource, and economic strength, specifically shown in Table 5. The index of industry scale mainly reflects the scale level of the logistics industry, including five indices, such as total amount of logistics industry, annual output value of logistics industry, total freight volume, tonnage mileage, and fixed asset investment. The competitive strength should also include human capital factor, and the human resources index of the logistics industry includes two indices such as employee number, and university education background. The economic strength indices are selected according to macro economy and economic expectation, and four indices, such as GDP, per capita GDP, total export-import volume and economic growth rate.

The following provides simple definition and calculation description of the indices. The total amount of logistics industry refer to the cargo value of the logistic field (logistic link), and so according to the definition, the total amount of logistics industry represents the sale and market scale of the logistics industry, and manifests the competitive strength of the logistics industry. The annual output value of logistics industry is the index for analyzing the output value of logistics industry according to specific transport industry, the transport industry includes transportation industry, warehousing industry, mail business and corresponding processing industry, and the annual output value of logistics manifests the value creation process of the logistics industry. The total freight volume refers to total goods transported during a certain calculation period, including pipe, road, marine and air transportation. The tonnage mileage refers to the quantity of goods transported by all transportation modes during a certain period multiplied by corresponding haul distance, and may reflect the results of the transportation industry. The fixed asset investment refers to the fixed asset investment scale of the industry. The employee number, and the number of employee above bachelor degree are people-based index, the former shows the absolute scale of employees, and the later shows employee quality and is soft index. The GDP and per capita GDP are indices reflecting national economic development level, the shows the absolute economic level and the per capita GDP shows relative economic level. The total export-import volume is the important index reflecting opening level, and important foundation for measuring the international openness of the logistics industry. The GDP growth rate refers to the growth rate of this year' GDP relative to previous year's GDP, and reflects the economic growth, and from the view of the industry, faster the economic development is, the stronger the competitive strength of logistics industry is.

**Table 5    Evaluation Index for Competitive Strength of Logistics Service Trade**

| Hierarchy 1 Index | Hierarchy 2 Index | Hierarchy 3 Index | Meaning |
|---|---|---|---|
| Competitive strength | Industrial scale index | Total amount of logistics | Reflect logistic scale |
| | | Annual output value of logistics industry | Reflect logistic scale |
| | | Total freight volume | Reflect freight scale of logistics |
| | | Tonnage mileage | Reflect operation ability of logistics |
| | | Fixed asset investment | Reflect investment condition of logistics industry |
| | Human resources index | Employee number | Reflect human resource of logistics industry |
| | | University education background | Reflect senior human resource of logistics industry |
| | Economic strength | GDP | Reflect economic strength of country |
| | | Per capita GDP | Measure economic development level of country |
| | | Total export-import volume | Reflect trade volume of country |
| | | GDP growth rate | Reflect economic growth of country |

(2) Evaluation index for competitive potential of logistics service trade.

The competitive potential of logistics service trade mainly reflects the potential ability of the logistics service trade to take part in competition. In this paper, the indices are selected for measuring from three aspects of logistics industry, such as industrial development, infrastructure level and relevant supporting industry. The industrial development indices include growth rate of industrial Increase, growth rate of freight volume, growth rate of fixed asset and Total Social Logistics Cost. The infrastructure level indices include railway network density, tonnage of port ship, cargo handling capacity of airport, and relevant support industry indices include the increase of primary industry, increase of secondary industry and increase of wholesale trade and retail industry.

The following provides simple definition and calculation description of the indices. The growth rate of logistics industry refers to the growth rate of logistics industry in current period relative to the increase of previous period, and reflects the growth of the logistics industry. The growth rate of freight volume refers to the growth rate of logistics freight volume of current period calculated quantitatively relative to the freight volume of previous period, and reflects transportation demand degree. For fixed asset level under accumulation of the logistics industry, and its growth rate reflects the growth speed of the fixed asset. Total Social Logistics Cost refer to total expenses of all national economic aspects for social logistics activities, including transport cost, loading and handling cost, distribution processing cost, distribution cost and cost for other logistic links. Total Social Logistics Cost includes transport cost, storage cost and management cost. From the view of the enterprise, the logistic cost is the product operation cost of the enterprise. The railway network density refers to the ratio of railway operating mileage to national territorial area, and reflects the development degree of railway construction. The higher the railway network density is, the higher forward effect the logistics industry has. The tonnage of port ship refers to the tonnages of ten thousand tons ship, and reflects the goods loading and handling capacity of the main port. The higher the tonnage of port ship is, the higher forward effect the logistics industry has. The cargo handling capacity of airport refers to the maximum cargo handling capacity of existing airport, and reflects the freight capacity of the airport. The higher the handling capacity is higher, the higher forward effect the logistics industry has. The increase of primary industry is the added output value of the primary industry, and as the primary industry relates to the logistic transportation from production to sale, the higher the increase of primary industry is, the higher logistic potential is. Similarly, the increase of secondary industry is the added output value of the secondary industry, and as the secondary industry, i.e. sale of industrial products, relates to the logistic transportation, the higher the increase of secondary industry is, the higher logistic potential is.

Table 6   Elevation Index for Competitive Potential of Logistics Service Trade

| Hierarchy 1 Index | Hierarchy 2 Index | Hierarchy 3 Index | Meaning |
|---|---|---|---|
| Competitive potential | Industrial development | Growth rate of industrial Increase | Describe scale development potential of logistics industry |
| | | Growth rate of freight volume | Describe transportation capacity development potential of logistics industry |
| | | Trowth rate of fixed asset | Describe fixed asset investment development potential of logistics industry |
| | | Gotal Social Logistics Cost | Reflect development change in cost for logistic process |
| | Infrastructure level | Railway network density | Reflect development degree of railway construction |
| | | Tonnage of port ship | Reflect cargo transportation capacity of port |
| | | Cargo handling capacity of airport | Reflect cargo transportation capacity of airport |
| | Relevant supporting industry index | Increase of primary industry | Reflect the change trend of primary industry |
| | | Increase of secondary industry | Reflect the change trend of secondary industry |
| | | Output value of wholesale trade and retail | Reflect the change trend of wholesale and retail industry |

The increase of wholesale trade and retail industry is the added output of wholesale trade and retail industry, the wholesale trade industry generally means that employers' transport of the products of enterprise to their region for wholesale, and so it has significant impact on the logistics industry.

(3) Competitive capacity indices of logistics service trade.

The competitive capacity refers to the ability of the logistics service trade to transfer the competitive strength and the competitive potential into the competitiveness of actual logistics business. In this paper, the indices are mainly selected for measuring from two aspects such as industrial efficiency and internationalization degree. The industrial efficiency indices include labor productivity, cost-profit ratio, ratio of industrial increase to GDP, ratio of industrial Increase to Increase of tertiary industry. The internationalization indices include ratio of import and export trade in international market, ratio of GDP to gross world product, and ratio of GDP growth rate to average world growth rate. The labor productivity is the ratio of increase of logistics industry (expressed in total output value in the industries) to employee number, and is often used for measuring the labor efficiency of the industry, and also the competitive capacity index. The cost-profit ratio is the ratio of total profit of the industry (enterprise) to industrial cost, and may be used to reflect the operation performance of the industry, and show the competitive capacity. The ratio of industrial increase to GDP refers to the ratio of increase of logistics industry in GDP and is used to measure the ratio of the increase of the logistics industry to GDP, and reflect the mature condition of a country's logistics industry. The ratio of industrial increase to increase of tertiary industry refers to the ratio of the increase of the logistics industry to the increase of tertiary industry, and reflects the ratio of the logistics industry in the service industry. The ratio of GDP to gross world product refers to the ratio of a country's value of import and export to value of world import and export, and is used for scale comparison with the Chinese import and export trade, and as all import and export trade relates to logistic transportation process, the higher value of trade is, the higher the competitive capacity of the logistics industry is. The ratio of GDP growth rate to average world growth rate refers to the ratio of a country's GDP to world total GDP, and used to reflect the economic scale of the country. Theoretically, the larger the economic scale is, the higher the competitive capacity of the logistics industry is. The ratio of GDP growth rate to average world growth rate refers to the ratio of GDP growth rate of a country to average world economic growth rate, and is used to reflect potential economic growth rate, and the macroeconomic growth ratio may influence the development of macroscopic industry and microcosmic enterprises.

**Table 7   Evaluation Indices for Competitive Capacity of Logistics Service Trade**

| Hierarchy 1 Index | Hierarchy 2 Index | Hierarchy 3 Index | Meaning |
|---|---|---|---|
| Competitive capacity | Industrial efficiency | Labor productivity | Reflect work efficiency of logistics industry |
| | | Cost-profit ratio | Reflect profitability of logistics industry |
| | | Ratio of industrial Increase to GDP | Reflect contribution of logistics industry development to national economy |
| | | Ratio of industrial Increase to Increase of tertiary industry | Reflect contribution of logistics industry development to tertiary industry |
| | Internationalization degree | Ratio of import and export trade in international market | Reflect the relative scale of China total trade volume |
| | | Ratio of GDP to gross world product | Reflect relative scale of Chinese economic aggregate |
| | | Ratio of GDP growth rate to average world growth rate | Reflect economic development ability of country |

### 2.2.3   Setting of valuation index weighting based on AHP

After international competitiveness evaluation system is established for the logistics service trade, on one hand, index statistic data is searched by various statistic approaches, on the other hand, the index weight is set, and in such a way, international competitiveness of logistics industry is determined finally by weighting. Many methods are available to set index weight at present, including fuzzy evaluation, principal component analysis, analytic hierarchy process, subjective decision method. Considering that more indices are used in this paper but 2-4 indices are approximately used every hierarchy, it is more suitable to use the analytical hierarchy process (AHP). Therefore, the weight of Hierarchy 1 Index, Hierarchy 2 Index and Hierarchy 3 Index for evaluation system is determined by AHP.

AHP is a qualitative and quantitative multi-objective decision analysis method, and a simple and practical analysis method for analysis of correlative and inter-inhibitive complex problems. In this process, the component elements of the problems are broken down according to problem nature and objective to be achieved, the elements is hierarchical according to element interrelation to form a hierarchical structure model, analysis is performed hierarchy by hierarchy to finally obtain the importance weight of lowest hierarchy to highest hierarchy (general objective). The principle of AHP is described as following, and the weight of qualitative index for enterprise credit evaluation is determined by this process. In AHP, the elements involving with complex problem of logistic system is grouped to form ordered hierarchical structure model, the relative importance of each element in each hierarchy is reflected by constructing judgment matrix, and consistency check is performed, specially as below:

(1) Establish hierarchical structure model.

After deep analysis of decision problem, the elements involved are divided into objective hierarchy, index hierarchy, scheme hierarchy and measure hierarchy, and hierarchical structure and the affiliation of the elements are described in a block diagram.

(2) Construct judgment matrix.

From the element of the highest hierarchy, two elements of the next hierarchy are compared by using a certain element of previous hierarchy as a judging criterion to establish the judgment matrix. The judgment matrix is recorded as B. The element bj of the judgment matrix B shows the relevant importance of the element Bi to Bj under judging criterion $A_K$:

$$b_{ij} = \frac{w_i}{w_j}$$

Where, $W_i$ and $W_j$ are respectively the measured importance value of $B_i$ and $B_j$. Here, for, the scaling method proposed by Professor Sattin, 1-9 and their reciprocal, is generally used.

(3) Calculate weight vector.

We also need to find the method for determining the impact of different elements in a certain hierarchy on the elements in previous hierarchy. Square root method is generally used for approximate calculation, and calculation steps are given below:

Step 1: Calculate the product $M_i$ of the element of each line in judgment matrix B

$$M_i = \prod_{i=1}^{n} b_{ij} \quad (1, \ 2, \ \cdots, \ n)$$

Step 2: Calculate $n^{th}$ root $\overline{w}_i$ of $M_i$

$$\overline{w}_i = \sqrt[n]{M_i}$$

Step 3: Normalize vector $w = (\overline{w}_1, \ \overline{w}_2, \ \cdots, \ \overline{w}_n)^T$ to obtain vector $w = (\overline{w}_1, \ \overline{w}_2, \ \cdots, \ \overline{w}_n)^T$. The normalized result is the relevant importance (weight) $w_i$ of $A_k$ to $B_i$, i.e. weight vector

$$w_i = \frac{w_i}{\sum_{i=1}^{n} \overline{w}_i} \quad (1, \ 2, \ \cdots, \ n)$$

(4) Consistency check.

In actual execution of AHP, different views are caused by cognitional diversity and the complexity of objective factor, and so it is impossible that each judgment matrix is uniform completely, especially for the problems with many element and large scale. Therefore, it is required to perform the consistency check to verify whether the results obtained by AHP are basically reasonable. Generally, 1 or 2-order judgment matrix always has full consistency (specific consistency check steps are not detailed here, and found out in relevant literature).

**2.3   Evaluation result of international competitiveness of Chinese Logistics Service Trade**

After establishing the evaluation system for international competitiveness of Chinese Logistics Service Trade, the data is selected for quantitative calculation of the competitiveness.

As more indices are selected for the competitiveness in this paper, detailed statistical description of each index is not provided herein, and the trend is mainly calculated for international competitiveness of Chinese Logistics Service Trade.

To not conflict with above, the data period is still 2004-2013 (as 2015 China Statistical Yearbook is not issued, the data of 20104 is unavailable). Due to difference in orders of magnitude of all index data, to avoid the impact of the orders of magnitude on the weight for index calculation, the indices are standardized by the following formula:

Direct Index: $Y_{ij} = \dfrac{X_{ij} - \min(X_j)}{\max(X_j) - \min(X_j)}$ ;

Inverse Index: $Y_{ij} = \dfrac{\max(X_j) - X_{ij}}{\max(X_j) - \min(X_j)}$

After acquisition of the indices, the index weight is set. As described above, in this paper, the index weight is determined for all indices by AHP. Considering that there are more evaluation system hierarchies and indices, only Hierarchy 3 Index under industrial development (Hierarchy 2 Index) under logistic competitive potential (Hierarchy 1 Index) is used as a case to describe determination of the weight by AHP.

Firstly, establish the judgment matrix:

**Table 8　Judgment Coefficient Matrix**

| A2 | Growth Rate of Industrial Increase | Growth Rate of Freight Volume | Growth Rate of Fixed Asset | Total Social Logistics Cost |
|---|---|---|---|---|
| Growth Rate of Industrial Increase | 1 | 1 | 2 | 3 |
| Growth Rate of Freight Volume | 1 | 1 | 2 | 3 |
| Growth Rate of Fixed Asset | 1/2 | 1/2 | 1 | 3/2 |
| Total Social Logistics Cost | 1/3 | 1/3 | 2/3 | 1 |

Calculate the weight vector by above AHP weight calculation method:

$\bar{w}_1 = \sqrt[4]{1 \times 1 \times 2 \times 3} = 1.5651$

$\bar{w}_2 = \sqrt[4]{1 \times 1 \times 2 \times 3} = 1.5651$

$\bar{w}_3 = \sqrt[4]{1/2 \times 1/2 \times 1 \times 3/2} = 0.7825$

$\bar{w}_4 = \sqrt[4]{1/3 \times 1/3 \times 2/3 \times 1} = 0.5217$

After normalization processing, obtain the normalized and estimated weight:

$w = [0.3529 \quad 0.3529 \quad 0.1765 \quad 0.1176]$

Check the weight of the judgment matrix according to the consistency check steps. First calculate BW vector and the largest eigenvalue:

$$B_0 \cdot W_0 = \begin{bmatrix} 1 & 1 & 2 & 3 \\ 1 & 1 & 2 & 3 \\ 1/2 & 1/2 & 1 & 3/2 \\ 1/3 & 1/3 & 2/3 & 1 \end{bmatrix} \cdot \begin{bmatrix} 0.3529 \\ 0.3529 \\ 0.1765 \\ 0.1765 \end{bmatrix} = \begin{bmatrix} 1.4118 \\ 1.4118 \\ 0.7059 \\ 0.4706 \end{bmatrix}$$

$$\lambda_{max} = \sum_{i=1}^{n} \frac{(BW)_i}{nW_i} = \frac{1.4118}{4 \times 0.3529} + \frac{1.4118}{4 \times 0.3529} + \frac{0.7059}{4 \times 0.1765} + \frac{0.4706}{4 \times 0.1176} = 4.00$$

According to above CI calculation formula, $CI = \dfrac{\lambda_{max} - n}{n - 1} = \dfrac{4.000 - 4}{4 - 1} = 0.00 < 0.1$, and so the result passes the consistency check. During actual calculation, the matlab software may be used for calculation.

According to the step of AHP, the index weight may be calculated for the whole evaluation system for international competitiveness of logistics service trade, specifically shown in the following table:

**Table 9　Index Weight Value**

| Hierarchy 1 Index | Hierarchy 2 Index | Hierarchy 3 Index |
|---|---|---|
| Competitive Strength 0.5396 | Industrial Scale Index 0.5472 | Total logistic cost 0.3197 |
| | | Annual output value of logistics industry 0.3197 |
| | | Total freight volume 0.1836 |
| | | Tonnage mileage 0.1091 |
| | | Fixed asset investment 0.0680 |
| | Human Resources Index 0.2631 | Employee number 0.5 |
| | | University education background 0.5 |
| | Economic Strength 0.1897 | GDP 0.3529 |
| | | Per capita GDP 0.1176 |
| | | Total export-import volume 0.3529 |
| | | GDP growth rate 0.1765 |
| Competitive potential 0.1634 | Industrial development 0.4000 | Growth rate of industrial Increase 0.3529 |
| | | Growth rate of freight volume 0.3529 |
| | | Growth rate of fixed asset 0.1765 |
| | | Total Social Logistics Cost 0.1176 |
| | Infrastructure level 0.4000 | Railway network density 0.1634 |
| | | Tonnage of port ship 0.5396 |
| | | Cargo handling capacity of airport 0.2970 |
| | Relevant support industry index 0.2000 | Increase of primary industry 0.3333 |
| | | Increase of secondary industry 0.3334 |
| | | Output value of wholesale trade and retail 0.3333 |
| Competitive capacity 0.2970 | Industrial efficiency 0.3333 | Labor productivity 0.3529 |
| | | Cost-profit ratio 0.3539 |
| | | Ratio of industrial Increase to GDP 0.1765 |
| | | Ratio of industrial Increase to Increase of tertiary industry 0.1176 |
| | Internationalization degree 0.6667 | Ratio of import and export trade in international market 0.5396 |
| | | Ratio of GDP to Global Gross Product 0.2970 |
| | | Ratio of GDP growth rate to global average growth rate 0.1634 |

After obtaining the index weight, the standardized value of each index of 2004-2013 is calculated. Table 10 show the international competitive strength index of the logistics industry, Table 11 shows the international competitive potential index of the logistics industry, and Table 12 shows the international competitive capacity index of the logistics industry. According to Table 10, it can be seen that the industrial scale, human resource and economic strength of Chinese logistics industry under the competitive strength basically trend to rise year by year. The international competitive strength of the logistics industry obtained by weighting also trends to rise.

**Table 10   Trend of International Competitive Strength Index of Logistics Industry**

| Year | Industrial Scale | Human Resource | Economic Strength | Competitive Strength |
|---|---|---|---|---|
| 2004 | 0.0000 | 0.0409 | 0.0660 | 0.0233 |
| 2005 | 0.0789 | 0.0135 | 0.1745 | 0.0798 |
| 2006 | 0.1668 | 0.0360 | 0.3001 | 0.1577 |
| 2007 | 0.2899 | 0.0939 | 0.4538 | 0.2694 |
| 2008 | 0.4016 | 0.1335 | 0.4151 | 0.3336 |
| 2009 | 0.4759 | 0.1827 | 0.3709 | 0.3789 |
| 2010 | 0.6236 | 0.1990 | 0.5850 | 0.5046 |
| 2011 | 0.7695 | 0.3292 | 0.7115 | 0.6427 |
| 2012 | 0.8966 | 0.3729 | 0.7367 | 0.7285 |
| 2013 | 0.9939 | 1.0000 | 0.8239 | 0.9633 |

According to Table 11, it can be seen that the industrial development, infrastructure level and relevant supporting industry of Chinese Logistics Service Trade under the competitive potential basically trend to rise year by year while specific rule is found out in the change trend of industrial development. The international competitive potential of the logistics industry calculated by weighting rises generally.

**Table 11   Trend of International Competitive Potential Index of Logistics Industry**

| Year | Industrial Development | Infrastructure Level | Related Supporting Industry | Competitive Potential |
|---|---|---|---|---|
| 2004 | 0.6633 | 0.0000 | 0.0000 | 0.2653 |
| 2005 | 0.5714 | 0.1330 | 0.0471 | 0.2912 |
| 2006 | 0.6049 | 0.1850 | 0.1126 | 0.3385 |
| 2007 | 0.7393 | 0.2702 | 0.2316 | 0.4501 |
| 2008 | 0.6506 | 0.3836 | 0.3636 | 0.4864 |
| 2009 | 0.4481 | 0.5214 | 0.4158 | 0.4710 |
| 2010 | 0.7510 | 0.6780 | 0.5742 | 0.6864 |
| 2011 | 0.7247 | 0.7945 | 0.7614 | 0.7600 |
| 2012 | 0.5763 | 0.8813 | 0.8811 | 0.7592 |
| 2013 | 0.3629 | 1.0000 | 1.0000 | 0.7452 |

According to Table 12, it can be seen that the industrial efficiency and internationalization degree of Chinese logistics industry under the competitive capacity trend to rise year by year. The international competitive potential of the logistics industry obtained by weighting rises generally.

**Table 12   Trend of International Competitive Capacity Index of Logistics Industry**

| Year | Industrial Efficiency | Internationalization Degree | Competitive Capacity |
|---|---|---|---|
| 2004 | 0.2941 | 0.0000 | 0.0980 |
| 2005 | 0.3695 | 0.1497 | 0.2229 |
| 2006 | 0.4148 | 0.1888 | 0.2641 |
| 2007 | 0.4638 | 0.3029 | 0.3566 |
| 2008 | 0.4738 | 0.4349 | 0.4479 |
| 2009 | 0.4193 | 0.5282 | 0.4919 |
| 2010 | 0.4993 | 0.5814 | 0.5540 |
| 2011 | 0.5804 | 0.6730 | 0.6421 |
| 2012 | 0.6599 | 0.7796 | 0.7397 |
| 2013 | 0.6401 | 0.8739 | 0.7960 |

After obtaining the indices on the competitive strength, competitive potential and competitive capacity of the logistics service trade, international competitiveness index of Chinese Logistics Service Trade may be obtained by final weighting, and the specific index trend is shown in Fig. 5. As shown in Fig. 5, international competitiveness index of Chinese Logistics Service Trade trends to rise linearly year by year, and this shows improvement of the comprehensive ability of Chinese Logistics Service Trade to take part in international competition. From the view of three component factors, the competitive strength has the trend of accelerated rise and more rapid rise in 2010 than in the years before 2010; the competitive capacity has same trend with international competitiveness, and rises linearly; the competitive potential has the trend of S-type rise: rise in 2004-2008 and fall after rise due to the impact of

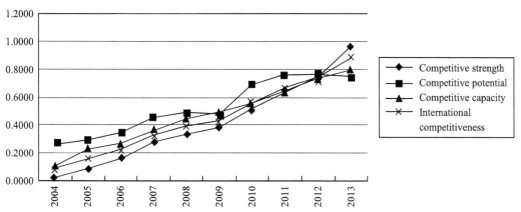

**Fig. 5   Trend of International Competitive Indices of Chinese Logistics Service Trade**

the financial crisis, rise due to potential development advantages provided for the logistics industry by national revitalization planning for logistics industry in 2010-2011, and fall in 2012-2013.

## 3. Strategy to participate in international competition of Chinese logistic service trade

Under the background of economic globalization, all industries hope to go abroad for more overseas business and development opportunities. For internationalization of the logistic industry, the government, the logistics industry association and the enterprises are required to take measures respectively and make systematic integration to form joint force and infuse the international market in industrial strategic attitude.

**3.1 The developing strategy of our government's reply to improve logistic service trade**

3.1.1 Improvement of policy

At present, the State Council and relevant departments have established more policies to promote the development and "going-abroad" of the logistics industry. However, there are many difficulties for the enterprises to implement the policies, even there is no governmental department governing logistics industry in some regions, and this results in poor implementation of preferential policies for the logistics industry. On the other hand, up to now, formal legal documents are issued for the logistics industry, only some simple normative regulations are available, which lead to nonstandard operation, cutthroat competition and poor market supervision of the whole logistic industry. For this purpose, China takes measures in two aspects: Increase policy support for "going abroad" of the logistics industry, and establish the laws and relevant rules and regulations for the logistics industry to protect the "going abroad" of the enterprises legally.

3.1.2 Establishment of standard

The logistics, as an emerging producer service industry, develops rapidly in recent years. However, larger defect exists in its industrial standardization, and mainly reflected in content and implementation of standard. For example, Chinese standard is not consistent with international standard mainly due to Chinese long-term plan economic system, less consideration is paid to the consistency with the international standard during establishment of the industrial standard. This results in the failure of the logistics enterprises to meet the international standards during international business, the cost increase of logistics enterprises, and a barrier for Chinese international trade. For this, National Bureau of Standards should quicken the establishment and perfection of suitable and reasonable industrial standard to provide powerful base for the overseas development of the enterprises.

### 3.1.3    Improvement of reform

At present, the state-owned enterprises, including COSCO, have large loss, mainly due to their confusion and redundancy. Under the state-owned system, the enterprises cannot ake targeted measures timely for market response, for example, for the project with continuous loss and excessive redundant personnel, responsibility of enterprises for continuous propulsion and local employment protection makes the enterprises governance inefficient. The advantages of state-owned enterprise reform lie in not only delegation of powers to the enterprises, but also the acceleration of state-owned enterprise merger to avoid internal competition of domestic enterprises in the international competition, and compete with large foreign logistics enterprises jointly.

## 3.2    The promotion strategy of logistic industry association

### 3.2.1    TO promote enterprises to go abroad

The logistics industry association can establish strategic alliances of the logistics industry to incorporate the qualified or interested logistics enterprises into such "internationalization" strategic alliances, and then participate in international competition in the form of supply chain. Such enterprises can complement their advantages in Geography, personnel and equipment, etc., against the competition from external enterprises by cost reduction, high efficiency and the third party's logistics pattern.

### 3.2.2    Set up higher regulation of market access

In the end of 2005, China opened the logistics industry officially based on the commitment made in joining "WTO". The opening of logistics industry enables the foreign-invested enterprises to come into China successively for purpose of getting a slice of cake in the logistic market, which will decrease the trade logistics of domestic logistics enterprises and additionally go against "internationalization" to be achieved by domestic logistics enterprises. Therefore, the industry association and ministry of commerce, etc develops the solution for raising admittance threshold of foreign logistics enterprises, by which the domestic logistics enterprises are protected.

### 3.2.3    Suggestion of cooperation

The industry association can enhance cooperation among various manufacturing industry associations, trade industry association and logistics industry association, and further to promote the cooperation among manufacturing enterprises, trading companies and logistics enterprises, and advocate priority selection of the domestic logistics companies when the domestic manufacturing enterprises export products and the trading companies import foreign products, thus provide the business basis for "internationalization" of the domestic logistics enterprises.

### 3.3 Participation in international challenge strategy of logistic service trade enterprises

#### 3.3.1 Seize the opportunity of "the Belt and Road"

After "the Belt and Road" strategy has been put into implement, many logistics service trade companies may consider internationalization business after developing to an extent in China. This is also the national strategy at this stage in our country and should be supported. At present, the scale and high-level business of the logistics enterprises in China are generally lower than those in Europe, America and Japan. This shows the enterprises face great pressure, but it does not represent the enterprises are unable to achieve "internationalization". Therefore, the logistics enterprises must be confident and emphasis on emerging market, grab chances to lay foundation for subsequent globalization development.

#### 3.3.2 Improve the system for international competition

In general, the logistics enterprises in China have disadvantages of small scale and imperfect systems currently, which have adverse effect on internationalization. For this reason, the logistics enterprises should strengthen self-construction including cultivation of internationalization business talent, be familiar with various factors in internationalization such as politic, law and market, as well as various business processes such as tax rate, exchange rate, customs and surrender document, establish the network platform system and develop the logistics with the view of internationalization, and especially give more attention to management and risk control (Jinkai Li, 2008; Xiang Zhang, 2013).

#### 3.3.3 Choose correct marking position for global race of services in trade

The diversified development at this stage becomes one of business modes of large-scale enterprises, but some scholars believe based on research finding, that the diversified development may probably impair long-term development of enterprises. With respect to the logistics enterprises, the multi-business diversification will certainly appear in internation-alization development, in which shipping, land transportation, freight forwarding and air transportation, etc. are all included in the business scope. Nevertheless, the experience of many large-scale enterprises shows that, diversified development increases income of enterprises, but its profit. the profit. is decreased. Therefore, the logistics enterprise should make orientation analysis before achieving "internationalization" if it makes high investment on the field in which the enterprise never set foot (Qiangbin Ouyang, 2009; Fang Fang and Liangyou Shu, 2007).

**References**

[1] Chen Ling. *Discussion on Internationalization Strategy of Chinese Logistics Enterprises* [J]. Enterprise Economy, 2010(4).

[2] Sun Xiaomei. Internationalization Trend of Modern Logistics Development [J]. Commercial Economy, 2011(2).

[3] Shen Liang, Dong Qianli and Liu Ruijun. Threshold of Opening, the *Production Efficiency of Logistics Industry and Manufacturing Industry* [J]. Technoeconomics & Management Research, 2014(11).

[4] Zhang Lina. *Study on International Competitiveness of Chinese Modern Logistics Industry* [J]. Master's Thesis of Shanxi University of Finance and Economics, 2010.

[5] Li Li and Xue Donghui. *Evaluation Research on International Competitiveness of Chinese Logistics Industry based on Fuzzy Analysis* [J]. China Mechanical Engineering, 2010(12).

[6] Li Li, Dong Hong and Liu Henan. *Study on Construction of International Competitiveness Production Model of Modern Logistics Industry* [J]. Logistics Technology, 2007, 26(8).

[7] Li Jinkai. *Analysis on Competitive Situation of Chinese Modern Logistics Industry: Based on International Perspective* [J]. Business Economics and Administration, 2008(7).

[8] Zhang Xiang. *Research on Internationalization Operation and Performance of Chinese Enterprises* [D]. Doctoral Thesis of Southwestern University of Finance and Economics, 2013.

[9] Ouyang Qiangbin. *Research on Formation Mechanism and Cultivation of Modern Internationalization Logistics Enterprises* [J]. Academic Journal of Guangdong Financial Vocational College, 2009(2).

[10] Fang Fang and Shu Liangyou. *Risk Prevention in Internationalization of Chinese Logistics* [J]. Logistics Technology, 2007(9).

(Doctors Zhang Qi, Liu Qi of Graduate School of Chinese Academy of Social Sciences)

# The Study on International Competitiveness of China's Computer and Information Service Trade

## 1. Analysis on the international competitiveness of China's computer and information service trade

### 1.1    analysis on overall international competitiveness

In 2014, the export amount of China's computer and information service trade is USD 18.36 billion, got 19% growth in comparison with 2013; the import amount is SUD 8. 5 billion and increased 42% than that in 2013. During 2003 to 2014, the export amount of China's computer and information service trade has increased from USD 1.12 billion to USD 18.36 billion, with average annual growth rate at 38.2% and got the proportion accounted for China's service trade export total amount from 2.4% to 8.5%; the import amount has also increased from USD1.04 billion to USD8.5 billion, with average annual growth rate at 20% and got the proportion accounted for China's service trade import total amount from 1.9% to 2.2%; since 2003 China's computer and information service trade has got the consecutive surplus year after year, in 2014 the surplus even reached USD9.86 billion (see attached figure 1).

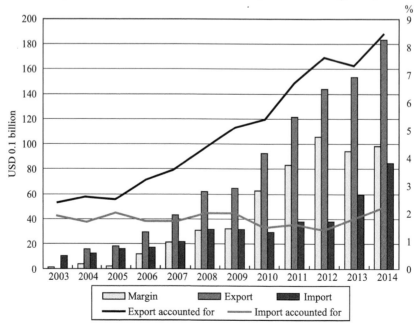

**Fig. 1    China's computer and information service import/export state from 2003 to 2014**
Data source: Sate Administration Foreign Exchange.

## 1.2    Analysis of international competitiveness in sub-industries

### 1.2.1    IT Outsourcing

Offshore IT Outsourcing refers to that the multinational contracting company consigns their own informatization construction process etc to the offshore contractor company with professional information technology for accomplishment. The offshore ITO usually includes following contents: informatization planning and consulting, equipment and software selection, network system and applied software system construction, daily maintenance, management and updates of the system network etc. The popularization of offshore ITO provides the great help for the enterprise realizing the digital business process, improving corporate work efficiency and saving informatization cost.

The ITO business in China has started quite earlier and currently it is just under the development period with high speed. In 2007 the revenue of China's ITO business was already USD 7.7 billion with growth rate at 23.3%. Thereinto, the system integration, hardware product and customized software have accounted for the largest market share. Till 2013 the business scale of ITO business has already reached USD31.17 billion, accounted for 56.4% total industry scale, with growth rate at 36.8% (as per shown in figure 2). The ITO business in China has even occupied more than 60% share of the service outsourcing. Till now, China has outpaced India and became to the first rank of the global offshore ITO contractor country, besides the support of government policy and human resource advantage, the main causing reason shall also be the increasingly strengthened corporate capacity and brand effect of those large service outsourcing companies such as NEU soft Group and AEGOVA etc. Currently the overall revenue amount of China's software service industry has only accounted for 0.2% of the GDP, in the US such ratio is already 1.5%. Therefore, it can be estimated that in coming 5 to 10 years, China's software service industry shall also continue its development in higher pace than that of GDP increase, so that to achieve the equilibrium status of national economic

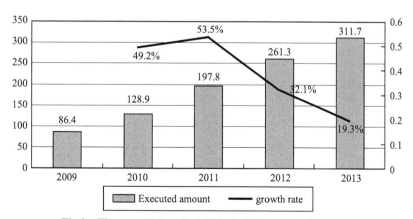

**Fig.2    The growth trend of China's ITO executed amount**

Data source: *China's service outsourcing development report 2012.*

379

structure, thus it can be seen that the ITO business in China still has the quire large space for improvement.

Being the important part of ITO, China has attached great importance to the development of offshore ITO since the beginning of such development (as per shown in figure 3.2). The offshore ITO business revenue in China has grown up to the USD 25.49 billion in 2013 from USD 3.21 billion in 2008, within the 6 years it has got the growth on nominal income amount by almost 7 times. The year-on-year growth rate has experienced the rapid initial increase above 50% at the very beginning then beyond 30% in average for the past years. In 2014 the global total ITO expenditure was USD 3800 billion with year-on-year growth rate by 3.6% (Zhang Ruili, Liu Jian, 2013). The slow recovery of the global economy and continuous decline of demand will impact the development of China's offshore ITO business, but under the push of domestic informatization investment and information consumption demand, the whole software industry will continue the slightly stable situation based on the stabilization with less decline in 2016, it was estimated that the growth rate in this year will be among 22%–25% accordingly.

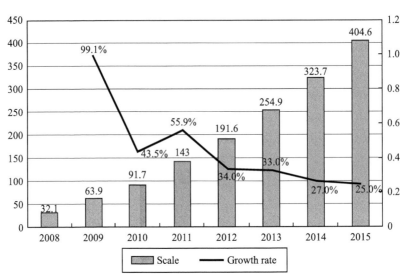

**Fig. 3    China's offshore ITO market scale trend  (unit: USD100 million)**
Data source: IDC official website: http://www.idc.com.

1.2.2    Cloud computing

The could computing is the addition, use and delivery pattern of relative service based on the internet, usually it may concern to provide dynamic extensible but usually virtual resources through the internet. In telecommunication service industry and computer service industry, the telecommunication infrastructure such as the server and network control equipment are usually shown in the "cloud" form in the diagram, so as to express its numerous and complicated characteristics, such a concept of clout computing is just abstracted from such illustration. Clout computing refers to provide the elastic and inexpensive distributed computing ability, it represents the dynamic extensible network application infrastructure by taking virtual technology as the core and taking lower cost as the target, it shall be the network computing technology and pattern as the most typical representative.

Cloud computing service, that is the cloud service, refers to provide the computer and information service through the cloud computing system, it can be the cloud computing products that can be taken as service for use, including the cloud host, cloud space, clout development, cloud test and comprehensive products etc. From this definition it can be seen that, the cloud computing service refers to that by depending on the cloud computing technology, to make the unified management and dispatch on plenty of computing resources connected through the network, forming the computing resource pool to provide the service upon user's demand. To outsource the computing ability in the form of service shall be the essential character of the cloud computing service. The cloud outsourcing rises in response to the proper time and conditions, representing such an outsourcing pattern that making the centralized processing on the computer and information service outsourcing by utilizing the cloud computing service. Under the cloud service platform,  so many service outsourcing resource clouds shall be integrated as the outsourcing resource pool, through the outsourcing service provided by the cloud management system, to achieve the convenient and flexible target, also reduce the cost and improve the efficiency accordingly.

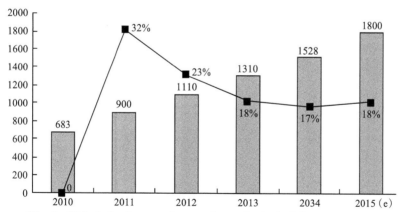

**Fig. 4    Global cloud computing market scale    (unit: USD 100 million)**
Data source: CCID Think Tank, research department of China Galaxy Securities.

The tides of cloud computing construction and cloud outsourcing development shows that, the overall competitive advantage of computer and information service industry is just converting in the pushing force for the industry development and informatization construction. At present, we are just at the beginning of the third information technology revolution tide due to the clout computing technology, the cloud computing could improve the social productivity and push the overall informatization of the society, and entirely overturn current business pattern and system. From perspective of industry, the "Y2K" problem in 1990s brought the development opportunities for Indian service outsourcing enterprises, now it's just the time for China's service outsourcing industry and enterprises grabbing such opportunity to exceed the traditional outsourcing power. In the cloud outsourcing time,. The outsourcing industry shall transform from the "straight line type", "plane type" toward the "matrix type", its division shall become more and more refined and much professional, the industrial form shall transform from linearity to the plane and three-dimension. In cloud outsourcing, the most important thing is the service, no application there's no service accordingly. This will create the new resource optimization, new pattern and industrial division.

### 1.2.3 Internet +

"Internet +" shall be the new format of internet development under the innovation 2.0, it's the new form of the internet form evolution and its created social-economic development with the drive of the knowledge society innovation 2.0. The "internet +" shall be the further practical results of the internet thinking, it represents such an advanced production relation to push the economic form changing and evolving continuously, so as to drive the vitality of social-economic entities, to provide wide network platform for the reform, innovation and development.

In China there was the third industrial revolution tide set off. With the continuously expanded internet market scale and the policy support in China, the "internet+" shall have the trend of significant development. In 2015 the internet market scale in China has accomplished more than 10 times growth in comparison with 2011, it was estimated that till 2017 it shall presents the multiple growth accordingly. In the two sessions, Prime Minister Li Keqiang has proposed that, being the direction of industrial transformation under China's economy New Normal, the "internet +" has been listed in the top design scheme of the country. Meanwhile the development of "internet +" in both depth and breadth also drove the upgrading and updating of traditional industries, greatly improved the industrial production efficiency.

China's mobile internet market scale during 2011-2018

"Internet + finance" has changed the competition pattern of financial industry. From the organization form, such combination has at least the three methods. The first one is that internet company deals with financial business: if such phenomenon occurred in a larger range and replaced those existed financial enterprises, that is the internet finance subversionism. The second one is the financial institutions in internet. The third one is the cooperation between internet company and the financial institutions.

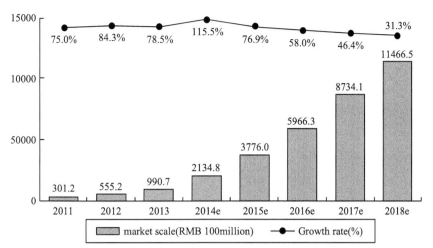

**Fig. 5    China's mobile internet market scale during 2011–2018**

Data source: CITICS.

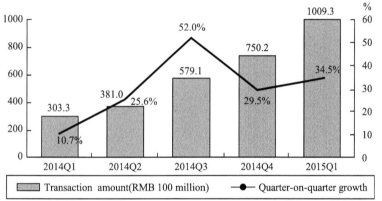

**Fig. 6    China's P2P internet loan market transaction scale during 2014 Q1–2015 Q1**

Data source: CITIC Securities.

Instruction: the P2P internet loan market refers to such the market where the P2P users realizing the online trading, both the user type, transaction quota, product type and product lifetime etc are not classified temporarily. The data is accessed through the estimation according to enterprise investigation, system capture and EnfoDesk method, the EnfoDesk may arrange find adjustment on the historical data according to the latest information.

**1.3    the measurement on international competitiveness of China's computer and information service trade**

The competitiveness of computer and information service trade refers to that by taking economic globalization as the background and regarding the improvement of national income and living standard as the target, the country or region shall have the ability to let its computer and information service industry participating in international competition, creating the added value and keeping the good balance of international payment accordingly, from the perspective of industry to analyze the international competitiveness level of China's computer and information service trade, there shall be mainly the three methods as market share, trade competitive power index and revealed competitive advantage.

1.3.1    The global market share in this industry

The international market share of the computer and information service trade is the ratio that the certain country or region accounts for the percentage of the total export amount of the world computer and information service trade, it reflects one country's (region) international competitive power on the computer and information service trade in a whole. The international market share of China's computer and information service trade is shown in Table 1.

Table 1    the international market share and export amount of China's computer and information service during 2007 to 2012

| Year | Export amount of China's computer and information service trade (USD 100 million) | Total export amount of global computer and information service trade (USD 100 million) | Market share (%) |
|---|---|---|---|
| 2007 | 43.45 | 1568.40 | 2.77% |
| 2008 | 62.52 | 1950.89 | 3.20% |
| 2009 | 65.12 | 1891.60 | 3.44% |
| 2010 | 92.56 | 2111.63 | 4.38% |
| 2011 | 121.82 | 2397.45 | 5.08% |
| 2012 | 144.54 | 2282.31 | 6.33% |
| 2012 | 144.54 | 2282.31 | 6.33% |
| 2013 | 154.30 | 2378.17 | 6.49% |

Data source: UN international trade center.

From table 1 it can be seen that the international market share of China's computer and information service trade was gradually increased in a stable basis, in 2013 the export amount of China's computer and information service trade was USD15.43billion, occupied the 4th ranking in the world, accounted for 6.49% of the export amount of global computer and information service trade, its international market share has got 3.72 percentage than that in 2007, it represented the increasing trend in whole, also reflected that the international competitive power of China's computer and information service trade has been improved increasingly.

In 2013, India, Ireland, Germany, China and UK have occupied the top five positions among the export amount ranking of global computer and information service trade, from the international comparison listed in diagram 7 it can be seen that even the international market share of China's computer and information service trade represented the increasing trend, but there still be the large gap in comparison with those major power in information service field such as India and Ireland.

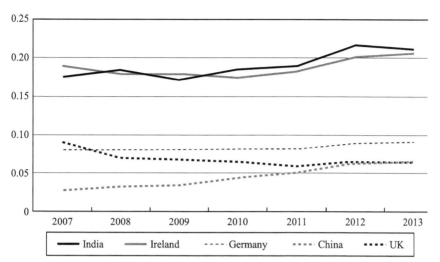

**Fig. 7    the international comparison on the computer and information service trade export**

Data resource: the UN international trade center

### 1.3.2    Analysis on the trade competitive power index

The trade competitive power index (TC) refers to the ratio of the import/ export trade balance of one country's computer and information service trade accounting for their total import/ export amount. This index reflects the production efficiency of one country's computer and information service, if the value of TC is larger than zero, it then implies that this country may have the high production efficiency on their computer and information service, vice versa, but such index cannot represent the influence the country may have in the world market. In this paper, it makes the comparison among the top five ranking country in the global computer and information service trade export amount according to the UN international trade center, details are shown in table 1.5.

The TC index can be represented by:

$$TC = \frac{E - I}{E + I}$$

There E refers to the export amount, and I the import amount.

From diagram 8 it can be seen that, the TC index of China's computer and information service is higher than that in Germany and UK, but still has the large gap in comparison with that in India and Ireland. The TC index of India represents the increasing trend from 2007 to 2012, and Ireland's is still keeping at a stable and higher level, China shall have the obvious difference from those two traditional powerful countries in information service, it implies that the overall competitive power of China's computer and information service is still at the "second echelon" among the international level, there's still quite large distance from the international leading advantages.

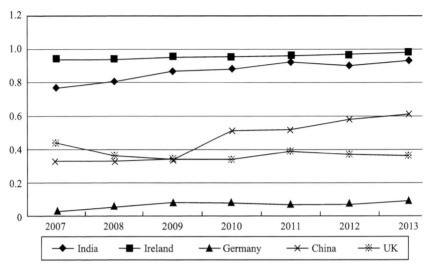

**Fig. 8    the international comparison on TC index of the computer and information service trade in different countries.**

Data source: the UN international trade center.

1.3.3    Revealed competitive advantage

The revealed competitive advantage (RCA) index was proposed by Balassa in 1975, according to the revealed competitive advantage principle, the RCA index could reflect the comparative advantage of one country's industrial trade. The RCA index for the computer and information service trade can be expressed by the ratio of the percentage that one country's computer and information service trade amount has accounted for in the country's total export amount divided by the percentage that the global computer and information service trade amount has accounted for in the world's service trade total amount. If the RCA index of one country's computer and information service trade is bigger than 1, it then implies that the country's computer and information service trade shall have the comparative advantage among the international market. In comparison with international market share index, this index eliminated the fluctuation effect of both the country's total amount and the world's total amount.

RCA index can be expressed by:

$$RCA_{ij} = \frac{X_{ij}/X_{tj}}{X_{iw}/X_{tw}},$$

There $X_{ij}$ represents the export value of product $i$ from the $j$-th country, $X_{ij}$ represents the total export amount of the $j$-th country, $X_{iw}$ represents the total world export amount of the product i, $X_{tw}$ represents the total world export amount.

From diagram 9, it can be seen that the RCA index of China's computer and information service trade was always less than 1 but always with the increasing trend, from 2010 till now its RCA index is always beyond 1, it can be seen that the competitive advantage of China's computer and information service trade in international market was increasingly strengthened, among the international comparison, the RCA index basically reflects the same conclusion with the TC index, the RCA index of the traditional information service powerful countries such as India and Ireland are always keeping the level above 5, the RCA index of China's computer and information service shall be at the "second echelon" and still has some differences with India and Ireland. This reflects that China's computer and information service industry may have certain comparative advantage, but shall not be at the absolute superiority among the international trade pattern.

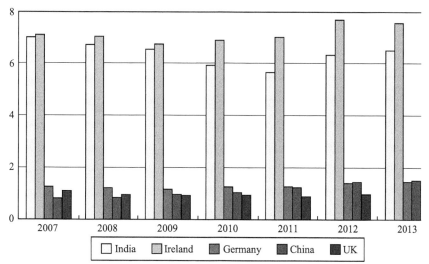

**Fig. 9  the international comparison on RCA index of the computer and information service trade in different countries**

Data source: the LIN international trade center with processing and finishing.

1.3.4    the evaluation and analysis on the export potentials of China's computer and information service trade

(1) The calculation method for export potential index.

According to technical content to calculate the export income index, then set up the model for relative export potentials of the computer and information service trade, to test and evaluate the relative benefits China's computer and information service industry may gain from the international  computer and information service market.

First of all, to determine the revealed competitive advantage index of each country's computer and information service trade.

$$RCA = \frac{X_i \left/ \sum_{i=1}^{m} X_i \right.}{\sum_{i=1}^{n} X_{ij} \left/ \sum_{i=1}^{n}\sum_{j=1}^{m} X_{ij} \right.}$$

There $\sum_{i=1}^{m} X_{ij}$ is the total export amount of the $m$ kinds services in the $i$-th economic entity;

$\sum_{i=1}^{n} X_{ij}$ 为 is the total export amount of the $j$-th service among the $n$ economic entities; $\sum_{i=1}^{n}\sum_{j=1}^{m}$

$X_{ij}$ is the total export amount of the $m$ kinds of services in the $n$ economic entities.

Secondly, to determine the value of revealed competitive advantage index after the process with the weight method as following:

$$rca_{ij} = \frac{RCA_{ij}}{\sum_{i=1}^{n} RCA_{ij}}$$

According to export technical content theory, the higher national income, there shall be higher technical content of their exported products, so the export income index of the computer and information service can be expressed as:

$EI_{ij} = r_{ij} \times Y_i$,   There $Y_i$ represents the average national income of such country

Then to calculate the average export income index of the five countries' computer and information service:

$$AEI_{ij} = \sum_{i=1}^{n} \left( \frac{x_j}{X_{nj}} \times EI_{ij} \right)$$

There, $x_j$ is the export amount of the $j$ service in a certain country, $X_{nj}$ is the total service export amount of the $j$ service in the fice countries.

Finally, to estimate the export income share of the certain country in the "five countries" model, that is the distributed relative export benefits, is:

$$F_{ij} = \frac{EI_{ij} \times (x_j/X_{nj})}{AEI_{IJ}} \times 100\%$$

(2) The data and calculation of export potential index.

In this paper, it sets up the "five countries" model of the export potentials, incorporating the five top ranking countries in the world's computer and information service trade export amount, including India, Ireland, Germany, China and UK, the data select interval is between 2007 and 2013. Thereinto, the $rca_{ij}$ can be found in diagram 10 and GNI data can be found in table 2.

Data is taken from ITC the export data statistics of computer and information service trade in each country, and with the calculation.

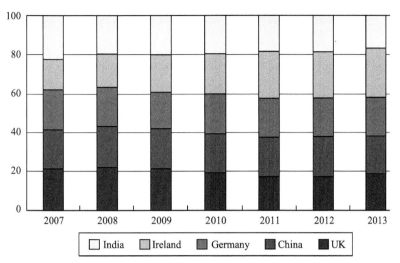

Fig. 10    $rca_{ij}$ data

**Table 2    national income level per capita in each country**

Unit: USD

| Country | GNI | | | | | | |
|---|---|---|---|---|---|---|---|
| | 2007 | 2008 | 2009 | 2010 | 2011 | 2012 | 2013 |
| India | 2480 | 3050 | 3610 | 4240 | 4900 | 5870 | 6710 |
| Ireland | 39440 | 42470 | 42550 | 43300 | 44560 | 46680 | 47240 |
| Germany | 960 | 1050 | 1170 | 1290 | 1450 | 1500 | 1530 |
| China | 44730 | 46010 | 41150 | 38390 | 38140 | 41010 | 42050 |
| UK | 48540 | 49700 | 44680 | 41800 | 39850 | 42160 | 44450 |

Data source: the world bank.

Through calculation it can get the export income shares of the computer and information service trade in each country among the market of computer and information service consisting by those five countries, that is the export potentials of computer and information service of each country. The results can be found in diagram 1.9.

(3) the analysis on the export potential index of China's computer and information service trade.

Through above estimation, from table 1.9 it can be seen that, China's export potential in computer and information service trade has grown up from 0.07% in 2007 to 0.83% in 2013, the relative export potential represents the certain increasing trend, this implies that the export benefits China's computer and information service has gained is continuously increasing, but in comparison with the export potentials of other four countries among the "five countries" model, China still has the large differences. From the perspective of export benefit index, there's asymmetry between the export potentials position and export scale of China's computer and information service trade, from this it can be seen that China shall only be the "big

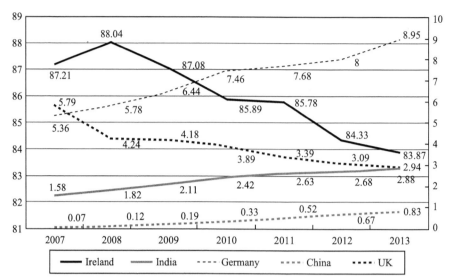

Fig. 11   the relative export potentials for computer and information service trade of each country among the "five country" model.

country" of computer and information service, not the "powerful major" of information service. China's computer and information service industry shall have the differences from the developed countries in the fields such as the core technology etc, thus makes it only depending on the traditional labor resource to expand its market scale, and getting the relatively lower export potentials than other export countries. This shows that the competitive power of China's computer and information service represents the increasing trend but still has the large differences from the development countries in the competitive advantage, meanwhile it also verifies that the HR resource advantage shall be gradually replaced by the technical advantage among the information service and information outsourcing, it may need to further promote the innovation level to increase the export benefits.

## 2. The study on the export potential of computer and information trade

Being the beneficial effects that China's economic and social development could gain from the openness, the research on the computer and information service trade export strategy should comprehensively consider of the influences from each aspect of economy and society. For the computer and information service industry, the openness brings the increase of trade import / export amount, the growth of foreign investment in China and the expansion domestic and abroad information service demand. At the same time, the innovation ability progress made in computer and information service technology also help improving the industrial structure, promote the transformation and upgrade of economic structure; the improvement of information security guarantee level could increase the stable factor for the society; by acquiring the consumer information service rights and benefits, it shall both improve the consumption structure and bring the beneficial factor for improvement of economic structure, and promote the satisfaction of the inhabitants, this shall be helpful for the optimization of social structure. Thus to study the export strategy of the computer and information service trade, it shall select the four aspects as economic growth, demands expansion, technical innovation, and information security for comprehensive consideration.

## 2.1 Economic growth

The economic benefit shall be the basic starting point for economic activities, also the primary aspect for observing the export strategy. To observe the economic strategy of the computer and information service industry in the openness, it shall mainly observe the four indexes as the trade amount, favorable balance, market scale, business income and domestic market cultivation.

2.1.1    With the increasingly growth of trade amount and favorable balance, the overall industrial competitive power has been improved during the openness period

At the beginning of industrial market opening, in a short time the service import increased significantly and there's the obvious deficit in the trade amount, later on, with the increasingly improved opening level, the industrial competitive advantage was emerged accordingly, and the trade amount rose up year by year, the favorable balance of export improved quickly and steadily. From 2001 to 2014, the total import / export amount of China's computer and information service trade has been increased from USD 810 million to USD 26.86 billion, with the expanded total volume by 22 times, the trade surplus has been increased from USD120 million to USD 9.86 billion, already the 82 times than that before the

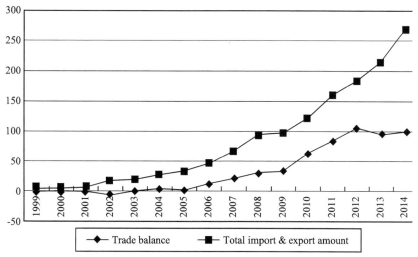

**Fig. 12    the trade amount and balance of China's computer and information service trade from 1999 to 2014**

Data source: the yearbook of China's Commerce.

openness.

Here it takes the trade competitive advantage index (TC index) to measure the overall competitive power of the computer and information service industry. The bigger value means that the production efficiency of such industry is higher than that of international level and has the competitive advantage accordingly. Since 2003 the TC index of China's computer and information service industry is always on the positive range, this is consistent with the time node for opening regional restriction within two years that China's computer and information service industry committed while being approved to join in WTO, it shows that the enterprise's strength has got the progress during the competition, later on during the further deepening process of the openness degree, the trade competitive advantage index continued to enlarge accordingly, the competitive power of China's computer and information service industry has gained the great progress.

2.1.2　　The market scale has been expanded during the openness, to lay the foundation for the accomplishment of the interests for the scale economy

The opened market created the fierce competitive environment, during the process of the domestic market expanding toward the international market, the market range has been expanded and provide the foundation for the accomplishment of the interest for the scale economy. China's computer and information service export are mainly the outsourcing service and built-in system software export. The increasing enlargement of China's offshore service outsourcing market shows that during development in past years, China's software information service industry has been gradually melted in the globalized international division of labor system, under the background that the domestic service outsourcing market still need cultivation, the enlargement of international market scale shall be beneficial to China's computer and information service industry to further explore the space for trade development.

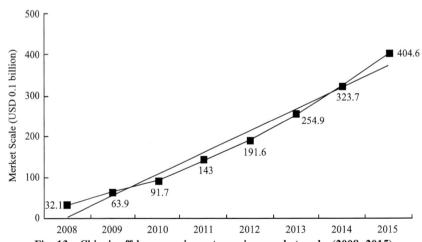

**Fig. 13　China's offshore service outsourcing market scale (2008–2015)**

Date source: International data corporation

2.1.3   The business income increased continuously, the enterprise's economic benefit has been get significant progress after the openness

With the deepening openness degree, the business income of China's software and information outsourcing enterprises kept the continuous increase, it can be represented through the economic benefits directly, the enterprise has got the practical interests during opening toward overseas. In 2014 China's software industry has got the RMB 3005.8 billion business income, with growth by 18.51%, such increasing rate is 16 percentages higher than that of electronics information manufacturing industry. In recent years, the business income growth of China's software and information outsourcing enterprises always keep above 20%. From the information service outsourcing international business income keeping the high growth, it implies that the economic crisis has only limited impact to the industry, the enterprise's economic benefits has got increasing progress during the openness.

To take Huawei Company as the example, since 2002 the Industry and Informatization Ministry and China Software industry association have released the statistical data of the top 100 enterprises with the largest software business income in China, this company always occupied the top rank. The annual software business income of Huawai has been increased from RMB6.22 billion in 2004 to RMB 191.77 billion in 2013, the annual average compound growth rate of software income has reached 36.4%. During the openness toward overseas, the income of China's information technology enterprises has increased steadily.

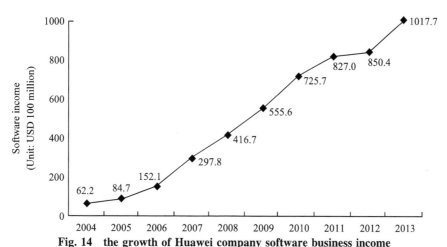

**Fig. 14   the growth of Huawei company software business income**
Data source: Industry and Informatization Ministry, China electronic information yearbook.

2.1.4   Domestic demand has been got expanded rapidly, the industrial openness shall also play the positive role on other fields of national economy

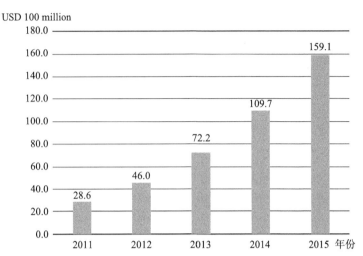

**Fig. 15   the diagram of China offshore service outsourcing market scale**

unit: USD 100 million.

Data Source: International data corporation.

## 2.2   Demands expansion

The openness of computer and information service trade could obviously improve the information service level that Chinese consumer may face to. Through opening the industry, on one hand it can break the deadlock of that the deficient competition among domestic information service departments currently, on the other hand to increase the opportunity for learning advanced technology and experience from the transnational corporation, so as to reduce service price while enriching the service contents, during such process, Chinese consumer shall become the major receiver of those benefits. Here below the consumer benefit is mainly observed through the series indexes such as service price level of such department, service content and service quality etc:

2.2.1    With enlarged market competition, the information service price level did also decrease

For ordinary users in China, the competition induced by the further openness of computer and information service industry shall bring the direct effect - that is the increase of consumer welfare. After the openness, the consumer shall have wider choice options, the market competition may bring more benefits to the consumer. During the industry opening toward overseas, China's information service industry has been experienced the market integration in so many times, the market competition becomes gradually severe. During the industrial competition, China's network speed has been improved gradually, the broadband downloading speed has got the higher ranking among the global market and the matching expenses has also been reduced.

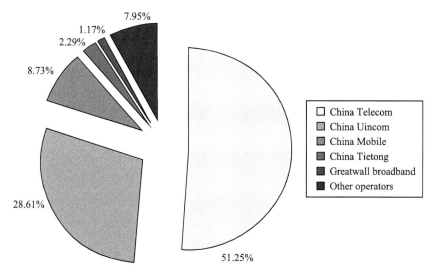

**Fig. 16   the market share of China's major network access providers in 2014**
Data source: China internet data center

2.2.2   With the richer service content and upgrading form and style, the consumer's demand has been got fulfilled

The industry opening enables the service products getting the leaping improvement in quantity, fulfilling the demand of consumer on the information service. The opened market also expands the type of service products to the horizontal extent, satisfies the user's preferences, greatly improves the user's experience feeling of internet information technology, increases the welfare of consumer.

The total amount of China's internet web has increased from the less 4.5 billion in 2006 to the 150 billion in 2013. From 2006 to 2013, the application form of China internet has also generated the huge changes, the internet information service does not only stay on the information access, but also become as the providing means for telecommunication, consumption, entertainment and recreation, the network service means continue to become richer. From the perspective of service content, after the openness, both the content and types of internet information service has been got extremely enriched, to fulfill the consumer's information demand to the great extent.

However, the existing internet management mechanism in China cannot let the foreign enterprises such as Facebook entering in. Consumer cannot make the contact with the world through these tools, without those powerful rivals, domestic information service market still need to enhance the independent R & D capacity, and such situation is also adverse to further improve the information service quality for the consumer.

2.2.3    With improved information service quality, the receiving effect of consumer has been improved accordingly

After the industry opening, the market supervision and industrial regulation have been gradually perfected, the information service quality has also been got the steadily progress. According to the statistics on the results of test performed by state application software products quality supervision and inspection center, in recent years the average first-pass yield of Chinese software has been got increased year by year, from the level about 20% during 2002-2005, rose up to the level about 30% during 2005-2008, and till 2014 this figure has been already risen up to about 50%, in some region and fields it even reached to above 70%. Generally said, the opening toward overseas has brought the welfare to the consumer of China's information service industry. Till now, for Chinese consumer, along with the expanded competition in information service industry market, the price of computer and information service has been reduced and the information service can be reached to more consumers accordingly. After the telecommunication operator's restructuring, the telecommunication and internet service comprehensive price level has declined by 10%. During the opening process, both the content and types of information service has been got enriched, the internet web quantity has been increased at the annual average growth with 79.4%, further fulfill the information demand of the consumer. In addition, the quality of information service has been got improved steadily, the surfing time of netizen has raised by nearly 3 times, there's also the enhancement in the effect of consumer receiving service.

### 2.3    Technical innovation

Technical innovation shall be the powerful driving factor for economic and social development, without the innovative ability it shall not master the development process of future economy. For one country, the independent innovative ability shall be both the important symbol for dividing the economic growth stage, also the crucial factor for determining the future economic growth potentials. One of the important consideration for the country all over the world implementing the policy of opening towards overseas is to fully play the positive effect of technical innovation shall make during the economic and social progress process. The independent innovation shall be the specific expression of export benefits, it also play the deep influence on the export benefits size China may enjoy accordingly. On the technical innovation layer of computer and information service industry during the openness, it mainly observes the three indexes as R & D expenditure, patent application quantity and copyright registration scale accordingly.

2.3.1    Investment on the R & D expenditure increased greatly, technical innovation has been raised on to the strategical height of the corporate development

China has the quite late beginning in the computer and information technology field, its technical level is under the level of Europe and US, the technical development have had to follow up with the information technology leading areas such as the US for a long time. Among the fierce competition after the openness, China's enterprises realized that the technology shall be the lifeline for corporate development, and continued to increase the scientific and technological R & D input so as to improve the corporate competitive power. Such a huge increase implies that the enterprise shall have the enough awareness on the importance of technical innovation from the micro level, especially in internet and information technical service fields, the upgrading of technology shall mean the survival or extinction for a batch of enterprises, the technical innovation has been already raised to the strategical height accordingly.

2.3.2    The patent application quantity has narrowed the gap with the international range, the independent innovation ability has enhanced significantly

Through long-term development, China has got the abundant results in the aspect of the scientific research and development in information technology field. Among the enterprise applying patents in China, even though there still have the large gap of the patent number applied by China's enterprises in comparison with overseas enterprises, but the industrial leading enterprises has approached to the level of the transnational corporation in applied patent quantity. From 2007 to 2014, the patents quantity applied by China's enterprises has been already narrowed with the total patents quantity applied by the transnational corporation in China. The independent innovation ability of China's enterprise has been enhanced significantly, and they have entered into the independent innovation period comprehensively. Although China's enterprises have narrowed the gap gradually with foreign enterprises, but the core part of information technology was still masted by the scientific and technological powers such as US etc, the technical spillover effect shall never bring the leading position of the information technology, the deficiency of the independent innovation ability shall always make the industry being located in the follower position.

2.3.3    The patent application in information industry field accounted for the major ratio, with high innovation degree, this shall be the important motive force for China's economic development

The information technology field shall be the place gathering the most active technical innovations and fast accumulation of patents in China, it's also the worthy high-tech industry with intensive knowledge and technology. In 2006, the patent application in information technology field has accounted for 32.24% of the total applied patents quantity, with the annual average growth rate at 23.67%, it's much higher than the average growth of all applied patents quantity in 18.11%. In addition, for the invention patent aspect that can mostly reflect the innovation degree, the invention patents of information industry has occupied 42.14% ratio among all the invention patents.

Taken together, China's information service industry has got the significantly increased technical independent innovation ability during the opening toward overseas. In technical innovation field, China's computer and information service industry has got extremely significant contrast before and after the openness, the investment of R & D expenditure represents the increasing trends by multiple times, the software and information technological service industry has got the growth rate by 785.6%.

### 2.4　Information security

In a short period, information security risk shall be the certain hidden danger of safety existed in the openness toward overseas of computer and information service trade, in a long period, the ability to handle with information security risk and guarantee the construction of information security shall improve the comprehensive strength of one country's information security, the improvement of the national information security comprehensive strength can be regarded as one of the important export interests. In this paper, the so-called information security mainly include two aspects as the network space security and public security.

China government has continued increasing its ability for handling network information public security. The network information public security refers to the ability that the government may handle with social unsteady factors caused by the network and create the positive and harmonious social circumstance. During China's information service industry opening and gradually improved technology level, the government departments at all levels have improved their ability to deal with public security risk significantly. In the statement that the general secretary Xi Jinping have made to the third plenary of 18th session referring to the *decision of CPC central committee made about several important problems on fully deepening the reform*, it especially emphasized the particular significance of the internet security. The central committee has set up the leading team for network security and informatization, the general secretary Xi Jinping assumed the leading role of such team personally, this reflects that the central committee has incorporated the information security into national overall reform strategy, and took information security, society harmony and national stability as a whole for integrated consideration. As the government departments of China in each level has gradually perfected the information security system and policy, there shall be the solid guarantee for handling with the public security risk caused by the network.

Generally, only the continuously opening could handle with the information security risk that the information service industry may face to. Although with the opening process of internet information service, it may increase the risk of network space security and public security accordingly, but expanding the openness should still be the only one mean to reduce the security cost and gain the export benefits. The globalization and informatization should be the future trend of the world, to set seclusion in information field can only increase national future security risk. To steadily expand the openness degree, positively promote technology progress, improve management level, these shall be the only way during the information service industry achieving the export benefits. Now the information service industry is just integrating relative constitutional functions with the authorities, to form the joint-force of internet management both from the technology to the content, from daily security to beating criminals, to significantly enhance the guarantee ability for network information security.

## 3. summary for the export strategy of information service trade

The reform and openness shall be the fundamental guarantee for China gaining the splendid achievement during past 30 years nearly, only continuing the opening and catching up with the trend of informatization and globalization can help seizing the opportunity of economic and social development. In general, during the process of opening toward overseas, the computer and information service industry has got the huge export benefits, but there still have the certain space to open then.

### 3.1    To continue the openness shall be the prerequisite for keeping industrial fast development

The opened industry brings the funds and technology, the computer and information service industry has also experienced the adjusting, integrating and exceeding period during such process. Since the opening toward overseas, both the domestic and international market scale of China's computer and information service industry has been expanded by multiple times, the trade amount of information service industry also got rapid growth, the overall business income kept the growth in high speed, its growth is much high than that of manufacturing industry in the same category. Local enterprises have continued to increase the R & D input, absorb and transform the advanced technology, so as to enable the industrial overall competitive power getting improved during the openness. In addition, the information service enterprises shall have even clear division during the openness, the industrial value chain has been developed from the dispersed chain into the closed loop recycle structure, the structure was becoming more complete. The rapid development of such industry cannot be without the opening toward overseas, to expand the opening toward overseas could bring the significant benefits.

### 3.2    The opening toward overseas drives the convergence of industries, the public attribution of information service industry has been highlighted accordingly

The opened industry expanded the market of information service industry, also accelerated the change of information service industry type. Besides being the carrier for other service, the information service industry also created the fresh business form during the integrating process, this more expressed the limitation of industrial classification. By integrating with the distribution service, the information service industry formed the brand new industry-E-commerce; by integrating with financial service, the information service industry given the birth of internet financial industry. The information service industry did also expand to other fields such as manufacturing industry, focusing on its core business. Among the informatization tide, the information service industry has gradually expanded into further more fields, has became the important foundation for society and economy.

From the social significance, the information resource should be such a semi-public article, the information service shall have the public attribution. Its public attribution was distinctly expressed in that being the objective risk of information service industry, the information security threat shall concern to social stability, the public security shall be the important aspect of information security. Among the opening toward overseas, the technical level of information service industry has been got great progress, the relative policies of administrative authorities have also been perfected gradually, only with the continuously opening toward overseas, the information security shall have the fundamental guarantee.

### 3.3　There still be quite large opening space for industry, the information service industry shall have the huge potentials for further opening

For the aspects of national treatment and the permission of foreign investment, China's information service industry shall also have great opening space. Although China's information service enterprises have got the rapid development, but in comparison with foreign same industry there is still the certain gap. The 100 domestic top stronger companies shall also have the significant differences from those world 100 top strongest companies, the limited openness could temporarily protect the immediate interests of those enterprises, but this shall be adverse to improve the enterprise's competitive power. The information service demand in domestic market shall be released during the openness, the development of information service enterprises shall also mutually promote the expansion of market demand, these shall be expressed as the booming development of outsourcing market. That is to say, the expansion of domestic demand shall have the positive effect for the improvement of China;s public service quality and the transformation of governmental function. In addition, further opening shall benefit to promote the primary telecommunication service etc reducing the expenses, improving the quality, so as to bring more benefits to the consumer. After expanded the opening, it shall further mine the export benefit space of the information service.

（Hui Rui, Master，Foreign Economic and Trade International Financial Research Center of the China Academy of Social Sciences; Doctor Qiu Ying, assistant professor of Jiangxi University of Finance and Economics）

# Research on the Path and Strategy Integrating China's Trade in Distribution Services into the International Market

## 1. Analysis of the International Competitiveness of China's Trade in Distribution Services

### 1.1    Analysis of the Industrial International Competitiveness of China's Trade in Distribution Services

1.1.1    Stable increasing of foreign direct investment

After the financial crisis in 2008, the net amount and stock of foreign direct investment of the Chinese wholesale and retail industries has been increasing in a stable manner, which demonstrates that the foreign capital output performance of China's trade in distribution services has been intensified. As shown in Table 1, the net amount and stock of foreign direct investment of China's wholesale and retail industries in 2009 reached 6.136 billion USD and 35.695 billion USD, respectively and reached 18.291 billion USD and 102.957 billion USD in 2014, respectively, 2.98 and 2.88 times those in 2009, respectively Of which, the investment stock was more than 100 billion USD, and ranked No. 4 of all industries. The growth of foreign direct investments in China's wholesale and retail industries is sound. In the year 2014, the flow and stock of foreign direct investments increased by 18.6% and 23.0%, respectively. The continuous growth and complementarity of overseas investment flow and stock of wholesale and retail industries demonstrate that the industrial competitiveness of China's trade in distribution services has been improved. Of all non-financial foreign direct investments, the ratios of wholesale and retail industries are very high, kept above 10% from 2009 to 2014, and

**Table 1    Net Amount and Stock of Foreign Direct Investments in China's Wholesale and Retail Industries**                                    Unit: 100 million USD

| Year | 2009 | 2010 | 2011 | 2012 | 2013 | 2014 |
| --- | --- | --- | --- | --- | --- | --- |
| Net amount of foreign direct investments in wholesale and retail industries | 61.36 | 67.29 | 103.24 | 130.49 | 146.47 | 182.91 |
| Stock of foreign direct investments in wholesale and retail industries | 356.95 | 420.06 | 490.94 | 682.12 | 876.48 | 1029.57 |

Data source: National Bureau of Statistics.

reached 17.1% in 2014. The distribution service industry plays a key role in China's foreign investments, it is the most active sector of foreign direct investments, and it shows a continuously intensified industrial international competitiveness of China's trade in distribution services.

### 1.1.2   Centralized foreign direct investment areas

China's foreign direct investments are scattered in almost 80% of the countries and regions in the world, but the invested areas are concentrated. The foreign investments in wholesale and retail industries show the same features. In the year 2014, over 80% of the investments flowed into Hong Kong, and then into ASEAN, Europe, America, Russia and other countries and regions. It can be seen that the foreign direct investments in China's wholesale and retail industries is mainly scattered in Asia, and Hong Kong gathered the most foreign direct investments in China's wholesale and retail industries, and it is a major area for investment. The foreign investment scale of China's distribution services has gradually increased, the invested area is wide, and it is mainly scattered around Asia. Although investments in European and American countries have expanded, the ratio is still low. The contrast between the unbalance of investment areas and the increasing investment scale means that the international competitiveness of China's trade in distribution services has much room for improvement.

### 1.2   Analysis of the Corporate International Competitiveness of China's Trade in Distribution Services

#### 1.2.1   Relatively small scale of domestic distribution enterprises

Domestic distributors make themselves larger by M&A and O2O, and realize local expansion, but they are relatively small and decentralized on the market. In view of a global comparison, according to the report entitled *Global Powers of Retailing 2015*, jointly issued by DTT and STORES Media, there are only 8 retailers from Mainland China listed in the Top 250 largest retailers, including Suning, GOME Electrical Appliances, Shanghai Friendship Group, JD.COM, Dashang Group, Chongqing Department Store, NGS Supermarket and Yonghui Supermarket. It can be seen that, on the global retailing markets, the total scale of Chinese retailing enterprises is relatively small. In terms of sales, in the year 2014, the sales of GOME Electrical Appliances were 143.5 billion yuan, ranking No. 1 of the Top 100 retailing enterprises in China; however, the scale is only 1/20 of Wal-Mart. The total sales of the Top 100 retailing enterprises in China in 2014 was 2.1 trillion yuan, only approximately 70% of the total sales of Wal-Mart. Table 2 lists the comparison in strength of domestic and foreign large-sized retailing enterprises in 2014. We can see that the scale of domestic distribution enterprises was relatively small, the average proceeds of the stores was relatively low, and further intensification of the international competitiveness of China's distribution enterprises was limited.

**Table 2  Comparison of the Strength of Domestic and Foreign Retailing Enterprises in 2014**

|  | Wal-Mart | Wal-Mart (China) | Gome Group | Suning Commerce |
|---|---|---|---|---|
| Number of stores | 10942 | 411 | 1698 | 1696 |
| Sales (100 million yuan including tax) | 28842 | 724 | 1435 | 1428 |
| Average sales of stores(100 million yuan including tax) | 2.64 | 1.76 | 0.85 | 0.84 |
| Ranking | World Retailing Top 100 No. 1 | China Chain Store Top 100 No. 5 | China Chain Store Top 100 No.1 | China Chain Store Top 100 No.2 |

Data source: data of Suning Appliance Group, Gome Group and Wal-Mart (China) is from the China Chain Store & Franchise Association. Data of Wal-Mart is from the Company's annual report; the middle rate for exchange of USD on December 31, 2013 was 1 USD=6.0969 CNY.

### 1.2.2    The weak cross-border business capacity of the distribution enterprises

At present, there are several ways that domestic distribution enterprises can enter into international markets: first, small-sized retailing enterprises can "go global", such as Beijing Tongrentang; second, petty commodities wholesale and retail enterprises are represented by the Yiwu Mode; third, the distribution business can be carried out by large-sized state-owned enterprises in their transnational diversification, such as the distribution business carried out by CNPC and Sinopec in overseas countries. Although domestic enterprises attach great importance to international business more and more, there are no typical enterprises with a relatively large scale in China, and cross-border business performance is even inferior. According to data from *Global Powers of Retailing 2014*, the Top 250 enterprises enter the markets of 10 countries and regions on average, and the number of countries and regions entered by the Top 3 enterprises in China Suning, GOME and Shanghai Friendship are 3, 3 and 1, and the number of countries and regions entered by Wal-Mart, TESCO, Carrefour and Metro are 28, 13, 31 and 32. The international market exploration by China's retailing tycoons is not only much lower than that of international retailing tycoons, but also is lower than the average level of the Top-250 retailing enterprises worldwide. Retailing proceeds of the Top 250 retailing enterprises from the overseas market account for 24.3% of the total proceeds on average, and international proceeds of China's retailing enterprises are very few and do not reach this level. It can be concluded that domestic distribution enterprises should further reinforce international competitiveness and combine into an international market better.

In summary, in terms of the industrial tier, the flow and stock of foreign direct investments in China's trade in distribution  services are continuously increasing, the international market is expanding, international competitiveness is enhanced, but mainly distributed around Hong Kong, and the competitiveness of domestic distribution enterprises in developed countries should be reinforced; in terms of enterprise, China has no large distribution enterprises "going global" successfully. The scale of domestic distribution enterprises is relatively small, internationalized business is low, and it seriously restricts the improvement of the international competitiveness of domestic distribution enterprises.

## 2. New Commercial Activity of Trade in Distribution Services – Cross–border E–commerce

With economic development, the fierceness of competition and the improvement of orientation towards technology, information and a network of distribution services, the new commercial activity in distribution service-E-commerce-was born. Cross-border E-commerce is an innovation of the conventional distribution and trade modes, it has become a key mode for the exportation and importation of distribution services and it has promoted a continuous increase in proceeds from the exportation of distribution services. Due to low transaction costs and breaking through restrictions in time and space, E-commerce causes a great impact on the conventional distribution industry. E-commerce is the inevitable trend in the revolution of the distribution system. Against the background of a slow-down in the growth of foreign trade in China, cross-border E-commerce has become a new developmental approach for promoting China's foreign trade. According to a monitoring report by the China E-business Research Center, the scale of transactions in China's cross-border E-commerce in 2014 reached 4.2 trillion yuan, an increase of 33.3% compared with the same period of the previous year, much higher than the 3.4% growth of conventional foreign trade in the same period. Cross-border E-commerce will become the new point of growth for China's foreign trade exportation and the bridgehead for opening up to the outside world on the part of distribution services.

### 2.1 Current Developmental Situations of China's Cross–border E–commerce

2.1.1 Cross-border E-commerce boosts growth

As shown in Table 3, the scale of transactions in China's cross-border E-commerce is increasing, and it reached 4.2 trillion yuan in 2014, approximately 4 times that of 2010. The total importation and exportation of goods in China in 2014 increased by 2.3% , and cross-border E-commerce transactions increased by 33.3% . Against the background of a slow-down in the growth of conventional foreign trade, E-commerce has boosted the growth of China's foreign trade. From 2010 to 2014, the ratio of cross-border E-commerce to the total import and export of goods increased and reached 15.91% in 2014. Such a ratio will continue increasing under the rapid development of cross-border E-commerce, which plays a key role in foreign trade in China.

Part V   Research on Hot Issues in the Fields of Trade in Services

**Table 3   The Scale of Transactions and Total Imports and Exports of China's Cross–border E–commerce**

| Year | 2010 | 2011 | 2012 | 2013 | 2014 |
|---|---|---|---|---|---|
| Scale of transactions of the cross-border E-commerce market (trillion yuan) | 1.1 | 1.7 | 2.1 | 3.15 | 4.2 |
| China's total imports and exports (trillion yuan) | 20.2 | 23.6 | 24.4 | 25.8 | 26.4 |
| Ratio (%) | 5.45 | 7.20 | 8.61 | 12.21 | 15.91 |

Data source: National Bureau of Statistics, the China E-business Research Center

2.1.2   Change in the export and import structure of cross-border E-commerce

Seen from Figure 1, the import and export structure of cross-border E-commerce has changed slowly. From 2010 to 2014, exports account for more than 80%, but the ratio of exports decreased slowly, and ratio of imports increased slowly. When the export and import structure changes slowly, the cross-border E-commerce becomes a key component of the distribution services. In terms of imports, the scale of the transactions of overseas purchasing on behalf of other users reached 74.4 billion yuan in 2013 and exceeded 100 billion yuan in 2014; in terms of exports, the research results show that, by the year 2018, online shopping requirements for commodities from China by America, the U.K., Germany, Australia and Brazil will have reached 144 billion yuan. Powerful domestic and overseas requirements on cross-border E-commerce show that cross-border E-commerce will play a key role in the process of distribution services being combined on the international market.

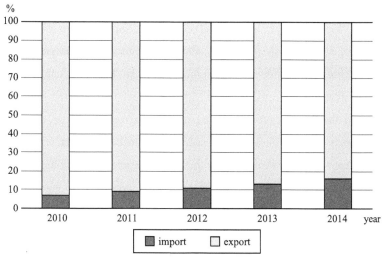

**Fig. 1   The Import and Export Structure of China's Cross–border E–commerce**

Data source: the China E-business Research Center

2.1.3   The expanding corporate scale of cross-border E-commerce

With increasing development of cross-border E-commerce, more and more enterprises focus on cross-border E-commerce. According to data by the Ministry of Commerce, the number of enterprises for cross-border E-commerce in 2014 was more than 200,000, and the number of platform enterprises was more than 5,000. The number of cross-border E-commerce enterprises is increasing, the scale is expanding, and the mode has been innovated. In terms of exports, Osell launched the "cross-border O2O" program to enter the offline wedding photography market into Russia, and it has covered over 500 wedding photography stores. In terms of imports, developing the cross-border E-commerce as a free-trade zone and a bonded area, etc., such as Tmall International "bonded import+ direct overseas mailing", Suning overseas shopping "self-operating+ business attraction" and JD's overseas shopping "self-operating not a platform operation". With the intensification of the enterprise layout and continuous mode innovation, cross-border E-commerce will continue developing.

2.1.4　Developmental opportunities for cross-border E-commerce

Prosperous development of cross-border E-commerce is benefited from advantageous policies in China. In the year 2012, the Ministry of Industry and Information issued the *"Twelfth Five-Year Plan" for E-commerce*, which encouraged large enterprises to go global if permitted by conditions, to challenge the global resource market and to actively carry out cross-border E-commerce, and issue network invoices, inspection and quarantine and other supporting policies; in August, 2013, the Ministry of Commerce and other authorities issued the *Notice on the Implementation of Policies Supporting Cross-border E-commerce Retailing Exports* and proposed 6 supporting measures, including establishing a new customs supervision mode for exports in E-commerce and making specific statistics to solve the statistic problem of customs supervision in retailing exports. Meanwhile, four pilot cities—Shanghai, Chongqing, Hangzhou and Ningbo—have started to establish a cross-border E-commerce platform; in the year 2014, the Ministry of Finance and the State Administration of Taxation issued the *Notice on Tax Collection for Cross-border E-commerce Retailing Exportation* to clarify tax discounts on cross-border retailing exports; in the year 2014, the General Administration of Customs issued the *Announcement on Supervision over Inward and Outward Goods and Articles for Cross-border E-commerce to* specify the supervision for cross-border E-commerce by customs officials. During the NPC and the CPPCC in 2015, Premier Li Keqiang proposed the "Internet+" action plan, and emphasized the development of E-commerce and the expansion of pilot projects of E-commerce. Competent state authorities issued opinions and methods to promote or standardize the development of E-commerce. Benefited by policies, the development of cross-border E-commerce is prosperous.

## 2.2   Restrictive Factors for the Development of Cross-border E-commerce in China

E-commerce is a collection of business flow, information flow, capital flow and logistics to reduce transaction costs and increase transaction efficiency. Due to the development of domestic E-commerce advantageous in laws, market, currency etc., transactions are smooth. Cross-border E-commerce challenges many restrictive factors such as policy, law, currency and practice. The existing restrictive factors of E-commerce will be analyzed as the first step in solving the bottleneck to the development of E-commerce and promoting the development of cross-border E-commerce.

(1) Commodity flow, namely the commodity flow for transactions between the E-commerce platform and the consumer. Cross-border E-commerce faces overseas consumers, and the first major restrictive factor is the language barrier, which reduces the number of consumer groups and reduces consumption. "Cross-border" means that the consumer group will be changed, with changes in consumption habits and philosophies. Cross-border faces risks of culture discount. If cross-border E-commerce cannot satisfy the consumption philosophy and consumption habit of its consumers, sales cannot be increased, and cross-border E-commerce will have little significance.

(2) Information flow, namely information communication between the E-commerce platform and the supplier. The E-commerce platform exhibits the commodity information of a supplier to achieve sales. The E-commerce platform does not provide services free of charge, and it relates to the profit mode of E-commerce. The main profit modes in China include the membership fee mode, the transaction commission mode, the product price difference mode, outcome-based payment, etc. Cross-border E-commerce means increasing costs. If the correct mode cannot be achieved, the E-commerce mode may suffer from losses.

(3) Logistics, namely the transportation of the commodity. The development of domestic E-commerce is affected by outdated logistics methods, and the final outcome of cross-border E-commerce is the cross-border transfer of the commodity, which increases the difficulties of international logistics. Cross-border E-commerce satisfies small-batch foreign trade requirements with frequent orders and small amounts per order, which inhibit activity for logistics enterprises' involving E-commerce. Many logistics companies only take commodity transportation of E-commerce as an auxiliary business. China cross-border logistics include airway package, mailing and express service, without logistics companies exclusively serving cross-border E-commerce. It increases logistics costs and restricts the development of cross-border E-commerce.

(4) Capital flow, namely the process by which consumers pay, is a key link in cross-border E-commerce and the core step for realizing commodity value. The security of payment

in E-commerce is the major factor restricting the development of E-commerce. The disclosure of information in E-commerce payment may cause great losses to customers. In addition, the development of a third party's payment platform in China falls behind, payment in cross-border E-commerce is monopolized by foreign-funded organizations, and impairs the competitiveness of cross-border E-commerce in China.

For the purpose of protecting the domestic enterprises' interests, some countries restrict the development of cross-border E-commerce. Conflicts among different state policies and laws limit the development of E-commerce. International codes on cross-border E-commerce are unavailable worldwide, development and codes of cross-border E-commerce vary, and risks of return and unavailability of professional talents are disadvantageous factors for this kind of commerce.

### 2.3 Trade in Computer and Information Services

Of the 12 categories of China's trade in services, trade in computer information services and distribution trade in services are key components. Since the year 2014, the environment of distribution service enterprises in China has involved many changes, and cross-border E-commerce is a kind of new commercial activity of the distribution services. The overseas warehouse is the innovation of E-commerce in exclusive line logistics; it provides solutions for overseas express delivery, precise overseas stock management, flexible sales strategies and decision-making support, while also enhancing customers' experiences. The rising overseas warehouse in the past several years has been regarded as the "solution" for logistics by many people. The total costs of logistics for overseas warehouses are relatively low, making E-commerce customers obtain rapid logistics with low costs. The disadvantages include warehouse management, warehousing leasing and fund circulation, and selection for warehousing products. The unavailability of an "overseas warehouse" has a great impact on cross-border E-commerce, and an increase in the scale of operations in cross-border E-commerce needs the cooperation of an "overseas warehouse"; the major reasons are:

(1) An "overseas warehouse" solves many difficulties of cross-border logistics and affords an excellent shopping experience to customers. Direct local shipping from an overseas warehouse reduces delivery time; use of local logistics can provide online delivery status to obtain full-course tracking; the first phase of the overseas warehouse is the conventional foreign trade logistics, customs clearance is operated according to the usual process to remove customs clearance barriers; the local transfer process reduces the fees for damaged package loss; the overseas warehouse stores kinds of commodities and articles that can be returned easily. It can be concluded that the "overseas warehouse" eliminates almost all of the difficulties in cross-border logistics.

(2) The "overseas warehouse" expands coverage of transported articles and reduces

Part V    Research on Hot Issues in the Fields of Trade in Services

logistics costs. Small mailing packages and exclusive international logistics restrict the weight and volume of transported articles, and many large articles and valuable articles can be delivered by international express. The birth of the overseas warehouse breaks through restrictions on weight, volume and value, and makes prices lower than those of international express.

(3) The "overseas warehouse" increases sales. The overseas warehouse overcomes difficulties of cross-border logistics, brings customers a better shopping experience, encourages more consumers to buy a second time and increases sales. The warehousing service experiment in the U.K. surveyed and researched Chinese sellers, and the results show that sellers with an overseas warehouse receive increased browsing count, better sales prices, an increased quantity of sold items, better total sales and transaction rates, etc.

(4) The "overseas warehouse" avoids freight in busy seasons. Because of consumption habits and holidays in different countries, customs clearance costs and transporting costs are subject to time and season. The birth of the overseas warehouse avoids risks of high transporting costs in busy seasons. Meanwhile, based on the customs policies, the articles are assembled or disassembled to avoid tariffs and to reduce costs.

(5) The "overseas warehouse" helps slow sellers in China to "go global". In past development, the domestic market for many labor-intensive products and the products causing "great pollution" in their production were complete, and a lot of stocks and slow sellers had to seek new markets; examples of such products with the above characteristics are heavy tiles and tires. The layout of the overseas warehouse solves the difficulties. The "overseas warehouse" in Germany cooperates with the local Carrefour, and has solved the problem of excessive production capacity of tiles and sanitary ware in Foshan.

Seen from the above analysis, the overseas warehouse overcomes difficulties in cross-border logistics, expands the varieties of transported articles, reduces logistics costs and is beneficial for increasing sales. As a new mode for cross-border electronic business, the overseas warehouse supplements and promotes E-commerce, and plays an active role in China's foreign trade.

### 2.4   Suggestions for the Development of Cross-border E-commerce in China

Accelerating the development of cross-border E-commerce means solving the disadvantages in commodity flow, information flow, logistics and capital flow, promoting the circulation of various elements, and guaranteeing smooth cross-border transactions.

2.4.1   Increase service-based proceeds

The main profit modes in China include the membership fee mode, the transaction commission mode, the product price difference mode and the outcome-based payment mode; these modes are risky, such as sunk costs from a forecast outcome that was not achieved, reduced revenue because of reduced members and compressed product prices due to severe competition. Therefore, cross-border E-commerce adheres to diversified business profit modes on a long-term basis. First, focus on miscellaneous service income, such as advertisements and technology services. At present, miscellaneous service income has become a major source of profits in E-commerce, such as Amazon advertisements and cloud computing. Second, attach great importance to Internet financial services. With the advantage of the Internet, provide financing for medium and small-sized enterprises, which would create proceeds and reinforce both parties' business relations. Finally, powerful enterprises can develop a third party's business to create proceeds, such as a payment platform, logistics and transporting.

### 2.4.2   Perfect international logistics system

The logistics industry is a necessary support for the development of cross-border E-commerce. The outdated development of international logistics seriously restricts the development of cross-border E-commerce. International small package and express delivery are choices for most E-commerce operators and these methods increase costs for cross-border E-commerce operators, so providing special services to cross-border E-commerce operators is urgently needed. Due to extensive coverage and risks of cross-border services, average logistics enterprises are unable to get involved. So the government could set up special international logistics companies that serve cross-border E-commerce. This practice is exercised by contracting professional logistics companies and it is supervised by the government to attain financial revenue. By application of the government's contribution, the logistics company's operation and separation of ownership and operation, the cross-border E-commerce operators can obtain freight advantages at lower costs. In addition, powerful E-commerce operators intensify the construction of overseas warehousing, reinforce cooperation with local logistics enterprises, advance localized operations, avoid trade barriers and achieve global resource integration.

### 2.4.3   Advance construction of a cross-border payment platform

The cross-border payment platform is significant for cross-border E-commerce. China's cross-border E-commerce started quite recently and the development of its cross-border payment platform is outdated, disadvantageous to the development of cross-border E-commerce operators. China should cultivate local third party's payment platforms, and the government should provide more support for the cross-border E-commerce payment platform, that is support in terms of policy and technology, integration of bank resources, and the formation of coordinated development of a third party's payment platform and bank system. Meanwhile, there should be an acceleration of building a payment management system for cross-border E-commerce and supervision over cross-border fund circulation should be reinforced to ensure that cross-border funds are operated as usual and smoothly.

### 2.4.4    Produce the function of policy support

Policy support is a powerful backup force for the development of distribution enterprises. The government should reinforce its strength in negotiating with developed countries, reduce restrictions from technology barriers, green barriers and other non-tariff barriers, and China's cross-border E-commerce should be treated equally. In practice, many problems of cross-border E-commerce are produced by different policies, different laws and different trade practices. The Ministry of Commerce, the Ministry of Industry and Information, the General Administration of Customs, the General Administration of Quality Supervision, Inspection and Quarantine, the State Administration of Foreign Exchange and other functional departments should reinforce coordination, increase customs clearance efficiency, provide fund support and provide high-quality public services for cross-border E-commerce.

### 2.4.5    Improve brand competitiveness

Cross-border E-commerce sells made-in-China products. The quality of the products must be assured in order to maintain the image of "made-in-China" and reduce risks of goods return. In conventional foreign trade, the prices of products made in China are low, but the quality is frequently very bad, and cross-border E-commerce is also of made-in-China and will encounter the same problems. As cross-border E-commerce is just at its beginning, it should avoid false products and provide high-quality products at the beginning, so as to establish sound brand images.

### 2.4.6    Establish a linking mechanism between talents and practice

What cross-border E-commerce needs are all-round talents covering E-commerce, international trade and foreign languages. The setup of E-commerce specialty should improve practical skills and train the ability to convert knowledge into a productive force, and focus on training comprehensive quality and innovation awareness. The majority of E-commerce businesses should establish talent training standards for talents who have the same professional basis but in different fields of skills, to meet various requirements of E-commerce in technology-based talents, business-based talents and all-round talents. Simultaneously, advanced overseas educational institutes could be brought into play in order to learn from advanced educational methods. Reinforce training of cross-border E-commerce talents and inject new forces for development of E-commerce are other important actions to be taken.

With the improvement of information technology proficiency, the world's distribution field has been changed significantly, and the key to distribution enterprise competition has been converted from price competition to competition in business modes, service, logistics, technology and information. Cross-border E-commerce has developed rapidly against this background. China's E-commerce enterprises have developed rapidly, and some large-sized cross-border E-commerce operators have been trained to provide forces for the exportation of

China's distribution services.

## 3. Formulation of an Export Strategy for China's Trade in Distribution Services

### 3.1    Medium and Long–Term Modes of China's Distribution Services Enterprises

According to the requirements and conditions of distribution enterprises in China, there are six "going global" modes available:

(1) The "going global" developmental mode for China distribution enterprises' acquiring a share of the market. China distribution enterprises expand their market shares in order to pursue economic benefits. When the domestic market is full and/or is restricted by anti-monopoly laws, China distribution enterprises need to explore overseas markets and obtain new market shares. The principle means to do this include sales through brokerage, self-built sales channels, acquiring foreign brands and channels, joint ventures or cooperating with foreign businessmen. Foreign trade is easily affected by non-tariff barriers, anti-dumping investigations and friction from trade surplus. Direct investment in establishing factories for local production and sales increases labor employment and taxes, and could be treated as more popular local enterprises. Many China distribution enterprises as OEM for foreign businessmen or China distribution enterprises selling via foreign agents obtain few profits. To receive high profits in sales and get closer to overseas customers, they usually choose to extend the downstream sales. Product source modes in cross-border E-commerce could be developed diversely, and advantageous resources of markets in all tiers could be fully utilized to increase the distribution profits of product localization.

(2) The "going global" developmental mode for China distribution enterprises to acquire technology. In earlier times, many Chinese manufacturing industries processed and assembled for European and American companies who provided drawings and equipment, Chinese enterprises provided labor forces and workshops; technology research and development were controlled by European and American companies. According to the strategy of "market exchange for technology", many enterprises are on the route towards introduction, learning, assimilation and re-innovation. The road has not been very successful. Because many foreign businesses only transferred outdated technology and the most advanced technology and R&D were controlled by themselves, Chinese enterprises always fell behind and were on the road towards introduction, learning, assimilation and re-introduction. It did not change the capability for powerful copying and weak research. The financial crisis made enterprises in many countries get into economic difficulties, so it is a good chance for China distribution enterprises to implement the "going global" strategy via cross-border E-commerce and the "bringing in" strategy. While China distribution enterprises are establishing their own network

platform, they consider acquiring foreign businesses' offline distribution management philosophies, localized distribution networks, production qualifications of special industries, acquiring and merging technology patents and R&D departments, or jointly establishing R&D institutes with foreign businesses, and improving China's R&D performance in some industries.

(3) The "going global" developmental mode for China distribution enterprises to acquire resources. Overseas resource development is a hot spot for foreign investments by China distribution enterprises. China has become the plant of the world. Regardless of satisfying or not domestic requirements or overseas requirements, domestic requirements are not sufficient, and they face increasingly serious environmental pressure and raw material price fluctuations on the international market. By developing the energy enterprises of cross-border E-commerce, in particular, energy and mineral development and raw material processing, China's enterprises should focus on developing, utilizing and controlling overseas mineral resources. At present, the world's high-quality mineral resources are controlled by the Western energy mineral tycoons. They administer international energy and mineral prices and obtain extra profits, and Chinese energy and mineral enterprises are always exploited by them. Besides, energy and mineral resources are regarded as strategic resources and are controlled by countries. So Chinese enterprises have to develop resources in remote, poverty-stricken countries and in countries experiencing social unrest, where development is difficult and risky. Cross-border E-commerce can use the network platform on a barter basis to exchange strategic resource products of other countries with small Chinese commodities, to attain the whole products by importing part-by-part.

(4) The "going global" developmental mode for China distribution enterprises to exert their competitive advantages. China distribution enterprises have products with "intermediate technological advantages", "low-cost and skillful labor advantages" and "capital advantages". Intermediate technology is suitable for developing countries and is cheap. Through copying and innovating, Chinese enterprises have mastered a lot of intermediate technologies in general manufacturing fields. Through cross-border E-commerce, the "intermediate technology advantage" of Chinese enterprises is transferred to developing countries, it can extend the service cycle of product technology and obtain more profits. Chinese laborers are skillful, experienced, endure hardships and receive low salaries. In particular, in project construction, they have experienced many world-class projects, and have learned the design, construction, management and operations of large complicated projects; moreover, they have a "low-cost labor advantage" compared with European and American companies, a "skillful labor advantage" compared with developing countries, and they are powerful forces in international project contracting. The future mode of cross-border E-commerce will be

changed from product output to project technology output.

(5) The "going global" developmental mode for the industrial upgrading of China distribution enterprises. At present, on the chain of multinational corporations, due to cheap and high-quality Chinese laborers, China distribution enterprises engage in the processing and assembling of products with low profit, while the Western multinational corporations control R&D, design, key raw materials and partial manufacturing, sales and service links, with relatively higher profits. With China's increasing labor costs and corporate performance, China distribution enterprises must shift to products and procedures with high profits, namely they must go into product upgrading and industrial chain upgrading. By cooperation between cross-border enterprises in acquiring R&D, design, key raw materials and partial manufacturing, sales and service links, they will achieve existing industrial chain upgrading; through developing new products by cooperating, they can upgrade products and enter higher-level industrial chains; through independently developed new products, they can create their own brands, act as the chain owner, and build new industrial chains worldwide.

(6) The "going global" developmental mode for China distribution enterprises to optimize resource allocation. The labor division of modern international production has been intensified by different products in different working procedures of the same product, which can make full use of the advantage of production factors in different countries. Supported by modern information and logistics technology support, a global industrial chain and production network should be established by multinational corporations, and they should realize global R&D, global production and global sales. To obtain the kind of global competitiveness that Western multinational corporations have, China distribution enterprises should develop by "going global", organize a global industrial chain, a production network and a warehousing network led by themselves, and in this way, the birth of the overseas warehouse would be achieved by the optimization of resources. Competitive advantages of different countries should be used, namely, research and development in areas with centralized talents, development in areas with rich resources, production in areas with minimum costs, marketing in areas with the largest market, financing in areas with minimum interest rates, to realize global resource allocation and optimization, which is the top territory of internationalization.

China distribution enterprises may choose one or several developmental modes at the same stage, and choose different developmental types at different stages. After corporate strategy demands have been changed, the "going global" cross-border E-commerce strategy will also be changed. Of course, the distribution enterprises are not based on strategy requirements, and can choose suitable developmental modes based on conditions, opportunities and environment. Choose which kind of "going global" strategy types is related to the general developmental mode of distribution services. To combine with the international market better, China distribution enterprises should choose different developmental modes: a developmental mode with transverse spreading, and overseas investment focuses on yielding competitive advantages and increasing the production and sales scale of the market; a developmental mode with longitudinal spreading, and overseas investment focuses on resources, technology, sales and other procedures with high added value in the upper and lower reaches; a developmental mode with hybrid spreading, and foreign investment focuses on industrial upgrading, establishing a global industrial chain and optimizing resource allocation. With respect to the kind of developmental mode chosen, it aims to combine with the international market with its own advantages and resources, and thus advance further development of China's foreign trade.

### 3.2   The Development Path of China's Distribution Services Enterprises

3.2.1   Choose professional talents and brokerage services

The development path of Chinese distribution enterprises' "going global" by cross-border E-commerce carries certain market risks, and professional strategic development needs inter-disciplinary talents and professional talents with knowledge and experience in international investments, international trade, international finance, technology, law, finance and accounting, etc., establishing a special operating organization, and setting up a professional decision-making, planning and implementing platform. Even an overseas investment department at the headquarters of the Group should be established to plan and manage overseas investments and development as a whole. When accessing different countries, cross-border E-commerce needs brokerage services like laws, auditing, accounting, investment banks, information, public relations, etc. There should be cooperation with domestic and overseas brokerage institutions, in order to form a complete brokerage service network. The brokerage fee needed is high, because, except for providing various services, they bear risks with enterprises, and the brokerage fee is the cost which cannot be saved in the development of distribution enterprises in China. Domestic and overseas medium and long-term brokerage services should assure quality and lower service fees in the form of complete platform outsourcing, etc.

3.2.2   Innovation and development of the distribution enterprise management

The development route for China distribution enterprises' "going global" is quite different from the developmental route for domestic investments; the existing flow, provisions and systems for domestic distribution enterprise management are not applied, the corporate management system for overseas investments and business activities is specially prepared, involving investment decision-making, investment management, asset management, financial management, risk control, human resources, performance assessment, etc. The corporate management system takes the developed practice of transnational investment in domestic and overseas enterprises into account, and optimizes according to rules and provisions. Due to the peculiarity, complexity, high risk and high pressure of Chinese distribution enterprises' "going global", the overseas investment and business management team should choose incentives and a restrictive mechanism that is different from domestic practices. Learning from the practices of Western transnational distribution enterprises, material benefits and treatment should be geared to international practices. They are far away from headquarters, and should be fully trusted and respected. Their safety should be of primary concern, and preparations for emergency should be made. Their psychological health should be cared for, and the pressure of work should be relieved. Domestic headquarters should reinforce the support and services for overseas business. Assessment on overseas investments and business activities should be reinforced, and those who make achievements should be rewarded. "Going global" development is a long-term plan, and it is a process that takes effect after efforts have been made, and as acting on one's own wishes with an eagerness for quick success and instant benefits are not allowed. According to the general strategy of distribution enterprises, the following actions should be taken: prepare medium and long-term "going global" development plans, describe objectives, principles, orientations, key actions and safeguard measures, prepare an annual implementation plan, determine key tasks, objectives and progress of the annual plan, key actions for major trends and areas, and the financial budget and the personnel allocation, and clarify who the responsible subjects are and establish assessment indexes for them.

### 3.2.3    Establish a risk prevention mechanism for distribution enterprises

The "going global" developmental plan for China distribution enterprises should consider the fact that the social, political and cultural environment is completely different from the domestic environment, many risks that never occurred domestically might occur, and risk control difficulties and consequences are much difficult than those in the domestic environment. The main profit modes for China's E-commerce include the membership fee mode, the transaction commission mode, the product price difference mode and the outcome-based payment mode; these modes carry certain commercial risks, such as sunk costs from a forecast outcome that was not achieved, reduced revenue because of reduced members and compressed product prices due to fierce competition. China should establish a regular risk prevention mechanism and plan, do research on country-specific risks and project risks, and prepare special reports as the decision-making basis. Moreover, China should assess the risk-taking capability, and buy commercial insurance to take risks beyond its own risk-taking capability. Selecting investment time and entry point according to the country-specific risk analysis is the risk control means which is the most cost-effective.

3.2.4 Involve entry time and entry mode

The time for China distribution enterprises' "going global" is crucial, so one must clearly know about time requirements for actions, reinforce the tracking and analyzing of international situations, domestic situations, the host country's situations, the enterprise's situations and the competitor's situations, and actions should be carried out during the most advantageous period. Foreign investment is a long-term action, and countries with low comprehensive risks should be selected. We usually choose countries and regions with stable political situations, a perfect law system, similar cultural and historical backgrounds and adjacent geographical conditions; focusing on China, we should carry out research and development in countries with centralized talents, manufacture in countries with low costs, market in countries with a large market, and set out globalized marketing. Various means of entry are taken into account for overseas development of China distribution enterprises. For instance, cross-border E-commerce can utilize the "The Belt and Road" convenient logistics and overseas warehouse, and can also try to make acquisitions and establish new enterprises. Because of different requirements for financial and integration performance in countries, requirements for enterprise management and control are different: holding and equity participations have different requirements for enterprises' management and control capabilities; joint and sole proprietorships are related to enterprise resources and risk-taking capabilities. The enterprises should know all about the various entry means and characteristics, their requirements regarding capabilities and resources, adaptability with the environment of the host countries and they should select the entry mode after considering all of these factors. In view of learning and risks, acquiring minor shares or jointly establishing connections with domestic and local enterprises, then cross-border E-commerce through self-operating, shareholding or joint venture is a reliable way.

3.2.5 Utilize state diplomatic resources

Under the framework of the WTO, member countries are obliged to promote and protect transnational investments. For such a purpose, the countries sign bilateral and multilateral trade protection protocols, to promote the establishment of various free trade zones and overseas developmental regions. Promoting economic development through international free trade and investment is one of the key diplomatic activities of all countries. The overseas investment activities of China distribution enterprises should combine state diplomatic activities and diplomatic resources, and know everything about international trade and investment protection protocols in order to obtain support, protection and assistance. The Ministry of Foreign Affairs, local foreign affairs authorities, embassies and consulates abroad as well as retired diplomats are diplomatic resources to be utilized.

3.2.6   Optimize financial tools and the management and control mode

With the development of the distribution enterprises' "going global", financing will be internationalized, involving currencies, financing and financial hedging tools that are various, and financing and exchange rate risks are high. It is difficult for China distribution enterprises just at the beginning of "going global" to obtain loans from foreign banks, so it becomes necessary for domestic banks to open overseas branches and provide financial services for enterprises that are "going global". The cross-border payment platform is crucial to cross-border E-commerce. According to relevant data statistics, in the field of cross-border payment, the foreign-funded organization Paypal accounts for almost 80% of the market share, it wields a monopoly on the market and has complete competition advantages. China should cultivate a local third party's payment platform, reinforce its support for a cross-border E-commerce payment platform, and form a coordinated kind of development between a third party's payment platform and the banking system in policy, technology and bank resources.

How the headquarters of domestic distribution enterprises manage and control the overseas warehouse is related to the overseas warehouse's shareholding ratio, importance and function orientation. Management and control over the overseas warehouse with share participation involves corporate governance and is specified in the Articles of Association. As for China distribution enterprises, how shareholding and sole proprietorship enterprises apply transnational culture management and transnational enterprise management to local or overseas staff is a great challenge. As for investments in the overseas warehouse, if the objective is localized operation for a regional market, operation and decision-making powers should be delegated, and domestic headquarters should only be in charge of strategy management and control, and financial and material management and control; if local country integration operation is exercised as the local national industrial chain, management and control over operations, finance and strategy should be reinforced.

3.2.7   Establish a data analysis platform

According to the "going global" development strategy and the objectives, principles, direction, time and region determined in the annual implementation plan, project information should be actively and specifically collected and screened to increase the efficiency of information gathering and to improve the quality of project screening. Moreover, practices of opportunism should be prevented, and unreliable individual information channels should be avoided. Governments of all countries have platforms for issuing policies on business and investment attraction, the World Bank and other international developmental organizations also issue project information, and industrial associations, brokerage organizations, international conferences and exhibitions and media advertisements are approaches for obtaining overseas investment information. In terms of data analysis of cross-border

E-commerce, mathematical models should be established to forecast, analyze and estimate product sales. Different marketing strategies can be used for different countries, and various promotion means can be used, such as globalization of promotional activities on "November 11".

### 3.3   Selection of a Strategy for the Development of China's Distribution Services Enterprises

When China distribution enterprises have needs and basic qualifications for "going global", they start to conceive the developmental philosophy of "going global". The "going global" development of China distribution enterprises does not only impact the enterprise development, but it also impacts domestic development, local development, relevant enterprise development, development of the country receiving the funds and competitor development. This is a multilateral strategy and a process of interaction, and it is different from a bilateral strategy that is only taken into account for competitors domestically. Therefore, conceiving the "going global" development strategy for China distribution enterprises is not only considered as a component of a general development strategy, but it also refers to a development strategy for China, a development strategy for local areas where enterprises are located, a development strategy for relevant enterprises, a development strategy for the countries to be invested in and a development strategy for competitors.

3.3.1   Distribution services enterprises in China and the overseas economic and social development strategy

In formulating a new round of trade protocols, China distribution enterprises should actively and prudently pursue a maximization of import and export benefits, they should require the overseas economy and society to: reduce discriminative treatment, emphasize offering national treatment to China distribution enterprises, create a fair environment for competition, emphasize different discounts and treatment for developing countries, reduce technical and trade barriers, establish unified international standards of E-commerce, and obtain initiatives for China distribution enterprises' "going global". China should adhere to multilateral trade negotiations, intensify its strength in foreign trade negotiations by developing imports and exports and by developing cross-border E-commerce, reflect the interests of developing countries and avoid negative standings in international disputes.

3.3.2   Distribution services enterprises in China and the domestic economic and social development strategy

Special national conditions make China distribution enterprises with distinctive national and regional characteristics and a high sense of responsibility for the state and society. China is the largest and most potential market in the world, and the "going global" development of China distribution enterprises does not mean that these enterprises are abandoning the domestic market and moving abroad. The strategy center of China distribution enterprises is still in China, domestic development is supported by overseas development, and the transnational index is no more than 50%; headquarters and key procedures are still in China; otherwise, it would no longer be a development strategy of transnational companies' "going global". It cannot be all of the general development strategy of China distribution enterprises, but it is only a key component, not only for internationalization. It solves some key issues which cannot be solved by a domestic development strategy, and it should be coordinated with the domestic development strategy so as to realize the general strategic objectives of the enterprises. Therefore, formulating the "going global" development strategy should be in accordance with the requirements of the general development strategy of the enterprises and coordinated with the domestic development strategy so as to yield the coordinating effects. The "going global" development of China distribution enterprises is taken into the national and regional development strategy by the Chinese government and plays a key role. When formulating the "going global" development strategy, the distribution enterprises should consider their position and function in the layout of the national and regional development strategies and try to receive support from the government.

3.3.3　China's distribution services enterprises and the development strategy of affiliated enterprises

In general, distribution enterprises establish supporting and cooperative industrial relations with local enterprises, and enterprises in the upper and lower reaches. One enterprise may follow the supporting enterprises in "going global", and may drive affiliated supporting enterprises to develop because of their "going global"; in particular regarding countries with weak industrial supporting conditions, resulting in industrial chains or industrial cluster investments. Strategic interaction exists in industrial clusters and industrial chain enterprises. When China distribution enterprises develop in overseas countries at the beginning, they find it difficult to establish a relationship of industrial support, and "going global" with domestic affiliated enterprises is advantageous to increasing strength, avoiding risks and overcoming difficulties in industrial supporting and market exploration. The Chinese government has negotiated with some countries to establish China distribution enterprise parks abroad to serve China distribution enterprises and create conditions for China distribution enterprises' "going global". Therefore, the development strategy for "going global" formulated by China distribution enterprises should consider strategic cohesion with affiliated enterprises.

3.3.4　China's distribution services enterprises and the host countries' strategy for economic, social and environmental development

The host countries' opening-door policy serves local economic, social and environmental development objectives and determines its attitude towards foreign funds. When formulating their "going global" development strategy, China distribution enterprises should consider the host countries' objectives for economic, social and environmental development, and the distribution enterprises' plans for the introduction of foreign funds cannot be in conflict with, and should be beneficial for the realization of, the host countries' objectives for economic and social development. Social and environmental responsibilities should be welcomed by host countries. At present, the countries propose higher requirements on bearing social and environmental responsibilities. China is a socialist country, China distribution enterprises must exercise social and environmental responsibilities, and also exercise social and environment responsibilities abroad, advance the economic development and the environmental protection of the host countries and the project area, establish a responsible image and brand of China distribution enterprises, endorse the philosophy of "peaceful development, cooperation and win-win", cultivate and develop soft powers, and create an environment that promotes the overseas development of China distribution enterprises and an external environment for China's national development.

3.3.5    China and foreign distribution services enterprises' joint development strategies in China and worldwide

The main competitors of China distribution enterprises at home and abroad are Western transnational companies. Internationally, overseas distribution enterprises spread with the advantages of state power, products, information, brands and channels, they establish industrial chains and production networks around the world and become global production organizers and coordinators. In China, with China's policy of reform and opening up, overseas distribution enterprises use the advantages of Chinese labor and joint ventures, cooperation and the three forms of OEM and compensation trade to take China distribution enterprises into the global industrial chain and production network. They have always helped China distribution enterprises aiming at controlling China distribution enterprises on their established industrial chains. Once China distribution enterprises obtain strength, they will want to upgrade the industry, reconstruct the industrial chain or "go global" for development; domestic and overseas distribution enterprises will come into conflict and then China distribution enterprises will be put under pressure. Once China distribution enterprises do not have advantages of labor elements, the overseas distribution enterprises will remove China distribution enterprises from the industrial chain. Therefore, the "going global" development strategy of China distribution enterprises is also made for a strategy of global competition.

The top objective for the "going global" of China distribution enterprises is to become transnational companies with a global resource allocation, and this is gradual internationalization. Set the objective of internationalization level when formulating the plan for the "going global" development strategy. The enterprise's internationalization level is assessed via a transnational index. If the transnational index is bigger, the enterprise's internationalization degree is higher. A transnational company should have an international index of more than 40%. The United Nations Conference on Trade and Development (UNCTAD) ranks the total overseas assets and transnational indexes of the Top 100 transnational companies worldwide annually. At present, large Chinese enterprises are still at the beginning of internationalized operations, and there are rare truly transnational companies. The internationalization of the China distribution enterprises is the inevitable trend, but not every China distribution enterprise will become a transnational company, and China distribution enterprises should determine the objectives of internationalization according to national conditions and their own situation. China distribution enterprises with a relatively large scale or that are dominant worldwide can set relatively higher internationalized business, and those with a relatively small scale or that are dominant on the domestic market can set relatively lower internationalized business. Different from enterprises in small European countries, China distribution enterprises do not need to pursue an extremely high internationalization for a long period of time, because of national situations. Its wide area, massive population, prosperous economy, stable political situations and the world's 2nd largest economic entity make China the world's largest and most potential market and so it attracts worldwide investors. China has a great amount of room for development, and it is a key market for Western transnational companies. In the near future, China distribution enterprises should place their main resources and energy on the development and operations of the domestic market. Most China distribution enterprises adopt the development strategy of "centering China, doing transnational business, taking care of the domestic and overseas markets, and promoting mutually", compete on the domestic and overseas markets with domestic and overseas resources, keep their standing and profitability within domestic competition and guarantee new room for the overseas market, which are the requirements for the sustainable development of China distribution enterprises and for the sustainable development of the Chinese economy.

"Going global" development is the inevitable requirement when China's economy and China distribution enterprises enter a new stage, and it is the advantageous choice made against the background of economic globalization and global financial crisis. As a national strategy, the implementing body for "going global" development is the enterprise, and whether to "go global" and how to "go global" are key strategic issues for independent decision-making by China distribution enterprises. China distribution enterprises have the power and the requirements for "going global", as well as the basic qualifications for "going global". China distribution enterprises are at the primary stage of transnational business, and their "going global" development encounters great opportunities and enormous challenges. Formulating and implementing the "going global" of China distribution enterprises are peculiar, and it is a process of multilateral strategic interaction. Combined with national and their own requirements, and starting from internal and external conditions, a strategic conception and selection have to be carried out, proper internationalization objectives must be set, and an effective implementation mechanism must be established, all of which will ensure the success of the "going global" drive of China's distribution services enterprises.

### References

[1] Yu Lixin. Cross-border E-commerce and Internet Financing as New Economic Growth of China, PPT 2015.

[2] Yu Lixin. Report on Research of China's Trade in Services (No.1), *Economic Management*, 2011

[3] Bi Xiuying. Discussion on the Influences of E-commerce on the Social Economy [J]. *Business Economy*, 2006(2): 117-118.

[4] Chai Yueting. Greatly Promote E-commerce Service Industry, *Science and Technology Daily,* 2011-03,16(11).

[5] Chen Boliang. Analysis on E-commerce Industry Market Structure under SCP Paradigm [J]. *Journal of Fujian Commercial College*, 2008(6):20-22, 53.

[6] Dong Hanliang. Analysis of the Macroscopic Economic Performance of the E-commerce, [D]. Jilin University, 2006.

[7] Du Rong. Analysis of the Interactive Influences of the E-commerce and Social Economy [J]. *Market Modernization*, 2005(11):165-166.

[8] Fan Gang. Analysis and Outlook of Element Factors for the Economic Growth of China [J]. *Capital Markets*, 2008(04):10-13.

[9] Fan Yuzhen. Empirical Study on Economic Growth by E-commerce Development of China [D]. Shanghai Normal University, 2010.

[10] Fei Jinhua. Reflections on Cost Computation of Chinese Websites [J]. China Management Informatization, 2006(01):48-50.

[11] Hu Ganglan, Lu Xianghua and Huang Lihua. E-commerce Ecological System and Its Evolution Route [J]. *Economic Management,* 2009(06).

[12] Han Lihong, Wang Yinan. Analysis of the Competitive Advantages of Corporate Value Chains Based on the E-commerce Mode [J]. *Academic Exchange*, 2008.

[13] Jin Feng. Taobao Accounts for 70% of the Market Share of the Domestic E-commerce, *Communication Information News*, 2010-06-04.

[14] Ma Bin, Xu Yueqian. On the Interactive Development of Professional Markets and E-commerce-Zhejiang Province as an Example [J]. *Journal of Business Economics*, 2005(03):15-19

[15] Ma Li, Xue Simin. Boost Western China Economic Development with E-commerce [J]. *China Management Informatization*, 2010(5):107-109.

[16] Liang Chunxiao. E-commerce of Medium and Small-sized Enterprises Entering Platform Era [J]. *Machinery Industry Information and Network*, 2007(01): quoting-52.

[17] Liang Wenguang. Empirical Analysis of the Economic Growth Element of Zhejiang Province [J].

*Knowledge Economy*, 2010(12):6-8.

[18] Li Zhongmei. Discussion on E-commerce Services [J]. *HLJ Foreign Economic Relations & Trade*, 2007(12):54-55.

[19] Liu Maohong, Zhang Tao and Liu Cuihong. Analysis of the Dynamic Factor for the Economic Growth of China [J]. *Reform and Development*, 2009(09):1-2.

[20] Liu Zuotai. Discussion on the Development of E-commerce and County Economy, *Rural Economy,* 2007(6):44-45.

[21] Lou Cequn. Discussion on Relations between Electronic Political Affairs and E-commerce [J]. *Journal of Central China Normal University* (Humanities and Social Sciences) , 2002(2):131-135.

[22] Ma Chunmei. Influences of the E-commerce on the Economy and the Development Strategy of China [J]. *Economic Forum*, 2005(24):63-64.

[23] Shi Shaogong. Explorative Research on Forming a Mechanism for E-commerce Service Cluster of China and Development Countermeasures [D]. Huaqiao University, 2009.

[24] Ming Xiaobo, Peng Lan. Types of E-commerce Service Industry and Its Standing in Western China E-commerce Development-Survey and Researched Based on the E-commerce Service Industry in Chengdu City [J]. *E-Business*, 2010(12): 14-16.

[25] General Office of the CPC Central Committee and the General Office of the State Council, the State Informatization Development Strategy from 2006 to 2020.

[26] Ouyang Zhonghui, Jiang Desen and Ma Jinyu. Analysis of the Mode of Economic Development Boosting by Information Economy, [J]. *Fujian Tribune* (Humanities and Social Sciences), 2008(06):107-111.

[27] Pei Ping, Cao Yuanfang. Analysis of the Power of the Economic Growth of China [J]. *Nanjing Journal of Social Sciences*, 2008(11):1-5.

(Associate professor Feng Xiaoling from Dalian Maritime University and researcher Yu Lixin, the director of Foreign Economic and Trade International Financial Research Center of the China Academy of Social Sciences)

# Research on the Export Strategy of China's Trade in Maritime Transport Services

## 1. Analysis of the International Competitiveness of China's Trade in Maritime Transport Services

### 1.1    Trade in Maritime Transport Services Accounts for the Largest Ratio and is the Most Important Sector of Trade in Transport Services

China is a large country for worldwide merchandise trade. The year-by-year increasing volume of merchandise trade drives the development of the derived trade in transport services; trade in maritime transport services accounts for the largest ratio and is the most important sector, and 80% of global merchandise trade is completed by maritime transport. After China's entry into the WTO, against the background of trade liberalization, huge maritime transport requirements each year make China become a large country for worldwide trade in maritime transport services.

1.1.1    Analysis of the international market share of trade in maritime transport services

The industrialization of an industry can be measured by that industry's share in the world market. As for trade in maritime transport services, share in the international market rejects the internationalization of each country's trade in maritime transport services.

**Table 1    Comparison of International Market Share of Trade in Maritime Transport Services from 2001 to 2010**

Unit: %

| Country(Region) | 2001 | 2002 | 2003 | 2004 | 2005 | 2006 | 2007 | 2008 | 2009 | 2010 |
|---|---|---|---|---|---|---|---|---|---|---|
| The USA | 15.63 | 15.52 | 13.56 | 13.26 | 11.73 | 11.24 | 11.10 | 11.10 | 11.07 | 12.16 |
| Germany | 6.53 | 5.97 | 5.99 | 7.34 | 7.14 | 6.68 | 6.73 | 6.69 | 6.38 | 6.75 |
| Japan | 7.42 | 7.75 | 7.01 | 6.97 | 6.54 | 6.50 | 6.35 | 6.63 | 6.60 | 6.69 |
| Great Britain | 6.13 | 5.53 | 5.27 | 5.13 | 5.22 | 5.44 | 5.52 | 5.69 | 5.84 | 5.99 |
| France | 6.46 | 5.92 | 5.33 | 5.43 | 5.43 | 5.12 | 5.09 | 5.08 | 5.06 | 5.32 |
| Denmark | 2.25 | 3.33 | 4.73 | 3.77 | 4.67 | 4.37 | 4.63 | 4.57 | 4.49 | 4.61 |
| Korea | 3.65 | 3.96 | 4.02 | 3.73 | 4.11 | 4.53 | 4.23 | 4.33 | 4.18 | 4.26 |
| The Netherlands | 6.63 | 6.35 | 5.87 | 5.06 | 5.05 | 4.74 | 4.01 | 4.26 | 4.31 | 4.43 |
| Hong Kong | 3.72 | 4.13 | 4.23 | 4.04 | 3.34 | 3.43 | 3.44 | 3.45 | 3.37 | 3.48 |
| Greece | 2.40 | 2.47 | 2.43 | 2.37 | 2.22 | 3.31 | 3.01 | 3.10 | 2.97 | 3.14 |
| Norway | 3.13 | 2.96 | 3.13 | 3.12 | 3.02 | 3.01 | 2.76 | 2.59 | 2.61 | 2.73 |

Continued

| Country(Region) | 2001 | 2002 | 2003 | 2004 | 2005 | 2006 | 2007 | 2008 | 2009 | 2010 |
|---|---|---|---|---|---|---|---|---|---|---|
| Italy | 3.13 | 2.76 | 2.41 | 2.65 | 2.53 | 2.63 | 2.79 | 2.57 | 2.54 | 2.58 |
| Singapore | 1.56 | 1.63 | 1.72 | 1.80 | 2.85 | 2.78 | 2.76 | 2.58 | 2.60 | 2.72 |
| China | 1.26 | 1.40 | 1.52 | 1.75 | 1.98 | 1.99 | 2.11 | 2.26 | 2.17 | 2.39 |
| Spain | 2.43 | 2.36 | 2.42 | 2.76 | 2.83 | 2.64 | 2.70 | 2.56 | 2.54 | 2.64 |

Data source: calculated according to WTO international trade statistics.

The above table lists the international market share of trade in maritime transport services regarding 15 representative countries and regions in global trade in maritime transport services from 2001 to 2010. As powerful countries of trade in maritime transport services countries, the percentage of share in the international market of maritime transport services in America, Japan, The Netherlands and Germany is much higher than that of the other countries. In particular, in America, its international market share is almost twice that of Japan which ranks No. 2. After comparing, China's trade in maritime transport services share in the international market ranks last among the 15 countries. Although its international market share increases year by year, the total increase is not significant, still a long way from the developed countries, keeping at approximately 2%. It means that the internationalization of China's maritime transport is relatively low and should be improved.

1.1.2　The trade competitive advantage index for maritime transport services

The trade competitive advantage index is an effective tool for analyzing the international competitive force of some industries. It reflects that whether the same kind of products manufactured by domestic enterprises is at a competitive advantage or a disadvantage compared with other products on the international market. When TC is valued (-1, -0.6), extremely competitive disadvantages exist; when TC is valued (-0.6, -0.3), relatively large competitive disadvantages exist; when TC is valued (-0.3, 0), weak competitive disadvantages exist; when TC is valued (0, 0.3), weak competitive advantages exist; when TC is valued (0.3, 0.6), relatively powerful competitive advantages exist; when TC is valued (0.6, 1), extremely competitive advantages exist.

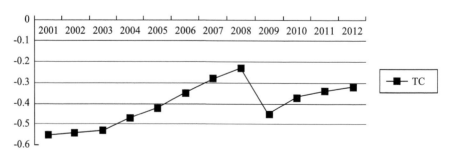

**Fig. 1　Trade Competitive Advantage Index of China's Maritime Transport Service from 2001 to 2012**
Data source: calculated according to WTO international trade statistics.

The above figure shows the changes in the trade competitive advantage indexes for China's maritime transport service from 2001 to 2012. From 2001 to 2008, the competitiveness of China's maritime transport services enhanced year by year, and the competitive advantage index in 2007 and 2008 reached the range of (-0.3, 0) which shows a weak competitive advantage. In the year 2009, affected by the deterioration of the global economic environment, China's maritime transport competitive index dropped by 51%. After 2009, with the recovery of the international market, the competitive advantage index of China's trade in maritime transport services started to rise but it did not reach the optimal values of 2008. In a general view, except for the years 2007 and 2008, the competitive advantage index of China's trade in maritime transport services was in the range of "relatively large competitive disadvantages". Although the indexes are increasing year by year, the fluctuation is large and easily affected by international economic situations, and the overall situations are not optimistic and should be improved further.

1.1.3   Ranking of the worldwide maritime transport liner companies

Except for the maritime transport international market share and competitive advantage, the index visually reflects the international competitiveness of China's trade in maritime transport services and that the development of the trade in maritime transport services enterprises is one of the key indexes for measuring the industrial competitiveness of trade in maritime transport services. As for the maritime transport enterprises, the scales of the quantity and tonnage of ships represent the overall developmental scale of enterprises. The total ranking of maritime transport enterprises of one country shows the development of the maritime transport service of that country.

Table 2   Ranking of the Top 20 Liner Companies in 2014

| Ranking | Company name | TEU | Total number of fleet (the number of vessels) |
| --- | --- | --- | --- |
| 1 | Mersk Line (Denmark) | 1,142,700 | 567 |
| 2 | MSC (Switzerland) | 1,330,234 | 474 |
| 3 | CMA-CGM (France) | 980,490 | 425 |
| 4 | Evergreen Marine (Taiwan) | 383,558 | 204 |
| 5 | COSCO (Mainland China) | 367,701 | 160 |
| 6 | Hapag-Lloyd (Germany) | 341,312 | 150 |
| 7 | APL | 315,345 | 121 |
| 8 | Hanjin Shipping (Korea) | 312,087 | 112 |
| 9 | CSCL (Mainland China) | 160,310 | 129 |
| 10 | MOL (Japan) | 340,776 | 111 |
| 11 | Hamburg Sud (Germany) | 211,619 | 105 |
| 12 | NYK Line (Japan) | 157,016 | 102 |
| 13 | OOCL (Hong Kong) | 144,269 | 86 |
| 14 | PIL (Singapore) | 123,436 | 172 |

Continued

| Ranking | Company name | TEU | Total number of fleet (the number of vessels) |
|---------|--------------|-----|------------------------------------------------|
| 15 | YML (Taiwan) | 161,751 | 84 |
| 16 | KLINE (Japan) | 221,243 | 67 |
| 17 | HMM (Korea) | 233,980 | 59 |
| 18 | ZIM (Israel) | 194,136 | 85 |
| 19 | S.A.G. (Arab) | 76,336 | 49 |
| 20 | CSAV (Chile) | 192,119 | 54 |

Data source: Alphaliner statistical data as on February 10, 2014.

Table 2 lists the Top 20 liner companies as in February, 2014 with statistics made by Alphaliner. The data show that, the famous Danish Mersk Line ranks first among the global liner companies, and COSCO and CSCL of Mainland China rank No. 5 and No. 9, respectively. The ranking of liners in Hong Kong and Taiwan, Hong Kong OOCL ranks No. 13; Taiwan ship companies Evergreen Marine and YML rank No. 4 and No. 15, respectively. Although China's liner companies are developing more rapidly than ever, a great gap still exists with the Danish Maserk and the Swiss MSC.

Seen from the above analysis, the international market share of China's trade in maritime transport services is low, and carries relatively large competitive disadvantages. The scale of China's maritime transport enterprise is relatively small, showing a relatively low internationalization of the maritime transport service industry and weak international competitiveness. The above shows that China's trade in maritime transport services encounters many problems in internationalization, and it is urgent that the "going global" of the maritime transport service industry be sped up.

### 1.2 Analysis of the Factors for the Lack of Competitiveness of China's Trade in Maritime Transport Services

The internationalization of China's trade in maritime transport services is low, and its international competitiveness is weak, and the profound causes are:

1.2.1 China's harbor and port berths have poor professionalism and can be easily affected by foreign business

Cargo harbor throughput directly affects the throughput of China's trade in maritime transport services competitiveness; therefore, China's cargo harbor and port berth throughput directly affects the development of China's trade in maritime transport services. In the past several years, development of China's harbor and port berths has been accelerated, the annual throughput ranks top in the world, the investment and construction of infrastructures are increasing, and management has been improved. Meanwhile, existing problems of China's harbors and ports are obvious, and the port berth structure and professionalism do not match the existing requirements; in addition, Sino-foreign shares in China's harbor construction and operations are larger and affect the development of container ports of domestic maritime transport enterprises.

Seen from the data in Table 3, from 2003 to 2012, the total number of harbor and port berths of China's coastal and inland river areas and berths with tonnage of 10 thousand tons and above are increasing year by year. In terms of ratio of port berths with tonnage of 10 thousand tons and above to the total number of berths, most harbor and port berths in China are small and medium-sized, the number of berths with tonnage of above 10 thousand tons occupies approximately 8.8%, and the trend towards development is not obvious. At present, the water depth of many harbor berths in China is not sufficient, and cannot satisfy the needs of large vessels. Besides, the throughput capacity of container ports is insufficient, plus being short of large professional containers, ore and crude oil and other deepwater berths, large vessels, in particular the oil vessels, must be unloaded with the help of transfer vessels. This extends the demurring time of cargoes and vessels, reduces the operation efficiency of harbors and increases the maritime transport costs.

**Table 3    Details of Berths in China's Coastal and Inland River Harbors**

| Year | 2003 | 2004 | 2005 | 2006 | 2007 | 2008 | 2009 | 2010 | 2011 | 2012 |
|---|---|---|---|---|---|---|---|---|---|---|
| Tonnage | 8449 | 9787 | 10652 | 10848 | 12131 | 14205 | 20091 | 20333 | 20524 | 20450 |
| 10 thousand tons | 771 | 837 | 955 | 1108 | 1217 | 1335 | 1507 | 1511 | 1706 | 1822 |
| Ratio | 9.1% | 8.6% | 9.0% | 10.2% | 10.0% | 9.4% | 7.5% | 7.4% | 8.3% | 8.9% |

Data source: *based on China Statistical Yearbook* over the years.

Except for the above, at present, harbor and port operations in China have been widely opened up, and the entry of foreign capital is slack, so it attracts a lot of foreign-funded enterprises to invest in the construction and operation of harbors in China. The continuous increase in foreign capital relieves tight fund issues in the construction of harbors and ports in China, brings more advanced technology and business philosophy, and plays an active role in the utilization of harbors and their operational efficiency; meanwhile, because of interests, foreign investors invest in harbors and ports on the principle of maximized benefits; therefore, harbors and ports invested in by foreign business are located at China's shipping hubs. Once foreign business applies control over harbors and ports in China by increasing its share, the development of container ports by domestic maritime transport enterprises will be affected, and the overall planning of harbors and ports in China will also be affected.

Existing problems regarding the construction and operation of harbors and ports in China, and the current situations of insufficient throughput capacity and low professionalism greatly affect the development of China's trade in maritime transport services, and the improvement of its international competitiveness is also restricted.

**1.2.2    The relatively small fleet and shipping capacity of China's maritime transport enterprises**

Seen from the data in Table 4, in the ranking of the shipping capacity of the world's ship-owning countries (regions), China ranks No.4. Although the ranking is high, compared with the developed countries, the fleet size of the maritime transport enterprises in China falls behind. By the end of 2011, the total scale of the fleet in China only accounted for approximately 8% of the Top 10 commercial fleets in the world, so the gap with the world's No.1, the Greek Fleet, and No.2, the Japanese Fleet, needs improving. The ratio of the size of the Greek fleet is 15%, that of the Japanese fleet is 14%; China has a gap of 0.6 percentage points from the No.3 German Fleet, 6 percentage points from the No.2 Japanese Fleet and 7 percentage points from the No.1 Greek Fleet. In conclusion, the total scale of Chinese vessels needs improving.

In addition, due to the unbalanced structure of the fleet of maritime transport enterprises and the limited shipping capacity in China, much of China's foreign maritime transport trade is carried by overseas maritime transport companies; meanwhile, the ratio of transport services for China and other countries by Chinese maritime transport service enterprises is low. In terms of water transport, China is the largest demanding country in the world. Foreign trade transporting demands via water in China in 2012 were approximately 4.2 billion tons, including 1.4 billion tons of bulk, 600 million tons of petroleum, 1.7 billion tons of container load freight and 500 million tons of general cargo. Statistics show that, of foreign trade cargo transported by sea, approximately 25% is undertaken by Chinese ship companies, of which 24% for container and bulk, 17% for petroleum, and 36% for groceries. The remaining

**Table 4    Fleet Size of the Top Ten Countries  (Regions)**

| Ranking | Country (region) | Total tonnage of fleet (million tonnage) | Proportion of total in the world (%) | Proportions of different types of vessels in the world (%) | | | Proportion of vessels with domestic flag (%) | Proportion of vessels with flag of convenience (%) |
|---|---|---|---|---|---|---|---|---|
| | | | | Oil vessel | Bulk vessel | Container vessel | | |
| 1 | Greece | 217.1 | 14.9 | 18.2 | 17.1 | 5.8 | 29.9 | 70.1 |
| 2 | Japan | 209.8 | 14.4 | 11.1 | 20.3 | 7.5 | 9.9 | 90.1 |
| 3 | Germany | 125.5 | 8.6 | 4.4 | 4.2 | 33.2 | 13.9 | 86.1 |
| 4 | China | 115.6 | 8.0 | 4.1 | 11.9 | 5.6 | 43.4 | 56.6 |
| 5 | Korea | 54.5 | 3.7 | 2.5 | 5.5 | 2.9 | 31.8 | 68.2 |
| 6 | The USA | 44.5 | 3.1 | 3.9 | 2.8 | 1.7 | 11.6 | 88.4 |
| 7 | Hong Kong | 42.4 | 2.9 | 2.6 | 3.9 | 1.4 | 63.3 | 36.7 |
| 8 | Norway | 40.6 | 2.8 | 3.7 | 1.6 | 0.2 | 35.2 | 64.8 |
| 9 | Great Britain | 40.3 | 2.8 | 2.5 | 2.7 | 4.0 | 32.7 | 67.3 |
| 10 | Taiwan | 37.7 | 2.6 | 1.7 | 3.2 | 3.8 | 11.2 | 88.8 |

Data source: Institute of Shipping Economics and Shipping (ISL), data as of December 31, 2011.

approximately 75% is carried by overseas ship companies; the maritime transport demand and supply are extremely unbalanced, and the development of China's trade in maritime transport services and its international competitiveness are affected significantly.

1.2.3   Great shortage of senior sailors in China's maritime transport enterprises

At present, China is one of the large countries of maritime transport in the world, and its harbor throughput, in particular its container throughput, has ranked No. 1 in the world for three consecutive years. The size of the present commercial fleet, China's total shipping capacity rank top in the world, and the size of its maritime transport fleet has increased year by year. An inevitable outcome is that the demand for sailors by maritime transport enterprises is also increasing year by year. At present, the total number of Chinese sailors is approximately 650,000, including approximately 162,000 sailors with senior qualifications. Nevertheless, compared with huge demands for sailors, the number of Chinese sailors is by far insufficient; there is a great shortage of backup forces, and the backup forces have a trend towards reduction and draining. The shortage of sailors with senior qualifications in China is 37,000. Experts of the Sailor Sector of the Maritime Bureau of the Ministry of Transport figured out that the shortage of sailors is caused by long training cycles and limited supply of professional colleges. There are about 70 institutes such as the maritime university, the maritime occupational college, the secondary technical school and training centers, but the number of sailors conveyed to the maritime transport service industry cannot satisfy the requirements of talents by the maritime transport industry. Besides, due to the rapid development of the maritime transport industry, one vessel can be finished in several months and launched; however, several, or more than 10, years are needed for training a sailor, from receiving sailing education to practice, until receiving a captain's certificate.

1.2.4   The government's insufficient support for the development of maritime transport

After China's entry into the WTO, the government opened up the market of maritime transport , and many foreign maritime transport enterprises entered China. Depending on powerful economic strength, the level of technology and supporting governmental policies, these overseas enterprises have stabilized advantageous standings in the competition for China's domestic maritime transport market. At present, many countries actively create an advantageous developmental environment for domestic maritime transport enterprises, including shipbuilding loan discounts, cargo retaining systems, maritime transport business subsidies, tax discounts and exemptions, fleet update subsidies, etc. On the contrary, with China's opening up of the maritime transport market, shipbuilding discount loans, the imported vessel tax discounts and exemptions, harbor charge discounts and cargo retaining systems formerly entitled to China's maritime transport enterprises have almost been cancelled. Meanwhile, foreign maritime transport enterprises on the Chinese market are entitled to more discounts than the domestic enterprises. Such unfairness causes an unfair competitive environment on China's maritime transport market, and greatly affects the competitiveness of China's maritime transport enterprises.

In fact, the importance of the government's support for the development of maritime transport and the improvement of its international competitiveness can be seen from existing cases: as for the losing country in World War II, Japan, the active intervention of supporting policies issued by the Japanese Government is an important reason why the maritime transport industry can be developed rapidly and even in a superior way to that of the U.K., America and other countries. After World War II, the Japanese Government started to greatly support the maritime transport industry, it continuously issued discount loans and taxation policies, making it possible for Japan to become the 2nd largest maritime transport country in only 20 years. At present, most countries in the world adopt various preferential means to support the development of their domestic maritime transport industries and their commercial fleets. As for China, proper preferential and protection measures are unavailable, and some policies make overseas maritime transport enterprises entitled to excellent national treatment. For example, in the field of investment and operation of harbors and ports, foreign businesses are entitled to preferential treatment, and the domestic maritime transport enterprises are restricted if they want to invest in, build and operate their ports. Except for the above, a tendentious subsidy policy is applied to the shipbuilding industry in China: if a foreign shipyard builds ships in China, the shipbuilding sector is entitled to grant credit loan discounts, while the Chinese shipyard is not entitled to such a subsidy. Seen from the above, the Chinese Government's support for the maritime transport industry is not enough, which impairs the international competitiveness of China's maritime transport enterprises and makes them at a disadvantage compared with their foreign competitors.

In addition, since the beginning of the global financial crisis, the international maritime market has been in a downward trend, and the prospects are not optimistic. Such difficult situations make China's maritime transport industry incur great losses; even for the state-owned maritime transport industry the government's assistance is needed. As for as the maritime transport policy in China, many restrictive policies have been issued in coordination with the liberalization of the maritime transport market, such as the "Cooperative Implementation Plan for Trade, Shipping and Shipbuilding", the "Code for Awarding Maritime Transport Investments" and the "Long-term Program for Expansion, Rejection and Updating of the Domestic Fleet" issued by China in 1987, 1990 and 1992. At present, China is short on supporting policies for trade in maritime transport services, and no substantial discount is provided by the "Code for Promoting Maritime Transport Upgrading (1991)" and the "Policy on Awarding Development of the Domestic Fleet" (1999). In the year 2012, due to China's long-time downward trend in the maritime transport industry, the Chinese transport sector decided to issue supporting policies for the sustainable development of the maritime transport industry on behalf of the government. The Ministry of Transport figured out that the Government should establish a cargo retaining system, and some large and medium-sized strategic materials should be provided with priority given to designated carrying vessels or domestic vessels. In terms of taxation, "at present, taxes on international maritime transport enterprises are low, and only value-added tax is paid; taxation on Chinese maritime transport enterprises is higher, and value-added tax, business taxes and other taxes must be paid. The Ministry of Transport is communicating with competent authorities, trying to obtain tax discounts and make taxation on domestic maritime transport enterprises identical with that on international maritime transport enterprises.

## 2. Research on the Export Strategy of China's Trade in Maritime Transport Services

The scale of exports of China's maritime transport service is large, and plays a key role in the world's maritime transport service market. However, the competitive advantages of China's maritime transport service are not obvious, the market share is small, and the export potential is low and does not match the export scale. The poor competitive force of the maritime transport service is a major cause for this outcome. In the 1930s, a U.K. scholar, D.H. Robertson proposed the theory of the "export engine". Exportation has the function of boosting the domestic economic growth and of spreading the economic growth among countries. The main opinions are described as follows: if the export trade growth is fast, the social resources can be concentrated on the export sector, and so the efficiency of the resource configuration would increase on the whole. The expansion of the scale of exports is a tool for the industrial scale economy, and yields correlation effects on relevant industries. The growth in exports is also beneficial to the free circulation of capital and technology. According to this theory, the breakthrough for the current export potential, the export scale and the market share is to expand the export trade of China's maritime transport service. Based on this theory, China should correct the draft of the maritime transport trade export strategy, so as to actively increase the export scale and promote the internationalization and the enhancement of its international competitiveness.

### 2.1   The Significance of Drafting an Export Strategy for the Maritime Transport Service Sector

2.1.1   Beneficial to the reduction of China's trade in services deficit

According to the data in Table 5, the total import and export of trade in services in 2013 was 536.546 billion USD, including 206.018 billion USD for service exports, an increase of

7.6% compared with the previous year; 330.528 billion USD for service imports, an increase of 17.6%, the trade deficit was 124.51 billion USD, an increase of 38.7 percentage points compared with 89.747 billion USD in 2012; the trade deficit gap of trade in services was expanding. Trade in services exports of China's maritime transport in 2013 was 25.825 billion USD, a drop of 4.6 percentage points compared with the previous year, and the imports were 70.62 billion USD, an increase of 5.8 percentage points compared with the previous year, and the trade deficit was 44.795 billion USD, an increase of 13 percentage points compared with the previous year.

**Table 5    Total Imports and Exports and the Trade Deficit of the Maritime Transport Service and China's Trade in Services**                        Unit: 100 million USD

| Year | 2007 | 2008 | 2009 | 2010 | 2011 | 2012 | 2013 |
|---|---|---|---|---|---|---|---|
| Total exports of maritime transport services | 198.62 | 254.5 | 148.07 | 229.28 | 240.44 | 270.81 | 258.25 |
| Total imports of maritime transport services | 351.34 | 405.4 | 361.52 | 492.88 | 629.94 | 667.27 | 706.2 |
| Trade deficit of maritime transport services | 152.71 | 150.9 | 213.45 | 263.61 | 389.51 | 396.46 | 447.95 |
| Total exports of trade in services | 1222.1 | 1471 | 1294.76 | 1621.65 | 1860.1 | 1914.3 | 2060.18 |
| Total imports of trade in services | 1301.2 | 1589 | 1588.56 | 1933.21 | 2476.54 | 2811.8 | 3305.28 |
| Trade deficit of trade in services | 79.1 | 118.1 | 293.8 | 311.56 | 616.45 | 897.74 | 1245.1 |

Data source: based on data of the UN Trade in Services.

Seen from Table 5, the trade deficit of China's trade in services is in the trend of spreading along a half-U shape, and the trade imbalance gap is increasing. Compared with the general trade in services deficit, the growth of the trade deficit of trade in services is relatively small. In the year 2013, the trade deficit of trade in services increased by 38.7%, and that of the trade in maritime transport services increased by 13%. Seen from the Figure, the deficit of trade in services in the years 2007 and 2008 came from the deficit of the maritime transport sector. In the past several years, the growth of the deficit of the trade in maritime transport services has been smaller than that of trade in services, although the deficit has increased year by year. Therefore, the export trade has developed in the maritime transport sector and is beneficial to the reduction of the deficit of maritime transport services, further relieving the growth of the deficit of China's trade in services, and it is an effective tool for reducing the deficit of trade in services.

2.1.2    Beneficial to the foreign direct investments in maritime transport

International trade theories and practices prove that the expansion of the scale of exportation is accompanied by an increase in foreign direct investments. The foreign direct investments in transport, warehousing and postal industry is used to replace the foreign direct investments in China's maritime transport. In the year 2012, the net foreign direct investments in China's transport, warehousing and postal industry was 2.988 billion USD, an increase of 14.2% compared with the previous year, foreign direct investment stock was 29.227 billion USD, an increase of 15.7% compared with the year before, about 2.42 times the net foreign direct investments in 2007. The increase in foreign direct investment stock means that China's maritime transport industry is developing rapidly, the foreign direct investment stock is proportional to the development of the maritime transport industry, the fund is supplemented for the further expansion of the scale of exportation, and that a virtuous cycle has started.

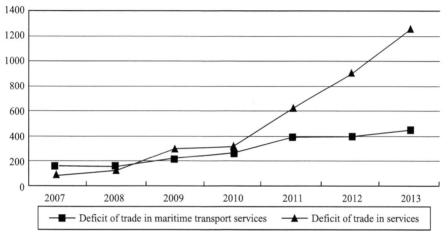

**Fig. 2    Deficit of China's Trade in Maritime Transport Services and Trade in Services**
Data source: based on data of the UN Trade in Services.

Meanwhile, seen from Figure 3, although amount of foreign direct investment stock in China's transport, warehousing and postal industry is increasing steadily, the net foreign direct investment is not increasing steadily, in particular for the years 2008 and 2009, affected by the financial crisis of 2008, the net foreign direct investment by China's transport, warehousing and postal industry dropped sharply, and increased rapidly in 2010, increasing by 174.5% compared with the previous year, and dropped down in 2011. Such instability is also affected by China's transport industry, in particular it affects the export trade of the maritime transport service industry.

2.1.3    Beneficial to the development of related industries

The maritime transport service industry cannot be developed independently, as it relies on the supply of shipyards from the shipbuilding industry in the upper reaches, on carrying cargo, harbor infrastructures and port carrying capacities in the middle reaches, on cargo exporters and importers in the lower reaches, and it is also supported by information technology,

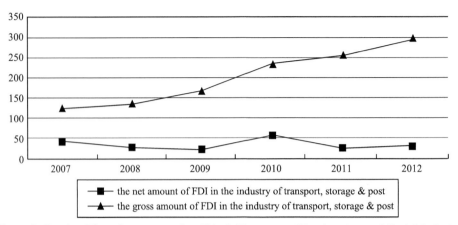

**Figure 3  Foreign Direct Investments by China's Transport, Warehousing and Postal Industry**

Data source: China Statistical Yearbook.

electronic technology, etc. With the continuous expansion of the maritime transport service industry, China increases its demands on the supply in the upper reaches and support in the middle reaches. This paper selects the number of maritime transport vessels, net carrying capacity of those vessels, the number of harbor and port berths, cargo exports and transport service exports in order to analyze the influences by increasing the maritime transport service exports.

Increasing the maritime transport service directly affects the development of China's shipbuilding industries, and determines the supply and demand of ocean liners in China. Table 6 lists the number of waterborne transporting vessels in China. It can be seen that the number of waterborne transporting vessels dropped down in the period under analysis. Affected by the financial crisis, the number of vessels dropped by approximately 4 percentage points compared with 2008, but the net carrying capacity increased. The net carrying capacity in 2013 was 244.0103 million tons, an increase of 6.8%; the average net carrying capacity was 1,414.11 tons/vessel, an increase of 10.5%. China's vessel tonnage is upgrading, vessels with tonnage of 10 thousand tons are increasing in number, and vessels with smaller tonnage are decreasing in number, which is more beneficial to the development of China's shipbuilding industry. Meanwhile, the costs of the maritime transport  industry are reduced, and competitiveness is improved.

**Table 6  The Number of Waterborne Transporting Vessels and China's Net Carrying Capacity from 2007 to 2013**      Unit: 10 thousand vessels, 10 thousand tons

| Year | 2007 | 2008 | 2009 | 2010 | 2011 | 2012 | 2013 |
| --- | --- | --- | --- | --- | --- | --- | --- |
| Number of vessels (10 thousand vessels) | 19.18 | 18.42 | 17.69 | 17.84 | 17.92 | 18.17 | 17.26 |
| Net carrying capacity of vessels (10 thousand tons) | 11883 | 12418 | 14609 | 18041 | 21264 | 22849 | 24401 |

Data source: Statistical Bulletin of the Ministry of Transport of the People's Republic of China.

Part V  Research on Hot Issues in the Fields of Trade in Services

As seen in Table 7, the number of harbors in China is increasing steadily. However, seen from the point of view of the regulation of port structure, port construction has two features: first, large ports have been constructed, there is especially a growth in the number of berths with a capacity of 100,000 tons or above; second, professionalism has become obvious, and petroleum, coal, iron ore, container, roll on-roll off shipments and other professional factors in large deep-water berths account for 57.6%.

**Table 7    The Number of Harbor and Port Berths in Coastal and Inland River Areas in China from 2003–2012**

Unit: berth

| Year | 2007 | 2008 | 2009 | 2010 | 2011 | 2012 |
|---|---|---|---|---|---|---|
| Coastal areas | 3970 | 4914 | 5372 | 5529 | 5612 | 5794 |
| Inland river areas | 8161 | 9291 | 14719 | 14804 | 14912 | 15019 |
| Total | 12131 | 14205 | 20091 | 20333 | 20524 | 20813 |

Data source: *China Statistical Yearbook* over the years and statistical data of the Ministry of Transport of the People's Republic of China.

Cargo exports drive the exports of maritime transport services, and an increase in the export service of maritime transport services facilitates the exportation of cargo and forms the coordinated development of industries in the upper and lower reaches. Seen in Table 8, cargo exports in China were more than 2 trillion USD in 2012, increasing by 67.9% compared with 2007. The total value of exports for China's transport service in 2012 reached 38.91 billion USD, increasing by 9.4% compared with the previous year, and increased by 7.59 billion USD compared with 2007 with an increase of 24.3%. The above figures show that, since the year 2007, with the expansion of the export trade of the maritime transport service sector in China, industries of the upper and lower reaches were boosted.

**Table 8    Exports of China's Cargo and Transport Services**

Unit: 100 million USD

| Year | 2007 | 2008 | 2009 | 2010 | 2011 | 2012 | 2013 |
|---|---|---|---|---|---|---|---|
| Cargo exports | 12204.6 | 14306.9 | 12016.1 | 15777.5 | 18983.8 | 20487.1 | 22096.1 |
| Exports of transport services | 313.2 | 384.2 | 235.7 | 342.1 | 355.7 | 389.1 | 376.46 |

Data source: National Bureau of Statistics; Ministry of Commerce; State Administration of Foreign Exchange.

2.1.4    Beneficial to the expansion of international influences of maritime transport

According to the statistical data by Alphaliner Company as of February, 2014, of the Top 20 liner companies, China occupies 5 of them. Of them, COSCO and CSCL from Mainland China rank No.5 and No.9, and COSCO operates 160 container vessels with a carrying capacity of 67701TEU. In overseas areas, its network covers Europe, America, Asia, Africa and Australia, and realizes all-round and all-weather "barrier-free" services. COSCO focuses on quality management of its transporting service, occupational health safety management and environmental protection, it strictly observes international protocols and domestic laws and regulations, and engages in intensifying its internal management. It passed the quality management system certification in 1998 and environmental management system and occupational health safety management certification in 2003. COSCO reinforces its capabilities of being able to adapt to the market and get involved in international competition; it is well-known worldwide and contributes to the maritime transport industry and world environmental protection. Some of China's maritime transport companies have gone abroad and have been accepted by the world. However, China's overall ocean service export is disadvantageous. Two of China's liner companies depend on new vessel building and charting in order to expand their carrying capacities, and they develop slowly. The maritime transport service sector expands the opening up and is beneficial to China's maritime transport enterprises' more active involvement in international competition. Meanwhile, the influences of China's maritime transport services have been intensified and the trade deficit will gradually be changed.

### 2.1.5 Beneficial to the expansion of national employment

In view of foreign trade, in particular in view of the WTO *General Agreement on Trade in Services* (hereinafter referred to as "GATS"), international trade in maritime transport services is not limited to waterborne cargo and passenger transporting services, but includes maritime transport auxiliary services, harbor services and other maritime transport services. Therefore, exports of maritime transport services increase employment in the ocean service chain and promote employment. As shown in Figure 4, the number of people employed in waterborne transport is affected by maritime transport trade, and increasing exports in China's maritime transport trade increases the employment rate. Meanwhile, the reduction of exports

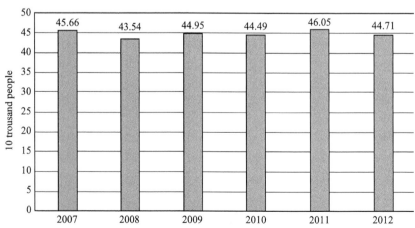

**Fig. 4   Employment in the Waterborne Transport Industry from 2007 to 2012**
Data Source: China Statistical Yearbook over the years.

of maritime transport also reduces those of the waterborne transport industry in China, mainly caused by the exportation of China's maritime transport services, thus driving the exports of related services, and has a leverage effect which influences the increasing or decreasing of employment. Increasing exports of China's maritime transport services makes China's maritime transport services more vigorous and competitive, it lowers transport costs, drives cargo exports, and China's trade in services, and indirectly increases employment in related industries. Therefore, in consideration of the availability of data, this paper only uses employment in the waterborne transport industry to measure influences on employment in China.

2.1.6    Beneficial to the expansion of overseas market

With regional economic cooperation in full swing in areas of the world, in particular in the Asia Pacific Area, the convenience of trading will be realized among countries to promote the volume of trade. China is actively participating in regional economic cooperation, proposed the construction of a new Maritime Silk Road in 2013. The construction of the New Maritime Silk Road will cover 20 countries and regions, from China's coastal harbors, southwards, across the South China Sea, through Malacca, Lombok and the Sunda straits, along the northern part of the Indian Ocean, to the Persian Gulf, the Red Sea, the Gulf of Aden and other areas. To be specific, based on the philosophy and spirit of the "Silk Road", the New Maritime Silk Road will be used to integrate various on-going cooperations to attain the effect of "one and one is more than two". It advances the requirements of maritime transport services; therefore, China should actively expand maritime transport exportation and seize the opportunity in the construction of the New Maritime Silk Road, which can be beneficial to the maritime transport sector of China to explore the overseas market better and reinforce its overall competitiveness.

In summary, expanding exportation of maritime transport services will result in obvious and active economic benefits, including: increasing the exports of China's maritime transport service industry, and reducing China's trade deficit in trade in services; favor increased foreign investments, and intensify international competitiveness; fully play the leading function of related industries, and promoting an increase in employment in the industries of the upper and lower reaches; increasing exportation provides more employment, increases employment of industries in the upper and lower reaches and promotes national employment. With respect to domestic active influences and overseas market expansion, the expansion of the scale of exportation of maritime transport services results in obvious export benefits and is the method we adhere to.

## 2.2  Analysis of the Macroscopic Route of the Export Strategy of the Maritime Transport Service Sector

### 2.2.1  Improve vessels, harbors and other infrastructures

The development of the export trade of maritime transport services makes more production elements in the maritime transport service sector, which is beneficial for the improvement of vessel equipment and promotes the development towards electronics and information in the entire maritime transport sector. As shown in Figure 5, the investments in water transport construction in China is 152.846 billion yuan, 1.72 times that of the year 2007. As seen from the above analysis, the number of China's 10-thousand-ton vessels is increasing, and the carrying capacity of China's maritime transport enterprises is intensifying, as shown in Table 9. The vessel power of China's maritime transport enterprises is growing. In the year 2012, the vessel power of Chinese enterprises reached 66.469 million kW, an increase of 11.7% compared with the previous year, 1.69 times that of 2007. Meanwhile, as shown in Figures 6, 7 and 8, the improvement of harbor infrastructures increases harbor cargo throughput in China, China's foreign trade cargo throughput and harbor container throughput. In the year 2013, harbor cargo throughput in China was 11.77 billion tons, an increase of 64% compared with the year before; foreign trade harbor throughput was 3.36 billion tons, an increase of 9.8% compared with the previous year; container harbor throughput was 190.21 million TEU, an increase of 7.1% compared with the previous year, so the competitiveness of the maritime transport sector will be improved.

**Table 9  Details of the Vessel Power of China's Maritime Transport Enterprises from 2007 to 2012**

Unit: 10 thousand kW

| Year | 2007 | 2008 | 2009 | 2010 | 2011 | 2012 |
|------|------|------|------|------|------|------|
| Power | 3936.7 | 4355.1 | 4620.9 | 5330.4 | 5949.7 | 6646.9 |

Data source: Statistical data of the Ministry of Transport of the People's Republic of China.

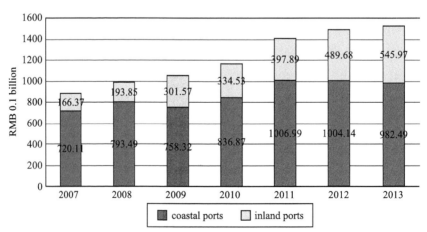

**Fig. 5  Investment in the Build–up of China's Water Transport Industry from 2007 to 2013**

Data source: Statistical Bulletin of the Ministry of Transport of the People's Republic of China.

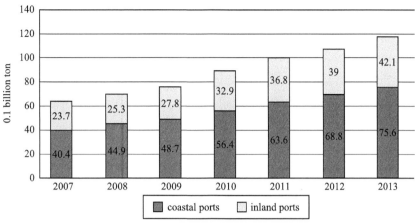

**Fig. 6    Cargo Throughput in China's Harbors from 2007 to 2013**

Data source: Statistical Bulletin of the Ministry of Transport of the People's Republic of China.

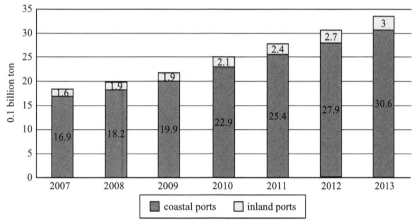

**Fig. 7    Foreign Trade Cargo Throughput in China's Harbors from 2007 to 2013**

Data source: Statistical Bulletin of the Ministry of Transport of the People's Republic of China.

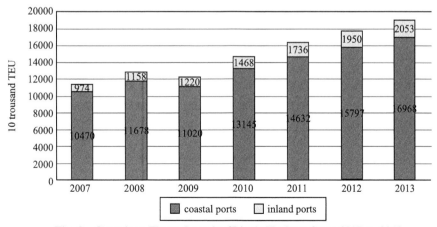

**Fig. 8    Container Throughput in China's Harbors from 2007 to 2013**

Data source: Statistical Bulletin of the Ministry of Transport of the People's Republic of China.

Part V    Research on Hot Issues in the Fields of Trade in Services

2.2.2  Information-oriented development promotes the expansion of exports

With the development of the world's prosperous economy marked by electronic computer and information technology, the maritime transport industry is realizing electronics and information orientation, and the birth of the Internet and electronic commerce is triggering the third revolution of the maritime transport industry. To increase the utilization rate of maritime transport resources and competitiveness of enterprises, maritime transport enterprises must establish an integrated and globally-shared information network. Application of information technology lowers management costs, improves service and reinforces competitive advantages for maritime transport companies. Among the Chinese maritime transport enterprises, COSCO has realized information management. To utilize the integration network effectively, COSCO tracks international advanced online marketing means and launches online ordering, transfer enquiry, information announcement and other international cargo online service systems via the Internet, and global Internet users can carry out their business online.

2.2.3  Improve the core technology of China's maritime transport

The core competitiveness of China's maritime transport service industry is not powerful, and expanding the scale of exports is beneficial to expenditures in research and development so that maritime transport services in China will be able to improve technology, in particular core technology. At present, China's largest traffic and transport comprehensive technology research and development base—the Shanghai Ship and Shipping Research Institute (Ship Research Institute), is the leader in ship and warship automation, intelligent transportation, environmental engineering and vessel water dynamics, and it has many hi-tech talents. In the year 2010, the State Council took it into the maritime circle and attached great importance to research and development of maritime transport. The maritime transport sector participates in TISA negotiations to expand its opening-up, and more domestic enterprises will get involved in international competition. On the current international maritime transport service market, with the transfer of industrial core competitiveness, technology and talent are dominant on the market. In terms of talent training, the Ministry of Transport has proposed to make the occupational qualification system of the maritime transport industry perfect, and to establish an maritime transport talent training mode in conformity with internationalization requirements; it also proposed to speed up the development of modern occupational education for sailors, and to reinforce skill training on sailor eligibility and improve the sailor examination and assessment base to cover all of China. More things that should be done are: standardize the sailor labor market and the management of the dispatching organization, make the sailor equity guarantee mechanism perfect, and establish a sailor's credit management system; increase the force of selection and training for maritime transport science & technology talents and professional talents; and introduce and train multi-disciplinary talents on navigation laws, navigation finance, maritime arbitration, shipping brokerage and liner services.

Expanding the exportation of maritime transport service trade is beneficial to investments in R & D funds of the maritime transport service industry and boosts the development of domestic maritime transport. Meanwhile, we shall attach importance to some harmful elements to the environment by maritime transport, and apply eco-friendly maritime transport, such as researching and developing energy saving and emission reduction, cutting down on the emission of contaminants, better implementing the low-carbon economic strategy, and developing utilization of solar energy, in particular wind energy; reinforcing the construction of a system of standards for eco-friendly maritime transport, and preparing norms and standards on vessel energy, clean energy and power vessel inspection; perfecting the vessel contamination prevention system, enforcing the limits on vessel contaminants and reinforcing the construction of contamination prevention facilities.

## 2.3   Selection of microscopic routes towards the creation of an export strategy for the maritime transport service sector

More than 90% of the transportation of foreign trade materials in China is completed by sea, and China has the largest demand on maritime transport. Of them, imported materials to China via maritime transport are mineral fuels, mineral oil and distilled products, asphalt materials, mineral wax, mineral slag, mineral ash and base metal, and the three kinds of products account for 47.41% of the total imports via maritime transport in China. China's maritime transport service will directly affect the adequate supply of the strategic resources which are related to the national economy and the people's livelihood. It can be seen that maritime transport is a strategic channel for China to fill in economic globalization, and is a key support for China's fully utilizing international and domestic resources, crucial to the national livelihood.

### 2.3.1   Serves for the internal and external enterprises

Any service development could not be isolated, maritime transport service industry can't develop lonely either. It is based on the supply of shipbuilding industry manufacturers, undertakes the goods transportation, relies on the support of the port infrastructure and port capacity situation; furthermore, it needs to face directly the f goods import and export business. It also requires the support of information technology, electronic technology and other industries. As a result, maritime transport service industry should provide services for other industries, while also needs the support of other industries serving the domestic and foreign enterprises at the same time. In addition, the scope of the international trade in maritime transport services is not limited to the maritime passenger and cargo transportation services. It should also include many ancillary services of maritime transport, ports and other maritime transport service. Therefore, the maritime transport service export will pull the whole maritime transport service chain of adding workers, promote employment, and improve the level of national welfare. Therefore, no matter from the positive economic effects of internally, or expansion of the external market, development is should stick to the direction of the maritime transport service industry.

2.3.2   Increase passenger carrying capacity of maritime transport in China

Meanwhile, as can be seen from Figure 9, the passenger carrying capacity of waterway transport in China is slowly increasing, and domestic waterway transport in China is improving, and under sound conditions. As shown in Figure 10, the passenger throughput of harbors in China drops down, 206 million passenger throughput at harbors in 2007, dropping in the following several years, and increasing after 2011, with an increase of 9.6% compared with 2010. The throughput still decreased in the previous 2 years. We can see that the value in 2007 is the peak value, and passenger throughput at harbors in China is in a decreasing trend;

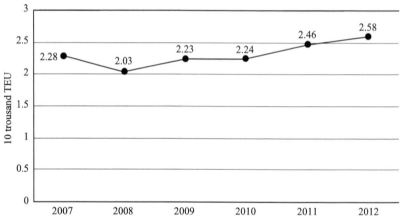

**Fig. 9    Passenger Carrying Capacity of Waterway Transport in China from 2007 to 2013**
Data source: Statistical Bulletin of the Ministry of Transport of the People's Republic of China.

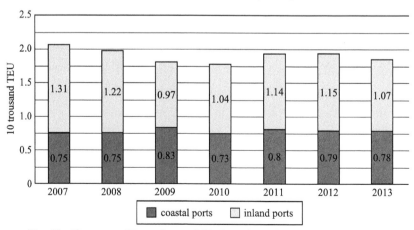

**Fig. 10    Passenger Throughput of Harbors in China from 2007 to 2013**
Data source: Statistical Bulletin of the Ministry of Transport of the People's Republic of China.

and Chinese consumers' overall interests are impaired.

2.3.3    Expand export trade, and encourage China's maritime transport companies to unite

Improvement of the vessel equipment of the maritime transport service sector and information orientation of the sector can bring export benefits through technology innovation, and expenditures of research and development is the key means of this innovation. The opening up of the maritime transport service market expands communication and cooperation between China's maritime transport service sector and overseas enterprises. Through cooperating with overseas maritime transport services, against the background of international service competition, depending on technology overflow effects, China's maritime transport service sector can learn advanced maritime transport technology and acquire management experience, it can accelerate phases of China's maritime transport, and the competitiveness of the maritime transport sector will be enhanced.

Meanwhile, expanding exports will encourage the government to lead the combination and reconstruction of maritime transport enterprises. For instance, COSCO and China Shipping have united to satisfy the current situations, provide scale advantages by innovative cooperation, emphasize low-cost advantages, revitalize competitive advantages so as to resist downward market conditions and powerful competitors and bring the enterprises out of trouble. On the other hand, trade in services exportation further advances talent strategy and improves the competitiveness of maritime transport enterprises. The international market competitiveness of one enterprise is the competition of talent, and enterprises cannot be developed without high-quality talents. In this view, China's maritime transport enterprises should learn from overseas enterprises, and focus on and retain talents.

(Associate professor Feng Xiaoling and Master Biao Ma from Dalian

Maritime University)